The Age of Paper

In the first detailed examination of Britain's transition to paper currency, Hiroki Shin explores how state, nation and community each played their respective roles in its introduction. By examining archival materials and personal accounts, Shin's work sheds fresh light on societal, institutional, communal and individual responses to the transformation. The dominance of communal currency during the Bank Restriction period (1797–1821) demonstrates how paper currency derived its value from the community of users rather than the state or the intrinsic value of precious metal. Shin traces the expanded use of the Bank of England note – both geographically and socially – in this period, revealing the economic and social factors that accelerated this shift and the cultural manifestations of the paper-based monetary regime, from everyday politics to bank-note forgeries. This book serves as an essential resource for those interested in understanding the modern monetary system's historical origins.

Hiroki Shin is Associate Professor in the School of History and Cultures at the University of Birmingham. His research focuses on the evolution of the modern economic system.

Technically assured and intellectually ambitious, Hiroki Shin has given us in *The Age of Paper* a fascinating account of a unique era in British financial history – an account that, to his book's huge benefit, embraces the broader political, social and cultural dimensions as well as the more narrowly economic.

David Kynaston, author of *Till Time's Last Sand: A History of the Bank of England, 1694–2013*

A fascinatingly written account of how the Bank of England note became Britain's most important currency. Erudite and thought-provoking, Shin opens up, and challenges, key debates about the experience and acceptance of paper money. A 'must read' for all scholars of the long eighteenth century.

Anne Murphy, author of *Virtuous Bankers*

The author eloquently communicates and cogently analyses everything there is to learn about this seminal episode in British monetary history and theory.

Patrick Karl O'Brien, author of *The Economies of Imperial China and Western Europe: Debating the Great Divergence*

This book offers valuable insights into the transformative forces shaping the history of Britain during the Bank Restriction period and beyond, shedding light on the transition to paper currency and its enduring impact. I highly recommend it.

Nuno Palma, University of Manchester

Cambridge Studies in Economic History

Editorial Board

Cambridge Studies in Economic History comprises stimulating and accessible economic history which actively builds bridges to other disciplines. Books in the series will illuminate why the issues they address are important and interesting, place their findings in a comparative context, and relate their research to wider debates and controversies. The series will combine innovative and exciting new research by younger researchers with new approaches to major issues by senior scholars. It will publish distinguished work regardless of chronological period or geographical location.

A complete list of titles in the series can be found at:
www.cambridge.org/economichistory

The Age of Paper

The Bank Note, Communal Currency and British Society, 1790s–1830s

Hiroki Shin

University of Birmingham

CAMBRIDGE
UNIVERSITY PRESS

Shaftesbury Road, Cambridge CB2 8EA, United Kingdom

One Liberty Plaza, 20th Floor, New York, NY 10006, USA

477 Williamstown Road, Port Melbourne, VIC 3207, Australia

314–321, 3rd Floor, Plot 3, Splendor Forum, Jasola District Centre,
New Delhi – 110025, India

103 Penang Road, #05-06/07, Visioncrest Commercial, Singapore 238467

Cambridge University Press is part of Cambridge University Press & Assessment,
a department of the University of Cambridge.

We share the University's mission to contribute to society through the pursuit of
education, learning and research at the highest international levels of excellence.

www.cambridge.org
Information on this title: www.cambridge.org/9781009503273

DOI: 10.1017/9781009503280

First published 2025

A catalogue record for this publication is available from the British Library

Library of Congress Cataloging-in-Publication Data
Names: Shin, Hiroki, author.
Title: The age of paper : the bank note, communal currency and British society,
    1790s-1830s / Hiroki Shin, University of Birmingham.
Description: Cambridge, United Kingdom; New York, NY : Cambridge
    University Press, [2024] | Series: Cambridge studies in economic history |
    Includes bibliographical references and index.
Identifiers: LCCN 2024026425 (print) | LCCN 2024026426 (ebook) |
    ISBN 9781009503273 (hardback) | ISBN 9781009503297 (paperback) |
    ISBN 9781009503280 (epub)
Subjects: LCSH: Paper money–Great Britain–History. | Bank notes–Great
    Britain–History.
Classification: LCC HG944 .S55 2024 (print) | LCC HG944 (ebook) |
    DDC 332.4/941–dc23/eng/20240726
LC record available at https://lccn.loc.gov/2024026425
LC ebook record available at https://lccn.loc.gov/2024026426

ISBN 978-1-009-50327-3 Hardback

Contents

Figures and Illustrations

Tables

Acknowledgements

It has been a long journey to the completion of this book, and along the way I have become indebted to many people. The book originated as my PhD project, and the manuscript has undergone a significant transformation – now far removed from its original thesis form. Still, I owe my greatest debt to the supervisor of my PhD thesis at the University of Cambridge, Martin J. Daunton, for his enduring patience and insightful comments on my work. I was fortunate enough to be able to shape my ideas about Britain's historical experience with paper currency through conversations with this great mentor in the master's lodge at Trinity Hall. After I left Cambridge, he gave me gentle nudges towards publishing my work as a monograph, chiefly through his annual Christmas cards, which always included a line enquiring when I would be completing 'the book'.

Craig Muldrew and Julian Hoppit, who served as examiners for my thesis, have been a continuous source of encouragement and motivation from the inception of my project to its fruition, first as a thesis and now as a book. While their work has always been an inspiration for my work, their practical support and advice have been invaluable in guiding this work to publication. I would also like to express my gratitude to the general editors of Cambridge Studies in Economic History for their decision to include my book in the series, as well as their subsequent editorial advice on how to improve the manuscript. The constructive criticism from an anonymous reviewer has been instrumental in refining my arguments and evidence. Special thanks are also due to Michael Watson and Rosa Martin at Cambridge University Press for their indispensable support and guidance throughout the book's production process.

During my PhD studies, I received generous financial support from the Cambridge Trust, the Business Archives Council and the Ellen McArthur Fund. More recently, I received school research funding from the School of History, Anthropology, Philosophy and Politics, Queen's University Belfast. I am deeply thankful for these financial benefactors, as they have been crucial to this publication's progress and completion.

My gratitude also extends to the British Museum's trustees for giving permission to include images from their print collection.

The collection held at the Bank of England Archives has long been the core of my research. I want to express my deepest thanks to the Bank of England's governors and trustees. The archives' current and former staff, particularly Mike Anson, Margherita Orlando, Kat Harrington, Evie Stevenson, Hannah Cleal, Holly Waughman and Joseph Hettrick, also provided invaluable assistance, showed much patience and became indispensable to my research. Furthermore, the Bank of England Museum staff, particularly John Keyworth, have my sincere gratitude, as the museum's collection played a key role in deepening my understanding of the Bank of England note as part of material culture in Bank Restriction Britain.

My investigations led me to numerous libraries, record offices and archives, each offering unique insights and resources. I was unable to include all the fascinating stories from various collections and records, that is, the following list is much shorter than it should be. I am particularly grateful that the following institutions gave me access to their invaluable collections: University of Cambridge Library, British Library, Guildhall Library, National Archives, National Archives Scotland, National Library of Wales, Public Record Office of Northern Ireland, HBOS Group Archives (now part of the Lloyds Banking Group Archives), Royal Bank of Scotland Archive, Bank of Ireland Arts Centre and the Royal Society of Arts Archive (with thanks to Eve Watson especially).

My work on British monetary history also took me to North America, where I served as a visiting fellow at the Lewis Walpole Library and Beinecke Rare Book & Manuscript Library, Yale University. The fellowship programme, the exceptional atmosphere and the library's collection were immensely beneficial to my research, and I extend my heartfelt gratitude for the library staff's hospitality.

Throughout this book's gestation, numerous individuals have provided their generous wisdom and encouragement. Frank Trentmann, with his extensive experience, provided practical insights on publishing a book, while offering intellectual stimulation through our conversations and his work on consumption history. At the University of York, Colin Divall helped me immensely, not only by giving me my first academic job in the UK but also by reinforcing my ties with the Bank of England Archives. My gratitude extends to individual scholars, including Patrick O'Brien, Nuno Palma, Anne Murphy, David Kynaston, Perry Gauci, John Turner, Matt Thompson, Alex Metcalfe, Jane Fiske and the late Peter Mathias.

Queen's University Belfast's collegial atmosphere enabled me to complete this long-term project. I am equally thankful to the audiences at the various conferences, seminars and workshops where I presented some parts of my research. Lyrabelle Yorong, Katrina Lising and Jesie Baltazar helped me create the database of historical lost-note claims. Furthermore, Anny Mortada went through my manuscript as a patient and diligent proofreader. All the remaining errors are mine.

I am proud to have received my first formal education in British history from such esteemed Japanese scholars as Yoichi Kibata, Takao Tomiyama and Tamotsu Nishizawa. The intellectual and moral support provided by my Japanese friends Atsushi Iguchi, Kenichi Natsume, Haruki Inagaki, Takeshi Nakamura and Toshihiko Iwama has been a driving force during my journey. Special thanks must be given to Toshio Kusamitsu, my mentor of many years, who introduced me to the art of being a historian. From my days as a student in Tokyo and Cambridge until this day, Kusamitsu *sensei* has enlightened me on British history and culture's depth and nuances continuously.

My family – Yutaka, Yumiko and Kuniaki Shin – has been the bedrock of my academic pursuits, enabling me to dedicate myself to study and research. Last, but certainly not least, I want to express my profound gratitude to my wife, Aya, for her enduring patience with my frequent absences on research trips and her invaluable assistance with digital technology. I lovingly dedicate this book to Aya, who understands the practicalities and nuances of money much more than I do.

Abbreviations

BE	Bank of England Archives
BIAC	Bank of Ireland Arts Centre, Dublin, Ireland
BL	British Library
CD	Bank of England, minutes of the Committee of Directors
CT	Bank of England, minutes of the Committee of Treasury
CWPR	*Cobbett's Weekly Political Register*
HBOS	HBOS Group Archives, Edinburgh (now part of the Lloyds Banking Group Archives)
NAS	National Archives of Scotland
PRONI	Public Record Office of Northern Ireland, Belfast
RBS	Royal Bank of Scotland
RO	Record Office
TNA	The National Archives, Kew

Introduction

On 1 March 1797, Edmund Burke, an aged politician and celebrated writer, sent a letter to his young friend George Canning expressing his concern regarding the ongoing war with France, the stability of government and the tenuous state of public credit.[1] Burke's apprehension was related less to the fragility of the nation's security and more to his fear that the way the government responded to the current financial instability might undermine the foundation of public credit. On the previous Sunday, the Privy Council had ordered the Bank of England to suspend payments in cash in order to fend off a large-scale run on the banks. The measure overturned the long-established rule that paper currency was convertible into precious metals. The idea of Britain's conversion to a paper-based currency system was particularly odious to Burke, whose *Reflections on the Revolution in France* fiercely attacked the French fiat paper currency *assignat* as representative 'not of opulence but of want, the creature not of credit but of power'.[2] It was a manifestation of French monetary despotism, fictitious wealth and an unsound economic idea – all of which were entirely foreign to the English situation, where there was flourishing commerce, solid credit and 'the total exclusion of all idea of power from any part of the transaction'. Burke elaborates on what set apart the paper money in England from that in France:

They forget that, in England, not one shilling of paper-money of any description is received but of choice; that the whole has had its origin in cash actually deposited; and that it is convertible at pleasure, in an instant, and without the smallest loss, into cash again. Our paper is of value in commerce, because in law it is of none. It is powerful on Change, because in Westminster Hall it is impotent. In payment of a debt of twenty shillings, a creditor may refuse all the

---

[1] Edmund Burke, *The Correspondence of Edmund Burke*, ix: *May 1796–July 1797*, ed. R. B. McDowell and J. A. Woods (London, 1970), 267–9.

[2] Edmund Burke, *Reflections on the Revolution in France*, ed. J. C. D. Clark (Stanford, CA, 2001), 401.

paper of the bank of England. Nor is there amongst us a single public security, of any quality or nature whatsoever, that is enforced by authority.[3]

In this brief exposition of the two foundations of Britain's paper currency, written with Burke's characteristically lucid style, the convertibility of paper into a precious metal formed only part of the contrast he intended to draw between the British and the French currencies. It was only by detaching it from the idea of 'authority' that Britain's paper currency could be completely set apart from the French currency. The value of Britain's paper did not rest on law or compulsion by political power but on British citizens' voluntary acceptance of it 'of choice'. In an early publication in the 1760s, Burke had already expressed the voluntary nature of credit, which could not be coerced because 'power and credit are things adverse, incompatible'.[4] The idea of voluntary acceptance had a close affinity with the core argument of Burke's condemnation of the French Revolution, which hinged upon his alienation of the French Revolution from the democratic tradition of Britain's Glorious Revolution. Just as the revolution of 1688 had the voluntary support of the nation, Britain's currency value was rooted in the nation's choice. However, what had appeared in 1790 to be an unassailable contrast between English and French national traditions came to be undermined by the suspension of currency convertibility in early 1797. Suspending the Bank of England's cash payments decoupled Britain's paper currency from the metallic standard, and it also threatened the fundamental principle of voluntarism that the nation's monetary and political systems had long upheld. For Burke, the British government was on the verge of following the fatal precedent of the French *assignat* by introducing political authority into the currency system. The subsequent course of events demonstrated that Burke's earlier recognition of British monetary voluntarism held true: the Bank of England note continued to base its value on voluntary acceptance rather than on law.[5]

****

What was the nature of the transformation that Britain experienced in the period following the suspension of cash payments in 1797? The era of

---

[3] Burke, *Reflections on the Revolution in France*, 401.

[4] Edmund Burke, *Observations on a Late State of the Nation* (London, 1769), 401. See also Richard Bourke, *Empire and Revolution: The Political Life of Edmund Burke* (Princeton, NJ, 2015), 348.

[5] In his letter to Canning, Burke stated, 'if you keep the Currency where it is and support it with vigour, necessity will draw out the Gold and silver'. Burke, *Correspondence of Edmund Burke*, ix, 269.

inconvertible paper currency in Britain offers a fascinating insight into a broad economic and social transformation triggered by a monetary regime change. Since its establishment in 1694, the Bank of England's promissory notes had been, in England if not across the British Isles, a widely recognised form of payment, but it was during the Bank Restriction period (1797–1821) that the Bank of England note truly became the nation's foremost currency.[6] At the end of the eighteenth century, money was omnipresent in British society. It was central to economic policy and to commercial transactions. In an industrial and commercial nation like Britain, money was the blood that circulated throughout its public and private spheres. Money was also crucial when a nation was engaged in major military conflicts, as the warring state sucked up a tremendous amount of financial resources. This was indeed the case for Britain at the end of the eighteenth century when it was fighting a war against revolutionary France. Money was equally essential for everyday economic transactions that concerned all sections of society, from wealthy aristocrats and business people to those who were barely making ends meet. In a society where the possession of money increasingly defined one's worth, money constituted a fundamental part of its denizens' world view and social relations. While a drastic change in the monetary order compelled Britons to rethink their ideas of monetary value, the social realities of monetary transaction were reshaped according to the new monetary regime.

Britain's Bank Restriction period and inconvertible paper currency were unique in several respects. First, despite some years of high inflation, especially around 1800 and 1813, Britain's paper currency generally retained its value throughout more than two decades of inconvertibility – over the period, the annual inflation rate was relatively moderate, at around 3 per cent, and the peak years of high inflation did not lead to financial collapse.[7] The relative stability showed that the new monetary regime was successfully operated. In contrast, similar experiments with paper currency in other European countries and in America ended with rampant inflation, or, as in the case of the two French experiments, the Mississippi scheme and the *assignat* led to devastating economic and

---

[6] In this book, Bank of England notes are referred to as 'Bank notes' to distinguish them from other banks' notes.

[7] Stephen Broadberry, Bruce Campbell, Alexander Klein, et al., *British Economic Growth, 1270–1870* (New York, 2015), 255–6; Youssef Cassis and P. L. Cottrell, *Private Banking in Europe: Rise, Retreat, and Resurgence* (Oxford, 2015), 103. See also Pamfili Antipa, 'How Fiscal Policy Affects Prices: Britain's First Experience with Paper Money', *Journal of Economic History*, 76 (2016), 1044–77.

social consequences.[8] Second, it was during the Bank Restriction period that the foundation of Britain's modern currency and banking systems was laid down, namely the gold standard in both theory and practice. The de facto gold standard, already in operation in England since 1717, came to be institutionalised by the legal recognition of gold as the principal standard of value and by the return to paper currency convertibility in 1821 at the 'ancient standard' gold price of £3 17s 10½d an ounce. Third, and particularly important for this book, Bank Restriction Britain saw a nationwide debate on a number of issues related to paper currency, a social and cultural phenomenon that cut across politics, intellectual controversy, legal courts, the business community, cultural politics and Britain's everyday life. It was the sheer volume and scope of the public discussion that make the Bank Restriction period so fascinating not only to economic and political historians but also to scholars of social and cultural history.

The Nature and Culture of Paper Currency

For the major part of monetary history, money existed in the form of metallic currency, especially gold and silver, and the historical association between money and metal has significantly shaped the way writers' in the past understood the nature of money. The classical definition of money's functions – money as a medium of exchange, a unit of account and a store of value – is a description that has a natural affinity with metallic currency. However, since the last decade of the twentieth century, academic interest in inconvertible currency, or fiat money, has significantly intensified. The growing scholarly interest in money can be traced to various sources, from the emergence of supranational currency (the euro), local currency and digital currency to the destabilisation of the financial system culminating in the 2008 global financial crisis. More importantly, money in the contemporary world – especially after the demise of the Breton Woods system – almost without exception consists of inconvertible currency. The recent surge in interest in money has led to a revision of the established understanding of money, often drawing inspiration from historical experiences and ideas. Particularly notable in the rejuvenated discussion on money is the emergence of neo-chartalism or Modern Monetary Theory.[9] An early systematic expression

---

[8] The classic work is Charles P. Kindleberger, *Manias, Panics, and Crashes: A History of Financial Crises* (London, 1978).

[9] L. Randall Wray, *Understanding Modern Money: The Key to Full Employment and Price Stability* (Cheltenham, 1998).

of the idea of chartalism was offered by Georg Friedrich Knapp, who in his *The State Theory of Money* (originally published in 1905) argued that money was fundamentally a ticket or token (the term chartal is derived from the Latin word *charta*).[10] Knapp identified the source of monetary value in the political authority's power to enforce certain means of payment. The state was able to determine what materials were acceptable as a legitimate payment method, thereby giving a chosen medium a privileged status in public transactions. Such a de jure form of money was enforced when public offices only accepted a designated means of payment for taxes and made payments to subjects in the same manner. Following Knapp, the idea of money as a 'creation of the state' has been discussed by Mitchell Innes, Joseph A. Schumpeter, John Maynard Keynes, Hyman Minsky and Abba Learner, constituting an alternative theory to metal-based monetary theory.[11]

According to chartalism, the central role of currency is being 'a unit of account' because what matters to the stability of a monetary system is to have a stable unit – such as the pound sterling or the dollar – rather than what material constitutes money.[12] By serving as a unit of account, money mediates credit and debt relations as fiat currency is 'nothing more than debt' and its function is that 'it can be used to retire liabilities to the government – such as tax liabilities'.[13] For the modern proponents of the chartalist view of money, the dominance of fiat currency since the late twentieth century offers a demonstration that money is fundamentally credit money.

The neo-chartalist view of currency offers an opportunity to reconsider the historical development of modern currency. Notably, the economic sociologist Geoffrey Ingham has applied a neo-chartalist perspective in his explanation of the creation of modern capitalist currency.[14] According to Ingham, the historical currency system, which first emerged as a unit of account imposed by a political authority, grew into a capitalist monetary system through the fusing of public money and private credit. In eighteenth-century Europe, as the volume of commercial operations grew, public monetary transactions were no longer the dominant domain of monetary space. Large banks that operated at the

---

[10] Georg Friedrich Knapp, *The State Theory of Money*, abridged edition, ed. J. Bonar (London, 1924); Wray, *Understanding Modern Money*, 23–9.

[11] Wray, *Understanding Modern Money*, chs. 2–3. See also Joseph A. Schumpeter, *History of Economic Analysis* (London, 1954), 717.

[12] Geoffrey Ingham, 'Money Is a Social Relation', *Review of Social Economy*, 54.4 (1996), 517.

[13] Wray, *Understanding Modern Money*, 12.

[14] Geoffrey Ingham, *The Nature of Money* (Cambridge, 2004).

national and international scale served to mediate between public and private monetary transactions, thereby creating 'a wider and more abstract monetary space based on impersonal trust and legitimacy'.[15] Thus capitalist money was characterised as the hybridisation of public currency and mercantile credit, in which the security of private transactions was ultimately guaranteed by the state.

While neo-chartalist reinterpretation of the history of modern money gives a proper place to the tremendous growth of credit currency in early capitalistic developments, it provides relatively less attention to historical variations and fluctuations. Why is it that modern monetary order has not always been stable? How did monetary regimes change and from what causes, and how were new monetary regimes naturalised? In particular, the fact that historical changes in monetary order often took place outside the control of monetary authorities warrants a study of money that gives equal attention to the monetary system and to the substantive level of money, that is how money has been used.[16] Viviana Zelizer's work on currency differentiation remains the best scholarly work highlighting the significance of monetary practice.[17] Zelizer argues that money users appropriated and modified money, attaching 'social meaning' to it, and that this currency appropriation could be observed even when a homogenous currency had been established. Zelizer discusses several strategies used to personalise currency, from mental accounting and 'earmarking' (separating money according to its origins and purposes) to physically altering notes and coins (adding personal marks and writings to them). While Zelizer stresses the personal nature of these practices, the appropriation of money through use could occur collectively. Alongside rules enforced by political authorities, users themselves may establish their own rules through everyday practice and social customs, creating a distinctive culture of money.

What Zelizer's study on the substantive level of money suggests is that money users can create and modify a monetary order. Nigel Dodd further investigated money users' constitutive role: he identified many instances 'in which money *already is* actively created by ordinary users – even those

---

[15] Ingham, *Nature of Money*, 126–31.

[16] Political scientist Eric Helleiner has discussed the creation of territorial currencies by investigating how the creation of the nation state and the dual growth of the state's financial operations and its disciplinary power, along with the advancement of technology to produce homogeneous currency, contributed to a situation that resulted in a nation having a single national currency. These factors, which Helleiner sees as the condition for the 'birth' of national currency, were more concerned with the consolidation of national currency, as his main example – Britain in the early nineteenth century – was antecedent to the establishment of the nation's money of account, the pound sterling. Eric Helleiner, *The Making of National Money: Territorial Currencies in Historical Perspective* (Ithaca, NY, 2003).

[17] Viviana Zelizer, *The Social Meaning of Money* (New York, 1994).

monies that states and banks produce'.[18] Money therefore is highly malleable and capable of reinvention. While the malleability of money has created distinctive monetary cultures and economic realities in different nations, communities and groups, money's capacity for reinvention provides a strong rationale for tracing the history of money. As Dodd rightly points out, to recognise money users' ability to mould and reinvent money is not to 'dispense with the need to understand the broader structural conditions of production of particular monies'.[19] Indeed, as much as money users are not entirely hedged in by rules set by the monetary authority (the state or banks), their use of money is not entirely free from certain sets of rules and structures that existed in moments in history.

A historical study of the substantive level of money can draw useful insights from how commodities were used in the past. In his influential essay in *The Social Life of Things*, Arjun Appadurai argues that studies of the circulation of commodities or things need to pay attention to a particular cultural and historical setting – what he calls the 'regime of value' – in which things were used.[20] The use of things is deeply connected to how they were designed, manufactured and distributed. Commodity use also includes both legitimate and illegitimate uses because users of things have not been entirely bound by the rules set by the commodities' makers. Such an insight perfectly applies to the history of the use of money. Like other things, money has an impassioned history of manufacture, including design, printing and counterfeiting. Money has been used, abused, stolen, lost, destroyed, prized, coveted and despised. There were material dimensions to the use of credit money, and, around its use, distinctive material cultures were formed. As will be discussed in this book, makers and users of paper currency equally took part in shaping the course of Britain's monetary history.

The history of money is also about culture. The use of money involves economic value and a shared belief regarding how such a value was generated. The foundation of monetary value was extensively discussed during the Bank Restriction period, and such discussions drove policy and everyday practice as they came to be widely accepted and formed part of contemporary culture. Money constituted a part of a broad cultural process, especially so during the Bank Restriction period because, at the time, there was a strong cultural tradition of seeing money

---

[18] Nigel Dodd, *The Social Life of Money* (Princeton, NJ, 2014), 272.
[19] Dodd, *Social Life of Money*, 306.
[20] Arjun Appadurai, 'Introduction: Commodities and the Politics of Value', in Arjun Appadurai, ed., *The Social Life of Things: Commodities in Cultural Perspective* (Cambridge, 1986), 15.

as a model of linguistic and visual representation. The monetary analogy of representation was founded on the idea of the intrinsic value of metallic currency. While the value of precious metal was thought to be the source of monetary value, metallic value and monetary value were supposed to have perfect correspondence. Before the Bank Restriction, the convertibility of paper currency into metallic currency guaranteed this correspondence. Once paper currency's convertibility was lost, the relationship no longer existed. Cultural historian Marc Shell found that the diffusion of paper currency foregrounded the issue of representative value in linguistics, aesthetics, literature and visual art, especially when paper wealth demonstrated its susceptibility to value fluctuation.[21] Inconvertible paper currency, by severing the bond between the representational medium of paper currency and what it purported to represent (gold and silver), posed a serious challenge to the traditional understanding of representation. This 'problematic of representation' concerning the epistemology and social existence of money had a profound impact on British culture.[22] The paper currency that appeared in James Gillray's caricatures, Samuel Taylor Coleridge's lectures, Percy Bysshe Shelley's poetry and Thomas De Quincey's prose was symptomatic of contemporary preoccupation with the question of the new relations between representation and value.[23]

Turning attention to everyday monetary operations, one could employ the concept of culture for heuristic purposes, as a way of identifying a set of beliefs and attitudes that shaped the ways the economic system operated on the ground. The research on the history of private credit serves as a case in point. Craig Muldrew's study of the English provincial economy demonstrates that ordinary economic transactions in the early modern period depended heavily on personal credit transactions that were grounded in a distinctive set of cultural norms and social expectations.[24] As purchases of daily necessities and household goods were conducted mostly on informal credit rather than cash, early modern consumers were entangled in a continuous credit relationship that formed the 'serial

---

[21] Marc Shell, *Art & Money* (Chicago, IL, 1995); Marc Shell, *Money, Language and Thought: Literary and Philosophical Economies from the Medieval to the Modern Era* (Berkeley, CA, 1982).

[22] Mary Poovey, *Genres of the Credit Economy: Mediating Value in Eighteenth- and Nineteenth-Century Britain* (Chicago, IL, 2008), 6, 16.

[23] Alexander Dick, *Romanticism and the Gold Standard: Money, Literature, and Economic Debate in Britain 1790–1830* (Basingstoke, 2013); Matthew Rowlinson, *Real Money and Romanticism* (Cambridge, 2010).

[24] Craig Muldrew, *The Economy of Obligation: The Culture of Credit and Social Relations in Early Modern England* (Basingstoke, 1998).

sociability of the culture of credit'.[25] At a time when long chains of credit relations connected households, contemporary culture had a strong emphasis on trust in one another. The local community closely monitored and communicated the state of personal credit that was built, demonstrated and maintained by individuals and households. Interpersonal trust, constant bargaining, reciprocity and leniency characterised the operation of what Muldrew calls the economy of obligation, in which, in its early phase, moral and economic obligations were intertwined.[26]

Historians of England's long nineteenth century have discovered the continued relevance of the traditional forms of personal credit operations. As Paul Johnson and Margot Finn demonstrate, consumer credit and credit-related litigations (as well as imprisonment for debt) were a part of everyday life in nineteenth-century England, existing alongside, on the one hand, non-monetary and non-contractual exchanges such as gift giving and, on the other, dry calculation-based economic transactions.[27] Finn, extending the chronology of the personalised economic relationship, has unearthed a wealth of personal experiences and literary depictions of consumer debt in her historical account of the piecemeal changes in debt-enforcing institutions. The mechanism for debt recovery in Victorian Britain still strongly featured personal bargaining and moral obligation, the operation of which was mediated and often defined by the equity tradition, extralegal obligations, negotiations and concessions, which worked in complicity with the cultural and social constraints of class and gender. As Finn writes, 'the enforcement of credit contracts was repeatedly mitigated in the practice of everyday life by contemporaries' reluctance to countenance notions of strict contract and individual liability'.[28]

What is at issue in the recent historiography of personal credit is the historical trajectory of the development of modern economic relations. Famously, Georg Simmel characterised modern money for its 'anonymity and colourlessness', qualities that detached it from money users'

---

[25] Muldrew, *Economy of Obligation*, 150–1.

[26] Muldrew observes an increasing dominance of institutionalised and centralised credit, such as the national financial market, the Bank of England and other joint-stock companies, which to some extent absorbed credit that previously circulated only in the local community. What Muldrew recognises as the growth of institutionalised credit corroborates Ingham's thesis of the historical hybridisation of public and private credit under the national monetary order. Muldrew, *Economy of Obligation*, 116.

[27] Margot C. Finn, *The Character of Credit: Personal Debt in English Culture, 1740–1914* (Cambridge, 2003); Paul Johnson, *Saving and Spending: The Working-Class Economy in Britain 1870–1939* (Oxford, 1985).

[28] Finn, *Character of Credit*, 98.

identity and personality.[29] After Simmel's seminal work, it became commonplace to assume depersonalisation in modern monetary relations – a separation between economic and social relationships – as a historical fact. However, credit currency has never existed entirely independent of social relations. Political power, communal practices and social networks remained factors that determined the circulation of credit currency. The assumption that modern money brought with it anonymous economic transactions is also questionable when it is tested against what we know about everyday life in nineteenth-century Britain, where face-to-face transactions remained the norm.

The continued relevance of personal credit relations points to a historiographical blind spot that exists between institutional provision and economic practices in terms of how they interacted in the past. Institutional credit provision involving the state and the Bank of England – on which the chartalist account of monetary history is grounded – was constantly subject to challenges and modifications. Among eighteenth-century authors, opinion was divided about the meaning of 'money of account' when the value of the Bank note and metallic currency diverged. The suspension of cash payments in 1797 shook the very foundation of monetary value, and such a systemic shock solicited a societal response from money users. Ultimately, interactions between the system, money users and their practices shaped a distinctive monetary landscape for Britain. Writing a history of money without money users is to miss a crucial component of the dynamics of the monetary regime and a driving force of regime change. Proper attention to money users is also indispensable when studying a period in which the constituency of money users saw a dramatic expansion – Britain's late eighteenth century being one such period. In particular, the Bank Restriction period saw the user-base of paper currency expand on an unprecedented scale. The introduction of small denomination notes in 1797 extended the reach of Bank notes to those who had previously not been accustomed to using paper currency in everyday transactions. As an increasing number of new members expanded the note-user community, the entire system of monetary circulation was restructured to accommodate them. In the resulting dense network of credit-money exchange, money users' practice transformed institutional provision. In other words, the institutionalised credit-money system was not entirely a product of deliberate policy or design, but it emerged at the juncture between institutional structure and note users' agency.

---

[29] Georg Simmel, *The Philosophy of Money*, ed. David Frisby (London, 1990 [1978]), 385.

This book draws upon the structural approach of neo-chartalism and the investigation into the substantive dimension of the use of money and its users. Rather than focusing on the genesis of credit money, its main interest lies in the dynamic process of credit money's evolution in one of the most turbulent eras of Britain's history. In particular, the book sheds light on the voluntarist and communal tradition in the history of credit money, though it by no means excludes other key forms of social entity, namely the state and nation. As Dodd argues, the three concepts – state, nation and community – offer alternative perspectives on the social aspects of money, which 'are not mutually exclusive and should not be run together'.[30] This book aims to describe how state, nation and community played their respective roles in shaping the history of Britain's paper currency.

Ideas of Paper Money and the Bank Restriction

Frank Fetter, who wrote extensively about the Bank Restriction period, notes that 'The two decades before 1797, despite the economic growth of the country and the expansion of banking, had been almost devoid of any fundamental analysis of the monetary standard, of banking theory, or of the position of the Bank of England'.[31] In terms of the development of monetary theory in Britain, the eighteenth century was only sparsely populated by major publications. One may even argue that the most fertile period of monetary debate prior to the Bank Restriction period was the 1690s, when the Great Recoinage debate produced numerous tracts that presented what became orthodox and heterodox theories of money. Monetary orthodoxy came to be represented by John Locke, whose claim that currency had an immutable metallic standard had subsequently been entrenched by the adoption of the de facto gold standard in 1717 by the Royal Mint under Isaac Newton's mastership.[32] On the other hand, the idea of flexible monetary standards, advocated by Locke's rival William Lowndes and the followers of Samuel

---

[30] Dodd, *Social Life of Money*, 8, 309. In contrast, Knapp distinguished between private and public 'pay communities'. Wray, *Understanding Modern Money*, 27.

[31] Frank W. Fetter, *Development of British Monetary Orthodoxy, 1797–1875* (Cambridge, MA, 1965), 1.

[32] Joyce Appleby, *Economic Thought and Ideology in Seventeenth-Century England* (Princeton, NJ, 1978); Joyce Appleby, 'Locke, Liberalism and the Natural Law of Money', *Past & Present*, 71 (1976), 43–69; John Locke, *Locke on Money*, ed. Patrick Hyde Kelly (Oxford, 1991); Kepa Ormazabal, 'Lowndes and Locke on the Value of Money', *History of Political Economy*, 44 (2012), 157–80.

Hartlieb – such as Cheney Culpeper and William Potter – fell into obscurity in the early eighteenth century.[33]

Eighteenth-century advocates of the paper-based currency system were generally discredited by its poor record of implementation. John Law, a Scotsman who contended that paper currency linked to the value of land was more stable than metallic currency, was to be remembered for his role in bringing about a devastating financial crash in France, where he put his idea into practice.[34] Mainstream economic writers in England and Scotland largely shied away from embracing paper currency that was not based on the metallic standard, with some exceptions, such as James Steuart and Bishop Berkeley, whose practical influence hardly matched that of their contemporary metallists, such as Joseph Harris, the Master of the Mint.[35] The Scottish thinker David Hume had a profound impact on the contemporary conception of money, though not because of his ideas about fiduciary money but because of his consolidation of the classical quantity theory of money.[36] As expressed by Hume, quantity theory saw a direct linkage between the quantity of money and the price level in a nation. When money was in excess of the volume required for a

[33] C. R. Fay, 'Locke versus Lowndes', *Historical Journal*, 4 (1933), 143–55; Carl Wennerlind, *Casualties of Credit: The English Financial Revolution, 1620–1720* (Cambridge, MA, 2011), 76, 129, 239; Carl Wennerlind, 'Money: Hartlibian Political Economy and the New Culture of Credit', in Philip Stern and Carl Wennerlind, eds., *Mercantilism Reimagined: Political Economy in Early Modern Britain and Its Empire* (New York, 2013), 81–5.

[34] Fetter, *British Monetary Orthodoxy*, 7–8.

[35] Schumpeter, *History of Economic Analysis*, 288–91. On Steuart, see Noboru Kobayashi, 'The First System of Political Economy', in Hiroshi Mizuta, Noboru Kobayashi and Andrew S. Skinner, eds., *An Inquiry into the Principles of Political Œconomy* (London, 1998), pp. lxxix–lxxxiii; Maria Luisa Pesante, 'Steuart's Theory of Money and Sovereignty', in Ramón Tortajada, ed., *The Economics of James Steuart* (New York, 1999), 186–200. On Berkeley, see Joseph Johnston, 'A Synopsis of Berkeley's Monetary Philosophy', *Hermathena*, 30 (1940), 73–86; Douglas Vickers, *Studies in the Theory of Money, 1690–1776* (London, 1960). Much less has been written on Harris, despite Schumpeter's comment that his work on money 'has some claim to being considered one of the best eighteenth century performances in the field of monetary analysis'. Schumpeter, *History of Economic Analysis*, 291.

[36] David Hume, 'Of Money', in Eugene F. Miller, ed., *Essays, Moral, Political, and Literary* (Indianapolis, 1985), 281–94; David Hume, 'Of the Balance of Trade', in Eugene F. Miller, ed., *Essays, Moral, Political, and Literary* (Indianapolis, 1985), 308–26. There has been a re-evaluation of Hume's monetary thought by scholars who interpret Hume's writings as being much more open to fiat currency than previous historians have acknowledged. Skaggs claims that 'Hume accepted the concept of fiduciary money to at least a limited extent'. Neil T. Skaggs, 'Credit Where Credit Is Due: Henry Thornton and the Evolution of the Theory of Fiduciary Money', *History of Political Economy*, 44 (2012), 451–69. Schabas and Wennerlind go further to suggest that Hume saw money's essence as trust and confidence. Margaret Schabas and Carl Wennerlind, 'Retrospectives: Hume on Money, Commerce, and the Science of Economics', *Journal of Economic Perspectives*, 25 (2011), 217–30; Wennerlind, 'Money', 86.

nation's trade, it would cause a general price increase, and, as high domestic prices deterred exports and attracted goods from abroad, the international payment medium, metallic currency, would be drawn out of the nation. This automatic mechanism of international adjustments – or the specie flow mechanism – would eventually settle the amount of domestic currency at a 'right' level.[37] Given the role of metallic currency in acting as the primary adjustment medium, quantity theory was firmly grounded in the metallic standard.

Like his contemporaries, Adam Smith based his views on paper currency on the metallist tradition, which is evident in his famous statement that compared the 'highway' of gold and silver money with 'the Daedalian wings of paper money'.[38] While admitting that the use of a paper medium would improve economic production, Smith saw convertibility as the necessary condition to guarantee the natural operation of the commodity money system.[39] Smith's attachment to convertibility as the precondition for secure paper currency was accompanied by a somewhat abstract notion of 'real transactions'.[40] Based on his observation of contemporary events, in particular the collapse of the Ayr Bank in 1772, Smith maintained that secure forms of paper instruments were based on concrete economic transactions as opposed to 'fictitious' or 'accommodation' bills that were created solely to supply credit. The real bills doctrine was to be reiterated during the Bank Restriction period, often being paired with the idea that excess credit currency would return to the issuers – which was called the law of reflux.[41] In hindsight, one may identify some embryonic ideas among British and other European writers concerning how credit currency operated. As yet, however, those early ideas had not grown into a coherent theory on inconvertible paper.[42]

The absence of a dominant orthodoxy in monetary theory, especially regarding inconvertible paper currency, resulted in an intense debate on currency and finance during the Bank Restriction period. Indeed, the period produced one of the most extensive debates on monetary issues in

---

[37] Fetter, *British Monetary Orthodoxy*, 4–5; D. P. O'Brien, *The Classical Economists Revisited* (Princeton, NJ, 2004), 169–75.

[38] Adam Smith, *An Inquiry into the Nature and Causes of the Wealth of Nations*, ed. R. H. Campbell, A. S. Skinner and W. B. Todd (Oxford, 1976), 321.

[39] Arie Arnon, *Monetary Theory and Policy from Hume and Smith to Wicksell: Money, Credit, and the Economy* (Cambridge, 2011), 38–44. See also Wray, *Understanding Modern Money*, 21–2.

[40] Smith, *Wealth of Nations*, 304.   [41] Fetter, *British Monetary Orthodoxy*, 10.

[42] The important contributions to currency theory by Ferdinand Galliani and Richard Cantillon were largely unknown in Britain; so were the previous Swedish debates on inconvertibility. Schumpeter, *History of Economic Analysis*, 706.

British history, known as the Bullionist Controversy, which culminated in 1809–11 with the publication of a parliamentary report on the high price of gold. Essentially, the debate revolved around the propriety of continuing with inconvertibility by inquiring whether the inflation experienced at the time could be attributed to the excessive issue of Bank notes. Those who took part in the debate often turned to Locke, Hume, Steuart and Smith, but these authorities from previous generations offered little direct insight on inconvertible currency, giving commentators on monetary issues in Bank Restriction Britain considerable room for theoretical latitude.[43]

Historians have traditionally depicted the development of monetary theory during the Bank Restriction by identifying two opposing camps: bullionists and anti-bullionists. According to this scheme, bullionists were adherents to the metallic standard, and they believed that money was an exogenous factor to the economy; that is, an increase in the volume of money did not affect the scale of economic activity.[44] Following quantity theory, they argued that when a greater amount of money was thrown into circulation, the excess money would raise the domestic price level, the principal indicator of which was the market price of bullion, until international specie flow eventually adjusted the price level, cancelling out the effect of excess currency. According to bullionists, the international distribution of the precious metal predetermined the amount of money that a nation could accommodate; hence issuing excess currency beyond the metallic reserve would harm the economy by causing inflation.[45] In contrast, anti-bullionists did not recognise the inflationary effect of excess currency, as they believed that additional money would stimulate economic activity – money as an endogenous factor – and that a nation's metallic reserve did not constrain the volume of money.[46] They claimed that the market price of bullion was primarily determined by its supply and demand rather than by the amount of circulating media. While bullionists regarded the metallic standard as an indispensable mechanism to rein in excessive currency

[43] Jacob H. Hollander, 'The Development of the Theory of Money from Adam Smith to David Ricardo', *Quarterly Journal of Economics*, 25 (1911), 429–70.

[44] Arnon, *Monetary Theory and Policy*, ch. 8; Edwin Cannan, 'Introduction', in Edwin Cannan, ed., *The Paper Pound of 1797–1821: A Reprint of the Bullion Report* (London, 1919), pp. vii–xlvi.

[45] Classic explanations are James W. Angell, *The Theory of International Prices: History, Criticism and Restatement* (Cambridge, 1926); D. P. O'Brien, ed., *Foundations of Monetary Economics*, ii: *The Bullionists* (London, 1994); Jacob Viner, *Studies in the Theory of International Trade* (New York, 1937).

[46] D. P. O'Brien, ed., *Foundations of Monetary Economics*, iii: *The Anti-Bullionists* (London, 1994).

creation, anti-bullionists did not see the need to link metallic and non-metallic currency, thereby advocating a paper-based monetary system. This schematic understanding of rival monetary theories, however, glosses over the wide spectrum of opinions and, at the same time, obscures some shared assumptions.[47] Dividing bullionists into 'rigid' and 'moderate' groups, as D. P. O'Brien has done, is one way to introduce a more nuanced understanding, but one should not assume that contemporary views always allow a neat categorisation.[48]

Arguably, we can set an earlier starting point for the British debate on inconvertible paper currency – in the early 1790s; by doing so, we begin to understand the political nature of the early debate and how the politics of the paper currency debate generated some shared understandings about paper currency among British writers prior to the Bank Restriction. What defined this early debate, and was the principal reference point for British writers, was the French experience of fiat currency during the French Revolution. As Linda Colley has argued, Britain's national identity between 1688 and 1815 was consolidated by envisaging the French nation as 'the Other', the plainest marker of which was the two nations' religious affiliation: Protestant Britain pitted against Catholic France.[49] The contrast did not stop there, and in the final phase of the 'protracted duel' between the two nations, beginning with the French Revolution and ending in the Battle of Waterloo, British society produced expressions of the French *otherness* in political, cultural and monetary terms. In this process, the British nation rediscovered their constitutional tradition, their cultural uniqueness and their economic system that owed much to robust industrial activity, the free market and a dependable currency.[50] Given the symbolic role that national currencies played in consolidating the collective consciousness of modern nation states across the world, the idea that there was a monetary dimension in the debate on British national identity formation was hardly far-fetched.[51] To British writers and politicians, the French paper currency *assignat* was a powerful symbol of the otherness of the French polity, which came to wield authoritarian power over the nation's economy. The *assignats*, originally issued in 1789 as a form of government

[47] Anna Gambles, *Protection and Politics: Conservative Economic Discourse, 1815–1852* (London, 1999), 90.

[48] O'Brien, *Classical Economists Revisited*, 176–7.

[49] Linda Colley, *Britons: Forging the Nation, 1707–1837* (New Haven, CT, 1992), 5–7, 18, 322.

[50] Colley, *Britons*, 24.

[51] For currency and national identity, see, for example, Eric Helleiner, ed., *Nation-States and Money: The Past, Present and Future of National Currencies* (London, 1999).

bond to cover state expenditure and reduce national debt, were backed by confiscated church estates.[52] Its creators originally envisaged that the holders of *assignats*, which bore 5 per cent interest, would use the bonds – amounting to 400 million francs – to purchase the confiscated land. When they exchanged the bonds for land, the *assignats* were supposed to be cancelled and burnt. However, not only did *assignats* remain in circulation after land purchases were completed, but the state's need for financial resources led to a prodigious further issue, or over-issue of the bonds, which then circulated as currency. Eventually, in April 1790, the French government decreed that *assignats* were legal tender and enshrined their place by printing small-denomination notes. Far from being the representation of secure property, the French paper currency became a medium for speculation and a major cause of inflation. The discussion on *assignats* served as a dress rehearsal for the subsequent British debate on inconvertible paper currency. William Huskisson, a young British expat in Paris with ambitions towards a political career – who would later become a leading authority in currency matters in his own country – made his name by applying Humean quantity theory to the *assignat* in his speech at the Societe de 1789 in Paris in August 1790. He told his French audience that, with the enormous amount of paper money in France, 'your prices in *paper* will go to any amount: your gold and silver will rise in *paper* price, like all other things'.[53]

Edmund Burke, whose animosity towards the revolution was fuelled by the way *assignats* were created, voiced the most celebrated critique against the French paper currency. As the intellectual historian J. G. A. Pocock astutely observed, Burke regarded the financial operation that gave birth to the *assignat* 'the central, the absolute and the unforgivable crime of the Revolutionaries'.[54] Burke's animadversion of the French currency was rooted in his rejection of any analogy between the English Revolution in 1688 and the French one in 1789. While the credit of the Bank of England, established as part of the Glorious Revolution, was supported by investments and deposits coming from citizens' voluntary

---

[52] Michael Bordo and Eugene White, 'A Tale of Two Currencies: British and French Finance during the Napoleonic Wars', *Journal of Economic History*, 51 (1991), 303–16; Jagjit S. Chadha and Elisa Newby, 'Midas, Transmuting All, into Paper: The Bank of England and the Banque de France during the Revolutionary and Napoleonic Wars' (Bank of Finland Research Discussion Papers 20/2013, 2013), 27–9; Eugene N. White, 'The French Revolution and the Politics of Government Finance, 1770–1815', *Journal of Economic History*, 55 (1995), 227–55.

[53] John Wright, *A Biographical Memoir of the Right Honourable William Huskisson* (London, 1831), 14.

[54] J. G. A. Pocock, 'The Political Economy of Burke's Analysis of the French Revolution', *Historical Journal*, 25 (1982), 334.

contribution, the French system was based on confiscation and forced-currency circulation, which amounted to the denunciation of private property.[55] Burke laid out the historical foundation of English public credit, centred around two pillars or conditions. The first pillar was the convertibility of Bank notes into precious metal, the core component of the Bank note as a 'promise to pay'. The second pillar was the principle that Bank notes were accepted only *by choice*. The credit of the Bank was ultimately guaranteed by its treasures, but acceptance of its notes was not compulsory but voluntary. No law, but custom enforced convertibility and voluntary acceptance. In England, papers issued by banks had no value 'in law', Burke explains, 'Nor is there amongst us a single public security of any quality or nature whatsoever, that is enforced by authority'.[56] It was this very denial of despotic power in the monetary order that safeguarded the English monetary system from degenerating into a system of forced monetary circulation like that which was emerging in France.[57] Burke drew a line between money that was 'enforced by authority' and money that was received voluntarily. The distinction between 'money by authority' and what his contemporaries called money of confidence was not Burke's invention, but political discussion of paper currency was most powerfully expressed in Burke's writing in the contrast between Britain's democratic money and the 'paper-money despotism' in France.[58]

Britain's early discussion on paper currency was not without division of opinion. A young medical student from Scotland, James Mackintosh, made an impassioned defence of the French Revolution against Burke's diatribe, in which he strove to cast a positive light on the new French system of finance.[59] Mackintosh argued that the National Assembly revived, rather than destroyed, public credit in France after the *Ancien Régime* had debilitated the French nation politically and financially.[60] Mackintosh's case for the regeneration of public credit soon lost ground as the continental wars put pressure on French finances, leading to a greater reliance on paper money, which was issued much beyond the

---

[55] Pocock, 'Burke's Analysis of the French Revolution', 347.

[56] Burke, *Reflections on the Revolution in France*, 401.

[57] On the forced circulation of the *assignat* in contrast to other voluntary currencies in France, see Rebecca L. Spang, *Stuff and Money in the Time of the French Revolution* (Cambridge, MA, 2015), 8–9.

[58] Pocock, 'Burke's Analysis of the French Revolution', 338.

[59] James Mackintosh, *Vindiciae Gallicae: Defence of the French Revolution, and Its English Admirers, against the Accusations of the Right Hon. E. Burke* (London, 1791).

[60] Steven Blakemore, *Intertextual War: Edmund Burke and the French Revolution in the Writings of Mary Wollstonecraft, Thomas Paine and James Mackintosh* (Madison, NJ, 1997), 204–7; Mackintosh, *Vindiciae Gallicae*, 22–35, 146–61.

estimated value of the confiscated property.[61] Private commercial transactions in France, including those involving specie, were severely restricted, and prices and wages came to be controlled by the Laws of the Maximum.[62] Legal sanctions, with the threat of the death penalty, were the principal tool to maintain the value of the currency, which proved to be ineffective against the rapid depreciation. In 1793, William Playfair estimated that the value of the *assignat* was more than half its previous level.[63] By 1796, the *assignat* had become practically worthless.

In the run-up to the French Revolutionary War, Burke's rhetorical assault on French paper money led to a practical rejection of its circulation in Britain. During most of the eighteenth century, payments in foreign paper currency between private individuals on British soil were valid with the agreement of the concerned parties.[64] The legality, or indeed the propriety of such practice came into question when John Wilkinson, who was a successful industrialist and brother-in-law to the radical thinker Joseph Priestley, circulated small-denomination *assignats* among workers and tradespeople at Bersham near Wrexham, Wales, where Wilkinson operated an ironworks.[65] The local circulation of French paper money came to the notice of Lord Chief Justice Kenyon, and subsequently parliament discussed the issue in December 1792.[66] The leading supporter of the bill to prevent the circulation of the *assignat* was Edmund Burke, who declared that its circulation was a 'treasonable fraud' that would serve 'no other purpose than that of assisting the

---

[61] Blakemore, *Intertextual War*, 205.

[62] Thomas J. Sargent and François R. Velde, *The Big Problem of Small Change* (Princeton, NJ, 2002), 505.

[63] William Playfair, *A General View of the Actual Force and Resources of France* (London, 1793), 52–3. Echoing Burke, Playfair later condemned the despotism of the Jacobins, who '[rule the nation] by means of a printing press and reams of assignats, pillage the nation, and excite massacre and bloodshed'. William Playfair, *The History of Jacobinism, Its Crimes, Cruelties and Perfidies* (London, 1795), 730.

[64] *Jordan's Parliamentary Journal* (1793), i, 186.

[65] W. H. Chaloner, *Industry and Innovation: Selected Essays*, ed. W. O. Henderson (London, 1990), 46; George Selgin, *Good Money: Birmingham Button Makers, the Royal Mint, and the Beginnings of Modern Coinage, 1775–1821* (Ann Arbor, MI, 2008), 57–8.

[66] R. H. Thompson, 'French Assignats Current in Britain: The Parliamentary Debate', *British Numismatic Journal*, 51 (1981), 200. Original papers: Letter from Peter Whitehall Davies to Lord Kenyon, 19 Dec. 1792, Lancashire Record Office (hereafter RO), DDKE/HMC/1373; Letter from Thomas Griffith to Lord Grenville, 7 Dec. 1792, The National Archives, Kew (hereafter, TNA), HO 42/23/98, fols. 226–8; Copy Out-letter to Thomas Griffith of Rhual from the Home Secretary, 10 Dec. 1792, TNA, HO 42/23/99, fols. 229–30; Letter from Thomas Griffith, 20 Dec. 1792, TNA, HO 42/23/100, fols. 231–2; Letter from Alexander Trotter, 29 Dec. 1792, TNA, HO 42/23/275, fols. 599–600; Letter from Thomas Griffith, 7 Jan. 1793, TNA, HO 42/24/22, fols. 48–9.

circulation of French principles'.[67] At the beginning of 1793, an act prohibiting the circulation of French-issued promissory notes was proclaimed, making French papers 'utterly void and of no effect in any payment within this realm'.[68] Offenders were to be fined five to twenty pounds for each note used.[69]

Burke, who died in July 1797, did not live to see how the new monetary regime of inconvertible paper unfolded – he only had a short glimpse of it from his death bed.[70] Nor is he remembered for his contribution to how his compatriots saw and understood the nature of paper currency that was no longer convertible to coins.[71] Burke's view on money was essentially political, and his inclination was closer to metallism than to nominalism, but he needed more than convertibility to set English paper currency apart from its French counterpart, which was, when Burke wrote his *Reflections* in 1790, still convertible into lands. The voluntarist basis of currency acceptance, rather than convertibility – which hardly distinguished Britain's paper currency from other convertible notes – was what made Burke's monetary contrast truly compelling and, at the same time, gave Burke's discussion of currency a logical coherence, especially by aligning it with his understanding of the English constitution. By introducing the voluntarist view of democratic money into his discussion, Burke practically resurrected the heterodox tradition in monetary theory, that is a credit-based theory of money. Equally importantly, Burke's discussion pointed to the distinctive way in which the contemporary discussion about paper currency was formulated. In addition to the rival theories of metallism and non-metallism, there was also a division within the latter. There were two forms of non-metallist view, or credit theory of money: one entailed an authority-based currency like the *assignat*, and the other a trust-based currency that was – as appeared in Burke's forceful discussion on Anglo-French monetary contrast – accepted voluntarily. That there were two sources of credit was a widely shared understanding of credit currency during the Bank Restriction period, an understanding that was reinforced by leading authorities in monetary discussion such as Henry Thornton and William Huskisson,

---

[67] *Jordan's Parliamentary Journal*, i, 186–8.   [68] 33 Geo III, c. 1 (1793).

[69] 33 Geo III, c. 1, s. 2.

[70] It is noteworthy, however, that Burke reiterated the voluntary and communal nature of Britain's public finance in 1797. Edmund Burke, *A Third Letter to a Member of the Present Parliament, on the Proposals for Peace with the Regicide Directory of France* (London, 1797), 102. See also, Robert Mitchell, *Sympathy and the State in the Romantic Era: Systems, State Finance, and the Shadows of Futurity* (London, 2007), 131–2.

[71] For example, Adam Smith denounced American colonies' enforcement of paper currency by legal tender laws. Wray, *Understanding Modern Money*, 21–2.

while rigid bullionists such as Walter Boyd and David Ricardo strove to diminish, though they found it difficult to repudiate in toto, the theoretical importance of the distinction within credit currency.

In terms of the history of monetary theory, what is significant is that the majority of British commentators on money did not attribute the value of paper currency to the state. Indeed, those who refused to associate Bank notes with any authoritative power of the state largely dominated the debate on inconvertible paper currency up to 1810. Of the two rival concepts of money in the tradition of monetary theory, which were identified by Charles Goodhart as metallism and chartalism, the latter was anathema to most monetary commentators in Bank Restriction Britain.[72] It was not that chartalism, the state theory of money, did not exist in Britain; it was avoided and marginalised in theory and policy because the majority view at the time deemed it incompatible with the nation's democratic society and their liberal economic creed.[73] As the following chapters will elaborate, the voluntarist idea of money had a profound impact on British society as Britons acted on the belief that their voluntary acceptance was the source of monetary value.

Communal Currency in Britain's Past

Throughout this book, the term *communal currency* is employed as a generic description of a dynamically evolving idea and practice concerning currency that manifested in writings and actions of Britons during the Bank Restriction period. It is an arbitrary term compared to currency voluntarism, which was more explicitly articulated by Burke and many of those who contemplated the nature of inconvertible currency in the period of our study. Still, such a historiographical intervention is warranted for capturing, in a proximate form, a strand of belief and practice in a coherent manner, while avoiding the distinctive connotations with which the term 'confidence' came to be associated. Economic writers during the Bank Restriction period frequently referred to confidence

---

[72] Charles Goodhart, 'The Two Concepts of Money: Implications for the Analysis of Optimal Currency Areas', *European Journal of Political Economy*, 14 (1998), 407–32. For the distinction between metallism and chartalism, see Schumpeter, *History of Economic Analysis*, 288–9.

[73] Neo-chartalists, following Knapp, do not see legal tender as a particularly important factor. Wray, *Understanding Modern Money*, 11, 26. For its rejection of legal tender and state power, Britain's communal trust theory should be distinguished from the romantic economic theory of Adam Müller, who, according to Schumpeter, 'confus[ed] the State with Society'. Schumpeter, *History of Economic Analysis*, 428.

when they described interpersonal trust in the monetary community.[74] Confidence is central to Thornton's historical and theoretical account of paper circulation in his *An Enquiry into the Nature and Effects of the Paper Credit of Great Britain* (1802) as he delineates a conjectural historical evolution of paper-based credit from personal trust among 'commercial men' to a more general trust. Commercial papers, he explains, first circulated based on 'confidence placed by each receiver in the last indorser [on the paper]'.[75] It is only when 'confidence rises to a certain height in a country' that paper instruments begin to circulate more widely and served as a common currency.[76] For Thornton, the British public's universal esteem of the Bank of England was the embodiment of this historical process. While Thornton's use of the language of confidence was hardly exceptional at the time, his analysis went beyond his contemporaries' largely static view of confidence. Thornton identified a dynamic level of confidence that modulated the velocity of paper circulation – a high degree of confidence would, for instance, increase the velocity of circulation, creating the multiplier effect of monetary circulation. Like his contemporaries, Thornton believed the confidence-based monetary order was what distinguished British paper currency from other, 'forced' currencies because, under the forced-currency system, there was a strong temptation for the state to manipulate the monetary value, and such political meddling did little to solicit general confidence, making the value of forced currency inherently unstable.[77] This was exactly the point Burke made in his contrast between the French *assignat*, which was circulated by authority, and the Bank of England note, which was accepted by choice. From the 1790s until the 1830s, various writers reiterated the idea of confidence as the basis of currency circulation, such as Thomas Attwood, who stated that any payment medium was 'created by confidence, supported by confidence, and discharged by

---

[74] On the proponents of the confidence theory in the 1790s, see Daniele Besomi, 'Paper Money and National Distress: William Huskisson and the Early Theories of Credit, Speculation and Crises', *European Journal of the History of Economic Thought*, 17 (2010), 64–5.

[75] Henry Thornton, *An Enquiry into the Nature and Effects of the Paper Credit of Great Britain* (London, 1802), 40. See also Arnon, *Monetary Theory and Policy*, 53; Friedrich A. von Hayek, 'Introduction', in Friedrich A. von Hayek, ed., *An Enquiry into the Nature and Effects of the Paper Credit of Great Britain (1802)* (London, 1939), 46–7; Neil T. Skaggs, 'Henry Thornton and the Development of Classical Monetary Economics', *Canadian Journal of Economics*, 28 (1995), 1214–15; Neil T. Skaggs, 'Thomas Tooke, Henry Thornton, and the Development of British Monetary Orthodoxy', *Journal of the History of Economic Thought*, 25 (2003), 183–4; Thornton, *Paper Credit*, 13–14.

[76] Thornton, *Paper Credit*, 37.   [77] Thornton, *Paper Credit*, 61–7.

confidence'.[78] The idea also manifested in money users' actions in Bank Restriction Britain. When money users held a strong belief that their voluntary acceptance was crucial in maintaining monetary value, their actions, especially at a moment of crisis, took a distinctively participatory form – there are examples throughout this book. Communal currency was not merely an idea, but something that guided the actions of Britain's money users and was embedded in the nation's monetary institutions.[79]

Our consideration of the money users' community begs the question about the constitution of such a community. For much of the eighteenth century, most Britons had only a limited experience of paper currency in their everyday life. With the suspension of cash payments in 1797 and the subsequent introduction of small-denomination notes, which substituted metallic currency to a significant extent, the notes issued by the Bank of England and other banking houses became familiar objects to an increasing proportion of the British population. In 1770, Thomas Bridge's humorous parable *Adventures of a Bank Note* described the Bank note as a status symbol, the possession of which made a humble poet into 'a Bank-dubb'd esquire'.[80] By 1805, when John Bounden, a shipwright at Plymouth dockyard, received his wages in Bank notes, being a note user had ceased to be a marker of aspirational economic status.[81] In the last decades of the eighteenth century, there was a dynamic development in Britain's credit currency, and the suspension of cash payments was undoubtedly the most important factor driving that development. In the new monetary landscape, in which Bank notes passed through the hands of diverse users from provincial shipwrights to wealthy bankers in the metropolis, the money users' community was reconstituted and had to be reimagined.

The exuberance of paper credit was a blessing and a curse for British society. From the 1770s onwards, the expansion of currency circulation by speculative bankers with weak or dubious credit had caused high-profile business failures such as the collapse of the Ayr Bank in the 1770s and that of the Manchester bank of Allen & Co. in the 1780s.[82] In 1793,

---

[78] Thomas Attwood, *Prosperity Restored; or, Reflections on the Cause of the Public Distresses, and on the Only Means of Relieving Them* (London, 1817), 30. See also David J. Moss, *Thomas Attwood: The Biography of a Radical* (Montreal, 1990), 58–9. Moss calls Attwood 'a student of Thornton' (p. 60).

[79] For discussion on the social aspects of state, nation and community, see Dodd, *Social Life of Money*, 8, 309. Compare Wray, *Understanding Modern Money*, 27.

[80] Thomas Bridges, *The Adventures of a Bank-Note* (London, 1770), i, 15. See also Poovey, *Genres of the Credit Economy*, 144–52.

[81] On this episode, see Chapter 3.

[82] On the Ayr Bank affair, see Tyler Beck Goodspeed, *Legislating Instability: Adam Smith, Free Banking, and the Financial Crisis of 1772* (Cambridge, MA, 2016); Henry Hamilton,

when Britain was witnessing another bout of business failures, an anonymous writer with the pseudonym of Colbert Jr attributed it, in a pamphlet entitled *The Age of Paper*, to the great increase of 'fictitious capital' that had proliferated in England. While being intended as a warning against the unbridled expansion of paper credit, the pamphlet was written when the memory of the French *assignat* was still fresh and contrasting the French and the English currencies was the foremost preoccupation of British writers on currency issues. Tellingly, the author dedicated the pamphlet to Edmund Burke, who sounded an alarm regarding the danger of the French Revolution and 'denounced the *despotism of capital*, which enchained arts, sciences, and industry itself'.[83] The pamphlet, which drew upon Burke's authority on financial matters, is just one example of the way British writers discussed monetary issues at the junction of political, literary and economic thought in pre-1797 Britain. After the suspension of cash payments in 1797, which heralded a new era in the monetary order, British writers became increasingly conscious of the social dimension of inconvertible currency, which was a dominant feature of paper credit in post-1797 Britain. Thornton and his contemporaries did not fail to notice the redistributional effect that the fluctuation of currency value produced, and they discussed, for instance, how the stickiness of wages made labourers' lives difficult during an inflationary period.[84] They discussed such topics primarily as problems associated with inconvertible paper currency, and their recognition that paper currency was creating new social relations and inequities was peculiar to this time, when a greater part of the British population – including an increasing number of wage labourers – had come to be caught in the web of paper credit. The anti-paper controversialist William Cobbett was acutely aware of social inequity, a prevailing feature of the age of paper currency, as he stated, 'Not such a creation as that of paper money, which only takes the dinner from one man and gives

---

'The Failure of the Ayr Bank, 1772', *Economic History Review*, 8 (1956), 405–17; Paul Kosmetatos, 'The Winding-Up of the Ayr Bank, 1772–1827', *Financial History Review*, 21 (2014), 165–90; Hugh Rockoff, 'Upon Daedalian Wings of Paper Money: Adam Smith and the Crisis of 1772', in Fonna Forman-Barzilai, ed., *Adam Smith Review*, iv (London, 2011), 237–68. On the episode of the failure of Allen & Co., see T. S. Ashton, 'The Bill of Exchange and Private Banks in Lancashire, 1790–1830', *Economic History Review*, 15 (1945), 28–9; Leo H. Grindon, *Manchester Banks and Bankers: Historical, Biographical, and Anecdotal* (Manchester, 1877), 45–6; Frank Stuart Jones, 'The Development of Banking Institutions in Manchester, 1770–1850' (unpublished PhD thesis, University of British Columbia, 1975), 31; L. S. Pressnell, *Country Banking in the Industrial Revolution* (Oxford, 1956), 455.

[83] Colbert Jr, *The Age of Paper; or, an Essay on Banks and Banking* (London, 1793), p. v.
[84] See Chapter 5.

it to another, which only gives an unnatural swell to a city or a watering place by beggaring a thousand villages'.[85] One thing historians have hitherto failed to appreciate is the extent to which the paper currency debate during the Bank Restriction period contributed to nurturing a new sensitivity to monetised social relations, which would later be called the 'cash nexus'. The idea of the cash nexus, as a fundamental critique on capitalistic, money-oriented social relations, would have been developed by Thomas Carlyle, Friedrich Engels, Karl Marx and John Ruskin in the Victorian period; but when these Victorian writers denounced society as being connected only by the cold chains or shackles of the monetised exchange of labour, they stood on the societal experience of over two decades of inconvertible paper currency.[86] It is worth noting that Carlyle, who called the era of the French Revolution the 'Age of Paper, and of the Burning of Paper', with a distinctive echo of Burke, belonged to the generation of Britons who were growing up when Britain departed from the metallic monetary standard and were probably the first generation that regarded paper currency as *cash*.[87]

Notwithstanding its contribution to the lineage of anti-capitalistic discourse, communal currency in the early part of the Bank Restriction was, in the main, a description of sanguine social relations mediated by monetary exchange. Jeremy Bentham, who, as an admirer of Thornton, was well versed in the contemporary idea of communal currency, pithily remarked,

The credit of paper is a disposition of public opinion, which is strengthened by general example and habit to such a degree that a time arrives when nobody thinks of converting it into cash: abstractly speaking, every body may know that the existing mass has no solid base, but this ideal reflection does not intrude into the ordinary transactions of life, and distrust does not attach to this or that individual piece of the paper. It is received as it is given. Others have trusted it, we can trust it as well.[88]

According to Bentham's account, note users based their decision to accept a note on the trust that had been shown by note users before then,

---

[85] William Cobbett, *Rural Rides*, ed. Ian Dyck (London, 2001), 256.

[86] On the cash nexus, see, for example, Niall Ferguson, *The Cash Nexus: Money and Power in the Modern World, 1700–2000* (London, 2001).

[87] Thomas Carlyle, *The French Revolution: A History*, ed. David Sorensen (Oxford, 1989), 154; Simon Heffer, *Moral Desperado: A Life of Thomas Carlyle* (London, 1995), 169–70; John B. Lamb, 'The Paper Age: Currency, Crisis, and Carlyle', *Prose Studies*, 30 (2008), 27–44; B. W. Young, *The Victorian Eighteenth Century: An Intellectual History* (Oxford, 2007), 33–4.

[88] Jeremy Bentham, 'The True Alarm', in *Jeremy Bentham's Economic Writings*, ed. Werner Stark (London, 1954), iii, 105–6.

and this decision was equally, though implicitly, based on the expectation that others in the future would judge the value of the note in exactly the same manner and accept it.[89] In such a way, personal trust is accumulated and shared among note users and therefore becomes *interpersonal* trust, while individual users perceive this interpersonal trust by identifying with other subjects.[90] The money users' community is a space in which interpersonal trust gives general currency to a payment medium. To be sure, this community has, for the most part, an abstract and notional existence; it is an 'imagined community' that is hardly visible in normal times.[91] Nor is the coherence and stability of such a community always guaranteed on account of social divisions by class, gender, geography and politics. It is all the more remarkable, however, that the obvious social divisions in eighteenth-century British society did not hinder contemporaries from embracing a community-based understanding of currency. Equally importantly, the decline of communal currency in the 1810s was not the result of teleological development of modern monies since historical contingency operated powerfully in discrediting communal currency and bringing about its eventual demise.

In its attempt to rediscover Britain's communal currency, this book departs from the conventional chronology of the Bank Restriction period, which starts in 1797 with the suspension of the Bank of England's cash payments and ends in 1821 when convertibility was restored. Instead, this book's narrative starts in the early 1790s, when the British had an initial engagement with inconvertible paper currency through their observation of the French monetary experiment. By contrasting the French *assignat* with their own paper currency, some British writers had early inklings that they were entering an age of paper, which turned into a conviction with the introduction of inconvertible paper currency in 1797. The choice of 1833 as the book's terminus ad quem defies the conventional narrative, which concludes with the resumption of cash payments in 1821 – the year when Britain's paper-based currency system came to an end. The early gold standard was hardly a stable system, and, for a study of Britain's communal currency tradition, 1833 is far more symbolic because, in that year, with the Bank note becoming the legal tender of the land, the voluntary foundation of the nation's currency was ultimately lost. The book's daring claim that

---

[89] This is unless the latest owner of the note decides to become the note's final user by bringing it to the original issuer for payment.

[90] Helleiner, *Making of National Money*, 45–6; Rowlinson, *Real Money and Romanticism*, 5.

[91] Benedict Anderson, *Imagined Communities: Reflections on the Origin and Spread of Nationalism* (London, 1983).

the Bank of England note was a *British* currency in the early nineteenth century may sound anachronistic. Admittedly, most of the events that the book narrates took place in England, but the fact remains that the notes issued by a bank based in London, without branches for most of the period of our study, were at the heart of contemporary discussion and imagination across the British Isles. And, as the following chapters strive to demonstrate, the English bank's notes did find a way to various parts of England, Wales, Scotland, Ireland and beyond.

This book's thematic chapters do not follow a strict chronological order, yet they are divided into two parts that correspond to the two distinctive stages of Britain's monetary regime that were dominated by paper currency. In the first part, Chapters 1–3, the book's discussion focuses on the early part of the Bank Restriction period, when communal currency and currency voluntarism became predominant features of Britain's monetary landscape. Chapter 4 serves as the bridge between the book's two parts by illuminating a number of events that occurred in the early 1810s that collectively constituted a turning point, in terms of theory, policy and institutional arrangements, in the fortunes of Britain's inconvertible currency system. The second part of the book, Chapters 5 and 6, describes how public hostility against the Bank and the 'forced' circulation of the Bank note undermined currency voluntarism, causing disenchantment among note users about communal currency, which was accompanied by radicalisation of the communal currency idea. Disenchantment and the disintegration of the money users' community, as it will be argued, were the main drivers that consolidated support for terminating the inconvertible currency system in 1821, and the same disenchantment eventually wiped away the remnants of voluntarist and communal features from Britain's currency in 1833. The Conclusion briefly summarises the book's main discussions. The demise of Britain's communal currency in early nineteenth-century Britain was largely forgotten by later monetary economists and historians of money. This remains the case in the early twenty-first century, but this book has benefited from substantial advancement in the historical approach to finance and money. Once neglected, financial and monetary history has been reinvigorated as some serious questions have been posed to the neoclassical and neoliberal world views and their ability to explain the humane, impassioned and often unpredictable nature of capital markets and the floating monetary standard, a recent notable manifestation of which was the 2008 international financial crisis.

The rise of new types of communal currency, from local currencies to the digital cryptocurrency, has tested established understandings of money and currency, and, at the same time, the intensifying critiques of neoliberal markets and capitalism appear as direct assaults on Wall Street and the banking system.[92] History shows us that what appear to be unassailable institutions and scientific truths have often emerged as a product of intense negotiation, struggles and historical contingencies, including the suppression of rival ideas, and this book aims to shed light on such historical contingencies in the emergence of Britain's modern currency order and in the way monetary transactions in capitalist society have been organised and imagined in British society. The very historicity of the modern monetary landscape makes it legitimate to question what appear to be entrenched and immutable social institutions by appreciating the human agency that moulded and sustained them. In the following chapters, my hope is to capture the social life of Britain's paper currency as much as that of the money users who took part in the making of a modern monetary system.

---

[92] See, for instance, Nigel Dodd, 'The Social Life of Bitcoin', *Theory, Culture & Society*, 35 (2017), 35–56.

1   The Beginning of the Bank Restriction Period

We may consider, with wonder and astonishment, the small space which the sun appears to fill in the firmament, while we know and see that every part of our globe benefits by the vivifying effects of its rays. The Bank of England is, to the Agriculture, Commerce, and Finance of Great Britain, its sun: and the circulation of fifteen millions and a half of its paper is the basis on which its convenience, property, and safety have hitherto rested.

Francis Baring, *Observation on the Publication of Walter Boyd* (1801)

The run upon the Bank continued to increase, until the day last mentioned, Saturday, the 25th of February, 1797, a day which will long be remembered, and which will be amongst the most memorable in the annals of England, as being the *last* (hitherto at least) on which the Bank of England was compelled, at the will of the bearer, to pay its promissory notes in gold and silver, agreeably to the tenor of those notes.

William Cobbett, *Paper against Gold* (1815)

On the morning of 27 February 1797, the Bank of England opened its doors to customers as usual. The day's business was, however, a far cry from normal. Since the end of the seventeenth century, the Bank of England note had been a 'promise to pay', meaning one could demand to exchange a Bank note into coins. On this day, the Bank of England announced it would no longer honour that promise – the Bank note became 'a promise to pay promises with promises'.[1] The crowd of people who came to the Bank that morning saw, possibly with a sense of imminent financial doom, a handbill stating that the Privy Council had ordered the Bank of England's directors to suspend exchanging notes into coins.[2]

---

[1] Kevin Barry, 'The Aesthetics of Paper Money: National Difference during the Period of Enlightenment and Romanticism', in David Duff and Catherine Jones, eds., *Scotland, Ireland, and the Romantic Aesthetic* (Lewisburg, PA, 2007), 55.
[2] *Cobbett's Parliamentary History of England from the Earliest Period to the Year 1803* (London, 1806–20), xxxiii, col. 333; John Ehrman, *The Younger Pitt: The Consuming Struggle*

It is the unanimous Opinion of the Board, that it is indispensably necessary for the Publick Service, that the Directors of the Bank of England, should forbear issuing any Cash in Payment until the Sense of Parliament can be taken on that Subject, and the proper Measures adopted thereupon, for maintaining the Means of Circulation, and supporting the Publick and Commercial Credit of the Kingdom at this important Conjuncture.[3]

The Privy Council's order heralded the beginning of the Bank Restriction period, during which the Bank suspended coin payments for its notes, a period that lasted for twenty-four years, until 1821. On the first day of the suspension, the Bank of England and other London banks made all payments in Bank of England notes except for fractional parts of transactions.[4] Similar scenes of paper transactions took place at public offices, where the majority of transactions were made in notes and small amounts of silver coin, though the latter was used sparingly and customers were asked to complete transactions only in paper currency and to allow bankers to do the same.[5] There was a great demand for the £5 note, the lowest denomination of banknote circulating in Britain, and the printing office at the Bank of England was operating at full capacity to satisfy the sudden demand for notes.[6] As soon as news of the stoppage reached provincial towns, banks stopped paying their notes in cash and 'not a guinea [was] to be had in exchange for Bank-notes on any of the public roads'.[7]

The suspension of cash payments in February 1797 was an event that had a profound impact on British society. In the weeks running up to the meeting of the Privy Council, the informed citizens in Britain's metropolis and commercial centres were well aware of the looming financial crisis, but only a few expected a measure as drastic as the suspension of the Bank's note convertibility. Since the Bank's establishment in 1694, its notes had been convertible into metallic currency, a practice that was broken only on two previous occasions and, in each case, for a short duration.[8] The scale of the suspension in 1797 was unprecedented, as the Bank of England's stoppage of cash payments was followed by all note-

(London, 1996), 6; George III, *The Later Correspondence of George III*, ed. A. Aspinall (Cambridge, 1963), ii, 541–2.

[3] The text of the Privy Council order can be found in the *London Gazette*, 28 Feb. 1797, 204–5. See also Wilfred M. Acres, *The Bank of England from Within, 1694–1900* (London, 1931), i, plate xxxiv.

[4] *St James's Chronicle*, 29 Feb. 1797.   [5] *The Oracle*, 28 Feb. 1797.

[6] *The Oracle*, 28 Feb. 1797.   [7] *Evening Mail*, 3 Mar. 1797.

[8] John H. Clapham, *The Bank of England: A History* (Cambridge, 1944), i, 31–2; William Robert Scott, *Constitution and Finance of English, Scottish and Irish Joint Stock Companies to 1720* (Cambridge, 1912), iii, 208–9; Richard David Richards, *The Early History of Banking in England* (London, 1929), 189–90.

issuing banks in the British Isles doing the same. Inconvertibility was eventually institutionalised, establishing a new monetary regime. How was this transition achieved? More crucially – as a monetary regime change affected the lives of millions – how did Britain's money users respond to the sudden transformation of the monetary order? And what persuaded them to accept the inconvertible paper currency? For the relatively wealthy part of British society in the late eighteenth century, who were already accustomed to the use of various paper instruments, the suspension brought about little change. In contrast, for the majority of the nation, pounds and guineas meant pieces of precious metal. For accustomed and new users alike, paper currency was no longer anchored in the metallic standard and that much was clear. If precious metal did not serve as the foundation of monetary value, however fictional it may already have been, the source of value had to be rediscovered. Previous experiments with inconvertible paper abroad, for instance, in the former American colonies and in France, offered no practical guide to Britain as they were far from success. The memory of devastating inflation in France, caused by the *assignat*, was still fresh, and in that recent memory, the state-imposed currency was closely associated with the Reign of Terror. Determined not to follow in the footsteps of its enemy state, the British nation responded to the suspension crisis in early 1797 in a distinctive, voluntarist manner.

The stakes were high. Money was an essential component of modern society that connected people, places and various social activities, affording vital functions in a society that was increasingly defined by industrial and commercial activities. The lives of entrepreneurs and workers in growing industrial cities, traders dealing in goods that were brought from across the globe and consumers enjoying all sorts of commodities all pivoted upon monetary transactions. Defending a prosperous country required monetary resources, too. For the fiscal-military state, survival and financial stability had become deeply entangled, as the state drew its physical strength from tax income and market borrowing. The interface between the fiscal and the military capacity of the modern state was nowhere more evident than in a state engaging in a major military conflict. In 1797, Britain was facing a formidable enemy that was gaining control of major parts of the European continent and was intent upon invading an island nation just across the Channel. The inconvertible paper currency emerged not out of the calm ocean of money's evolutionary process but from a turbulent sea of international conflict and financial uncertainty.

Fiat paper currency, which English writers and politicians had discussed as something foreign to their own nation, suddenly became a reality in 1797.[9] That inconvertible bank papers, which were issued by the Bank of England and other banks in England, Wales, Scotland and Ireland, were eventually accepted by the population at large does not mean that these nations effortlessly achieved the transition to inconvertibility. Nor was it fulfilled without the involvement of money users. Far from it: the success of the regime change rested on the tacit consent of Britain's money users, which was expressed in a series of public meetings across the nation. By doing so, they enacted the voluntary nature of paper currency, which, as Burke identified in 1790, made English paper currency unique and wholesome. In the crucial early months of 1797, the solidarity of Britain's monetary community replaced the metallic standard as the foundation of the circulating medium. With this vocal support from the community of money users, the inconvertible Bank of England note became the *nation's* paper currency.

The Bank of England Note and British Society in the 1790s

By the late eighteenth century, the Bank of England had become an indispensable part of British finance and the economy. Lord North, in his oft-quoted speech in 1781, described the Bank as virtually comprising 'a part of the constitution'.[10] The Bank's prominent role in supplying the nation with the means of payment was recognised in the embryonic discussion on the functions and responsibilities of major banks in a national-scale operation. However, the Bank was not, in the modern sense of the term, a central bank, though economic writers expressed their growing expectations that the Bank ought to behave differently from other private banking institutions. Francis Baring was one of the first writers to give the idea of a central bank a clear expression when he described the Bank's role as 'the dernier resort' within the nation's banking system in times of financial instability.[11] Following his predecessors, such as Adam Smith who likened the Bank to 'a great engine of the state', Baring wrote that 'the Bank must be considered solely as the centre or pivot, for the purpose of enabling every part of the machine to move in perfect order'.[12] According to Baring, the Bank's role of supplying the nation with its circulating medium had a greater importance than

---

[9] See Introduction.

[10] Clapham, *Bank of England*, i, 174; *Cobbett's Parliamentary History*, xxii, col. 519.

[11] Francis Baring, *Observations on the Establishment of the Bank of England, and on the Paper Circulation of the Country* (London, 1797), 22.

[12] Baring, *Observations on the Establishment*, 6–7; Adam Smith, *An Inquiry into the Nature and Causes of the Wealth of Nations*, ed. R. H. Campbell, A. S. Skinner and W. B. Todd (Oxford, 1976), 320.

its transactions with the government and the commercial world. For the Bank's status as a major supplier of currency, Baring later resorted to the analogy of the sun within the planetary system. Just as the sun benefited the earth with the 'vivifying effects of its rays', the Bank animated Britain's agriculture, commerce and finance, with its notes acting as beams of sunlight, which served 'for the invaluable purpose of melting down, finally, the whole produce of commerce, trade, agriculture into one general mass'.[13]

The manner in which the Bank note was created indicates how closely the Bank's operations were intertwined with British economy, both in its public and in its private spheres of operation.[14] Thomas Surr, a Bank of England clerk who later became a celebrated novelist, explained that there were four principal channels through which the Bank of England created its notes.[15] First, the Bank issued notes when it discounted commercial bills and notes. Between 1794 and 1796, the Bank held £2–£3.8 million in discounted commercial papers.[16] The annual volume of commercial discount must have been many times greater than the amount held by the Bank; hence the volume of Bank notes involved in this type of transaction would also have been significant.[17] Second, the Bank settled its purchase of gold and silver bullion by Bank note payments.[18] Third, the Bank defrayed outlays on the dividends on Bank stock, its employees' salaries and various other purchases in the course of its business. Fourth, the Bank's loans either to the government or to private individuals were paid by Bank note, as were the quarterly dividends on the public debt.[19] In 1797, the Bank's chief cashier, Abraham

---

[13] Francis Baring, *Observation on the Publication of Walter Boyd* (London, 1801), 14–15; House of Commons, *Report, Together with Minutes of Evidence, and Accounts, from the Select Committee on the High Price of Gold Bullion* (1810), appendix, 132.

[14] Patrick O'Brien and Nuno Palma, 'Not an Ordinary Bank but a Great Engine of State: The Bank of England and the British Economy', *Economic History Review*, 76 (2023), 305–29.

[15] Thomas Surr, *Refutation of Certain Misrepresentations Relative to the Nature and Influence of Bank Notes* (London, 1801), 23–7.

[16] Ian P. H. Duffy, 'The Discount Policy of the Bank of England during the Suspension of Cash Payments, 1797–1821', *Economic History Review*, 35 (1982), 82; Norman J. Silberling, 'British Prices and Business Cycles, 1779–1850', *Review of Economics and Statistics*, 5 (1923), 256.

[17] Clapham, *Bank of England*, i, 213.

[18] Clapham, *Bank of England*, i, 219–21; 'Third Report from the Committee of Secrecy on the Outstanding Demands of the Bank and the Restriction of Cash Payments', in House of Commons, *Reports from the Committee of Secrecy on the Outstanding Demands of the Bank and the Restriction of Cash Payments* (1797), 82.

[19] Surr, *Refutation of Certain Misrepresentations*, 23–7.

Newland, stated that only around one-tenth of such payments were made in coin and the rest was paid in Bank notes.[20]

The flow of the Bank note was intrinsically linked with the state of affairs in British society. The Anglo-French military conflict was the single most important factor that defined British society between 1793 and 1815, and several years thereafter.[21] What began in 1793 as part of the European war against revolutionary France became, after a brief respite in 1802–3, the war with Napoleonic France, continuing through to 1815. The war against France was a major destabilising factor for Britain's finance. The outbreak of war with France in February 1793 triggered a major banking crisis in England. The war was not the only cause; the crisis emerged on the heels of the speculative boom in the preceding three years. At the height of 'canal mania' in 1793, eighteen new canal proposals were submitted to parliament.[22] The failure of Lane, Son and Fraser, a corn trader deeply involved in speculation, shook the credit market.[23] Instability soon spread across the country, causing runs on banks in Newcastle, Manchester and Yorkshire, leading to more than 20 bank failures when total bankruptcy in England numbered more than 1,200.[24] An increase in the Bank's commercial accommodation and the government's issue of exchequer bills to the tune of £2.2 million assuaged the country's credit, but subsequently country bankers became cautious of expanding credit and reduced their note circulation.[25] The shortage of circulating medium became a problem in the following two years, leading to the lifting of the legal ban on the issue of £5 notes.[26]

[20] House of Lords, *Report of the Lords' Committee of Secrecy* (1797), 38.
[21] For the significance of warfare on the development of modern national currencies, see David Glasner, 'An Evolutionary Theory of the State Monopoly over Money', in Kevin Dowd and Richard H. Timberlake, eds., *Money and the Nation State: The Financial Revolution, Government, and the World Monetary System* (New Brunswick, NJ, 1998), 21–45; David Graeber, *Debt: The First 5,000 Years* (New York, 2011).
[22] Baron F. Duckham, 'Canals and River Navigations', in Derek Howard Aldcroft and Michael J. Freeman, eds., *Transport in the Industrial Revolution* (Manchester, 1983), 100–41; J. R. Ward, *The Finance of Canal Building in 18th Century England* (Oxford, 1974), 86–96.
[23] Henry Dunning Macleod, *The Theory and Practice of Banking* (London, 1856), ii, 382–7; L. S. Pressnell, *Country Banking in the Industrial Revolution* (Oxford, 1956), 456–7.
[24] Albert Edgar Feavearyear, *The Pound Sterling: A History of English Money* (Oxford, 1931), 178; Ron Harris, *Industrializing English Law: Entrepreneurship and Business Organization, 1720–1844* (Cambridge, 2000), 212; Julian Hoppit, *Risk and Failure in English Business 1700–1800* (Cambridge, 1987), 183; Francis E. Hyde, Bradbury B. Parkinson and Sheila Marriner, 'The Port of Liverpool and the Crisis of 1793', *Economica*, 18 (1951), 363–78.
[25] Feavearyear, *The Pound Sterling*, 178.
[26] John Ehrman, *The Younger Pitt: The Reluctant Transition* (London, 1983), 387. According to Clapham, the Bank of England's £5 notes filled the gap created by the reduction of country note circulation. Clapham, *Bank of England*, i, 265.

The total circulation of the Bank note increased from £10.2 million in August 1794 to £14 million in February 1795.[27]

The long-term impacts of the continuing wars were profound and far-reaching. The wars officially severed ties between Britain and France. As the French army seized control of European commercial centres, the international market inevitably changed its contours – the Paris Stock Exchange suspended its operations in 1793, and two years later, so did Europe's principal market in Amsterdam, which had come under French occupation.[28] International connection through financial transactions did not disappear, but it took a different form from when European trade still had an important share in Britain's commerce.[29] The international grain trade was crucial to Britain, especially during the series of bad harvests in the 1790s.[30] Precious metal moved across borders, and the money transfer now included a significant amount of British government subsidies for continental allies, notably Austria. As the Bank was the principal repository of the nation's bullion reserve, international financial transactions, which were conducted either by bills or bullion, affected the Bank's reserves. As later became a topic of heated debate, domestic monetary policy was hardly isolated from the foreign exchange and bullion price quoted in markets abroad.

The outbreak of war against France set in motion a series of structural changes in state finances. During the long eighteenth century, recurring wars were a major driver for the English state's development of an efficient financial system, which grew into what John Brewer called the fiscal-military state.[31] National debt and taxation were two wheels of the system, and they were ever-growing. In a country where citizens were already heavily taxed, the French wars put an additional burden on their shoulders as the nation had to pay not only for its own military forces but also for its continental allies in a military conflict that covered the major part of Europe.[32] In the first few years of the war, with an expectation that

---

[27] House of Commons, *Report from the Committee of Secrecy on the Bank of England Charter* (1832), appendix, 17.

[28] The relative importance of Hamburg increased. Youssef Cassis and P. L. Cottrell, *Private Banking in Europe: Rise, Retreat, and Resurgence* (Oxford, 2015), 83; Larry Neal, *The Rise of Financial Capitalism: International Capital Markets in the Age of Reason* (Cambridge, 1990), 225–9.

[29] See, for example, Ralph Davis, *The Industrial Revolution and British Overseas Trade* (Leicester, 1979), 88–9.

[30] Roger Knight and Martin Wilcox, *Sustaining the Fleet, 1793–1815: War, the British Navy and the Contractor State* (Woodbridge, 2010), 73–6.

[31] John Brewer, *The Sinews of Power: War and the English State, 1688–1783* (London, 1989).

[32] Peter Mathias and Patrick O'Brien, 'Taxation in Britain and France, 1715–1810: A Comparison of the Social and Economic Incidence of Taxes Collected for the Central Governments', *Journal of European Economic History*, 5 (1976), 606–11.

the war would not last long, the government resorted to the traditional way of paying for military conflict by raising loans. Between 1793 and 1796, the national debt increased from £241.6 million to £310.4 million.[33] The Bank of England maintained its vital role within the British financial system, though it was less dominant in direct state financing and commercial discounting than in the previous period.[34] For its long-term loans, by 1793 the government had come to rely chiefly on loan contractors such as the firms of Boyd, Benfield & Co., Hope & Co., Angerstein, Warren & Lock and Sir Francis Baring & Co., while the Bank remained the repository of money raised by state loans.[35] The Bank also played an important part in handling and regularly making advances on the government's short-term loans, such as exchequer bills.[36] The Bank's position in the state's taxation machinery was equally crucial.[37] When in 1796 the expectation of a short war was dashed by the collapse of the First Coalition, the government contemplated shifting the war finance from loans to taxation, which would eventually lead to the introduction of income tax in 1799.[38] Tax collection was conducted through a network of local tax collectors, receiver generals and local banks, the latter chiefly as remitters of collected tax money. Ultimately, money collected across the nation was sent to the Bank, which distributed public funds to the accounts of government departments.[39] For its role in managing public loans, tax revenue and Bank note issuance, the Bank occupied a pivotal place in Britain's public credit and monetary order, a role that it fulfilled without officially taking the crucial step to becoming a modern central bank.[40]

---

[33] Brian R. Mitchell, *British Historical Statistics* (Cambridge, 1988), 601.

[34] David Kynaston, *The City of London* (London, 1994), i, 27.

[35] Stanley D. Chapman, *The Rise of Merchant Banking* (London, 1984), 4.

[36] In the disposal of government bills, loan contractors played a greater role than the Bank. Arnold D. Harvey, *Collision of Empires: Britain in Three World Wars, 1793–1945* (London, 1992), 71–2.

[37] Cassis and Cottrell, *Private Banking in Europe*, 89–94; Sydney R. Cope, 'The Goldsmids and the Development of the London Money Market during the Napoleonic Wars', *Economica*, 9 (1942), 191–203; E. Victor Morgan and William Arthur Thomas, *The Stock Exchange: Its History and Functions* (London, 1962), 46–50.

[38] Patrick K. O'Brien, 'The Political Economy of British Taxation, 1660–1815', *Economic History Review*, 41 (1988), 1–32.

[39] See, for example, P. G. M. Dickson, *The Financial Revolution in England: A Study in the Development of Public Credit, 1688–1756* (London, 1967), 390.

[40] Timothy L. Alborn, *Conceiving Companies: Joint-Stock Politics in Victorian England* (London, 1998), 54; Forrest Capie, 'The Emergence of the Bank of England as a Mature Central Bank', in Donald Winch and Patrick O'Brien, eds., *The Political Economy of British Historical Experience, 1688–1914* (Oxford, 2002), 295–8; Forrest Capie, Charles Goodhart and Norbert Schnadt, 'The Development of Central Banking', in Forrest Capie, Stanley Fischer and Norbert Schnadt, eds., *The Future of*

Invasion Scare and Financial Instability

The financial crisis of early 1797 was less a sudden outburst of financial instability than the consequence of a series of events that had unfolded over the previous months. On 21 December 1796, a French fleet arrived in Bantry Bay, Ireland. Although there was no landing of the French forces, the fleet remained in the bay for two weeks, almost unchecked, as the British naval fleet was stationed at Spithead.[41] The attempted French invasion cast serious doubts as to the security of the territory under British influence and, at the same time, unsettled the financial situation in Ireland and Britain, two nations connected by formal and informal ties, including various types of monetary transaction.[42] In Ireland, a shortage of money manifested itself immediately after the French fleet's arrival, with the city of Cork, one of the largest financial centres in that country – and the closest major city to Bantry Bay – directly affected by the events.[43] On 6 January 1797, a Cork merchant reported that 'all Business here is at a stand, no Money in Circulation'.[44] Cork bankers briefly stopped cash payments, following the recommendation of the city of Cork committee.[45] Evidence suggests that the financial difficulties extended beyond the south-western part of the country and a similar suspension of cash payments was discussed in Dublin, albeit the city's bankers did not resort to the measure.[46]

After the French expedition to Bantry Bay, Britain was besieged with chronic invasion alarms, with rumours that the next target might be Aberdeen, or somewhere on the east coast of England.[47] Whatever the

---

Central Banking: The Tercentenary Symposium of the Bank of England (Cambridge, 1994), 5–6.

[41] Arthur Bryant, *The Years of Endurance, 1793–1802* (London, 1942), 167–71; Michael Carroll, *A Bay of Destiny: A History of Bantry Bay and Bantry* (Bantry, 1996), 239; E. H. Stuart Jones, *An Invasion That Failed: The French Expedition to Ireland, 1796* (Oxford, 1950); E. H. Stuart Jones, *The Last Invasion of Britain* (Cardiff, 1950), 19.

[42] Geoffrey Bolton, *The Passing of the Irish Act of Union: A Study in Parliamentary Politics* (London, 1966), 22–3; *Morning Chronicle*, 19 Jan. and 1 Feb. 1797; *The Telegraph*, 20 Feb. 1797.

[43] Marianne Elliott, *Partners in Revolution: The United Irishmen and France* (New Haven, CT, 1982), 120–1; Thomas Pelham to the Duke of York, 1 and 4 Jan. 1797, British Library (hereafter BL), Pelham Papers, Add Ms 33113, fols. 71–9.

[44] From C. Cayne, 6 Jan. 1797, Cork City and County Archives, Irish Distillers Copy Letter Book, 1794–1802, U15B.

[45] *Hibernian Chronicle*, 2 and 5 Jan. 1797.

[46] *Freeman's Journal*, 29 Dec. 1796. As Louis Cullen has pointed out, the Irish exchange rate was already below par – in both Dublin and London – by the end of January. L. M. Cullen, *Anglo-Irish Trade 1660–1800* (Manchester, 1968), 181.

[47] *Morning Chronicle*, 25 Jan. 1797. See also Ehrman, *Younger Pitt: Reluctant Transition*, 5; Trevor McCavery, 'Finance and Politics in Ireland, 1801–17' (PhD, Queen's University

source may have been, William Pitt the Younger's government took the same view on the target of the next invasion attempt, ordering reinforcements to defend the east coast. What the government probably did not know was that the French had already decided on their next targets, namely western ports and towns, from where the invasion forces were to proceed on to Bristol, Liverpool and Chester.[48] It was, however, the rumour of the anticipated French invasion on the north-eastern coasts that led to a run on the banks in Newcastle.[49] On February 18, banks in Newcastle were swarming with people trying to exchange local banknotes into coins. There had been a run on banks in Midlothian the previous day, but the Newcastle run was greater in scale and more profound in its impact.[50] The exact amount of banknotes brought in for exchange is not known, but that Newcastle banks were closed from the following day shows that locals withdrew a substantial amount of cash and that bankers expected further demand for cash would follow.

According to contemporary comments on the Newcastle run, the direct cause of the panic was a wartime procedure called 'driving the country', which was devised by the Duke of Richmond in 1793. The chief component of this procedure was to remove horses and other means of transportation from an area where an invasion was imminent, thereby retarding the movement of invading troops once they arrived.[51] Ironically, however, implementing 'driving the country' had incited an unintended panic in Newcastle.[52] The *Newcastle Chronicle* unreservedly blamed the government measure for what happened in Newcastle:

[A]n alarm arising from the absurd measures of Ministry, in causing returns to be made to the Government of the grain, live stock, carts, defensive instruments, &c. has created amongst the farmers a great degree of suspicion and apprehension of

---

Belfast, 1980), 310; Patrick K. O'Brien, 'Government Revenue, 1793–1815: A Study of Fiscal and Financial Policy in the Wars against France' (DPhil, University of Oxford, 1968–9), 112; Mark Philp, 'Introduction: The British Response to the Threat of Invasion, 1797–1815', in Mark Philp, ed., *Resisting Napoleon: The British Response to the Threat of Invasion, 1797–1815* (Aldershot, 2006), 1–18. On the rumour of the next target, see *Newcastle Chronicle*, 8 Jan. and 11 Feb. 1797.

[48] Stuart Jones, *Last Invasion of Britain*, 62–3.

[49] The Newcastle banker Rowland Burdon attributed the bank run to the 'apprehension of an immediate invasion'. House of Commons, *1797 Commons Committee on the Outstanding Demands of the Bank*, 143.

[50] William Forbes, *Memoirs of a Banking-House* (Edinburgh, 1859), 82. See also *Morning Chronicle*, 16, 17 and 18 Feb. 1797.

[51] Ehrman, *Younger Pitt: Reluctant Transition*, 261. The original plan is 'A plan for driving the country &c.', TNA, PRO 30/8/245. This strategy was also deployed in Bantry Bay. Carroll, *Bay of Destiny*, 253–4.

[52] The connection between the enquiry and the alarm was made elsewhere. *Morning Chronicle*, 22 and 24 Feb. 1797. See also Ehrman, *Younger Pitt: Consuming Struggle*, 5.

the stability of the Different Banking-house in this country; amongst others, those of this town.[53]

Intrusive data gathering by the state amplified the widespread anxiety caused by the rumour of a French invasion.[54] Just as reliance on statistical information was itself recent at the end of the eighteenth century, so too was the government's gathering of local information through local magistrates and constables, a practice that only started in the 1790s.[55] Following the population controversy and some local enumerations prompted by it, the British people's suspicion of 'numbering' might have been subdued to a certain extent, but it was yet to be totally dispelled.[56] Combined with the unsettling nature of the state's information gathering in the local community, the ministry's inquiry in early 1797, when the invasion attempt at Bantry Bay was still a fresh memory, was taken as a clear sign of a pressing danger. The preparatory measure, based on misinformation regarding the next invasion, was thus fanned into a blazing financial panic. As soon as news of the Newcastle panic reached London, some London bankers, such as Harley and Cameron, came under acute financial pressure and turned to the Bank of England – the 'dernier resort' for liquidity supply, in Baring's words.[57]

It was at this juncture that a French invasion attempt materialised, with French troops landing in Wales on February 22. It was by no means a successful invasion attempt: the 1,400 invading soldiers, consisting mostly of American prisoners, surrendered only four days later.[58] With this attack on the British mainland, the French revolutionary government aimed, first of all, to incite insurrection among the disaffected and poor in Britain, with the expectation that it would facilitate the progression of the invading troops into the inland cities. The second aim of the invasion

---

[53] *Newcastle Chronicle*, 25 Feb. 1797; House of Commons, 'Third Report on the Outstanding Demands of the Bank', 143.

[54] Rosalind Mitchison, *Agricultural Sir John: The Life of Sir John Sinclair of Ulbster, 1754–1835* (London, 1962), ch. 10; Stuart Woolf, 'Statistics and the Modern State', *Comparative Studies in Society and History*, 31 (1989), 588–604.

[55] Clive Emsley, *British Society and the French Wars, 1793–1815* (London, 1979), 45.

[56] Michael Drake, 'The Census, 1801–1891', in E. A. Wrigley, ed., *Nineteenth Century Society: Essays in the Use of Quantitative Methods for the Study of Social Data* (Cambridge, 1972), 8; David V. Glass, *Numbering the People: The Eighteenth-Century Population Controversy and the Development of Census and Vital Statistics in Britain* (Farnborough, 1973), 19–20, 90.

[57] Baring, *Observations on the Establishment*, 22; Clapham, *Bank of England*, i, 271.

[58] Studies on the landing include Phil Carradice, *The Last Invasion: The Story of the French Landing in Wales* (Pontypool, 1992); J. E. Thomas, *Britain's Last Invasion: Fishguard, 1797* (Stroud, 2007).

was to interrupt British commerce.[59] A contemporary observer, Lady Amabel Yorke, perceptively wrote in her diary,

People think it is a Scheme to incumber us with Prisoners who would mutiny in case of a real Invasion; I think it more likely to be Some Scheme to hurt our Credit by the Panic it would excite. All the Stories told since the Beginning of the Week have had that Tendency & have succeeded but too well.[60]

It is, however, not entirely plausible to attribute Britain's credit crisis to what Lady Yorke described as a 'very strange' invasion attempt because a substantial increase in cash demand had already started by the time of invasion.[61] The French invasion was, therefore, an aggravating factor in the already fragile state of finances. The suspension crisis needs to be seen as a sequence of events, starting with the invasion at Bantry Bay and the ensuing financial instability, which was followed by the French landing in Wales and the nationwide liquidity crisis. Describing the suspension of cash payments as a 'panic' – as opposed to the local panics preceding it – is a gross simplification of an event that had multiple causes, manifestations and responses, an event that cannot be reduced to a momentary loss of rationality and its eventual restoration. The panic perspective, with its assumption of social resilience to return to the previous state of things, misses the constructive aspect of the 1797 crisis, after which British monetary order never returned to its pre-1797 state. The 1797 crisis led to the setting down of institutional conditions and a general consensus about the new monetary order, factors that were fundamental to the ensuing era of inconvertible paper currency. To understand how the crisis served as a break between the age of metallic currency and the age of paper currency, we must examine the mode by which the British nation responded to the suspension crisis.

[59] Stuart Jones, *Last Invasion of Britain*, 63, 164. Thomas Paine's work was an inspiration for this strategy. John Keane, *Tom Paine: A Political Life* (London, 1995), 427–8; Thomas Paine, *The Decline and Fall of the English System of Finance* (Paris, 1796).

[60] Diaries of Lady Amabel Yorke, West Yorkshire Archive Service, WYL150/7/6/16, fol. 261. On the French assault on Britain's commerce, see also William Cobbett, *Paper against Gold and Glory against Prosperity* (London, 1815), i, 201; Gavin Daly, 'English Smugglers, the Channel, and the Napoleonic Wars, 1800–1814', *Journal of British Studies*, 46 (2007), 34–5; *True Briton*, 17 Feb. 1797.

[61] The amount of withdrawals from the Bank of England on February 23 and 24 was £90,000 and £130,000, respectively. Bank of England, minutes of the Committee of Treasury (hereafter CT), 24 Feb. 1797, Bank of England Archives (hereafter BE), G8/6, fol. 442; Clapham, *Bank of England*, i, 271. See also O'Brien, 'Government Revenue, 1793–1815', 112.

The Declaration Movement

How did the British public respond to the unprecedented measure of cash payment suspension? There was a real danger of the suspension exacerbating financial instability by signalling to the public the Bank's vulnerable position, when public credit was on tenuous ground. The market price of Bank stock had declined from £137 to £130 in the week preceding the suspension, and the announcement of the Privy Council's order on the morning of February 27 hardly offered a positive future outlook for investors in the stock market.[62] The suspension also disrupted Britain's economic transactions. Metallic currency was an essential part of the nation's monetary system, and the suspension, by prompting the withdrawal and hoarding of coins, could potentially strip the nation of the small-denomination currency that was vital to the functioning of the economy – though historians believe that small change had always been in short supply in eighteenth-century Britain. An economic standstill due to the lack of means of payment was not a far-fetched prospect when British law prohibited banks, including the Bank of England, from issuing notes of less than five pounds. If small-denomination coins ceased to circulate, how would labourers' wages and daily necessities be paid and all other small transactions be conducted?[63]

The public response to the suspension took a collective form, the prime example of which was the public meeting that was organised at the Mansion House in the heart of the City of London. The meeting, which started at midday on February 27, was attended by leading merchants, bankers and other dignitaries of the metropolis, who discussed the best means to support public credit at the time of crisis. The tangible end result of the meeting was a declaration expressing support for the suspension of cash payments and the circulation of Bank of England notes instead of specie.[64] Around a thousand people appended their names to the declaration:

[T]o prevent embarrassments to Public Credit, from the Effect of any ill-founded or exaggerated Alarms, and to support it with the utmost Exertions at the present important Conjuncture... That We, the undersigned, ... do most readily hereby declare, that we will not refuse to receive Bank Notes in Payment of any Sum of Money to be paid to us, and we will use our utmost Endeavours to make all our Payments in the same Manner.[65]

---

[62] *Course of the Exchange*, 21, 24 and 28 Feb. 1797.
[63] Such a fear was expressed in Ireland. General G. Lake (Belfast) to T. Pelham, 6 Mar. 1797, BL, Pelham Papers, Add Ms 33103, fol. 188.
[64] *St James's Chronicle*, 28 Feb. 1797.   [65] *The Times*, 28 Feb. 1797.

Historians have generally assumed that this London meeting was the only notable public reaction to the suspension, taking it as evidence that Britain achieved the transition from convertible to inconvertible paper money fairly smoothly. The economic historian John Clapham wrote that, after the order and the London declaration, '[a]lmost at once the metallic reserve began to improve'.[66] Similarly, Emmanuel Coppieters remarked that the meeting guaranteed the use of the Bank of England note between bankers and merchants.[67] One contemporary witness, a Plymouth banker, William Elford, who attended the Mansion House meeting, reported the sanguine effect of the London declaration on public credit as largely a metropolitan phenomenon yet to be extended to provinces:

I am just returned from a meeting of the Bankers Traders &c. at the Mansion House, where certain resolutions which will appear in the papers have been taken, and am happy to add, that the measure is so well received as to have elevated the Consols one & half per Cent – and the New Loan is fallen from a discount of almost eleven to eight and a quarter discount. It is suppos'd that resolution similar to those taken at the Mansion House, will be enter'd into by Gentlemen and others in the different provinces & districts, & Support Public Credit, as was done in 1745, the good effect of which will I doubt not soon be manifested.[68]

Its immediate effect on the financial market notwithstanding, the meeting was organised when there was a real sense of emergency. Prior to the order of the Privy Council, the need for such an emergency meeting had already been floated by the governor and deputy governor of the Bank of England on February 23, when they suggested to Pitt to hold 'some general meeting of the Bankers and chief Merchants of London ... in order to bring on some resolution for the support of the public credit'.[69] The Bank took the initiative on the morning of February 27 by inviting the lord mayor and some leading London bankers to a private conference, which preceded the public meeting at the Mansion House.[70] The Bank therefore anticipated and to some extent arranged the public meeting, but did that mean that the Bank and the government orchestrated the Mansion House meeting, as Cobbett later asserted?[71]

---

[66] Clapham, *Bank of England*, i, 272.

[67] Emmanuel Coppieters, *English Bank Note Circulation, 1694–1954* (The Hague, 1955), 37.

[68] William Elford to Earl Fortescue, 27 Feb. 1797, Devon Heritage Centre, 1262M/0/O/LD/12/41. The rise in stock prices was noted by contemporary newspapers. *St James's Chronicle*, 28 Feb. 1797.

[69] House of Commons, 'Third Report on the Outstanding Demands of the Bank', 104.

[70] Private minute book, BE, M5/472.

[71] Cobbett, *Paper against Gold*, i, 230–4, 240. See also, Michael T. Davis, ed., *The London Corresponding Society: 1792–1799* (London, 2002), vi, 128–33.

Contemporary evidence strongly suggests that the British nation's collective response to the suspension was spontaneous in its origin, as the London meeting was one among many such meetings that occurred in February and March 1797. Nine days before the London meeting, on February 20, the principal tradesmen in Newcastle had met together at Turner's Inn to take a collective measure against the run on banks that was forcing the local banks to stop payment. Issuing a public declaration was the measure adopted by this public meeting: 'THAT we, whose Names are hereunto subscribed, will receive the Notes of ALL the BANKS here, in Payment as usual'.[72] It is important to note that this meeting was held before Pitt and the Bank's representatives discussed a similar measure. Following the gathering in Newcastle, and prior to the Fishguard landing, at least five meetings issued declarations in Sunderland, Durham, Newcastle and South Shields.[73]

The London declaration was not the first, nor was it the last. After the Bank of England suspended its cash payments, a series of public meetings were held in cities and towns across Britain, and those meetings invariably issued declarations as news of the suspension spread around the country. On March 1, Bath, Hull, Northampton and Oxford issued declarations.[74] The *St James's Chronicle* reported, 'At Yarmouth, Lynn, Beccles, Canterbury, York, Bristol, Shrewsbury, and, in short, every town of consequence in the kingdom, the inhabitants have agreed to similar resolutions in support of their several Banks, and of the Bank of England'.[75] Local meetings appeared across Britain as swiftly as an electric shock running through the nation. In contemporary newspapers, about 150 such declarations in England, Scotland and Ireland can be identified (Figure 1.1) – due to the lack of local newspapers in the period, there is, however, no direct evidence about declarations in Wales, apart from one in Holywell, Flintshire.[76] Apart from major commercial centres, declarations were issued in places ranging from Plymouth, the

---

[72] *Newcastle Chronicle*, 25 Feb. and 4 Mar. 1797.

[73] *Newcastle Chronicle*, 25 Feb. 1797; *Newcastle Advertiser*, 25 Feb. and 4 Mar. 1797.

[74] The Bristol bankers were among the first to be informed of the Privy Council's decision by their London agents, which enabled the city to hold a meeting on the day of the suspension. Charles Henry Cave, *A History of Banking in Bristol from 1750 to 1899* (Bristol, 1899), 16–18; John Latimer, *The Annals of Bristol* (Bath, 1970), 522.

[75] *St James's Chronicle*, 28 Feb.–2 Mar. 1797.

[76] *The Star*, 8 Mar. 1797. There is no doubt that financial instability threatened Wales in late March 1797 when the London bank Harley & Co. stopped payment, and, as a consequence, the Brecon Bank came close to suspending its normal discounting business. On this occasion, William Taitt of the Dowlais Iron Company felt his company was compelled to 'devise some other mode for the payment of our men', indicating that financial distress was ensuing from the shortage of circulating medium caused by the Bank of England's suspension of cash payments. See Dowlais Iron

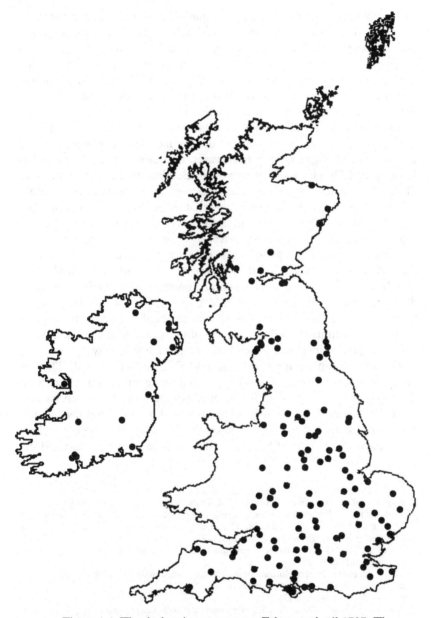

Figure 1.1 The declaration movement, February–April 1797. The spots mark the reported locations of declarations.

Sources: Aberdeen Journal; Bath Herald and Register; Berrow's Worcester Journal; Cambridge Chronicle; Cumberland Pacquet; Derby Mercury; Dublin Journal; Edinburgh Evening Courant; Exeter Flying Post; Felix Farley's Bristol Journal; Hampshire Chronicle; Ipswich Journal; Jackson's Oxford Journal; Kentish Chronicle; Leeds Mercury; Lincoln, Rutland, and Stamford Mercury; Manchester Mercury; Morning Chronicle; Norfolk Chronicle; Northampton Mercury; Norwich Mercury; Nottingham Journal; Portsmouth Gazette and Weekly Advertiser; Reading Mercury; Sheffield Courant; Shrewsbury Chronicle; Staffordshire Advertiser; The Star; Sussex Weekly Advertiser; The Times; York Courant.

Isle of Wight and Sandwich in England to Aberdeen and Banff in Scotland, and Londonderry and Limerick in Ireland.[77] For its geographical coverage, the declaration movement was anything but an action taken solely by merchants and bankers in the city and was something far broader in its scope. The movement went well beyond financial and commercial centres as it covered most of the major cities and towns – as well as some minor ones – of the British Isles.

Some of the meetings appear to have been organised around local political leaders – if not *by* them – from the fact that their names appear at the top of the signatories in most cases, for example the lord mayors in London and Dublin, the lord provost in Edinburgh and mayors of other places.[78] In major cities at least, bankers were at the heart of the process, evidenced by the bankers' conferences that preceded public meetings, but cooperation with the local community was crucial. One such case was Norwich, where, following the arrival of the news from London on the evening of February 27, local banks' proprietors held a meeting the next day, when banks suspended their business.[79] A court of mayoralty was then held at the city hall, and a resolution confirmed the bank proprietors' decision, which was further endorsed by the principal merchants at an even larger meeting.[80] The process, from the banks' decision to suspend payments to confirmation by the local authority and public endorsement, aimed to gain political legitimacy from the local community.

The suspension's impact went beyond England with speed. Thomas Coutts & Co., the Bank of Scotland's London agent, sent a dispatch on the day that the Privy Council convened (despite it being a Sunday and the Privy Council's order not being made public until the next day).[81] The dispatch arrived in Edinburgh on the Monday, and the three chartered banks – the Bank of Scotland, the Royal Bank of Scotland and the

---

Company letter books 1796–7, Glamorgan RO D/D/GD/A, fol. 293. An attempt to bolster local commercial credit on March 27 in the Welsh legal court closely followed the model of the declaration movement, as recorded by John Bird, clerk to the Marquess of Bute. Hilary M. Thomas, ed., *The Diaries of John Bird of Cardiff: Clerk to the First Marquess of Bute 1790–1803* (Cardiff, 1987), 97.

[77] There are several places where no record of a declaration has been found, such as Leicester and Cornwall.

[78] The Colchester, Exeter, Northampton, Plymouth, Shrewsbury, Winchester and York declarations were headed by the mayors.

[79] *Norwich Mercury*, 4 Mar. 1797.

[80] *The Diary of James Woodforde*, ed. Peter Jameson (Castle Cary, Somerset, 1998), xv, 43; C. B. Jewson, *The Jacobin City: A Portrait of Norwich in Its Reaction to the French Revolution, 1788–1802* (Glasgow, 1975), 77–8; Mayor's court book, 28 Feb. 1797, Norfolk RO, MF 632/4.

[81] Bank of Scotland, board minutes, 27 Feb. 1797, Edinburgh, HBOS Group Archives (hereafter HBOS), 5/1/8.

British Linen Company – and a private bank, Forbes & Co., immediately organised a meeting of bankers.[82] After this conference of bankers, the lord provost convened a public meeting. Impressed by the scale of the event, William Forbes of Forbes & Co. wrote, 'the greatest number of respectable citizens I ever saw met together to the number of Some hundreds; who all unanimously agreed to Support the Banks & the Credit of the Country'.[83] In Ireland, by the order of the lord lieutenant and the Irish Privy Council, the Bank of Ireland suspended its cash payments on March 2, three days after the Bank of England's suspension.[84] The following day, just as was the case in Scotland, the lord mayor of Dublin called a public meeting at the mansion house, attended by over 250 people, which duly and unanimously adopted a declaration.[85] On March 4, just as their English counterparts had, the Irish Privy councillors signed a resolution 'to accept on all occasions bills of the Bank of Ireland'.[86]

Further expressions of support followed the public meetings and their declarations. After declarations had been issued by public meetings, the wider community took part by appending their signatures to the declarations. The London declaration initially had about 1,000 signatories. On the day of the meeting, according to the *London Chronicle*, 'The Mansion-house was crouded [sic] for the whole day, by persons pressing forward to sign the … Resolution', while it was also placed in London's major taverns and streets, eventually garnering around 4,000 signatures.[87] In Newcastle, the declaration was placed in the Exchange to invite signatures.[88] A similar situation occurred in large cities and small towns. For example, in the small parish of Ashford in Kent, with a population of approximately 2,000, 'upwards of 100 persons' signed the local

---

[82] Charles Munn, *The Scottish Provincial Banking Companies 1747–1864* (Edinburgh, 1981), 54–5.

[83] Letter by William Forbes, 1 Mar. 1797, National Archives of Scotland (hereafter NAS), GD27/6/38.

[84] Bank of Ireland, Court of Directors transaction book, 4 Mar. 1797, Bank of Ireland Arts Centre, Dublin (hereafter BIAC), book 2, fol. 342. Also, Pitt to Earl Camden, 27 Feb. 1797, TNA, PRO 30/8/195, fols. 166–7.

[85] *Belfast Newsletter*, 3 Mar. 1797.

[86] Thomas Pelham to Charles Agar, 4 Mar. 1797, Hampshire RO, 21M57/C31/14.

[87] *London Chronicle*, 25–28 Feb. 1797; Cobbett, *Paper against Gold*, i, 228. Part of the list of names was published as *Declaration of the Merchants, Bankers, Traders, and Other Inhabitants of London, Made at the Mansion-House, February 27th, 1797: With a List of the Names and Places of Abode of the Subscribers Thereto* (London, 1797). Charles Hales wrote, probably with some exaggeration, that 'upwards of 10,000 signatures' were added to the declaration. Charles Hales, *A Correct Detail of the Finances of This Country* (London, 1797), 35.

[88] For a similar procedure, *Kentish Chronicle*, 3 Mar. 1797; letter from Robert Bristow, 7 Mar. 1797, TNA, HO 42/40/96.

declaration.[89] The *Leeds Mercury* reported that, in total, 689 people signed the declarations in Newcastle, Durham and Sunderland.[90]

It is clear that the meetings' participants did not deem declaration a sufficient means for assuaging the potential contagion of financial instability – attracting the widest possible support was the key to the success of suspension. The process of appending locals' signatures also shows that both the public meetings and their declarations were an act to consolidate, visualise and display public support for, or trust in, the financial system. Robert Mitchell argues that financial panics rendered state finance visible as a system, and the visibility of state finance made possible a connection between people 'through affective bonds of belief, "Opinion" and desire'.[91] At the level of popular politics, a sense of community rather than any recognition of the system dominated the British public's response to the crisis. For the most part, 'affective bonds' were the creation of a sense of solidarity within a community as it was foregrounded by the moment of crisis. Nevertheless, such unity was by no means achieved effortlessly, as nationwide solidarity required the binding of variegated and often conflicting interests.

Supporters of National Credit

The declarations issued by public meetings during the suspension crisis were couched in a language of voluntarism. All of the declarations expressed the need to support public credit by way of accepting banknotes. Noticeably, some declarations mentioned their willingness to accept local banknotes only, while others mentioned both local banknotes and the Bank of England note. Voluntary acceptance was crucial for private bankers as there were no legal grounds for their stoppage of cash payments. The suspension at the Bank of England was ordered by the Privy Council, but even that had to be sanctioned by retrospective legislation – and likewise for the Bank of Ireland.[92] In contrast, the nation's legislature did not grant local banks a similar legislative remedy and, theoretically, the holders of local banknotes could demand cash payments if they wanted. In other words, local banks' suspensions rested

---

[89] *Kentish Chronicle*, 10 Mar. 1797. It is highly likely that the declarations printed in the newspapers gave only a partial list of participants.

[90] *Leeds Mercury*, 4 Mar. 1797.

[91] Robert Mitchell, *Sympathy and the State in the Romantic Era: Systems, State Finance, and the Shadows of Futurity* (London, 2007), 5.

[92] John Craig wrote that the Privy Council 'illegally ordered' the Bank to cease cash payments. John Craig, *The Mint: A History of the London Mint from AD 287 to 1948* (Cambridge, 1953), 260.

upon public confidence, a voluntary agreement between bankers and their customers.[93]

The declarations were addressed to a broad community of Britain's note users, which included the nation's rent payers. A Newcastle declaration on February 22, for example, specifically stated that landlords would accept banknotes for rent payments.[94] As one of the most substantial types of cash payment for a large part of the population – and the suspension crisis coincided with the period of annual rent payments – assuring the acceptability of banknotes for rent payment was clearly important in convincing rent payers that paper currency was good for other forms of payments too. By securing the general public's acceptance, further bank runs would also be forestalled. Contemporaries such as the Newcastle banker Rowland Burdon believed that a collective demand for cash payments tended to come from occasional users of paper currency, but they nonetheless posed a direct threat to country banks.[95] Similarly, William Forbes identified those who demanded cash payments at Scottish banking houses as 'mostly of the lowest and most ignorant classes, such as fisherwomen, carmen, street-porters, and butcher's men'.[96] It is impossible to know whether such a class-based understanding of the bank runs was grounded in observation or a simple reflection of prejudice against lower classes of people. Yet with this contemporary understanding of the potential causes of local financial disquietude, it is clear that declarations were intended as a message directed at the general public, assuring them of paper currency's general acceptability. While Britain's business community and wealthy classes had already become accustomed to the use of paper currency, those who needed persuading to use banknotes were people who were not accustomed to handling good sums of money on a daily basis.[97] Thus, to achieve their purposes, the declarations had to address people across the social classes.

The declarations also showed the degree to which paper currency had become a binding agent within the national and regional economies. The declaration in Leeds, for instance, is a catalogue of well-established

---

[93] Baring, *Observations on the Establishment*, 67.   [94] *Newcastle Advertiser*, 25 Feb. 1797.

[95] Burdon identified small farmers as the main cause of the Newcastle run in mid-February. House of Commons, 'Third Report on the Outstanding Demands of the Bank', 45.

[96] Forbes, *Memoirs of a Banking-House*, 83. See also, Baring, *Observations on the Establishment*, 53–4.

[97] Robert Day, *Address to the Grand Jury of the Country of Dublin on the 10th of January, 1797* (Dublin, reprinted in Northallerton, 1797); Henry Thornton, *An Enquiry into the Nature and Effects of the Paper Credit of Great Britain* (London, 1802), 176.

merchants in and around the city, which was a regional commercial centre.[98] There is no indication of the initiator of the meeting, but heading the list of signatories was John Blayds, a prominent merchant and three-time mayor, who had a close connection with the local bank, Beckett's.[99] The incumbent mayor's merchant house, Clapham and Hall, was also listed among the signatories, who were drawn overwhelmingly from the city's mercantile community. That the Leeds merchants' scope of business extended to national and international realms is indicated by their pledge to accept both local banknotes and the Bank of England note. This interpretation is warranted by reference to a contemporary commercial directory, in which one can identify forty of the seventy-five signatories appearing in the declaration.[100] Those names include Leeds's leading merchant families, Smithsons, Rayners and Oats, the international trading family of Rhodes and the large-scale manufacturers of Wormald, Foundain and Gott, as well as those who were directly involved in banking, such as Bishoff's. The list of signatories in Leeds provides a snapshot of the business and social network that existed in the city at the time, showing the extent to which the use of paper currency mediated such a network. That said, the participants of the declarations were not always confined to bankers and their wealthy customers. In the Aylesbury declaration, for instance, the names of farmers, grocers, inn holders, butchers, bakers, a peruke maker, the vicar, and the dissenting minister appeared in the list of signatories.[101]

The published list of the signatories of the London declaration contains 3,455 names. About two-thirds of these are accompanied by an address, either their place of residence or their business premises. As in the case of the Leeds declaration, one can gain a detailed understanding of the occupational composition of the signatories by comparing the list with a contemporary commercial directory (Table 1.1).[102] Out of the 1,580 names thus identified, the largest occupational group is that of merchants, amounting to 584. Another conspicuous group is bankers. Fifty-nine bankers are found in the list, showing that most of the bankers in London participated in the declaration (the *London Directory* lists a

---

[98] *Leeds Mercury*, 11 Mar. 1797.

[99] Richard George Wilson, *Gentlemen Merchants: The Merchant Community in Leeds, 1700–1830* (Manchester, 1971), 241.

[100] *The Leeds Directory for the Year 1798* (Leeds, 1798).

[101] *Northampton Mercury*, 4 Mar. 1797.

[102] *A London Directory or Alphabetical Arrangement Containing the Names and Residences of the Merchants, Manufacturers and Principal Traders in the Metropolis* (London, 1797). The figures in Table 1.1 are revised from the data in Hiroki Shin, 'Paper Money, the Nation, and the Suspension of Cash Payments in 1797', *Historical Journal*, 58 (2015), 430–1.

Table 1.1 *Occupation/trade of the London declaration signatories*

Occupation/trade		Occupation/trade	
attorney/solicitor	13	insurer/insurance broker	22
banker	59	ironmonger	20
bookseller	13	jeweller	6
brewer	16	manufacturer	19
cheesemonger	10	merchant	584
chemist/druggist	22	oilman	12
coach maker	7	orangeman	6
cooper	6	packer	7
distiller	18	perfumer	7
draper	83	printer	10
dyer	6	seedsman	7
factor/broker	107	stationer	21
goldsmith	9	stockbroker	11
grocer	43	sugar refiner	26
haberdasher	34	tobacconist	9
hardwareman	7	tea dealer/broker	18
hat maker	8	upholsterer	13
hatter	10	warehouse/warehouseman	99
hosier	16	weaver	24
		others	172
		Total	1,580

Source: Declaration of the Merchants, Bankers, Traders, and Other Inhabitants of London, Made at the Mansion-House, 27 February 1797: With a List of the Names and Places of Abode of the Subscribers Thereto (London, 1797).

total of sixty-nine bankers). In contrast, only eleven stockbrokers and eighteen insurance brokers are present. In any case, a wide variety of trades appear in the list, such as eighty-three linen drapers, ninety-nine ware-housemen, forty-three grocers, thirty-four haberdashers, twenty-one stationers, twenty-six sugar refiners, sixteen brewers and twenty ironmongers.

In many ways, the list is incomplete, but it offers sufficient evidence to show that the participants did come from a broad range of backgrounds. This does not necessarily mean the declaration commanded cross-class support. In neither the declaration of Leeds nor that of London is there an instance in which a signatory's working-class background is suggested. Another conspicuous absence was women. The list of signatories to the London declaration may include female participants, but the overwhelming majority were men – a feature that was shared by other public meetings held in early 1797 for the support of public credit.

For this reason alone, the declarations could hardly represent the whole community of Britain's money users. Rather, declarations were a peculiar form of public act, reflecting the contemporary social structure and biases. At any rate, the signatories were a tiny proportion of the London population – around one million at the time. As a historical event, therefore, the geographical spread of public meetings and declarations across the country was far more important than the single meeting of London's leading citizens.

Historical Dimensions to the Declarations

Apart from the identity of participants, the London declaration offers some important clues as to the historical meanings of the declaration. The declaration meeting was chaired by Brook Watson, who was the lord mayor and a Bank of England director.[103] With the order of the Privy Council legalising suspension at the Bank of England – with its note circulation occupying a monopolistic status in and around the metropolis – there was no fundamental problem like that faced by the local banks' regarding the legitimacy of suspension. However, support for such an extraordinary measure could not be taken for granted. During the meeting, Benjamin Travers, a grocer known for his radical politics, suggested holding a 'more public Meeting' to consider the resolution's propriety. This suggestion was rejected by the majority due to a concern that 'the Jacobins would croud some public Hall early, and pass a negative Resolution'.[104] There was, therefore, a palpable tension around the political division, which could have jeopardised the solidarity of the meeting. It was in this tense atmosphere that Watson invoked the precedent of 1745, 'when it was unanimously agreed by the principal Merchants not to refuse Bank-notes in payment, but to give them every possible currency'.[105] This refers to the financial crisis of September 1745, which was caused by the Jacobites's successful military campaign at Prestonpans.[106] Facing a run by note holders fearful of the progression of the Jacobite troops into London, the Bank had tried to exchange its notes for silver, not gold – though the latter was then

---

[103] John Clarence Webster, *Sir Brook Watson: Friend of the Loyalists, First Agent of New Brunswick in London* (Sackville, Canada, 1924).

[104] *The Times*, 28 Feb. 1797. On Benjamin Travers, see Alfred B. Beaven, *The Aldermen of the City of London* (London, 1908), i, 293–310.

[105] *The Times*, 28 Feb. 1797.

[106] Maberly Phillips, 'The Old Bank: Bell, Cookson, Carr, and Airey, Newcastle-upon-Tyne', *Archaeologia Aeliana*, 16 (1894), 453. See also, Nicholas Rogers, 'Popular Disaffection in London during the Forty-Five', *London Journal*, 1 (1975), 5–27.

customary, to impede a torrent of withdrawals. To avoid a devastation of the Bank's finance, London merchants decided to take collective action. On September 26, prominent financiers, including Samson Gideon, Theodore Janssen and John Barnard, organised a meeting at Garroway's Coffee House, and a resolution was issued: 'We the under-sign'd merchants and others ... do hereby declare, that we will not refuse to receive bank notes'.[107] Under this declaration – identical to that of the 1797 London meeting – 1,140 signatures were gathered in five days and the 'hurry' ceased.[108] In February 1797, Watson and probably the Bank directors too were convinced that re-enacting the declaration of 1745 would be a powerful safeguard against the threat of financial debacle. The collective memory of London's business community was thus revived to support Britain's financial system once again.

The overlap between patriotism and currency voluntarism was a pro-nounced feature during the suspension crisis.[109] Amid the mobilisation of nationalistic spirit, financial instability was rhetorically transformed into a crisis that tested communal solidarity in British society. There was no mention of the French invasion in the 1797 London declaration. What was instead singled out as the cause of the crisis was 'the Effect of any ill-founded or exaggerated Alarms'.[110] With this rhetorical man-oeuvre, the 1797 declaration, and its 1745 equivalent alike, aimed at ensuring coherence within the community of note users. For Henry Fielding, a contemporary witness and fervent admirer of the 'ever-mem-orable Association in Defence of Public Credit' of 1745, the enemies – more obnoxious than the Jacobites – were those who were driven by cowardice and tried to withdraw money from the Bank, 'the Contrivers and Abettors of this detestable Scheme ... the most flagitious and profli-gate Enemies of their Country'.[111] Watson was not alone in invoking memories of 1745, and the analogy with the events of that year was made

---

[107] *Gentleman's Magazine*, 15 (1745), 499–500; Lucy Sutherland, *Politics and Finance in the Eighteenth Century* (London, 1984), 391. The list of names who signed the declaration can be found in the *London Gazette* 24–27 Sept. and 28 Sept.–1 Oct. 1745.

[108] Acres, *Bank of England from Within*, i, 180; David Joslin, 'London Bankers in Wartime, 1739–84', in L. S. Pressnell, ed., *Studies in the Industrial Revolution: Presented to T. S. Ashton* (London, 1960), 161.

[109] Matthew Rowlinson and Eric Helleiner have separately picked up this episode as demonstrating the link between nationalism and trust in finance. Eric Helleiner, *The Making of National Money: Territorial Currencies in Historical Perspective* (Ithaca, NY, 2003), 45–6; Matthew Rowlinson, *Real Money and Romanticism* (Cambridge, 2010), 51.

[110] *The Times*, 28 Feb. 1797.

[111] Henry Fielding, *The True Patriot and Related Writings*, ed. W. B. Coley (Oxford, 1987), 72.

elsewhere, publicly and privately.[112] From this historical linkage of financial crises, economic nationalism was only a small step away. The *Newcastle Advertiser*, for instance, explicitly made the connection when it described the declarations as having demonstrated a spirit equal to 'the patriotism of English merchants and capital Stock-holders that protected public credit, by supporting the Bank of England in the year 1745'.[113]

Another historical origin of the declaration movement was the anti-radical political movement of the early 1790s. In 1792, John Reeves initiated the formation of the Association for the Preservation of Liberty and Property against Republicans and Levellers with the aim of counteracting the radical societies, fashioning it as the defender of the 1688–9 constitution.[114] Towards the end of 1792, Reeves's and similar associations published declarations in the newspapers that expressed their loyalty to the constitution.[115] As the movement swiftly spread to the whole country, with newspapers serving as a vehicle of the association's political message, provincial meetings also issued similar declarations.[116] Inspired no doubt by Reeves's association, diverse groups of people congregated to issue similar declarations. Among these groups, and one of the most conspicuous, were the 'the Merchants, Bankers, Traders, and Other Inhabitants of London', which issued a declaration in December of that year.[117] The same group, representing London's commercial community, published a similar declaration three years later, amid the royalist backlash occasioned by an assault on George III's carriage.[118]

---

[112] *Dublin Journal*, 7 Mar. 1797; *Northampton Mercury*, 18 Feb. 1797; William Elford to Earl Fortescue, 27 Feb. 1797, Devon Heritage Centre, 1262M/0/O/LD/12/41.

[113] *Newcastle Advertiser*, 4 Mar. 1797.

[114] On the association movement, see Eugene Black, *The Association: British Extraparliamentary Political Organization, 1769–1793* (Cambridge, MA, 1963), 233–74; Harry T. Dickinson, 'Popular Loyalism in Britain in the 1790s', in Eckhart Hellmuth, ed., *The Transformation of Political Culture: England and Germany in the Late Eighteenth Century* (Oxford, 1990), 503–33; Robert Dozier, *For King, Constitution, and Country: The English Loyalists and the French Revolution* (Lexington, KY, 1983), 55–92; Kevin Gilmartin, 'In the Theater of Counterrevolution: Loyalist Association and Conservative Opinion in the 1790s', *Journal of British Studies*, 41 (2002), 291–328; Austin Mitchell, 'The Association Movement of 1792–3', *Historical Journal*, 4 (1961), 56–77.

[115] *The Times*, 24 Nov. 1792; Michael Duffy, 'William Pitt and the Origins of the Loyalist Association Movement of 1792', *Historical Journal*, 39 (1996), 943–62; Michael Duffy, *The Younger Pitt* (Harlow, 2000), 152.

[116] Donald Ginter, 'The Loyalist Association Movement of 1792–93 and British Public Opinion', *Historical Journal*, 9 (1966), 185.

[117] *Declaration of the Merchants, Bankers, Traders and Other Inhabitants of London Made at Merchant Taylor's Hall December 5th, 1792* (London, 1792). See also, *The Star*, 6 Dec. 1792. Nine of the twenty-three names that appeared in the 1792 declaration were of people related to the Bank.

[118] *Declaration of the Merchants, Bankers, Traders, and Other Inhabitants of London, Made at Grocers' Hall, December 2nd, 1795* (London, 1795). See also, *St James's Chronicle*, 1–3 Dec. 1795.

Allusion to the association movement of the early 1790s was common-place among participants of the declaration movement of 1797, not least because there was a clear overlap in membership. The London merchant Samuel Bosanquet, then one of the Bank of England's directors, exem-plifies this overlap. Bosanquet was the chair of the meetings held in 1792 and 1795 and was also one of the eminent signatories of the 1797 London meeting. In the immediate aftermath of the suspension, contemporaries often described the declarations as 'associations'. For example, the Earl of Chesterfield publicly announced that he was deter-mined to 'join any Association that might be formed here, for the Support of Public Credit', while 'associations' was the term usually employed to describe the declaration movement in parliament.[119] However, in spite of the temporal proximity of the 1797 declaration movement and the association movement, their similarity should not be overstated. In particular, reading too much into the aspect of loyalist propaganda in the two movements would oversimplify the matter. According to Donald Ginter, even the declarations of 1792–3 had a much wider scope than simple loyalist demagogy. The declarations were capable of representing 'every type of contemporary ideological position short of revolutionary republicanism'.[120] Declaration was therefore intended less as a rock-solid ideological touchstone, against which one's political allegiance was judged, than as creating a common ground for British citizens across many shades of political creeds. It was this inclu-sive nature of public declaration, rather than the narrowly defined mes-sage of loyalism, that was conveyed and exploited during the suspension crisis. The nationalism thus embodied in the declarations was directed at the preservation of public credit, rather than the constitution. In fact, there was hardly any mention of the king or government in the declar-ations of 1797. The success of the declaration movement was largely due to the fact that it obscured the social divisions created by political allegiances.

The declarations had layers of meaning, and, similarly, their legitimacy came from multiple sources. This probably reflected the situation of banknote circulation. The Bank of England was not the sole issuer of banknotes in eighteenth-century Britain. Far from it: there were hun-dreds of note issuers, including the chartered banks of Scotland and Ireland, as well as numerous country banks. The order of the Privy Council relieved the Bank of England from making cash payments, but

---

[119] *Cobbett's Parliamentary History*, xxxiii, 328, 330–1; *Northampton Mercury*, 4 Mar. 1797. See also, George Rose, *A Brief Examination into the Increase of the Revenue, Commerce, and Manufactures of Great Britain, from 1792 to 1799* (London, 1799), 67.
[120] Ginter, 'Loyalist Association Movement', 187.

it did not extend this special sanction to other banks. This meant that acceptance of banknotes – apart from those of the Bank of England and the Bank of Ireland – rested upon voluntary agreement.[121] Some provincial meetings tried to invest a semi-legal authority in the declaration by employing the legal platform of assizes and quarter sessions. Baron Hotham, as the judge of the Essex assizes, urged the grand jury to 'more than the ordinary exercise of their jurisdiction', after which the jury issued a unanimous resolution to receive banknotes.[122] In Surrey, the general quarter session made a declaration during its adjournment, thus imparting, as Cobbett cynically pointed out, 'something of a *magisterial* weight and authority'.[123]

Even where there was no recourse to semi-legal authority, the collective act of declaration undoubtedly had a certain binding power in the context of the socio-economic life of eighteenth-century Britain, where the traditional 'economy of obligation' still regulated a large part of everyday economic life.[124] At a time when economic transaction had yet to become a commercial exchange between anonymous economic actors, publicly committing oneself to an economic obligation meant that the economic community monitored the subsequent fulfilment of the obligation. The signatories of the declarations were living in a society that was still largely dependent upon what Margot Finn calls 'a scaffolding of extra-legal customs, obligations and expectations'.[125] The economic obligation implied in the declarations of 1797 did not go much beyond the acceptance of banknotes, but they served as a public record of one's economic obligation – a type of public collective act, for which there was a precedent. In 1793, to save the banks of Newcastle, which were hard hit by the outbreak of war with France (the early effect of which was particularly severe in the north), a public meeting issued a resolution with the aim of ensuring the acceptability of local notes.[126] This public expression of confidence was accompanied by an acknowledgement of economic

---

[121] Pressnell calls the suspension 'virtually legal recognition'. Pressnell, *Country Banking*, 159.

[122] *Norfolk Mercury*, 18 Mar. 1797. The Plymouth declaration went further by saying that they would not hesitate to undertake 'any Action or Suit ... at the Instance of any Person whatsoever, who may refuse to receive Bank of England Notes'. *Exeter Flying Post*, 16 Mar. 1797.

[123] Cobbett, *Paper against Gold*, i, 228–9, 398. The Norwich declaration also originated from the chief magistrates. *Norfolk Chronicle*, 4 Mar. 1797; *St James's Chronicle*, 28 Feb.–2 Mar. 1797. See also *York Courant*, 20 Mar. 1797.

[124] Craig Muldrew, *The Economy of Obligation: The Culture of Credit and Social Relations in Early Modern England* (Basingstoke, 1998).

[125] Margot C. Finn, *The Character of Credit: Personal Debt in English Culture, 1740–1914* (Cambridge, 2003), 95.

[126] Phillips, 'Old Bank', 461.

obligation as the signatories declared that, in case local banks failed, they would personally be liable to sums ranging from £500 to £20,000 per person.[127]

The suspension foregrounded the traditional economic network centred on obligation. In stark contrast to some historians' claim that economic transaction had become highly anonymised by the end of the eighteenth century, the declaration movement revealed the continuing relevance of interpersonal trust in Britain's monetised society.[128] The nuances of the nationalism expressed in the realm of finance also require a careful interpretation. It cannot be assumed that the nationalism of the London declaration was wholly identical to that of declarations in other places in England, such as Newcastle, Norwich and Aylesbury, let alone in Scotland and Ireland.[129] The geographically uneven circulation of the Bank of England note, given the varied degree of its use – a topic we will examine in Chapter 2 – does not entirely explain certain variations, such as the exclusion of the Bank of England note in some declarations. However, we are not so concerned here with the forms of diverse economic nationalism but with how the differences were translated into a unified expression.

The Nature of the Declaration Movement

The economic nationalism expressed in the declaration movement should be considered in the light of various social and geographical divisions in British society, where economic matters were often a major source of conflicts. As far as the suspension was concerned, the main areas of contention were mostly unrelated to different theoretical views on money. Conflicts were more likely to arise in three other areas: politics, geography and class. In particular, contemporary political divisions could have become a serious obstacle to achieving solidarity, with the most tangible threat undoubtedly coming from the political

---

[127] George Bain, 'Early Days of Banking in Sunderland', *Antiquities of Sunderland and Its Vicinity*, 6 (1905), 81; 'County Banking Reports', *Banker's Magazine* (1845), 215; Durham University Library, Archives and Special Collections, Cookson papers 4–1; *Newcastle Chronicle*, 13 Apr. 1793.

[128] Compare James Thompson, *Models of Value: Eighteenth-Century Political Economy and the Novel* (Durham, NC, 1996), 44–5.

[129] For the complexity of the British regional political dimension in this period, see David Eastwood, 'Patriotism and the English State in the 1790s', in Mark Philp, ed., *The French Revolution and British Popular Politics* (Cambridge, 1991), 146–68; Emma Macleod, 'British Attitudes to the French Revolution', *Historical Journal*, 50 (2007), 706–7; Katrina Navickas, *Loyalism and Radicalism in Lancashire, 1798–1815* (London, 2009).

radicals.[130] To late eighteenth-century British radicals, the financial system represented Old Corruption, growing hostility against which could flare up at any time into a physical assault on the Bank, as it did in 1780 during the Gordon Riots.[131] This 'portentous challenge to authority', as Nicholas Rogers describes it, served as a symbolic political act as well as a highly practical tactical assault at the heart of the state machine.[132] Although the suppression of radical societies in 1795 effectively contained the large-scale organised activities of popular radicalism, the surviving threat from radicals sufficed to warrant the government's fears that, with some encouragement from an invasion scare, violent action might at any time materialise, which likely involved an attack on the Bank.

By 1797, nascent anti-paper radicalism was emerging, especially after Thomas Paine provided some theoretical support in his pamphlet, *The Decline and Fall of the English System of Finance* (1796).[133] There were some signs of radical societies' slow awakening to the significance of the popular politics of paper currency. The March issue of the *Moral and Political Magazine* – the mouthpiece of the London Corresponding Society – carried a special report on the suspension, which underlined the Bank's 'real insolvency' and 'most precarious security', with a distinctive echo of Paine's prediction that the days of English finance were numbered.[134] However, unlike the period following the 1810s, the popular radicals of 1797 had yet to possess effective tactics for deploying anti-paper rhetoric for their cause. Nor is there any evidence to suggest the existence of an organised attempt to sabotage the acceptance of paper currency – precedents such as the United Irishmen's attempt to 'discourage the circulation of banknotes' were not repeated in England in 1797.[135]

By replacing the political implication of suspension with the objective of upholding public credit through accepting banknotes, the declaration movement appealed to the nation at large and was able to engage some radical elements, such as Benjamin Travers, who attended the London

---

[130] J. Ann Hone, 'Radicalism in London, 1796–1802: Convergences and Continuities', in John Stevenson, ed., *London in the Age of Reform* (London, 1977), 79–101.

[131] John Stevenson, *Popular Disturbances in England, 1700–1870* (London, 1979), 81.

[132] Nicholas Rogers, *Crowds, Culture, and Politics in Georgian Britain* (Oxford, 1998), 169. See also, Ian Haywood and John Seed, 'Introduction', in Ian Haywood and John Seed, eds., *The Gordon Riots: Politics, Culture and Insurrection in Late Eighteenth-Century Britain* (Cambridge, 2012), 5, 11; Dana Rabin, 'Imperial Disruptions: City, Nation, and Empire in the Gordon Riots', in Haywood and Seed, eds., *Gordon Riots*, 105–6; Stevenson, *Popular Disturbances in England*, 81–3.

[133] J. R. Dinwiddy, *Radicalism and Reform in Britain, 1780–1850* (London, 1992), 180; Paine, *Decline and Fall*, 36.

[134] *Moral and Political Magazine*, Mar. 1797, 130, 132.

[135] John Thomas Gilbert, ed., *Documents Relating to Ireland, 1795–1804* (Shannon, Ireland, 1970), 156; Roger Wells, *Insurrection: The British Experience, 1795–1803* (Gloucester, 1983), ch. 7.

meeting. The orderly proceedings through which even a renowned 'Jacobin' city such as Norwich issued declarations also pointed to the existence of a broad swathe of support for the movement beyond any narrow definitions of political allegiance. In the declaration movement of 1797, the collective memories of both the 1745 London meeting and the association movement of the early 1790s enforced the legitimacy of the reciprocal relationship between banks and banknote users. At the junction of these historical memories, the declaration emerged out of a collective initiative of the community of banknote users.

The broad range of support for the declaration movement showed that it was almost impossible to interpret the movement in terms of political factions, as the politics of paper currency was not always subservient to party politics. The caricaturist James Gillray probably did not fully comprehend the problematics of paper currency when he attempted to visualise the suspension with the language of party politics. Still, in his satirical depiction of the 1797 crisis, his artistic genius betrayed him by capturing the fundamental point (Figure 1.2). In the print, Charles James Fox exhorts John Bull, who is extending his hands to accept a Bank of England note, to insist on having coins, in order to make peace with the French. John Bull is adamant that he will accept the Bank of England note and let Pitt hold on to the gold, but only to give it to the Frenchmen when they arrive.[136] There is obvious logical confusion in John Bull's statement: he is choosing to accept the banknote both to keep away the French and, at the same time, with a view to offering gold to the invaders when they arrive. Placing John Bull in between Pitt and Fox failed to convey the meaning – which Gillray possibly intended – of sharp political contrast over the suspension; in effect, the picture offers a visual testimony that acceptance of the banknote was an act that defied the dominance of party-political logic. The politically ambiguous, if not entirely neutral, nature of the declaration explains the seemingly contradictory situation that ensued. In late March and April, numerous public meetings across the country, including one in London, petitioned for reform and for dismissal of the ministry, indicating the fragility of the support for Pitt's government.[137] The overwhelming support for the suspension

[136] British Museum, Department of Prints and Drawings, *Catalogue of Prints and Drawings in the British Museum. Division 1. Political and Personal Satires*, ed. Frederic George Stephens and Mary Dorothy George (1870–1954), viii, 336–7.

[137] Clive Emsley, *Britain and the French Revolution* (Harlow, 2000), 27; Jenny Graham, *The Nation, the Law, and the King: Reform Politics in England, 1789–1799* (Lanham, MD, 2000), ii, 745–6; J. Ann Hone, *For the Cause of Truth: Radicalism in London 1796–1821* (Oxford, 1982), 30; Jewson, *Jacobin City*, 79–80; William Wenman Seward, *Collectanea Politica: Or the Political Transactions of Ireland from the Accession of George III to the Present Time* (Dublin, 1801), 192.

Figure 1.2 James Gillray, *Bank-Notes, – Paper Money, – French Alarmists, – o the Devil, the Devil! – ah! poor John Bull!!!* (March 1797).
© Trustees of the British Museum

expressed in the declaration movement by no means points to the existence of indisputable unity under the banner of pro-ministry or loyalist sentiment.

The declaration movement reinforced nationwide support for the suspension, and this owed much to the equivocal nature of public credit, which could mean either national or local credit. In some declarations, where the participants pledged to accept only local banknotes, public credit meant local credit, but they clearly recognised that regional finance formed a part of national finance. At the notional level at least, the link between regional and national finance levelled out regional variations in economic patriotism. At the practical level, the erasing of difference in economic nationalism was grounded in the necessity of local finance. As local banks, as well as Scottish chartered banks, had no legal authority to suspend cash payments, they needed the pretence that they were following the example of the Bank of England, thereby gaining de facto sanction for their suspension. The public meeting in Norwich, for example, stated clearly that the city's banks were 'to follow the regulation of the Bank of England as far as possible', which entailed endorsing the

Bank of England's suspension, from which other banks' suspensions derived their legitimacy.[138] In other words, local declarations, the primary aim of which was to legitimise the suspension of country banks' cash payments, ultimately had the effect of endorsing the nationwide transition to a new monetary regime of inconvertible paper through creating notional and practical linkages between the Bank note and country banknotes. The declaration movement thus enabled political and regional tensions among the heterogeneous British nations to be diffused.

The long-standing dichotomy between moneyed and landed interests was, for a moment, obliterated during the declaration movement, as the landed elite played a part as crucial as that of the moneyed interest, as they were major customers for the banks and merchants, while being holders of national debt.[139] Immediately after the suspension, the Privy councillors, consisting of the nation's leading landlords, issued a declaration underlining the fact that they were committed to the Bank's suspension.[140] At a more local level, Newcastle landowners publicly denounced the run on banks and forced people to bring back the withdrawn cash: the landowners demanded rent payments in cash, threatening that those who failed to do so would be allowed no future arrears.[141] The cash thus collected was presumably to be paid into the local banks. Where such regurgitation of cash was not necessary, landowners, such as the Duke of Northumberland and the bishop of Durham, announced that they would accept banknotes for rent payments on their estates.[142]

The potential threat against achieving solidarity implied by the three levels of economic nationalism – political, geographical and social – was effaced, and they merged into a single national movement to support public credit. Therefore, the declaration movement was not, as some have assumed, a crude, momentary eruption of economic nationalism. It was grounded in the social and political conventions of collective action developed in the long eighteenth century. What happened in the period following the suspension was a societal process that translated various differences into social cohesion, in which the sense of solidarity was expressed in a collective action that was so potent that it gave British finance the much-needed resilience to thwart a nationwide financial crash. In other words, the declaration movement offers us a glimpse into

---

[138] *Norwich Mercury*, 4 Mar. 1797.

[139] '[T]he great and undoubted SECURITIES of this Association of the MONIED and LANDED INTEREST' was noted by a newspaper. *The Oracle*, 2 Mar. 1797.

[140] *London Gazette*, 28 Feb. 1797; *Morning Chronicle*, 2 Mar. 1797.

[141] *St James's Chronicle*, 4–7 Mar. 1797.

[142] Duke of Northumberland to Tm Matthew, 23 Feb. 1797; the same to the bankers of Newcastle, 27 Feb. 1797, Northumberland RO, Ridley Papers, ZRI 34/2.

the historical moment when trust in the financial system was consolidated and visualised into a tangible form in the face of a potentially devastating financial crisis.

The Aftermath of the Suspension

The extent to which the declaration movement helped normalise the financial situation cannot be shown in monetary or other objective terms, but, despite continued financial instability in the next few months, not a single bank run was reported following the suspension.[143] Given the severity of the systemic shock to Britain's finance and the profound nature of the transformation of the monetary system, Britain's management of the 1797 suspension crisis was so successful that it is no wonder later historians wrongly assume it was achieved effortlessly. Far from it: the containment of the financial crisis would not have been possible without nationwide support for public credit and the nation's collective action to preserve order in the national monetary system. On March 21, Newcastle banker Rowland Burdon was cautiously optimistic:

I apprehend that the alarm has not altogether subsided, and that the country people are still desirous of procuring Specie; but from the manner in which the leading interests of the country have come forward, and from the circumstance of the rents of the country being paid about this time, the Banks which are now opened for ordinary business, expect their Notes to pass currently.[144]

The tenuous situation – the Bank's effort to secure gold from Hamburg had been hampered by the hazardous state of shipping routes – continued until May, when the demand for circulating medium finally subsided.[145] Under the circumstances, the government had no difficulty in legalising the suspension. The acts relating to the suspension went through parliament swiftly. Legislation on March 3 confirmed the validity of Bank notes of less than £5, which was followed, on March 10, by the suspension of the acts of 1775 and 1777 that had prohibited the issue of small notes (£1 and £2 notes).[146] On March 20, the Bank Restriction Act came into being.[147] All this was completed within less than a month of the suspension, but the legal provisions were mostly retrospective,

---

[143] See, for example, *Diary of James Woodforde*, xv, 128.
[144] House of Commons, *1797 Commons Committee on the Outstanding Demands of the Bank*, 45.
[145] John Cookson, *The Friends of Peace: Anti-war Liberalism in England, 1793–1815* (Cambridge, 1982), 158.
[146] 37 Geo. III, c. 28, and 37 Geo. III, c. 32. See also Acres, *Bank of England from Within*, i, 278.
[147] 37 Geo. III, c. 45.

acknowledging the transformation of the British monetary landscape. The Bank of England, for instance, had begun issuing small-denomination notes on March 2, the demand for which was so intense on Monday the following week that the Bank's stock was exhausted in two hours.[148]

Soon after, in April and May, mutinies erupted at Spithead and Nore, diverting the public's attention away from the Bank's suspension of cash payments.[149] In parliament, Charles Grey's Parliamentary Reform Bill was defeated, which led Fox and some of his followers to abandon parliamentary politics, leaving only a small number of opposition Members of Parliament (MPs) to stand in the way of the government's financial policy in the legislature.[150] Thus, in June, when the Restriction Act had been originally intended to expire, Pitt summarily informed the Bank of England of his intention to continue the suspension, even though he knew very well that the Bank had sufficient reserves to resume cash payments.[151] Chadha and Newby argue that the Bank Restriction Act rendered the future resumption of the Bank's cash payments credible in the eyes of Britain's note users, thereby bolstering the value of inconvertible Bank notes.[152] With the far-reaching support from the country that had been shown during the suspension crisis, combined with the absence of the tangible challenge to his financial helmsmanship, there was no pressing reason for Pitt to relinquish the financial free rein gained by severing the link between precious metals and paper currency.[153] Nor did the Bank see any advantage of resuming cash payments, and it informed Pitt in October of that year that it was 'by no means their Wish the restriction on the Bank should be discontinued'.[154]

---

[148] '£1 Notes–£2 Notes', 28 Feb. 1929, BE, ADM 6/78, fol. 19c; *The Telegraph*, 7 Mar. 1797.

[149] Lord Westmorland to Charles Agar, 24 May 1797, Hampshire RO, 21M57/C31/62, fol. 4.

[150] *Cobbett's Parliamentary History*, xxxiii, col. 734; Richard Davis, *Dissent in Politics, 1780–1830: The Political Life of William Smith, MP* (London, 1971), 94–5, 101; Ernest Smith, *Lord Grey, 1764–1845* (Oxford, 1990), 65–7.

[151] William Pitt to the Bank, 12 June 1797, BE, letters to the Bank from William Pitt, M5/606, fols. 38 and 39; Pitt to the Bank, 12 June 1797, TNA, PRO 30/8/195, fols. 25–44. Also, court papers, BE, G6/129, fols. 56 and 59. Later that year, the same formality was repeated. Private minute book, 25 Oct. 1797, BE, M5/472, fol. 72.

[152] Jagjit S. Chadha and Elisa Newby, 'Midas, Transmuting All, into Paper: The Bank of England and the Banque de France during the Revolutionary and Napoleonic Wars' (Bank of Finland Research Discussion Papers 20/2013, 2013).

[153] Patrick K. O'Brien, 'Public Finance in the Wars with France 1793–1815', in Harry T. Dickinson, ed., *Britain and the French Revolution, 1789–1815* (Basingstoke, 1989), 180–1.

[154] Bank to the chancellor of the exchequer, 26 Oct. 1797, secretary's letter books, BE, G23/48, fol. 28.

As Gillray depicted in his caricature, Fox and Sheridan opposed the suspension in parliament, though they scarcely had support even from their fellow Whigs. Still, it is important to note that their attack on the suspension was tainted by the analogy between British paper currency and French *assignats*. Fox, whose idea of currency rested firmly on the metallic standard, categorically stated that gold and silver were the 'true circulating medium', while paper currency was a mere representative of metallic money.[155] He believed that inconvertible currency would become a compulsory paper currency, and it would inevitably lead to currency depreciation, just as the French had experienced with their *assignat*. Echoing Fox, Sheridan predicted that 'the idea of compulsion alone would produce a depreciation, and though not in the same rapid progress, the paper of this country would ultimately experience the fate of the French'.[156] The anti-government *Morning Chronicle* also drew upon the French analogy: 'Paper that could not instantly be exchanged for cash, could only be forced upon the people by a Government of regicide, and could only be available during the reign of terror'.[157] These early critics of inconvertible paper claimed that English paper currency had mutated into something resembling the devalued French paper. The memory of the depreciation of French *assignats* – which often drew upon Burke's imagery in his *Reflections* – loomed ever so large.[158]

The deep-seated suspicion against paper currency with legal tender status, grounded in anti-French discourse, was the cultural as well as political factor that deterred the government from attempting to legislate to that effect. In the House of Commons during the discussion on the Bank Restriction Bill, Pitt remained vague about his intentions regarding the legal status of the Bank note.[159] He appealed to the members of the House not to press for a discussion on that issue as 'it would not only be useless but improper' when there were many uncertainties. And 'as long as the circulation rested upon paper taken by general consent, he thought it would not be adviseable [sic] to have it taken by compulsion, which might have an injurious effect, and was at present superfluous'.[160]

In Scotland, the idea of inconvertible paper currency – and the idea of making the Bank note legal tender – was received more favourably than

[155] *Cobbett's Parliamentary History*, xxxiii, col. 73.
[156] *Cobbett's Parliamentary History*, xxxiii, col. 64.   [157] *Morning Chronicle*, 28 Feb. 1797.
[158] As Mitchell rightly points out, Fox and Sheridan draw upon Burke's comparison between British and French financial systems. However, Mitchell misses the point that Burke's Anglo-French comparison was shared by both pro- and anti-government commentators. Mitchell, *Sympathy and the State in the Romantic Era*, 136–40.
[159] Coppieters, *English Bank Note Circulation*, 36.
[160] *Cobbett's Parliamentary History*, xxxiii, col. 354.

in England. As paper currency was much more common in Scotland, hostility against fiat paper currency was largely non-existent and there were those who expressly supported making the Bank note legal tender.[161] As early as 27 March 1797, Lord Meadowbank sent a letter to Henry Dundas, war secretary in Pitt's government, putting forward a plan for making the Bank note legal tender, which was to be implemented alongside a ban on the circulation of other banknotes.[162] Coincidentally, Scottish banks, in particular the two chartered banks, the Royal Bank of Scotland and the Bank of Scotland, were considering seeking parliamentary legislation for legal tender status for their notes.[163] The Scottish banks' ambition was not necessarily a sign of their disaffection with the England-centred monetary order, unlike in 1826 when the Scots fiercely opposed the attempted integration of Scottish money under the unified British monetary regime, but was probably grounded in the assumption that the Bank of England note would soon become legal tender, and the Scottish bankers were merely trying to secure the same privilege for their own banknotes.[164] In contrast, giving the Bank of England note a privileged legal status excited fear among Irish politicians and bankers about a currency invasion from London. The Irish government's controversial proposal to import a large amount of Bank of England notes met fierce opposition from the Bank of Ireland. The Irish bank appealed to popular opinion, arguing that the loss of their own notes would mean a loss of economic and political independence, an appeal that was strongly supported by Dublin merchants, who were generally averse to the idea of leaving the issue of banknotes, a major source of credit supply, at the mercy of politicians and financiers in London.[165] The politicisation of the debate went too far, leading to the rejection of note exchange between Irish and English banks, which sowed

---

[161] Letter to Henry Dundas, 11 Mar. 1797, NAS, GD51/5/235; *London Chronicle*, 25–28 Feb. 1797. See also *Cobbett's Parliamentary History*, xxxiii, cols. 330–1, 354; Frank W. Fetter, *The Economist in Parliament, 1780–1868* (Durham, NC, 1980), 98.

[162] Alan Maconochie to Henry Dundas, 27 Mar. 1797, NAS, GD51/1/394.

[163] Letters from Robert Dundas of Arniston, lord advocate; James Fraser, treasurer of the Bank of Scotland; and William Simpson, cashier of the Royal Bank of Scotland, 11 Mar. 1797, NAS, GD51/5/235.

[164] S. G. Checkland, *Scottish Banking: A History, 1695–1973* (Glasgow, 1975), 436–7; Rowlinson, *Real Money and Romanticism*, 93.

[165] Robert B. McDowell, *Ireland in the Age of Imperialism and Revolution, 1760–1801* (Oxford, 1979), 22; William Edward Hartpole Lecky, *A History of England in the Eighteenth Century* (London, 1878), viii, 323–4; R. B. McDowell, 'The Age of the United Irishmen: Revolution and the Union, 1794–1800', in T. W. Moody and W. E. Vaughan, eds., *A New History of Ireland*, iv: *Eighteenth Century Ireland 1691–1800* (Oxford, 2009), 368.

the seeds of the Irish financial crisis that was to materialise in less than a decade.[166]

Events in high politics had, however, a relatively minor role in the suspension crisis. Rather, the financial crisis laid bare the government's limited control over Britain's immense financial system, especially when the French wars had greatly magnified financial uncertainties. The situation was fraught with ominous possibilities, which could well have caused a financial calamity on a significant scale. At the outset of the crisis, the government only exacerbated the situation, and, as we have seen, its defence policy blunder incited an initial financial panic. When trying to contain the crisis, the government had only limited power. Nor was the Bank of England central in ensuring the acceptance of its notes by the general public. Partly to regain public trust, the Bank had to concede a substantial amount of information for public scrutiny. In a parliamentary committee, instigated by Sheridan, for the first time in its history, the Bank of England's internal operation and its financial state were revealed to the public in order to prove its earlier statement that, despite the depletion of its metallic reserve, it was in an 'affluent and prosperous situation'.[167] What mattered to the government and the Bank was gaining public support for the new monetary order based on inconvertible paper currency. Grounded in historical precedents, the declaration movement and its layers of meaning gave legitimacy to the stoppage of cash payments not only for the government and the Bank of England but equally for other banks across the British Isles. The declarations not merely complemented the government and the Bank's limited control over the monetary system, but they worked to eliminate the potential threat to solidarity by dissolving political, regional and class division regarding the support of public credit.[168] Although the declaration movement by no means encompassed the entire nation, support for the financial system, the Bank of England and inconvertible paper currency emanated from more diverse social and geographical backgrounds than most historians have previously acknowledged.

---

[166] F. G. Hall, *The Bank of Ireland, 1783–1946* (Dublin, 1949), 83.

[167] Court papers, 6 Apr. 1797, BE, G6/129, fol. 28.

[168] Diffusing political tension had paramount importance in Britain during the French wars. Philip Harling, 'A Tale of Two Conflicts: Critiques of the British War Effort, 1793–1815', in Mark Philp, ed., *Resisting Napoleon: The British Response to the Threat of Invasion, 1797–1815* (Aldershot, 2006), 33–54; Joanna Innes and Arthur Burns, 'Introduction', in Joanna Innes and Arthur Burns, eds., *Rethinking the Age of Reform: Britain 1780–1850* (Cambridge, 2003), 19; Macleod, 'British Attitudes to the French Revolution', 696–9.

The cultural foundation of the declaration movement was the idea that the value of the Bank of England note – and, by extension, paper currency in Britain in general – rested on the voluntary acceptance by its users. To put it another way, the declaration movement enacted the very mode of currency voluntarism that Edmund Burke had identified as one of the chief pillars of Britain's democratic monetary order. To be more precise, it was a post-Burkean feat in the sense that, by adopting declarations, the British public agreed to do away with the convertibility of paper currency, to which Burke was still strongly attached. Burke was, to say the least, ambivalent about the long-term prospect of the new monetary order based solely on voluntary support because, for him, the natural state of the monetary system was constituted by the coexistence of credit, including credit currency, and metallic currency. While giving a nod to the resilience of his compatriots, Burke comments,

But, for the present, if the general interest is appealed to in support of Credit, Credit will be supported, and Cash will, by degrees, reappear, from the necessity of its reappearance but if a low Paper Currency is once admitted, the Market will be overloaded, Gold and silver will be more and more withheld and if Guinea Notes, or any thing resembling them, are once put into Currency, you will never see a Guinea; whereas if you keep the Currency where it is and support it with vigour, necessity will draw out the Gold and silver. Excuse, I beg you, these crude ideas. No man wishes more than I do, that all my ideas should be found vain and frivolous upon experience.[169]

Part of Burke's concerns – the disappearance of metallic currency from circulation – proved well founded. What he failed to recognise, however, was that the British economy and its money users were more than capable of adapting to the use of inconvertible currency. As with the majority of his contemporaries, Burke did not foresee that the paper-based currency system would continue for more than two decades with relative stability. Britain's experience with inconvertibility played out differently to what Burke had anticipated, and the inconvertible Bank of England note did not follow the fate of the French *assignats*. During the twenty-four years of the Bank Restriction period, the inconvertible paper currency was a major factor shaping Britain's economy, society and culture. It was a new era that opened with the British nation promising to accept paper as money; therefore note users agreed to substitute the 'promise to pay' printed on paper with their own voluntary acceptance. To what extent did this promise bind British money users, and how did it transform Britain's everyday life? One way to answer these

[169] Edmund Burke, *The Correspondence of Edmund Burke*, ix: *May 1796–July 1797*, ed. R. B. McDowell and J. A. Woods (London, 1970), ix, 269.

questions is to investigate how and by whom the promise was performed –
two inseparable topics that concern the money users who accepted and
circulated paper currency. The suspension of cash payments brought
about some important changes in Britain's monetised economy, among
which was a redefinition of the nature and constitution of the community
of note users. Chapter 2 will discuss the circulation of the Bank of
England note and, more crucially, the identity of note users.

2   The Users of the Bank of England Note

The immediate effect of the suspension of the Bank of England's cash payments and the ensuing Bank Restriction Act was a significant increase in the circulation of the Bank of England note. This statement requires qualification. In terms of the total amount of money circulating as paper currency, there was hardly a drastic change in the year of the suspension. In 1797, the highest point of Bank-note circulation was £13.3 million, a figure greater than £11.1 million in the previous year, yet smaller than £14.3 million in 1795.[1] In terms of the number of notes issued, however, the effect of the suspension was spectacular. Prior to the suspension, the number of notes issued by the Bank each month was approximately 100,000. In March 1797, it shot up to 700,000, and another 500,000 notes went into circulation in April.[2] There was a simple reason that the sudden increase of the notes does not appear in the statistical record: the majority of the additional issue was in small-denomination notes – £1, £2 and £5. With this statistical blind spot – which tends to discount the short-term impact of the suspension – it is beyond dispute that there was a dramatic increase in the circulation of the Bank of England note.[3] As the increase in small notes made only a modest addition to the total amount of money in circulation, the true impact of the suspension on Britain's monetary landscape cannot be gauged without taking into account both the amount and the *number* of the note issue. In the long term, the suspension transformed Britain's monetary composition, which became noticeable by the end of the eighteenth century with the rising amount of money issued as notes. A general increase in the total circulation was a constant trend between 1797 and 1821, punctuated by

---

[1] House of Commons, *Report from the Committee of Secrecy on the Bank of England Charter* (London, 1832).
[2] Court papers, 10 May 1797, BE, G6/129, fol. 44.
[3] In 1797 alone, approximately 1.5 million £1 notes were added. 'Bank Accounts: Periodical Fluctuations', BE, M5/549, fol. 155.

a powerful boost around 1800 and 1810 (Figure 2.1).[4] Then, what characterised the period was the combination of an exponential increase in the number of Bank notes and a significant and sustained increase in their overall amount.

Between 1797 and 1821, nearly 27 million small-denomination notes were thrown into circulation.[5] The Bank's issuance of small-denomination notes was a drastic departure from the previous period as, until March 1797, the law had prohibited Britain's banks from issuing £1 and £2 notes, albeit the legislature had lifted a similar ban on the £5 note in 1793. Made of paper, the life of a Bank note was limited compared to coins, but small-denomination notes usually stayed in circulation longer than larger-denomination notes. It was estimated in 1818 that the average life of £1 and £2 notes was 147 days, far longer than that of £100 notes (49 days) and £1,000 notes (13 days).[6] A Bank note did not necessarily only live once: even after notes were withdrawn from circulation and cancelled on the Bank's account, some of them were reissued.[7] Thus the constantly issued freshly minted notes and reissued notes made up the total circulation of Bank of England notes at a previously unimaginable scale, that is unimaginable except in Scotland where there had already been sizeable small-note circulation.[8] Bank notes, especially small-denomination notes, flooded the British monetary landscape, where there had previously been no equivalent paper currency, transforming the existing order of circulating media.

The data for note issue clearly shows that, although coins did not entirely disappear, British society was inundated with paper currency in a fairly short period of time, after the Bank announced the suspension of cash payments. This potentially profound change, however, has offered little evidence to historians with an interest in the use of money in everyday life. The aggregate statistics, those of either the amount or

---

[4] For the note circulation statistics, see 'Bank of England Liabilities and Assets: 1696 to 1966, Appendix', *Bank of England Quarterly Bulletin*, 7 (1967), 1–86; Timothy S. Davis, *Ricardo's Macroeconomics: Money, Trade Cycles and Growth* (Cambridge, 2005), 233–7.

[5] The ratio of newly issued £1 notes to £2 notes in the Bank Restriction period, by number, was 8.15:1, and, in value, it was £237,962,000:£58,360,000. '£1 and £2 Notes: 1797–1826', BE, C12/166.

[6] Derrick Byatt, *Promises to Pay: The First Three Hundred Years of the Bank of England Notes* (London, 1994), 207; 'Memorials, Contracts, Accounts for Parliament', BE, M5/601.

[7] '£1 and £2 notes: 1797–1826', BE, C12/166; appendix D gives the value of reissued £1 and £2 notes in 1818 as £3,286,000 and £174,000, respectively, compared to the amount in new notes of £17,070,000 and £1,760,000.

[8] The life of a country banknote was usually considered approximately three years. The basis for this calculation is not clear, and the estimate is far less reliable than that of the Bank of England. L. S. Pressnell, *Country Banking in the Industrial Revolution* (Oxford, 1956), 182.

Figure 2.1 Bank of England note circulation (quarterly), 1790–1821.
Sources: House of Commons, *Report from the Committee of Secrecy on the Bank of England Charter* (London, 1832), 79–80; House of Lords, *Reports from the Select Committee on the Expediency of Resuming Cash Payments* (1819), appendix, 320–2.

number of issued notes, do not tell us where those numerous notes went, let alone by whom and how they were used. Hence, the circulation statistics offer little to tell us what impact the increased number of Bank of England notes had on social and economic life in Britain. Was its impact limited to London, or was it felt further afield, in provincial cities and towns in England and beyond? Did the increase in the number of notes mean that people with modest means could get hold of them? These questions have eluded investigation primarily because of the lack of historical evidence. In normal situations, monetary transactions rarely left traces, apart from numbers scribbled in the account books. The less the amount of the transaction, the scarcer the records left for historians. This is especially true for transactions between non-merchants. Everyday transactions involving money usually disappear into the haze of distant time.

Historical records that capture the circulation and use of a discrete set of objects are much rarer than their production records, but the Bank of England note is an exception to this general rule as the Bank has meticulously recorded information about notes that have gone missing since the early years of its establishment, throughout the long eighteenth century and beyond. This type of use – or, rather non-use – was recorded as owners of missing notes came to the Bank to report those incidents. In contrast to macro data on note circulation, the record of lost-note claims offers fascinating insights into the everyday use of Bank notes, while the lists of claimants serve as snapshots of note users' collective profile. A consistent examination of the claim data across time periods would complement historians' speculations about the infiltration of the Bank note into British society. If we take the loss of notes to follow the general pattern of note use and circulation, the record of lost notes would illuminate these topics, on which historians have hitherto had fragmented evidence. The historical diffusion of paper currency, as this chapter elaborates, went beyond financial and commercial centres. Also, the same records offer a unique mode of revisiting the role of the state in the penetration of paper currency in Britain, a topic that has attracted scholars' renewed attention in recent years. Equally importantly, lost-note claims offer historical evidence that allows us to delineate a type of personal credit network and to determine the extent to which institutionalised credit replaced personal credit during the long eighteenth century.[9] Thus this seemingly innocuous record of lost property answers some fundamental questions about modern monetised society in Britain.

---

[9] Craig Muldrew, *The Economy of Obligation: The Culture of Credit and Social Relations in Early Modern England* (Basingstoke, 1998), 103–19.

The Landscape of Britain's Circulating Media

According to a contemporary estimate, Britain's monetary circulation prior to the suspension of cash payments consisted of £25 million in gold coins, £10.5 million in Bank of England notes and £7 million in country banknotes.[10] These circulating media had different degrees of acceptability and desirability, which were articulated in the velocity of circulation and the differentials between the denominated and actual value of these forms of currency (i.e. the premium and the discounts on them) and occasionally by money users' refusal to accept a specific payment medium. As Edmund Burke wrote in 1790, a creditor could well refuse payment of a Bank of England note because, until 1833, notes issued by this private joint-stock company were not legal tender. The Bank's practical monopoly on note issue, as a concomitant to its legal monopoly of joint-stock banking in London (where there were sixty-two private banks in 1792) and its environs by the mid-eighteenth century, was rarely challenged but by no means impregnable.[11] Throughout the eighteenth century and well into the nineteenth century, the Bank did not seek to dominate the nation's currency, and the increase in its total issue was slow at a time when the nation was experiencing a historical economic expansion. The Bank's note circulation hardly exceeded £5 million until the 1760s. In the following two decades, note circulation more than doubled; it reached £11 million at the end of the 1780s but settled at roughly that level until 1797. In the English provinces beyond the Bank's

[10] House of Lords, *Reports from the Select Committee on the Expediency of Resuming Cash Payments* (1819), 11. The figure excludes pre-union Ireland. Note that the figures relating to banknotes are the average number of circulating notes and not the total number of notes issued in that year. In 1792, the total number of notes issued by the Bank was 819,300, amounting to nearly £75 million. House of Commons, *Account of Number of Bank Notes and Post Bills Issued, and Calculation of Time of Circulation of Bank Notes, 1792 and 1818* (1819).

[11] The Bank's joint-stock banking monopoly was granted in 1708, and its monopoly of London's note circulation had been established by the 1770s as private bankers ceased to issue their notes in the metropolis. J. Lawrence Broz and Richard S. Grossman, 'Paying for Privilege: The Political Economy of Bank of England Charters, 1694–1844', *Explorations in Economic History*, 41 (2004), 56–7; Rondo Cameron, 'England, 1750–1844', in Rondo Cameron, ed., *Banking in the Early Stages of Industrialization: A Study in Comparative Economic History* (New York, 1967), 21–2; John H. Clapham, *The Bank of England: A History* (Cambridge, 1944), i, 162; Emmanuel Coppieters, *English Bank Note Circulation, 1694–1954* (The Hague, 1955), 31; Ian H. Duffy, 'The Discount Policy of the Bank of England during the Suspension of Cash Payments, 1797–1821', *Economic History Review*, 35 (1982), 67; Pressnell, *Country Banking*, 138. For the number of London banks, see Clapham, *Bank of England*, i, 165; *The London Directory for the Year 1792; Containing an Alphabetical Arrangement of the Names of Residences of the Merchants, Manufacturers and Principal Inhabitants in the Metropolis and Its Environs* (London, 1792), 161–2.

monopoly area, private banking developed in the late eighteenth century. While the law limited the size of each country bank – they were prohibited from having more than six partners – the total number of country banks in England and Wales increased from fewer than 50 in 1760 to about 230 by 1793, when country banks' note circulation stood around £11 million, matching that of the Bank of England.[12] Around the same time, out of forty English counties, thirty-one were served by more than two banks, with seven counties being served by more than ten banks.[13]

There were also multiple note issuers in Scotland and Ireland. As the Bank of England's monopoly did not cover Scotland, three chartered banks – the Bank of Scotland, the Royal Bank of Scotland and the Scottish Linen Bank – had been established by the mid-eighteenth century, and there were twenty-nine note-issuing houses in Scotland in 1789.[14] Nor was the Scottish banks' development hindered by a limitation on the number of partners, allowing banks to expand branch networks. As the accumulation of precious metal was much smaller there than in England, the notes issued by the Scottish chartered banks had an extensive circulation among the Scottish population. In 1797, the total note circulation in Scotland was estimated in the range of £1.2–£1.5 million.[15] Across the Irish Sea, the mainstay of banking in pre-union Ireland was the system of private banking until 1783, when the Bank of Ireland was founded after the English model. In the following decade, the Bank of Ireland established itself as the leading financial institution in Ireland; in 1797, around £737,000 in its banknotes was in circulation.[16] Up to this point, the Irish bank's circulation was moderate in scale partly due to it not having monopoly on banknote issue – the Bank of Ireland note circulated alongside private banknotes, especially in the southern part of the island.[17] The demand for paper currency, broadly speaking,

---

[12] Coppieters, *English Bank Note Circulation*, 154; Margaret Dawes and C. N. Ward-Perkins, *Country Banks of England and Wales: Private Provincial Banks and Bankers, 1688–1953* (Canterbury, 2000), i, 6; Albert Edgar Feavearyear, *The Pound Sterling: A History of English Money* (Oxford, 1931), 304; Pressnell, *Country Banking*, 11.

[13] Dawes and Ward-Perkins, *Country Banks of England and Wales*, i, 11–12.

[14] S. G. Checkland, *Scottish Banking: A History, 1695–1973* (Glasgow, 1975), 184; House of Commons, *Report from the Select Committee on Promissory Notes in Scotland and Ireland* (1826), 19.

[15] House of Commons, *Reports from the Committee of Secrecy on the Outstanding Demands of the Bank and the Restriction of Cash Payments* (1797), 80.

[16] House of Commons, *Appendix to Minutes of Irish Exchange Committee* (1804), 66.

[17] Andy Bielenberg, *Cork's Industrial Revolution 1780–1880: Development or Decline?* (Cork, 1991), 128–30; L. M. Cullen, 'Landlords, Bankers and Merchants: The Early Irish Banking World, 1700–1820', in Antoin E. Murphy, ed., *Economists and the Irish Economy: From the Eighteenth Century to the Present Day* (Blackrock, Ireland, 1984), 39–41.

was also limited by the general preference for metallic currency in the northern part of Ireland.

The expansion of private note issue in England and Scotland in the 1760s led to a series of laws to regulate currency creation. The first of these regulative rules was enforced in Scotland, where the banking industry had been enjoying relative freedom. The Bank Notes (Scotland) Act of 1765 prohibited the issue of notes under £1 in Scotland, the avowed rationale for which was to protect users of small notes, but the law was in fact driven by existing Scottish bankers to raise barriers to new entrant banks and to consolidate the business of banknote circulation.[18] Ten years later, complaints from incumbent bankers in Yorkshire about the abuse of small notes in northern England led to legislation that brought English paper currency under the same strict regulations on small-denomination notes as in Scotland.[19] Subsequently, the ban on small notes was relaxed when, in 1777, the minimum issuable denomination was raised to £5.[20] These laws against small notes were applied equally to those of the Bank of England and of other banks, until they were superseded by the Bank Restriction Act.

Throughout the eighteenth century, until the 1800s, cash normally meant coins, excluding bank papers. As the Bank note remained non-legal tender, the only legal tender in Britain was regal coins made of gold and silver (though, under legislation in the 1770s, silver's legal tender status was limited to up to £25 per payment). For most of the eighteenth century, the general shortage of small-denomination coins was a source of perennial complaint. This was chiefly due to the Royal Mint's inactivity in coin production. Between 1752 and 1801, the mint produced only £143,313 in silver coins.[21] The mint's production of copper farthings (¼d) and half pence had also been sparse until the recoinage of 1773–7, and in 1787, the mint ceased to issue copper coins altogether.[22] The

---

[18] Checkland, *Scottish Banking*, 121; Clapham, *Bank of England*, i, 160; Tyler Beck Goodspeed, *Legislating Instability: Adam Smith, Free Banking, and the Financial Crisis of 1772* (Cambridge, MA, 2016), ch. 3.

[19] 15 Geo. III, c. 51; Clapham, *Bank of England*, i, 162; Pressnell, *Country Banking*, 16.

[20] 17 Geo III, c. 30; Feavearyear, *Pound Sterling*; Charles Munn, 'The Emergence of Joint-Stock Banking in the British Isles: A Comparative Approach', *Business History*, 30 (1988), 72; Pressnell, *Country Banking*, 16. Shapiro notes that after the 1770s country banks continued to issue small notes illegally. Samuel Shapiro, *Capital and the Cotton Industry in the Industrial Revolution* (Ithaca, NY, 1968), 134.

[21] John Craig, *The Mint: A History of the London Mint from AD 287 to 1948* (Cambridge, 1953), 246; Graham P. Dyer and Peter P. Gaspar, 'Reform, the New Technology, and Tower Hill, 1700–1966', in C. E. Challis, ed., *A New History of the Royal Mint* (Cambridge, 1992), 434–6.

[22] Craig, *The Mint*, 251–2. For the Bank's general indifference to the state of coins, see Clapham, *Bank of England*, i, 175–6.

mint's reluctance to supply small-denomination currency stemmed partly from rampant counterfeiting, clipping and sweating – as the new issue of full-weight 'good' coins was quickly replaced by bad ones, that is light coins.[23] There was also the entrenched belief among mint officials that their chief responsibility was to produce coins of precious metals, not tokens of base metal (copper coins were legal tender only up to six pence).[24] Indeed, the mint was much more active in supplying the nation with gold coins. After the recoinage of the 1770s, there were about £20 million worth of guinea coins in circulation in the late 1770s, whereas a mere £32,000 copper coins are generally believed to have been in circulation in the 1780s.[25] The production of gold coins continued throughout the 1780s: from 1785 until 1794, the mint annually struck £1.1–£3.7 million gold coins. However, in the following period, the French wars and the suspension of cash payments made the mint's production highly unpredictable, and its gold coinage fluctuated from around £50,000 to £2 million.[26] In the first fifteen years of the nineteenth century, the annual addition to gold circulation was small and, in the early 1810s, almost negligible.[27]

As Nuno Palma discusses, the inflow of precious metals from America significantly increased Britain's money supply in the seventeenth century and the expansion of money stock continued well into the eighteenth century.[28] Private issue of tokens, which became conspicuous in the 1780s, was therefore a response to the scarcity of small-denomination currency in England – not a general coin shortage – which had been exacerbated by the prevalence of counterfeiting of regal coins.[29] Towns, merchants and industrial firms issued private tokens to fill the gap in the

[23] For the problems with clipping and coining in this period, see Constantine G. Caffentzis, *Clipped Coins, Abused Words, and Civil Government: John Locke's Philosophy of Money* (Brooklyn, NY, 1989); Peter Mathias, *The Transformation of England: Essays in the Economic and Social History of England in the Eighteenth Century* (London, 1979), 195–6; John Styles, '"Our Traitorous Money Makers": The Yorkshire Coiners and the Law, 1760–83', in John Brewer and John Styles, eds., *An Ungovernable People: The English and Their Law in the Seventeenth and Eighteenth Centuries* (London, 1980), 172–249.

[24] Mathias, *Transformation of England*, 193–4.

[25] Craig, *The Mint*, 244; Craig Muldrew and Stephen King, 'Cash, Wages and the Economy of Makeshifts in England 1650–1830', in Peter Scholliers and Leonard Schwarz, eds., *Experiencing Wages: Social and Cultural Aspects of Wage Forms in Europe since 1500* (New York, 2003), 159.

[26] Craig, *The Mint*, 418.

[27] Dyer and Gaspar, 'Reform, the New Technology, and Tower Hill', 454–5, 468–72.

[28] Nuno Palma, 'Money and Modernization in Early Modern England', *Financial History Review*, 25 (2018), 231–61; Forrest Capie, 'Money and Economic Development in Eighteenth-Century England', in Leandro Prados de la Escosura, ed., *Exceptionalism and Industrialisation: Britain and Its European Rivals, 1688–1815* (Cambridge, 2004), 228.

[29] Mathias, *Transformation of England*, 197.

means of payment for transactions of relatively small sums.[30] For instance, the leading issuer of trade tokens, the Parys Mines Company of Anglesey, produced 300 tons of pence and halfpence tokens between 1787 and 1791, which circulated in Liverpool, Birmingham and London.[31] Similarly, the ironfounder John Wilkinson's trade tokens, some of which were struck by Matthew Boulton in Birmingham, had an extensive circulation in the Midlands.[32] There were also numerous token issuers operating at a moderate scale, albeit they generally had limited circulation, usually being confined to small areas in each issuer's locality. An estimate of the national figure suggests that about 600 tons of tradesman's tokens were manufactured in England in this period.[33]

The eighteenth-century British monetary system was relatively uniform, yet various currencies coexisted in the British Isles. Private token issue was not suppressed until the 1810s, and the state made only a limited effort to eliminate the use of foreign currencies. Despite the legal prohibition on circulating foreign coins, Portuguese coins were not entirely uncommon in late eighteenth-century England.[34] Foreign paper money, such as the French *assignat*, until it was banned in 1792, could be offered as a legal means of payment for private transactions. The use of near money such as bills of exchange was as common in domestic business transactions as it was for international transactions. An eminent London banker, Henry Thornton, stated in 1802 that the amount of bills of exchange in circulation was possibly greater than the circulation of 'all the bank notes of every kind, and of all the circulating guineas'.[35] Notwithstanding, the use of commercial bills was confined to the business community and 'come[s] little under the observation of the public'.[36]

---

[30] Eric Helleiner, *The Making of National Money: Territorial Currencies in Historical Perspective* (Ithaca, NY, 2003), 24.

[31] Peter Mathias, 'Official and Unofficial Money in the Eighteenth Century: The Evolving Uses of Currency', *British Numismatic Journal*, 74 (2004), 69.

[32] F. Stuart Jones, 'Government, Currency and Country Banks in England, 1770–1797', *South African Journal of Economics*, 44 (1976), 258.

[33] George Selgin, *Good Money: Birmingham Button Makers, the Royal Mint, and the Beginnings of Modern Coinage, 1775–1821* (Ann Arbor, MI, 2008), 126; George Selgin, 'Steam, Hot Air, and Small Change: Matthew Boulton and the Reform of Britain's Coinage', *Economic History Review*, 56 (2003), 480.

[34] Craig, *The Mint*, 54, 240–1. On the circulation of foreign coins in other European countries, Helleiner, *Making of National Money*, 22.

[35] Henry Thornton, *An Enquiry into the Nature and Effects of the Paper Credit of Great Britain* (London, 1802), 43.

[36] Thornton, *Paper Credit*, 43. There is no reliable estimate of bill of exchange circulation during the Bank Restriction period. Cameron, 'England, 1750–1844', 44. Still, it is generally believed that there was a significant boost in circulation after the 1770s. T. S. Ashton, 'The Bill of Exchange and Private Banks in Lancashire, 1790–1830', *Economic History Review*, 15 (1945), 25–35; Jones, 'Government, Currency and Country Banks',

What Thomas Sargent and François Velde describe as a 'laissez-faire' regime of metallic-currency production equally applied to paper currency (except in London), as the government 'at least did not discourage' private suppliers of coins and notes as long as issuers adhered to the legal rules concerning small notes.[37] Also, neither the Bank nor the mint actively pursued a systematic approach to circulating their notes and coins in the provinces.[38] Britain's monetary landscape was thus characterised by a 'multiple currency' situation in terms of currency media though not of monetary unit.[39] Eric Helleiner notes that the ability of nation states to control and regulate monetary circulation 'stemmed from such features as its policing powers, its more pervasive role in the domestic economy, its centralized authority, and its stronger ability to cultivate the "trust" of the domestic population'.[40] Prior to 1797, some of these conditions did not exist in England, leading to Helleiner's observation that the formation of a national currency started in earnest only in the late 1810s, a period that saw the introduction of an official silver-token currency and the Bank's rigorous enforcement of measures against counterfeit notes. The Bank Restriction period was a crucial turning point in the making of Britain's national currency, during which some of the preconditions for the Bank note becoming a national currency began to emerge.

The existence of multiple currencies continued to characterise Britain's monetary landscape into the early nineteenth century. The number of country banks peaked in 1812 at 707, many of which issued their own banknotes.[41] The note issue of country banks significantly expanded during the Bank Restriction period – from around £5 million in 1796 to around £20 million in the early 1810s, according to an estimate; so did note issues by Scottish and Irish banks.[42] The total circulation of Scottish notes was estimated at £3.5 million in

261; Shizuya Nishimura, *The Decline of Inland Bills of Exchange in the London Money Market, 1855–1913* (Cambridge, 1971), 30. See also S. G. Checkland, 'The Lancashire Bill System and Its Liverpool Protagonists, 1810–1827', *Economica*, 21 (1954), 129–42.

[37] Thomas J. Sargent and François R. Velde, *The Big Problem of Small Change* (Princeton, NJ, 2002), 266.

[38] Clapham, *Bank of England*, i, 41; Selgin, 'Steam, Hot Air, and Small Change', 497.

[39] On multiple currencies, see Frank Perlin, *Unbroken Landscape: Commodity, Category, Sign and Identity: Their Production as Myth and Knowledge from 1500* (Aldershot, 1994), 118–19.

[40] Helleiner, *Making of National Money*, 7. See also Geoffrey Ingham, 'Further Reflections on the Ontology of Money: Responses to Lapavitsas and Dodd', *Economy and Society*, 35 (2006), 271–2.

[41] Dawes and Ward-Perkins, *Country Banks of England and Wales*, i, 6.

[42] Coppieters, *English Bank Note Circulation*, 154. Pressnell's relatively reliable estimate is £14.5 million in 1808–9. Pressnell, *Country Banking*, 145.

1815.[43] In the same year, the Irish national bank issued £3.3 million notes, while the annual banknote circulation by Irish private banks was in the region of £232,000–£343,000.[44]

Britain's multiple-currency situation was dominated by paper currency, while the mint produced only a limited number of gold coins – especially during the early part of the Bank Restriction – and when they were issued, those coins tended to be hoarded away and illegally exported as and when they fetched a good price abroad. During the Bank Restriction period, the Royal Mint, except in 1797–8, rarely produced gold coins to a value surpassing £500,000.[45] Silver coinage lacked standardisation and was in short supply despite the Bank's issue of silver-dollar tokens.[46] The dominance of paper currency in the nation's circulating media, or the lack of metallic currency therein, was vividly captured in George Woodward's caricature in 1804, in which a country banker is staring at the ghost of a guinea coin floating in mid-air, confessing that he had never seen a real guinea coin in his trade (Figure 2.2). Only when the Napoleonic wars had ended, did the state begin to address the problem of regal coinage.[47] The so-called Great Recoinage from 1816 increased the circulation of regal coins, both gold (sovereigns) and silver (crowns and half-crowns), with more than £4 million of gold coins and £2.4 million of silver coins being issued in 1817.[48] Still, in the same year, the Bank of England note circulation stood at £29.5 million, including around £8 million in small denominations. The Bank Restriction period was truly an age of paper currency: it dominated the nation's monetary landscape. Among the multiple currencies circulated, the Bank of England note was undoubtedly the most prominent form of Britain's paper currency, even if it was yet to become a national currency.

[43] House of Commons, *Report on Promissory Notes in Scotland and Ireland*, 7.

[44] House of Commons, *Report on Promissory Notes in Scotland and Ireland*, 15. The Irish paper-currency circulation was chiefly a feature of the southern part of Ireland, while in the northern part of Ireland, metallic currency remained predominant even after 1797. See Cullen, 'Landlords, Bankers and Merchants', 39–41.

[45] For the mint's output between 1800 and 1810, see Dyer and Gaspar, 'Reform, the New Technology, and Tower Hill', 455.

[46] Between 1797 and 1799, as an emergency measure to alleviate the acute shortage of coins, additional silver coins were issued by countermarking silver Spanish dollar coins, totalling £282,137. By the Act of 1798, the mint was officially prohibited from carrying out silver coinage, and it was the Bank that took on the issue of silver-dollar tokens from 1804 until 1815. Dyer and Gaspar, 'Reform, the New Technology, and Tower Hill', 449–59; E. M. Kelly, *Spanish Dollars and Silver Tokens: An Account of the Issues of the Bank of England, 1797–1816* (London, 1976), 89, 123; Selgin, 'Steam, Hot Air, and Small Change', 503–4.

[47] This was accompanied by tightened restriction on private coinage between 1812 and 1817. Mathias, 'Official and Unofficial Money', 83.

[48] Craig, *The Mint*, 419.

Figure 2.2 George Moutard Woodward, *The Ghost of a Guinea, and Little Pitts, or the Country Banker's Surprise!!* (1810).
© Trustees of the British Museum

Radius of the Bank of England Note

Historians of eighteenth-century British banking have long believed that, beyond the metropolitan area – a thirty-mile radius from the Bank of England – only very few Bank notes circulated.[49] Indeed, in the early part of the century, contemporaries often referred to the Bank of England as 'the Bank of London'. However, as John Clapham cautions, the characterisation of the eighteenth-century Bank of England as the Bank of London is not invariably true.[50] The Bank's direct commercial dealings may have been limited to London-based customers, but there is ample evidence that the Bank increasingly became indispensable for the operation of commerce and national finance in a broader area of Britain.[51] Also, during that century the Bank had become an important provider of circulating media, chiefly paper currency – a role that eventually matched in significance that of the Royal Mint in metallic currency.

On this topic, little is known about the Bank of England note's circulation outside London – or, indeed, if the Bank note found its way into other parts of the country. The total circulation figures serve only as an indication of the Bank's overall note issue, and these figures do not allow nuanced interpretation. Our understanding of the geographical reach of the Bank of England is equally lacking, which makes it difficult to gauge the impact of inconvertible paper currency on British society. The most ample evidence relates to intellectual debates and policy discussion in parliament or the Bank's parlour, but they often had limited relevance to the everyday life of the nation at large. Still, the fact remains that the Bank of England note did become a national topic that was discussed by metropolitan citizens as well as denizens of provincial cities and towns. The problematics of the Bank note cut across social boundaries, being a topic of conversation among various sorts of people, from common labourers, farmers, shopkeepers, clergy, merchants and economic thinkers to politicians of different persuasions. If Bank-note circulation was confined to in and around London, how was it possible for it to have such a profound impact on British society?

To better understand the extent of the Bank notes' penetration into British society, the following sections draw upon a method used by Clapham in a book published more than seventy years ago. In exploring what he calls 'the radius of the Bank of England note',

---

[49] Coppieters, *English Bank Note Circulation*, 30–1, 70; Pressnell, *Country Banking*, 15, 138.
[50] Clapham, *Bank of England*, i, 146–50; Coppieters, *English Bank Note Circulation*, 20.
[51] Anne Murphy, 'Performing Public Credit at the Eighteenth-Century Bank of England', *Journal of British Studies*, 58 (2019), 58–78.

Clapham traces the claims made on Bank notes that were lost. While Clapham's main source was the Court of Directors' decision on payments for lost notes, the following sections draw upon the Lost Note Books, which are a more complete record of lost-note claims made at the Bank of England.

The Bank note was a type of promissory note, for which the Bank was ultimately responsible for paying the denominated amount to the bearer of the note.[52] The nature of the Bank note as a promissory note meant that the rightful owner of a note could claim payment from the Bank even when the note was lost or destroyed. That was, of course, as long as the claimants could specify the notes they had lost; otherwise, the Bank was not obliged to repay the lost monetary value.[53] This requirement did not present a difficulty to claimants. Note users in the eighteenth and early nineteenth centuries in general kept surprisingly detailed records of the notes they handled. Accordingly, a typical entry in the Lost Note Books consists of the date of application; the name and abode of the claimant (s); and the serial number, issue date and amount of the notes that were lost. Besides the lost notes' details, the Lost Note Books often recorded the circumstances of how losses occurred. The entries contain a catalogue of situations for how things went missing. Notes were mislaid or stolen or slipped out of pockets.[54] The chance of one's pocket being picked or being robbed was high, constituting one of the major reasons for claims to be lodged.[55] Claims were also made for lost notes when they were paid to the wrong person, they paid for forged instruments, or an employee or runaway wife absconded with them.[56] Notes contained in mail could be stolen or robbed, and some of them simply disappeared. Some Bank notes were consumed by fire, some washed to pieces and some eaten by vermin.[57] During the Bank Restriction period, the Bank paid out around £5,000 annually for lost or destroyed notes, and 'very considerable sums' were also paid for mutilated notes.[58]

With Clapham's dictum, 'losses were more or less proportioned to use', one can draw upon the record of lost Bank notes as historical

---

[52] The payment here means payment in specie, in other notes or by crediting to an account.
[53] The claimants were required to have both the serial number and the date of issue. The Bank to George Lewis, 13 May 1799, secretary's letter books, BE, G23/2.
[54] Lost Note Books, BE, C101/21, fol. 278; C101/22, fols. 10, 64 and 69; C101/24, fols. 311 and 312.
[55] Lost Note Books, BE, C101/22, fol. 12; C101/24, fol. 327.
[56] Lost Note Books, BE, C101/22, fol. 102; C101/23, fol. 198; C101/24, fols. 322 and 340; C101/25, fol. 270.
[57] Lost Note Books, BE, C101/22, fols. 55 and 88.
[58] House of Commons, *Account of Number of Bank Notes and Post Bills Issued by Bank of England, 1697–1831* (1833).

evidence that reveals much more than a mundane side of the Bank's business in dealing with customers' trivial claims.[59] The Lost Note Books add significantly more detail to Clapham's early foray into the subject.[60] While Clapham, from the record of lost-note payments, could only speculate on the proliferation of the Bank of England note after the 1760s, the Lost Note Books reveal what happened in the last decades of the eighteenth century and thereafter. Up to the 1760s, the number of claims brought to the Bank remained constant, around 50 annually (Figure 2.3). In the following decade, the number of claims shot up, reaching 169 in 1775.[61] Claims further increased in the late 1780s, when their number surpassed 200.[62] More striking still is the increase in claims after the suspension of cash payments in 1797. In that year, 480 claims were lodged at the Bank, an increase of nearly 100 over the previous year.[63] Thereafter, annual claims increased constantly to reach 799 in 1810.[64] The apex of lost-note claims came in 1815, when there were 1,688 claims in a single year. While the increase in claims was extraordinary, we must, however, keep in mind that the claimed notes in the Lost Note Books represented only a small fraction of the total number and amount of circulated notes: the total value of claimed lost notes was £2,409 in 1800 and £17,877 in 1810, whereas the total amount of Bank-note circulation was about £15 million and nearly £25 million, respectively.[65] Notwithstanding, as relatively randomised data, the lost-note records are the invaluable source that helps us understand the use of the Bank note during this period. Among other things, the record furnishes us with note users' profiles, which are all but erased in the aggregated circulation statistics.

As meticulous as ever, the Bank clerks recorded the details of lost-note claims submitted to the Bank after its notes became inconvertible. On the day the Bank of England suspended its cash payments, 28 February 1797, four claims were recorded.[66] John Grace of the stock exchange lost a £50 note, for which he was able to provide the serial number and issue date, but he could not do the same for the two other notes he claimed to have lost alongside the £50 note. The record does not specify Grace's occupation, but he was apparently a stockbroker or investor as he stated that a receipt for a £500 stock subscription was also missing. Grace's personal devastation was narrowly averted for he was fortunate

---

[59] Clapham, *Bank of England*, i, 147–50.   [60] Clapham, *Bank of England*, i, 146–9.
[61] Lost Note Books, BE, C101/13–14.   [62] Lost Note Books, BE, C101/16–18.
[63] Lost Note Books, BE, C101/21–2.   [64] Lost Note Books, BE, C101/34–6.
[65] Lost Note Books, BE, C101/23–4 and C101/34–6.
[66] Lost Note Books, BE, C101/21, fol. 306.

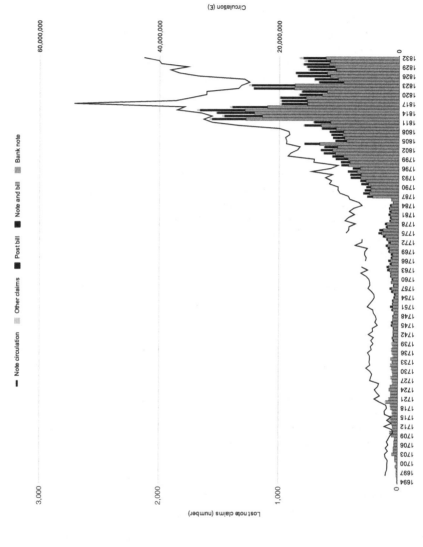

Figure 2.3 Bank of England note circulation and lost-note claims (selected years), 1694–1832.

Sources: 'Bank of England Liabilities and Assets: 1696 to 1966, Appendix', *Bank of England Quarterly Bulletin* (1967), 1–86; Lost Note Books, BE, C101, various years.

enough to find them later as an appended note to the entry reveals.[67] Thomas Polehampton of Eton College brought to the Bank the 'sinister' part of a £20 note – the other half he had lost – and the Bank paid him the full amount on security provided by a Leicester Fields saddler and a reverend. Henry Brookes of Brighton lodged a claim for a lost Bank Post Bill of £20 that had gone missing the previous night. The day's last entry was a payment to a Liverpool merchant, Charles Taylor, for his lost £10 note.

The first appearance of £1 and £2 notes in the Lost Note Books is on 16 March 1797, when Joseph Rogers of Old Broad Street applied to stop payment of freshly printed small-denomination notes.[68] These notes were sent to John Wilkinson of Chesterfield in Derbyshire but never reached their destination. On March 20, another loss of small notes was reported by Mess Tiplady & Co., a London warehouse, which applied to stop payment of sixteen small notes sent to Harborough, the circumstances of which are not stated. In the month of their first issue, the small-denomination notes were used, lost and stolen. John Wilson came to the Bank on March 24 to report that he had dropped three £1 notes in the Royal Exchange. Robert Chambers, a Hampstead tailor, was the unfortunate first victim of a small notes (£2) robbery, which took place when he was on his way home in the evening.[69]

Regarding the early geography of Bank-note circulation, the eighteenth-century record of lost Bank notes generally conforms with Clapham's assertion that, up until the 1760s, the geographical spread of the Bank's note circulation gradually expanded. Note circulation was initially concentrated in the metropolis: between the 1690s and the 1700s, in the first volume of the Lost Note Books, the proportion of claims that were from London/Middlesex was 62 per cent.[70] As Figure 2.4 shows, London's share declined after the 1720s – from 77 per cent in the 1710s to 72 per cent in the early 1720s and to 66 per cent in the early 1730s – then remained at the same level until the early 1760s, indicating a gradual diffusion of the Bank note outside London. Interestingly, even after the 1760s, when the growth of English provincial banking began, the share of London claims remained relatively low at 60 per cent between the 1760s and 1780s. It was in the early 1790s that the proportion of London claims showed a small increase to 62 per cent of the total claims, suggesting that the balance between the Bank note's

---

[67] Lost Note Books, BE, C101/21, fol. 306.
[68] Lost Note Books, BE, C101/21, fol. 316.
[69] Lost Note Books, BE, C101/21, fol. 329.
[70] In my analysis of the geographical distribution of lost-note claims, I have considered Middlesex as part of the London area.

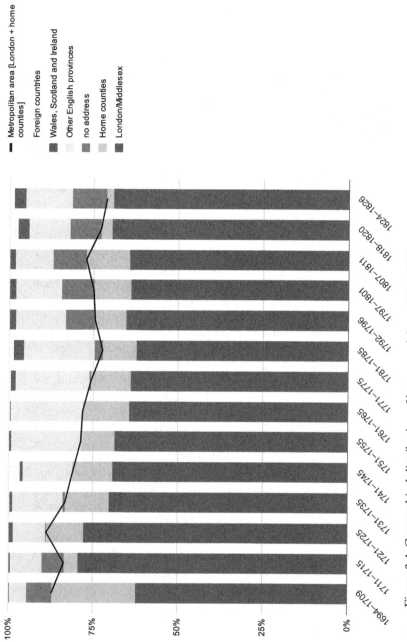

Figure 2.4 Geographical distribution of lost-note claims, 1694–1826.
Source: Lost Note Books, BE, C101, various years.

metropolitan circulation and its regional circulation had changed, thereby making its regional penetration less conspicuous than in the previous period. However, London's share declined again after 1797, and between 1807 and 1811 it stood at 57 per cent, implying that the country banks' note issue prior to 1818 had relatively little effect in checking the geographical expansion of Bank-note circulation.

A closer look at the data for lost-note claims recorded in the pre-suspension period (1792–6) and the post-suspension period (1797–1801) – totalling 1,920 claims and 2,566 claims, respectively – offers insights into the geographical distribution of note users. Claims from the metropolitan area, including London, Middlesex and some parts of Surrey and Kent, which in practice formed a greater part of London, were pre-dominant. In the pre-suspension period, apart from 1,195 claims relating to London/Middlesex (which had the greatest number), 67 concerned Surrey and 34 Kent. Still, the home counties were by no means dominant among lost-note claims outside London in this period, as other counties equally appeared in the Lost Note Books. Twenty-six claims relating to Hampshire were the largest in the second group, followed by Bristol (20) and Oxfordshire (20), Essex (19), Somerset (18), Warwickshire (18) and Wiltshire (16) (Table 2.1). Though fewer than these, claims came from far and wide: Bedfordshire, Cambridgeshire, Cheshire, Devon, South Wales, Yorkshire and Scotland. The geographical spread of the claims covers most of the English counties, and it becomes patchy beyond the English borders. In the post-suspension period, the geographical spread was retained, with a noticeable rise in the number of claims in some regions. Surrey, Kent and Sussex saw a relatively large increase in claims, probably due to their connection with London's economy. More interestingly, some counties at a distance from the metropolis, such as Hampshire, Devon, Lancashire, Somerset and Yorkshire, saw a surge in claims. A less pronounced rise in the number of claims was experienced in Hertfordshire, Norfolk and Northamptonshire. Claims related to Wales were not particularly conspicu-ous in terms of their number – 21 – but their geographical origin was spread widely: Glamorganshire, Monmouthshire, Powys and Gwynedd. Only 10 claims concerning Scotland were recorded between 1797 and 1801, while claims from Ireland increased from 7 to 15 after the suspension. Among claims from Ireland, five concerned Dublin and others were related to losses in Cork, Sligo, Wicklow, Meath, Waterford and Belfast. The Lost Note Books record occasional claims from overseas, which refer to places such as Berlin, Paris and Holland.

To some extent, the expansion of the Bank's sphere of influence was due to the development of the nation's postal service. Being well aware of the demand for monetary transaction over distance, the Bank began to

Table 2.1 *Geographical distribution of lost-note claims, 1792–1796, 1797–1801 and 1807–1811*

Place/Year	1792–6	1797–1801	1807–1811	Place/Year	1792–1796	1797–1801	1807–1811	Place/Year	1792–1796	1797–1801	1807–1811
No address	177	283	418	Essex	19	28	40	Shropshire	5	4	8
Bank of England	28	74	81	Gloucestershire	10	6	11	Somerset	18	25	23
Army	6	7	11	Guernsey	2	0	2	Staffordshire	5	6	7
Navy	5	16	7	Hampshire	26	38	50	Suffolk	6	14	5
Ship	7	23	7	Herefordshire	3	5	4	Surrey	67	94	117
General Post Office	7	21	25	Hertfordshire	7	13	16	Sussex	15	28	45
Public office	7	19	94	Huntingdonshire	0	2	5	Warwickshire	18	16	12
Bedfordshire	7	6	6	Isle of Man	0	0	0	Westmorland	0	2	1
Berkshire	17	16	11	Jersey	1	1	3	Wiltshire	16	14	7
Bristol	20	14	21	Kent	34	58	84	Worcestershire	8	5	6
Buckinghamshire	7	4	7	Lancashire	10	25	33	Yorkshire	14	24	34
Cambridgeshire	15	19	11	Leicestershire	6	2	7				
Cheshire	12	6	8	Lincolnshire	9	10	4	Ireland	7	15	12
Cornwall	4	9	5	London	1,195	1,482	1,862	Scotland	7	10	14
Cumberland	6	5	3	Norfolk	10	16	8	Wales	18	21	23
Derbyshire	2	4	2	Northamptonshire	8	14	5				
Devon	6	21	38	Northumberland	2	9	8	Other/foreign	3	1	0
Dorset	5	5	10	Nottinghamshire	9	6	2				
Durham	2	2	8	Oxfordshire	20	17	7	Total	1,920	2,566	3,245
				Rutlandshire	2	1	3				

Source: Lost Note Books, BE, C101/19–26 and C101/30–8.

provide a special form of paper instrument for that purpose in the early eighteenth century. The facility was originally introduced in 1728 – as a precaution against the then-frequent highway robberies – as 'bank bills', which were payable three days after the Bank's acceptance to prevent criminals from encashing stolen notes before the victims had reported their loss to the Bank. In 1739, it became the 'Bank Post Bill', payable seven days after acceptance.[71] Bank Post Bills were used – and often went lost – in transactions over both long and relatively short distances. In 1797, when the Bank Post Bill was already a well-established method for distant transactions, 62 claims for missing Bank Post Bills were recorded in the Lost Note Books.[72] Nonetheless, slipping Bank notes into an envelope – often cut in half – remained a common method of sending money.[73] From the Lost Note Books, it appears that this practice became prevalent after 1797 as the cases of loss by post increased from 171 in the pre-1797 period to 279 in the post-1797 period. Just as in the case of the Bank Post Bills, sending Bank notes by post served for both long-distance and short-distance transactions – for instance, between 1797 and 1801, twenty-four losses were recorded concerning transactions between London and Kent.[74] The loss of notes by the postal service was a problem no doubt shared by other banks. For example, between 1805 and 1807, the Bank of Ireland compensated 3,260 claims, amounting to £74,550 for the miscarriage of its banknotes and post bills sent by post.[75] The General Post Office and local post offices appear in the Lost Note Books, especially in the later part of the Bank Restriction period, as they lodged claims on behalf of the owners of lost notes.

The data of lost-note claims illuminate several factors that shaped the pattern of the Bank note's geographical distribution. Undoubtedly, the nature of the local economy affected the movement of Bank notes. T. S. Ashton observes that, in Lancashire, locals often preferred the Bank of

---

[71] Clapham, *Bank of England*, i, 144; Virginia Hewitt and John Keyworth, *As Good As Gold: 300 Years of British Bank Note Design* (London, 1987), 154.

[72] The total number of claims, including both Bank notes and Bank Post Bills for that year, was 544. Lost Note Books, BE, C101/21–2.

[73] On the extensive use of the post to send banknotes, see Howard Robinson, *Britain's Post Office: A History of Development from the Beginnings to the Present Day* (London, 1953), 97–9. See also B. Critchett, *The Post-Office Annual Directory for 1808* (London, 1808), 356.

[74] Similarly, fourteen claims related to notes lost between London and Sussex, and thirteen between London and Surrey.

[75] House of Commons, *Commissioners of Inquiry into Fees and Emoluments Received in Public Offices in Ireland, Ninth Report (General Post Office)* (1810), appendix, 5–7; House of Commons, *Commissioners of Inquiry into Collection and Management of Revenue in Ireland and Great Britain, Nineteenth Report (Post Office Revenue, Ireland)* (1829), appendix, 522.

England note to country banknotes.[76] The underlying reason was local suspicion as to the stability of private banks, rooted in the memory of a local financial crisis in 1788. The small number of note-issuing country banks in Lancashire, and hence the relative prominence of the Bank of England note, was also explained by 'the larger scale of business undertaking and the concentration of production in a relatively small area'.[77] Up until the 1790s, Lancashire's preference for the Bank note did not show up in the Lost Note Books. Only occasionally were lost-note claims made from that region. It was in the 1790s, and particularly after the suspension, that claims from Lancashire visibly increased, with most claims coming from Liverpool and Manchester, reflecting the centrality of these places in the regional economy.[78]

The record of lost-note claims cautions us against focusing our attention too much on the heartlands of industrialisation by providing evidence of Bank-note use in other regional commercial centres. Bristol is a good example of a city whose role as a long-standing trading hub had increased trade-related note circulation. As Clapham points out, note losses in Bristol were already conspicuous in the early eighteenth century.[79] In the subsequent period, although the growth of other major ports overshadowed Bristol's prosperity as a centre of West Indian and Peninsular trade, including the slave trade, it remained a sizeable mercantile city, with related movement of currency and credit.[80] Merchants in Bristol, trading across the Atlantic in goods from Birmingham and other English manufacturing towns, generated a large number of inter-regional transactions.[81] While this type of trade activity was commonly conducted on credit, Bank of England notes were also a legitimate means of payment and often preferred to local notes; as purchasers could expect some discount for ready-money (including Bank-note) transactions, some merchants would have opted for using paper currency in place of credit.[82] One can only speculate as to the actual volume of Bank-note circulation in Bristol, but the frequency of claims from Bristol merchants suggests that receiving and paying Bank notes was a common practice in the mercantile community in this south-western city. The London bank

[76] Ashton, 'Bill of Exchange', 31.   [77] Ashton, 'Bill of Exchange', 28.
[78] See General Gascoyne's comments in *Parliamentary Register*, xvii (1802), 513.
[79] Clapham, *Bank of England*, i, 147.
[80] Gordon Jackson, 'Ports 1700–1840', in Peter Clark, ed., *The Cambridge Urban History of Britain*, ii: *1540–1840* (Cambridge, 2000), 708–9.
[81] Kenneth Morgan, *Bristol and the Atlantic Trade in the Eighteenth Century* (Cambridge, 1993), 104–5; Kenneth Morgan, 'The Economic Development of Bristol, 1700–1850', in Madge Dresser and Philip Ollerenshaw, eds., *The Making of Modern Bristol* (Tiverton, 1996), 55–9.
[82] Morgan, *Bristol and the Atlantic Trade*, 108–9.

of Martin & Co. claimed for £85 sent by Bristol linen merchant John Innys Baker in 1795.[83] In the following year, Bristol mercer Prideaux & Thorn claimed, through John Pole in London, for a £20 note sent to them from Worcester.[84] A £10 note sent by William Jordan of Birmingham in 1810 went missing on its way to Hicks & Co. in Bristol.[85] Most lost-note claims from Bristol concerned London, but the Lost Note Books also record the movement of notes between Bristol and, for instance, Gloucester, Worcester, Brecon (Powys) and Moulton (Northamptonshire).

The use of the Bank note in inter-regional payments and for duty payments at trading ports suggests that the degree to which the Bank of England note complemented local note circulation and bills of exchange could have been significant. By the early 1760s, tax collectors at ports in Bristol and in Hull were accepting Bank notes for 'Duties of all Kinds as Specie'.[86] Merchants and traders in Lynn apparently found this a convenient practice as they requested the same arrangement in 1763. When the need for a relatively large payment arose regularly and frequently, coins were cumbersome to handle. The preference for paper currency, therefore, was quite natural in active commercial centres such as Bristol.

Economy was by no means the only factor that characterised the spread of Bank note use; there were cases for which social factors provided a better explanation than economic ones. A prime example is the frequent report of note losses from Bath, which was probably due to seasonal migration to this popular destination for a pleasure visit. Visitors from outside the city, many of them from London, would have avoided the trouble of going to local banks to obtain local notes by using notes they had at hand. Bath bankers, such as the Bladud Bank, were accustomed to handling notes of various geographical origins due probably to seasonal immigration from across the country.[87] Local banks in Bath were not inimical to the invasion of Bank of England notes: the 'High Street Bank' of Bath, Clement & Co. apparently accepted Bank of England notes, as shown by the bank's claim for forty-eight Bank notes amounting to £1,000 in April 1797.[88] Those of comfortable financial

---

[83] Lost Note Books, BE, C101/20, fol. 313.

[84] Lost Note Books, BE, C101/21, fol. 226.

[85] Lost Note Books, BE, C101/36, fol. 227.

[86] 'Petition of the Merchants and Traders in the Town of Lynn', 15 Nov. 1763, TNA, T 1/426/318–9.

[87] There is anecdotal evidence of the Bladud Bank's acceptance of the Bank of Ireland's notes in 1810. Steven Clews, 'Banking in Bath in the Reign of George III', *Bath History Journal*, 5 (1994), 114.

[88] Lost Note Books, BE, C101/21, fol. 339. On Clement & Co., see Clews, 'Banking in Bath', 106.

means who moved between Bath and London (and their country residence) were undoubtedly well acquainted with the Bank of England note. Dame Ellen Wrey, a wealthy widow in Bath, appears in the Lost Note Book in 1800 as a claimant for five £20 notes, four £10 notes and four £5 notes, which were sent from London to Bath.[89] Similarly, in 1810, Mrs Framel lodged a claim for banknotes sent by J. W. Boddington of London, some of which disappeared before arriving in Bath.[90] The existence of Bank-note users in the locality increased the chance of local traders handling the notes. A baker in Bath, who claimed for a lost £20 note, was possibly one such trader.[91]

As with the case of Bath, the culture of sociability provides a plausible explanation for the frequent loss of Bank notes reported from Oxford and Cambridge. In 1801, Mrs Gabbs, a resident of Abergavenny, Wales, reported the loss of a £10 note sent to her son at Jesus College, Oxford.[92] That she sent a Bank of England note rather than a country note from her locality showed the general belief in the acceptability of the Bank note in university towns, a belief that was probably shared by the families of university students. As a meeting place for scholars from diverse geographical backgrounds, a mongrel currency situation may have resulted unless there was a standard form of payment. Lost-note claimants such as John Wyatt of Jesus College Cambridge and William Palmer of St Edmund Hall Oxford were among those who lived in the heterogeneous cultural and monetary situation of these places, in which the Bank of England note was a generally accepted means of payment.[93]

More than anything else, the wars with France had a profound effect on the pattern of diffusion of the Bank note after 1797 and through to the end of the wars. Throughout the military confrontation, Hampshire remained the place that, after Surrey and Kent, reported the greatest number of lost notes. Losses related to the navy port towns of Portsmouth and Southampton accounted for most of the claims from Hampshire. The economy of Portsmouth (including Portsea) was defined by its connection with the Admiralty. Being a vital station for repairing and refitting ships, the expansion of Portsmouth dockyard started in the aftermath of the American War of Independence and

---

[89] Lost Note Books, BE, C101/24, fol. 209. For Dame Wrey's economic standing, see TNA PROB 11/1151/162.
[90] Lost Note Books, BE, C101/36, fol. 104.
[91] Lost Note Books, BE, C101/23, fol. 231.
[92] Lost Note Books, BE, C101/25, fol. 114.
[93] Lost Note Books, BE, C101/23, fol. 55; C101/22, fol. 305.

continued until 1815.[94] Wartime naval activity stimulated the local economy directly by creating employment for dockyard workers and indirectly by increasing demand for food, clothing, retailing and other services.[95] As Gillian Russell contends, the 'most innovative industrial centres' during the French wars were 'not the mill towns of the north but the naval dockyards' in port cities, and war-induced economic activities, a considerable part of which originated in state expenditure, brought Bank notes to port towns.[96] The increased number of claims concerning Devon shows a similar connection between Bank-note use and maritime activity in Plymouth. In some seafaring occupations and the navy, wages were usually paid by Bank note – a topic discussed in Chapter 3 – which they used at their ports of call. Sailors and seamen disembarked at the port, with wages in their pockets, and their spending undoubtedly affected the local composition of circulating media. The growing presence of mobile note users engaged in naval activity was also evident from the number of lost-note claimants with an address on board a ship, which increased more than threefold after the suspension (Table 2.1).

The record of lost-note claims for the period between 1807 and 1811 illustrates the intensified effect of the war economy on the pattern of Bank-note diffusion. After Surrey and Kent – the number of claims concerning these places is 117 and 84, respectively – Hampshire and Devon competed with other home counties in the number of lost-note claims. Out of 50 Hampshire claims, 29 related to Portsmouth (including Spithead and Portsea).[97] In 1807, the Hampshire bank Elford & Co. reported, 'Scarcely a day passes in which several [Bank of England small notes] are not tendered to us in the course of business'.[98] Although lagging behind Hampshire, Devon, with 38 claims, was still prominent in the Lost Note Books of this period. The frequent claims from Hampshire and Devon were a reflection of the heightened tension of the French war, and the Lost Note Books provide some insights into how military officers and sailors served as agents in mediating the geographical movement of the Bank note, albeit the record describes cases when the transactions did not go as intended. In 1809, a £10 note sent from

---

[94] L. V. Morgan, 'Historical Review of Portsmouth Dockyard in Relation to Our Naval Policy', *Transactions of the Institution of Naval Architects*, 90 (1948), 24.

[95] Barry Stapleton, 'The Admiralty Connection: Port Development and Demographic Change in Portsmouth, 1650–1900', in Richard Lawton and Robert Lee, eds., *Population and Society in Western European Port-Cities, c. 1650–1939* (Liverpool, 2001), 212–51.

[96] Gillian Russell, *The Theatres of War: Performance, Politics, and Society, 1793–1815* (Oxford, 1995), 7.

[97] Other claims concerned Southampton, Gosport, Winchester and the Isle of Wight.

[98] Elford Co. to the Bank, 10 Jan. 1807, BE, F2/165.

London to William Gill, a midshipman on HMS *Tartar*, never arrived at Plymouth.[99] Captain James Fynmore, on board HMS *Africa* at Plymouth Dock, reported in 1810 that a £2 note sent to Mrs Fynmore in Kent had gone missing.[100] Similarly, in 1808, Mrs Tarplitt in London sent a letter containing a £2 note, addressed to HMS *Repulse* in 'Plymouth, or elsewhere', which was not received by George Tarplitt, a seaman. The postal movement of Bank notes relating to official military business was probably on a greater scale than that conducted by individuals. The Navy Office and Victualling Office reported note losses, so did army and navy agents.[101] The broader war economy was enmeshed in the paper-money system, and the movement of Bank notes through private and official transactions involving navy employees was a clear manifestation of the relation between war and monetary circulation.

There was undoubtedly a significant diffusion of the Bank note in the metropolis as well as in the provinces during the Bank Restriction period. Between 1807 and 1811, the number of claims concerning the home counties remained high: 45 from Sussex and 40 from Essex. Nevertheless, the number of claims relating to Yorkshire (34) was equal to that of Berkshire, Buckinghamshire and Hertfordshire combined. There were also other places where the number of claims equalled or closely matched that from the home counties, such as Lancashire (33), Bristol (21) and Somerset (23), confirming the geographical patterns of Bank-note diffusion discussed above. This pattern of provincial penetration is in line with the comment made by the London banker Henry Thornton that as much as £2 million of metallic currency was substituted by the Bank note in the early phase of the Bank Restriction and of these additional Bank notes thus circulated 'some [were] in London, and many of them in the country'.[102] Another London banker, Samuel Hoare, echoed Thornton by testifying that the amount of Bank of England notes circulating outside London had increased from £1 million to £2.5 million after the suspension.[103] These contemporary testimonies confirm that the Bank of England note infiltrated British society widely. The geographical distribution of lost-note claims reveals that the radius of the Bank of England note was far-reaching at the end of the eighteenth century, and its scope had further expanded in the early nineteenth

---

[99] Lost Note Books, BE, C101/34, fol. 381.
[100] Lost Note Books, BE, C101/34, fol. 372.
[101] Lost Note Books, BE, C101/36, fol. 145.   [102] Thornton, *Paper Credit*, 224.
[103] House of Commons, *1797 Commons Committee on the Outstanding Demands of the Bank*, 53. See also, Jane Fiske, ed., *The Oakes Diaries: Business, Politics and the Family in Bury St Edmunds 1778–1827* (Woodbridge, 1990), i, 343; John A. S. L. Leighton-Boyce, *Smiths, the Bankers, 1658–1958* (London, 1958), 159–60, 167.

century. A conceivable reason for historians' long neglect of the penetration of the Bank note was that the transformation of the broader paper-money economy overshadowed the spatial diffusion of the Bank of England note. While Bank-note circulation increased from £9.2 million in 1796 to £19.6 million in 1809, the circulation of country banknotes saw a more significant growth from £5 million to £25 million in the same period. It is not difficult to imagine that the rise of the country banknote hampered the spread of the Bank of England note in the provinces to some extent, and the boost in country note circulation made the presence of the Bank note in the provinces less visible.

When the Bank of England suspended its cash payments, there were already a number of provincial users. Yet, it is clear that the Bank Restriction made the Bank note much more common in places far distant from London. The geographical coverage of the lost-note claims after 1797 was such that there were almost no provinces in England where a Bank of England note had not gone missing. Claims for lost notes came from Wales, Scotland, Ireland, Guernsey and, though less often, from places abroad, such as Jamaica, Portugal and America. According to the Lost Note Books, users of the Bank note included a schoolmistress in Banff, a reverend in Dublin, a surgeon in Yorkshire, a spinster in Cornwall, a widow in Monmouthshire and a shopkeeper in Cumberland.[104] In this short list of lost-note claimants, the variety of their social background is as striking as their geographical dispersion. Thus, the exploration of the radius of the Bank note leads us to the question of how deeply the Bank note had penetrated the social composition of the British nation.

Whose Money? The Social Distribution of Note Users

To what extent did the increase in the total circulation of the Bank note from the late 1790s lead to the use of the Bank note by wider social groups? Prior to 1797, the circulation of the Bank note had been relatively exclusive, as a combination of the limited volume of Bank notes and the equally limited classes of denomination kept the number of note users down. For most of the eighteenth century, the lowest denomination of the Bank note was £10.[105] Even when the Bank introduced the £5 note in 1793, those sums were rarely used in everyday transactions.

---

[104] Lost Note Books, BE, C101/22, fol. 156; C101/23, fol. 295; C101/25, fols. 94 and 223; C101/24, fols. 107 and 185.

[105] 'The Bank of England Note: A Short History', *Bank of England Quarterly Bulletin*, 9 (1969), 212.

It was only when £1 and £2 notes were introduced in March 1797 that the Bank note came to serve the need for small transactions, penetrating, as contemporary commentators described, the life of 'lower orders of the People'.[106] One major reason for the issuing of small notes was to accommodate everyday transactions, after a large amount of coin disappeared from circulation due to the suspension. This naturally led to a situation in which the Bank note appeared more frequently and in diverse, everyday situations. Yet, even the small-denomination Bank notes did not routinely find their way into the pockets of those with modest means – such as common labourers – for whom £1 and £2 were not trifling amounts. As the small-denomination notes had relatively large monetary value, they did not change hands as frequently as small change. They were more likely to appear when a round sum was transacted, such as the payment of wages. Indeed, the lack of means to pay labourers' wages was a serious concern in the immediate aftermath of the suspension because a delay in wage payment could potentially cause social unrest. The lord lieutenant of Gloucestershire, for instance, warned in early March 1797 that the delay in workmen's wage payment – caused by the shortage of cash – would incite a riot among local people 'within a week'.[107] Such a concern precipitated the issuance of small-denomination notes and token metallic currency.[108]

A factor that probably eased the shock of introducing inconvertible paper currency was the limited dependence on metallic currency in pre-suspension British society. As demonstrated by Craig Muldrew and Stephen King's study, the perennial shortage of small-denomination coins in the British economy contributed to the formation of an extensive network of personal credit.[109] In a broader sense, personal credit and paper currency emerged as an additional money stock and the prolific use of personal credit throughout the century provided the foundation for the later, more extensive circulation of credit currency.[110] Nevertheless, the large-scale introduction of paper currency, without the guarantee of convertibility, was an unprecedented social experiment in Britain. The timing was hardly ideal for such an experiment. While the country was engaged in a war with the formidable French revolutionary state, the social situation was volatile. In England and in certain parts of

---

[106] *Morning Chronicle*, 2 Mar. 1797; *St James's Chronicle*, 2–4 Mar. 1797.
[107] Letter from the Earl of Berkeley, 3 Mar. 1797, TNA, HO 42/40/136.
[108] *Hibernian Chronicle*, 2 Jan. 1797; William Tait to Thompson, 26 Mar. 1797, Glamorgan RO, Dowlais Iron Company letter books, 1796–7, D/D/GD/A, fol. 293.
[109] Muldrew and King, 'Cash, Wages and the Economy of Makeshifts', 156; Muldrew, *Economy of Obligation*, 100–2.
[110] Palma, 'Money and Modernization in Early Modern England', 235.

Scotland and Ireland, as we saw in Chapter 1, the declaration movement to a significant extent eased the impact of the introduction of inconvertible paper currency, laying the foundation for the inconvertible currency system as money users expressed their support and promised voluntary acceptance of the Bank note. In its aftermath, British society faced the challenge of maintaining the paper-money system with the greatly increased circulation of the Bank note. Did the British public at large honour their declarations? And if the promise was kept and the Bank note generally accepted, how extensive was the paper-money economy and what types of people were included in the community of note users?

The British public was far from homogeneous as a nation and as a community of money users. They were divided by class, politics, geography and gender – just to mention the obvious. Economic standing affected an individual's use of money and what kinds of payment methods they had recourse to. Generally, the better-off had a wider variety of money instruments at their disposal. In addition to paper and metallic currency, those belonging to the upper echelon of society usually had access to exclusive means of payment, premised on the availability of financial services, such as bankers' drafts and cheques. Choices for the less affluent were narrower. Still, personal credit and quasi-money existed to cater to their everyday needs in the forms of tokens and IOUs (albeit IOUs were also used by the wealthy). These various media of exchange complemented metallic currency, which was often in short supply, especially small-denomination coins.[111] The divide between those who had access to exclusive means of payments and those without recourse to them was an entrenched social reality. Nevertheless, with the introduction of inconvertible banknotes, the foundation of both of these economic spheres was now paper credit and paper currency acted as a nexus connecting the variegated monetary landscape. It was a landscape accommodating money users of different backgrounds, geographical locations and social status. This new monetary environment was probably more familiar to merchants, bankers and the wealthy, as paper instruments had already been incorporated in economic transactions involving relatively large sums. The increased circulation of paper currency, then, supposedly, took the form of downward penetration, infiltrating into the lives of common people, who had been less accustomed to handling paper currency. This remains a mere hypothesis unless it is supported by evidence. The note users' profiles, recorded in the Lost

---

[111] Mathias, *Transformation of England*, 191–7.

Note Books, provide some clues as to how inconvertible paper currency changed the social composition of note users.

The Lost Note Books offer a general guide to historical changes in the social composition of note users. The early volumes, which go back as far as 1694, show that those engaging in finance and trade formed the largest group of lost-note claimants: out of 733 claimants from the years 1694–1710, 1711–15, 1721–5 and 1731–5, 207 claimants belonged to this group, constituting 28 per cent of the total claims (see Table 2.2). Clearly, the Bank note in its early years was predominantly a means of carrying out various commercial and financial transactions. This may sound as though the Bank note was a highly exclusive means of payment available only to merchants, financiers and the wealthy, but this was not the case. Following financiers and merchants, the second-largest group of claimants belonged to the hand manufacturing and artisanal trade, such as cabinetmakers, clothiers, coopers, ironmongers and tailors, and the third largest was those in the retail trade, such as bakers, cheesemongers, druggists, haberdashers and linen drapers. There were 147 claimants in the hand manufacturing and artisanal trade, while 138 claimants, 19 per cent of the total, were in the retail and wholesale trade. Although the Lost Note Books do not provide information as to the scale of those claimants' activity, presumably only a few of them ran large-scale business operations and hence most were of relatively humble means. A modest proportion of claimants (12 per cent) were in service or in labouring jobs: barbers, clerks, inn holders, journeymen and servants. Some of them were probably representing their masters, but the Bank note was a familiar object for those in the service trade already in the early century.

Due to the limited sample size of the lost-note claims up to the 1790s, no definitive conclusion can be drawn regarding the social distribution of Bank notes in the eighteenth century. However, the data indicate a slow but steady social penetration, with those in finance and trade becoming less dominant while hand manufacturing and retail workers remain consistently present. Interestingly, professionals – lawyers, doctors and clergy – despite their privileged social status and traditional image of being a major group of note users, are not well represented. In contrast, those in service and in labouring work slowly increase their presence. This does not necessarily mean that the diffusion of Bank notes was most conspicuous in the relatively low-income groups. The number of claimants with hereditary or honorary titles, from duke, duchess, viscount, baronet, esquire to gentleman, who are counted separately from the occupational groups, shows an increase towards the mid-eighteenth century, when it declines in proportion (Table 2.3). From the Lost

Table 2.2 *Occupation of lost-note claimants, 1694–1785*

	1694–1710	1711–1715	1721–1725	1731–1735	1741–1745	1751–1755	1761–1765	1771–1775	1781–1785
Hand manufacturing	35	26	46	40	21	24	44	75	31
	25.4%	25.7%	18.5%	16.3%	8.8%	12.7%	17.7%	17.6%	16.1%
Construction	3	1	3	6	1	4	3	5	4
	2.2%	1.0%	1.2%	2.4%	0.4%	2.1%	1.2%	1.2%	2.1%
Professional	12	3	16	23	18	12	14	31	15
	8.7%	3.0%	6.4%	9.4%	7.5%	6.3%	5.6%	7.3%	7.8%
Retail	24	22	52	40	34	27	48	83	39
	17.4%	21.8%	20.9%	16.3%	14.2%	14.3%	19.4%	19.5%	20.3%
Military related and seafaring	6	5	20	8	13	9	15	17	11
	4.3%	5.0%	8.0%	3.3%	5.4%	4.8%	6.0%	4.0%	5.7%
Service and labour	11	10	27	42	39	35	29	67	30
	8.0%	9.9%	10.8%	17.1%	16.3%	18.5%	11.7%	15.8%	15.6%
Finance and trade	38	32	71	66	85	64	75	118	50
	27.5%	31.7%	28.5%	26.9%	35.4%	33.9%	30.2%	27.8%	26.0%
Large manufacturing	1	1	5	9	14	8	5	12	8
	0.7%	1.0%	2.0%	3.7%	5.8%	4.2%	2.0%	2.8%	4.2%
Agriculture/farming	5	1	3	2	11	2	12	12	3
	3.6%	1.0%	1.2%	0.8%	4.6%	1.1%	4.8%	2.8%	1.6%
Other	3	0	6	9	4	4	3	5	1
	2.2%	0.0%	2.4%	3.7%	1.7%	2.1%	1.2%	1.2%	0.5%
Subtotal	138	101	249	245	240	189	248	425	192

Source: Lost Note Books, BE, M2/2, C101/1–16.

Table 2.3 *Honorary/hereditary titles and female claimants in Lost Note Books*

	1694–1710	1711–1715	1721–1725	1731–1735	1741–1745	1751–1755	1761–1765	1771–1775	1781–1785
Honorary/hereditary	39	19	88	91	92	92	116	176	89
Gender (only spinsters and widows)	6	6	26	23	25	16	32	50	13
Other identifiable claims	138	101	249	245	240	189	248	425	192

Source: M2/2, C101/1–16.

Note Books, the spread of Bank notes among the middle classes was conspicuous from the 1720s onwards. The number of female claimants, ascertained either from the entries' indication of marital status (spinster or widow) or their title (Miss or Mrs), was consistently small – a topic that will be further discussed later in this chapter.

By the 1790s, when the number of lost-note claims increased significantly, the diversity of claimants' social background had become a pronounced feature. There are more than 200 different occupational descriptions in the entries covering 1792 and 1801, a considerable broadening of the coverage of occupations in the early volumes, in which only 70 occupational descriptions are found. Still, the variety and breadth of occupations represented in the entries are striking: basket maker, bookseller, calico printer, clock maker, coach maker, cooper, matchmaker, millwright, rope maker, saddler, shoe maker, soap boiler, tallow chandler, tanner, upholsterer, cleaner and waiter. With regard to shopkeepers and most merchants, the record does not always describe what sorts of goods and merchandise they dealt with, but entries include merchants of brandy, hop, timber and wine.

For the pre-1797 period (1792–6), the largest number of claims came from those belonging to finance and trade, such as factors, brokers, dealers and merchants (Table 2.4). The second-largest occupational group is retailing and wholesale, totalling 75 claimants (20 per cent of the total). In this group, there are 8 butchers, 7 stationers, 5 victuallers, 16 linen/woollen drapers and 7 apothecaries/druggists. The next conspicuous group is traditional or small-scale hand manufacturing (total 65), which includes blacksmiths, dyers, hosiers, haberdashers, shoemakers and tailors. The next group consists of professionals such as attorneys, surgeons and clerics, followed by military-related and seafaring occupations.

As noted earlier, lost-note claims in the eighteenth century came mostly from employees in the areas of finance/trade, traditional manufacturing and retail. There is some ambiguity about the data on financiers and merchants, as many London bankers and merchants appear in the Lost Note Books without occupational description either because they were account holders at the Bank or well known to the Bank; hence, the clerks felt no need to record the claimants' occupation. With this ambiguity in mind, leading London merchants and bankers, such as Boldero & Co., Coutts & Co., Down & Co., Drummond & Co., Esdaile & Co., Hoare & Co., Lefevre & Co., Robarts & Co. and Sir James Sanderson & Co., thus claimed lost notes multiple times in those years.[112] There is

---

[112] The figures in Table 2.4 show the numbers after eliminating double-counting.

Table 2.4 *Occupation of lost-note claimants, 1792–1820*

	1792–1796	1797–1801	1804–1812	1818–1820
Hand manufacturing	65	54	65	123
	17.6%	10.8%	12.3%	15.6%
Construction	13	12	22	13
	3.5%	2.4%	4.2%	1.6%
Professional	45	62	60	76
	12.2%	12.4%	11.3%	9.6%
Retail and wholesale	75	90	69	116
	20.3%	18.0%	13.0%	14.7%
Military related and seafaring	33	91	104	68
	8.9%	18.2%	19.7%	8.6%
Service and labour	29	49	53	84
	7.9%	9.8%	10.0%	10.7%
Finance and trade	87	119	125	262
	23.6%	23.8%	23.6%	33.2%
Large manufacturing	4	4	11	24
	1.1%	0.8%	2.1%	3.0%
Agriculture/farming	15	13	9	13
	4.1%	2.6%	1.7%	1.6%
Other	3	5	11	9
	0.8%	1.0%	2.1%	1.1%
Subtotal	369	499	529	788

Source: Lost Note Books, BE, C101/19–59, selected years.

also a potentially significant margin of error in identifying those claimants in the finance and trade category (including those who were known to the Bank) – despite this being the largest group of claimants, with 87 claims in the pre-suspension period and 119 in the post-suspension period – which needs to be recognised as there is a realistic possibility of them claiming notes on behalf of their customers.[113] Still, their greater presence indicates the increasing frequency of private bankers' involvement in Bank-note-related transactions.

In the post-1797 period (1797–1801), hand manufacturing, construction, large manufacturing and agriculture/farming reduced their share. The retail trade, including 19 grocers and 31 drapers, retained its place by increasing its number from 75 to 90. Compared to the pre-1797 period, there are more bakers, cheesemongers, fishmongers and shopkeepers among the lost-note claimants. Some of these cases concerned

---

[113] From the same reason, employees of the Bank of England and post offices were excluded from some considerations.

only small sums, such as Carnaby Street fishmonger William Taylor claiming for a £5 note.[114] The group of professionals and those in finance and trade slightly increased their share. Relatively more visible is the increasing share of those in service and labouring work, which grew from 29 to 49, though it is still smaller compared to most of the other groups.

The most striking change in the post-1797 period was the increase in claims from those in war-related and seafaring occupations, a category of note users that had hardly been noticeable prior to the 1790s. The number of claims from this group increased from 33 to 91, becoming the second-largest group of claimants after finance and trade. Various ranks of military personnel were represented in the group, ranging from a general, a rear admiral, majors, colonels and captains to pilots, gunners and seamen. Lieutenant Pierce Power in the Lancashire Fencibles sought payment for two £5 notes, which had been burnt.[115] Colonel Richard Bright of the Marines left his £40 note in a shop.[116] A seaman, Dennis Carty, and a surgeon, both on board HMS *Egmont* jointly lodged a claim for £20 and £5 notes.[117] The number of claimants in war-related occupations continued to grow in the period between 1804 and 1812. The share of this category grew from 18 per cent to 20 per cent of the total. Among the claimants were 46 captains, 25 lieutenants, 6 midshipmen, 5 seamen and 3 gunners. When we recall the prominence of navy towns in the geographical distribution of lost-note claims, discussed in the previous section, there is no doubt that the intensifying war with France had a tangible effect on the composition of the note-user community. After precipitating the suspension of cash payments, the French wars continued to define both the geographical and the social diffusion of the Bank of England note.[118] Apart from the war-related occupations, the four groups that increased their share were the hand manufacturing, construction, finance/trade and large manufacturing groups, though the increase was marginal. Other groups, such as professional, retail/wholesale and agriculture/farming decreased their share. However, the lost-note record for the 1804–12 period is less reliable than for other periods

[114] Lost Note Books, BE, C101/21, fol. 301.
[115] Lost Note Books, BE, C101/22, fol. 83.
[116] Lost Note Books, BE, C101/22, fol. 164.
[117] Lost Note Books, BE, C101/22, fol. 274.
[118] For the entire period examined here, large industrial manufacturers are conspicuous for their absence in the lost-note record. This is quite surprising, given that British society had gone through a historic industrialisation (claims from manufacturers numbered 4 in the pre-1797 period, 4 in the post-1797 period and 11 in 1804–12). Potential explanations are that large manufacturers delegated claims to their agent banks or that they preferred to use local banknotes.

due to the relatively small proportion of entries with occupational descriptions; hence we should not read too much into these minor changes.

One serious shortcoming of the lost-note record is its clear gender bias. Female claimants, usually accompanied by their marital status, that is Miss, spinster, Mrs, wife or widow, do appear in the Lost Note Books, but their number is consistently small.[119] In the early eighteenth century, female claimants constituted only 5 per cent of the total. In the early to mid-1790s, the underrepresentation of female claimants was sustained, though their number had increased to more than 127 out of the total 2,094 identifiable claimants. In the first five years of the suspension, their proportion declined to 5 per cent (122 out of 2,500 claimants were women). It would be absurd to assume that the lost-note record truly reflected the proportion of female note users, even when we admit the relatively limited economic opportunities for women in the eighteenth century.[120] The primary reason for the underrepresentation of female note users should be sought in the gender bias in the process of recovering lost property at the time. For instance, married women were more likely to claim lost notes as joint claimants with their husband. Or in some cases wives do not appear as claimants but are only mentioned in the description of losses, such as in the entry for Samuel Harper, who stated that he was seeking payment for a £10 note that 'his Wife has lost, but cannot say how – or when'.[121] Presumably, there were other, similar cases of husbands claiming for notes their wives had lost, but not necessarily vice versa.

The changes in the gender composition of lost-note claimants suggest that during the Bank Restriction period the gendered code for lost-note claims was relaxed, if only slightly. Between 1807 and 1811, 208 claims (7 per cent of the total) were made by women and the majority of these claimants – 127 – were described as 'Mrs'.[122] This contrasts well with previous periods, when widows and spinsters were more conspicuous than married female claimants. From this change, we may assume that the diffusion of paper currency during the Bank Restriction period made

---

[119] Lost Note Books, BE, C101/22, fol. 239. Examples include Ann Salt, 'Birmingham widow', and Sarah Chandler, 'Mortlake Surrey Spr'. Lost Note Books, BE, C101/21, fol. 299; C101/22, fol. 239.

[120] At Heywood's bank in Liverpool between 1788 and 1797, 27 per cent of account holders were women. Sheryllynne Haggerty, 'Women, Work, and the Consumer Revolution: Liverpool in the Late Eighteenth Century', in John Benson and Laura Ugolini, eds., *A Nation of Shopkeepers: Five Centuries of British Retailing* (London, 2003), 126.

[121] Lost Note Books, BE, C101/23, fol. 279.   [122] Lost Note Books, BE, C101/30–8.

it more socially acceptable for women to be claimants than in the previous period. Thus, in 1810 Fanny Chandler of Fitzroy Square reported to the Bank that she had lost a £15 note while shopping.[123] Mrs Frederickson of White Chapel lost a £50 note along with her pocketbook.[124] One may even argue that women gradually started to assert ownership of the Bank note in the official process of recovering lost monetary value. In the late 1800s, wives were claiming for notes their husband had lost as well as those they themselves had lost, for example Mrs Smith who lodged a claim for a £10 note in July 1810, of which her husband was robbed near the Hermitage Bridge.[125] These women represented the often-marginalised – historically and historiographically – group of female note users, whose presence was slowly becoming visible at a time when women's property rights were yet to be legally recognised.[126]

The Lost Note Books serve as a window through which we can see the faces of note users. The record shows a Strand plumber claiming for £20 and a Soho paper stainer claiming for a burnt £50 note.[127] A hawker, Moses Solomon, and his wife, Deborah, reported that he was robbed of a £20 note, while a cleaner of the Bank, Mr Simons, lodged a claim for £15 for his acquaintance, who had left it in a public house.[128] The Solomons and the Bank's cleaner belonged to the humbler occupations that were increasingly visible in the record, in which one finds a labourer in Wilstone, Hertfordshire, requesting payment for fragments of a £10 note that he found.[129] Sometimes, occupational description can be deceptive: one learns from the record that a nightman in Newington Causeway lost a £25 Bank note out of his pocket and a Worcester miner claimed for several £5 notes.[130] Some of the claimants may have been reporting notes that had been lost by their employers, as in the case of servants and clerks, or that they had lost Bank notes while in service. Still, the increase in claimants with humbler occupations is a manifestation of the downward penetration of Bank-note use after the suspension. The constant presence of retailers, such as butchers, fishmongers, grocers, cheesemongers, barbers and shopkeepers, is equally important, for it is

---

[123] Lost Note Books, BE, C101/34, fol. 254.
[124] Lost Note Books, BE, C101/36, fol. 171.
[125] Lost Note Books, BE, C101/35, fol. 260.
[126] On this topic, see Edward Copeland, *Women Writing about Money: Women's Fiction in England, 1790–1820* (Cambridge, 1995); Leonore Davidoff and Catherine Hall, *Family Fortunes: Men and Women of the English Middle Class, 1780–1850* (London, 1987).
[127] Lost Note Books, BE, C101/24, fol. 158; C101/22, fol. 329.
[128] Lost Note Books, BE, C101/21, fol. 340; C101/22, fol. 32.
[129] Lost Note Books, BE, C101/25, fol. 297.
[130] Lost Note Books, BE, C101/23, fol. 96; C101/22, fol. 151.

another indicator of the growing use of the Bank note in everyday transactions. Their note use may have been mostly related to business transactions, such as purchasing stocks of merchandise, but some of their lost notes were probably passed on to them by their customers. During the Bank Restriction period, the social background of claimants became more diverse, departing from the relatively limited range of claimants' occupations in the early eighteenth century. The Lost Note Books bring us closer to note users of this period. Somewhat ironically, people's material losses in the past serve as eloquent evidence of the material presence of the Bank of England note in Bank Restriction Britain.

Conclusion: The Presence of the Bank Note

In 1809 in the small village of Brignall in the North Riding of Yorkshire, a labourer, Joseph Foster, was indicted for stealing a leather pocketbook belonging to John Wilson, a local coachman. In the pocketbook, there were fifteen pieces of gold (with a value of six pence each) along with three Bank of England notes (one £2 and two £1 notes).[131] Six years later, in Northallerton, not far away from Brignall, John Robinson was prosecuted for stealing two Bank of England notes (a £1 and a £2 note) and ten £1 country banknotes.[132] The Bank's internal record suggests that these two incidents were by no means isolated cases of criminal incidents involving Bank of England notes in the provinces during the Bank Restriction period.[133] Those cases serve as testimony to the historical fact that notes issued by what was generally believed to be the 'Bank of London' found their way into the pockets of provincial note users, tucked in with coins and country banknotes. If private individuals held relatively small amounts in Bank of England notes, it is not difficult to imagine that provincial businesses such as country banks held a greater amount of it. Just as reports of theft provide occasional insights into individuals' possession of Bank notes, some criminal records on bank robbery offer a momentary glimpse of the extent of country banks' holding of Bank notes. In January 1800, the City Bank of Exeter was broken into and the contents of an iron chest, amounting to £7,000, were stolen. Included in the list of stolen money are the City Bank's own notes

---

[131] Bill of indictment, Joseph Foster, 1809, North Yorkshire County RO, QSB 1809 1/6/16.

[132] Bill of indictment, John Robinson, 1815, North Yorkshire County RO, QSB 1815 1/6/8.

[133] For instance, out of the ninety-nine reports regarding forgery crimes recorded by the Bank's Committee for Lawsuits between June 1802 and March 1807 only thirteen cases concerned London. Committee for Lawsuits, BE, M5/307.

(351 five-guinea notes) and 127 Bank of England notes (£1 and £2). The City Bank kept many fewer local notes – only eight of them – issued by other Exeter banks, showing that, next to its own notes, the bank dealt with the Bank of England note most frequently.[134] As much as it is impossible to go back 200 years and open every person's pocketbook, auditing provincial banks' holdings of different types of currency is beyond the means of historians. With regard to small-denomination notes, the past becomes foggier. The City Bank's holding of small Bank of England notes suggests that the Exeter bank's own note issue was concentrated on large denominations, while it catered to its customers' need for small-denomination notes by using Bank of England notes. Such a practice was mentioned by the Norwich banker Hudson Gurney, who stated that, in his city, no local banks issued notes lower than £5 and small-note circulation consisted mostly of Bank of England notes.[135] This coexistence of Bank notes and country notes may have been widespread, but the historical record is unable to prove – or disprove – it. At a time when small-denomination notes made up a relatively minor portion of a banker's portfolio, provincial bankers' holdings of small Bank of England notes rarely left traces in the aggregate statistics.

With the Lost Note Books, we now have a historical overview of the geographical and social penetration of the Bank of England note, where previously historians relied only on occasional and anecdotal evidence. The record has limitations, but in terms of its chronological coverage and its details of note users' profiles, it is exceptionally rich historical evidence. Among other things, lost-note claims point to several factors that significantly affected the pattern of how and where Bank of England notes were likely to be used in Bank Restriction Britain. Local economic activity, especially trade, was a major determinant of monetary circulation. The seemingly obvious connection between trade and the pattern of currency circulation has, however, been downplayed by contemporary and modern historians, whose attention has been drawn mostly to the apparent preference for the Bank of England note that was observed in the industrial heartlands in Lancashire. The reports of lost notes from Bristol and West Riding suggest that Lancashire may not have been exceptional for its extensive use of the Bank of England note. The lost-note claims equally highlight social and cultural factors in the

---

[134] A handbill issued by Milford, Clarke and Co., 20 Jan. 1800, Devon Heritage Centre, 47/14/2.

[135] House of Commons, *Reports from the Select Committee on the Expediency of Resuming Cash Payments* (1819), 250. In May 1800, Norwich bank Kett & Back's claim for Bank notes consisted of twenty-one notes, of which nineteen were £1 and £2 notes. Lost Note Books, BE, C101/24, fol. 117.

proliferation of paper currency. The culture of sociability, which was accompanied by people's movement to leisure or intellectual centres, created demand for Bank notes as a standard means of payment in places such as Bath, Oxford and Cambridge. Moreover, the French wars profoundly affected the patterns of geographical and social flow of the Bank of England note, not only by diverting capital to war-related industries but equally by incorporating soldiers, sailors and seamen into the community of note users. All the above factors worked alongside the overall increase in the circulation of the Bank note to shape the way paper currency penetrated into British society.

In most cases, what the Lost Note Books reveal may not properly be called the *circulation* of the Bank of England note in economists' terms – except for the cases in the conventional thirty-mile radius – but something more nuanced and attenuated. For its modest volume and elusive nature, it would be more plausible to call it the *presence* of the Bank note. By acknowledging the presence of the Bank note beyond the metropolitan zone of circulation, we begin to unravel two crucial historical questions. The first is the constitution of Britain's 'multiple currency' landscape in the long eighteenth century.[136] The Bank of England note coexisted with other notes issued by country banks in England and Wales, and, to some extent, with those issued by Scottish and Irish banks. Coins, tokens and other forms of currency also formed part of the monetary landscape. The users of money in this period had to cope with the variegated collection of currency options, some of which, such as country banknotes and tokens, had only limited geographical acceptability. The Bank of England note had a general acceptability that was recognised by provincial money users. This is why the theft of Bank notes in a small Yorkshire village was not necessarily an extraordinary case. Backed by its general acceptability, the Bank note travelled far and wide, complementing metallic and locally issued currency. The second is the unique status the Bank of England note held in Britain's multiple-currency situation. The Bank of England note was yet to achieve the status of a truly national currency because it was not a legal tender. Nor was it the most frequently used currency in many provincial cities and towns, especially where there were note-issuing country banks. Notwithstanding, note users in the metropolis and the provinces started to see the Bank of England note as a quasi-national currency – as *the* banknote in Britain. As far as its note circulation was concerned, the

---

[136] See Introduction.

Bank of England grew out of its 'Bank of London' phase in the early part of the Bank Restriction period.

Chapter 3 will elaborate on several factors that shaped the distinctive patterns of Bank-note circulation, some of which have been identified in this chapter. The presence of the Bank note in various parts of British society is premised on its use, and, indeed, several specific uses were closely related to its geographical and social diffusion. A consideration of the uses of the Bank note is essential for us to fully appreciate the dynamic nature of circulating media, the value of which was generated by movement from one economic agent to another, based on its capacity to transfer monetary value. Equally importantly, the manner in which Bank notes travelled from hand to hand was rooted in the customs and practices of everyday life in Britain. For these qualities, paper currency became meaningful in society. In other words, the social meanings of money were generated through social interactions between money users through their use of currency.

3 The Registers of Paper-Currency Use

From house to house, both far and wide,
I've travell'd, till I've lost my pride,
so many trades I now have seen,
That ev'ry circumstance to tell –
is utterly impossible.
From high life – now completely low –
and down hill yet, I seem to go;
Written o'er with many a name,
I scarcely now look like the same.

The Adventures of a One Pound Note: A Poem (1819)

John Bounden was a shipwright employed at His Majesty's dockyard in Plymouth. On the day of his quarterly wage payment, 6 April 1805, Bounden received a total of £24 and 9 shillings, paid to him in five Bank of England notes (two £10, two £1 and one £2 notes and a half-guinea coin).[1] Having received these notes, he 'immediately wrote the number of the ten pound notes, on his pay ticket' before he left the pay office. It was about half past three in the afternoon, and he set out towards the town of Plymouth with his friend Nicholas Adams. Together, they entered the State Inn, where they drank three quarts of porter. Leaving Adams in the inn, Bounden then went to Mary Folley's house, probably a brothel. After spending some time with the lady, Bounden headed to the house of Charles Bonnett, a local victualler, to settle his debt. Bounden intended to pay £20 to Bonnett – in two £10 notes – but one of them, with the serial number 7637, had gone missing. Two days later, before the justice of the peace, local hatter William Kingdon testified that Mary Folley paid a £10 note with serial number

---

[1] Depositions of John Bounden of Stoke Damerel, shipwright, and William Kingdon of Plymouth, hatter, against Mary Folley for stealing a Bank of England note. 8 Apr. 1805, Plymouth and West Devon RO, 1/695/43. For shipwrights' wages at the royal dockyards, see James M. Haas, *A Management Odyssey: The Royal Dockyards, 1714–1914* (Lanham, MD, 1994), 31–7, 52–7; James M. Haas, 'Methods of Wage Payment in the Royal Dockyards 1775–1865', *Maritime History*, 5 (1977), 99–115.

7637 to him on the day Bounden lost his note, when she purchased a beaver bonnet and a feather for 13 shillings and 6 pence. In the transaction, as Kingdon further explained, he paid the change in a £2 Plymouth banknote, some Bank of England notes and coins. The small episode of Folley's prosecution reveals fascinating details about users and uses of the Bank of England note in a naval port town far away from the metropolis.

During the eighteenth century, the Bank of England note had gradually been incorporated into the fabric of Britain's social and economic life. This process accelerated during the Bank Restriction period as paper currency replaced metallic currency in numerous transactions that had long been conducted by exchanging pieces of metal or on credit. The change was tangible, not least to William Cobbett, an astute observer of monetary issues, who wrote that the proportion of paper transactions to cash transactions was one to four in 1745, but in 1803 five out of six transactions were conducted in paper currency.[2] His observation is supported by a recent estimate of Britain's monetary circulation, which shows that the ratio between the amount in regal coins and the amount in Bank of England notes saw a drastic change from two to one in the pre-1797 period to one to eight in 1810.[3] The ascendancy of paper currency transformed the nation's monetary landscape – which consisted of a mixture of coins, notes, tokens and other near-monies, supported by various forms of credit, as paper currency replaced metallic currency in a wide range of economic transactions. How was this transformation manifested, and how was it experienced by Britain's money users? Moving beyond the conventional economistic analysis of money use, this chapter expands its investigation to multiple levels of money use, following Arjun Appadurai's analysis of the 'registers of use' in his seminal essay in *The Social Life of Things*, in which he conceptualises the use of things from the perspectives of social practice, meaning, knowledge and the interlinkage between the use of things and personality.[4] These registers of use inform the following sections' discussion of the use of paper currency in Bank Restriction Britain.

---

[2] Lewis Melville, *The Life and Letters of William Cobbett in England and America, Based upon Hitherto Unpublished Family Papers* (London, 1913), i, 191.
[3] Patrick K. O'Brien and Nuno Palma, 'Danger to the Old Lady of Threadneedle Street? The Bank Restriction Act and the Regime Shift to Paper Money, 1797–1821', *European Review of Economic History*, 24 (2020), 400.
[4] Arjun Appadurai, 'Introduction: Commodities and the Politics of Value', in Arjun Appadurai, ed., *The Social Life of Things: Commodities in Cultural Perspective* (Cambridge, 1986), 39.

A consideration of the modern usages of paper currency beyond the conventional functionalist approach, for one thing, illuminates the channels through which the Bank of England note penetrated into British society. At the end of the eighteenth century, Britain's circulating media were hardly standardised, with hundreds of currency issuers creating notes and tokens, albeit these private payment media generally functioned only as local currency with geographically limited circulation. There was evidence of the Bank note's diffusion to various parts of the British Isles, as we have seen in Chapter 2, but it was yet to become a dominant national currency. This selective penetration was chiefly due to the Bank note's limited *use* rather than the Bank of England's inability to produce and circulate it in sufficient amounts. As T. S. Ashton notes, 'each of the chief forms of money had its special use', but it was anthropologists and sociologists who developed the concept of 'special purpose money' (as opposed to general purpose money) that has been used to explain the sociocultural delimitation of monetary use in both traditional and modern communities.[5] The Bank of England note was a special purpose currency because its use was limited, especially outside the Bank's monopoly area, by its relatively narrow purposes of use in commercial and state-related businesses.[6] Rather than being a marker of the underrated status of the Bank note, the eighteenth-century Bank note's special purposes served as entry points for its penetration into the English provinces and beyond. During the Bank Restriction period, the state as much as the commercial sector tacitly contributed to broadening the use of Bank note by shifting transactions from a metallic to a paper medium. Dissecting the modes of Bank-note use sheds light on the respective roles of public and private monetary transactions in shaping the nation's monetary order.

This chapter's survey of Bank-note use is unavoidably selective – no historian can possibly cover the myriad ways money was used – but the range of Bank-note use examined here reveals some of the distinctive features of currency use in the age of paper. The following sections analyse a wide variety of sources from merchants' records, criminal court

---

[5] T. S. Ashton, *Economic Fluctuations in England 1700–1800* (Oxford, 1959), 106; Paul Bohannan, 'The Impact of Money on an African Subsistence Economy', *Journal of Economic History*, 19 (1959), 491–503; Karl Polanyi, 'The Economy as Instituted Process, Trade and Market in the Early Empires', in Karl Polanyi, Conrad M. Arensberg and Harry W. Pearson, eds., *Trade and Market in the Early Empires: Economies in History and Theory* (Glencoe, IL, 1957), 266; Viviana Zelizer, *The Social Meaning of Money* (New York, 1994), 21–4.

[6] For a parallel limitation regarding the historical use of coins, see Craig Muldrew, '"Hard Food for Midas": Cash and Its Social Value in Early Modern England', *Past & Present*, 170 (2001), 78–120.

cases and personal diaries to official accounts of institutional monetary arrangements in an attempt to describe the registers of Bank-note use. Such an examination is crucial in understanding not only the modes of paper-money circulation but also how it was embedded within a society. Departing from the assumption of modern money's de-individualised character, which often draws upon the study by Georg Simmel, our close examination of historical evidence reveals that anonymous transactions are not characteristic of the use of the Bank note in this period.[7] Britain's note users developed distinctive practices that reduced anonymity risks, while the same practices afforded note users a vision of a monetary space that was grounded in a sense of community rather than that of a faceless mass. It was within this identifiable membership of community and through face-to-face monetary transactions that social meanings for paper currency were generated, negotiated and sometimes contested – a process hardly confined to the narrowly defined *economic* realm of social life.

Wage and Salary

Despite Peter Linebaugh's caution that 'Any study of working-class power must begin by considering the form and value of payment', historians have paid little attention to the *form* of payment, focusing almost exclusively on the value of payment.[8] Among a number of uses for money, both metallic and paper, contemporaries placed particular importance on payment for human labour. What Linebaugh traces as a decline of traditional in-kind payment in Britain's naval dockyard at the turn of the nineteenth century is an example of the expanding dominance of monetary wages. Wage labour captured a growing proportion of the British population during the French wars. For instance, the expansion of enclosed land brought droves of agricultural workers to the wage-labour market, where they earned 7–13 shillings a week, equivalent to £18–£34 per annum.[9] In the late eighteenth century, skilled workers

---

[7] Georg Simmel, 'The Metropolis and Mental Life', in Kurt H. Wolff, ed., *The Sociology of Georg Simmel* (Glencoe, IL, 1950), 414.

[8] Peter Linebaugh, *London Hanged: Crime and Civil Society in the Eighteenth Century* (London, 1991), 374.

[9] The nominal agricultural wages are from A. L. Bowley, 'The Statistics of Wages in the United Kingdom during the Last Hundred Years. Part I: Agricultural Wages', *Journal of the Royal Statistical Society*, 61 (1898), 704–6. For other trades, see Elizabeth W. Gilboy, *Wages in Eighteenth Century England* (Cambridge, MA, 1934); John Rule, *The Vital Century: The Developing English Economy, 1714–1815* (London, 1992), 254–6. On the general monetisation of work, or wage labour, see Beverly Lemire, *The Business of Everyday Life: Gender, Practice and Social Politics in England, c.1600–1900* (Manchester,

earned more than £50, and the annual income of professionals could be more than £200.[10] In relation to the means of payment, it is important to note that for most of the eighteenth century payment of wages in gold coins or paper currency was relatively rare due to their high denomination values when low-paid labourers barely earned 10 shillings per week. As Craig Muldrew points out, for many labourers and servants, their wages were cancelled out against debts to their employer, such as rents and living-in expenses.[11] Nonetheless, the introduction of small-denomination paper currency in 1797, when the proportion of the wage-earning population was rising, combined with the general upward trend in nominal wages, undoubtedly served to increase the number of workers whose regular wage payments could be paid in paper currency.[12] According to an estimate, between 1797 and 1810 low-paid workers' average *nominal* earnings per year increased from less than £30 to more than £40.[13] These workers were more likely to be paid in banknotes, if not the Bank of England note, than in the previous period. Contemporary practice also needs to be taken into account, such as the prevalent custom of paying labourers on a weekly or longer-term basis; furthermore, as historian of country banking L. S. Pressnell points out, labourers often received their pay collectively rather than individually.[14]

Custom rather than contract usually dictated how wage and salary payments were made. Silver dollars (valued at 4s 9d) and, later, Bank tokens (5s) and copper coins, along with local notes and tokens, were paid out to those who earned relatively little money. Yet, use of these

2005), 88–90, 189–93; Joel Mokyr, *The Enlightened Economy: An Economic History of Britain, 1700–1850* (New Haven, CT, 2009), 24.

[10] Brian R. Mitchell, *British Historical Statistics* (Cambridge, 1988), 153.

[11] Craig Muldrew and Stephen King, 'Cash, Wages and the Economy of Makeshifts in England 1650–1830', in Peter Scholliers and Leonard Schwarz, eds., *Experiencing Wages: Social and Cultural Aspects of Wage Forms in Europe since 1500* (New York, 2003), 156, 161.

[12] A shortage of small-denomination currency often caused concern about the difficulty of paying workers, a concern frequently voiced in early 1797 as the suspension of cash payments led to hoarding of metallic currency. For example, Dowlais Iron Company letter books 1796–7, Glamorgan RO D/D/GD/A, fol. 293; *Hibernian Chronicle*, 2 Jan. 1797.

[13] With, of course, regional variations; see Gilboy, *Wages in Eighteenth Century England*. For the general trend of nominal and real wages, see Robert C. Allen, 'The Great Divergence in European Wages and Prices from the Middle Ages to the First World War', *Explorations in Economic History*, 38 (2001), 414–15; Stephen Broadberry, Bruce Campbell, Alexander Klein, et al., *British Economic Growth, 1270–1870* (New York, 2015), ch. 6; Jane Humphries and Jacob Weisdorf, 'Unreal Wages? Real Income and Economic Growth in England, 1260–1850', *Economic Journal*, 129 (2019), 2867–87; L. D. Schwarz, 'The Standard of Living in the Long Run: London, 1700–1860', *Economic History Review*, 38 (1985), 24.

[14] L. S. Pressnell, *Country Banking in the Industrial Revolution* (Oxford, 1956), 153.

currencies did not preclude the use of the Bank of England note. Especially in London, a considerable number of relatively low-paid workers were starting to receive their wages in the Bank note at the end of the eighteenth century. There are some scattered contemporary references to wage payments in paper currency, such as the case of an employee at linen draper John-Spicer Fisher's shop near Holborn Bridge, who, in August 1801, received a £1 note as part of a regular wage payment.[15] Similarly, Mr Kingsbury in Oxford Street paid three £1 notes to his housemaid Elizabeth Taylor, a widow.[16] Wage payment in paper money, in London and the provinces, became less uncommon in the Bank Restriction period. In the provinces, it was more likely that employers would use local banknotes for wage payments, such as in the case of Draycott Hall, Yorkshire, where lead miners were paid in £1–£5 local notes and silver coins in 1799.[17] When Cobbett remarked that 'now the day-labourer receives his wages in notes' in 1803, it was still a recent development. Even so, paper currency gradually appeared in transactions that provided people's basic source of income.[18]

For those with higher earnings, it became more likely that they were paid in Bank of England notes. This was especially true in London, where the Bank note was the principal paper currency.[19] Unsurprisingly, for employees of the Bank of England – at the end of the century, there were around 600 clerical and 30 non-clerical staff at the Bank – a large part of their salaries came in the form of the Bank note.[20] Other London banks, sixty-nine of which existed in 1797, and most of the established merchant houses in the metropolis probably adopted the same practice. As the major part of the government's financial resources were deposited in and administered by the Bank, members of the state bureaucracy (which expanded from 16,267 in 1797 to 24,598 in 1815, due largely to the military and associated economic activities during the war) received their salary in Bank notes, and the salary of

---

[15] Old Bailey Proceedings, 16 Sept. 1801, Peter Burn (t18010916-7). For Fisher's trade, see *A London Directory or Alphabetical Arrangement Containing the Names and Residences of the Merchants, Manufacturers and Principal Traders in the Metropolis* (London, 1797), 61.

[16] Old Bailey Proceedings, Sept. 1803, Sarah King (t18030914-85).

[17] Mining papers, 1707–1928, North Yorkshire County RO, Draycott Hall Manuscripts, ZLB/3/3/5. Also, Pressnell, *Country Banking*, 156.

[18] Melville, *Life and Letters of William Cobbett*, i, 191.

[19] Henry Thornton, *An Enquiry into the Nature and Effects of the Paper Credit of Great Britain* (London, 1802), 60.

[20] Wilfred M. Acres, *The Bank of England from Within, 1694–1900* (London, 1931), ii, 351, 377; Thomas Surr, *Refutation of Certain Misrepresentations Relative to the Nature and Influence of Bank Notes* (London, 1801), 26.

those civil servants was on the rise.[21] In nominal terms, the annual salary per head in the public service increased from £84.5 in 1797 to £130 in 1815, amounting to more than a 50 per cent increase in average salary.[22] Until the post-war revision of official salaries in 1815, the wartime civil government administration maintained a well-paid, hence expensive bureaucracy.[23] In the 1810s, the government's pay office remitted Bank of England notes for the salaries of consuls and government representatives in foreign lands, and they were 'receiving in specie only a portion of their just emolument'.[24] While this arrangement was often lamented by British officials abroad as they had to carry the loss from the exchange rate, government officials in Ireland gladly received their payments as the exchange rate was generally favourable to the English currency.[25] A major form of non-labour income, the annual interest from investment in public debt – which stood at more than £12 million at the end of the eighteenth century, its quarterly payments amounting to around £3 million – was paid mostly in the Bank of England note.[26] Similarly, chartered corporations paid their dividends in the Bank note – the total annual payout of the Bank of England between 1797 and 1804 was £814,968.[27]

During the Bank Restriction period, the largest and most expensive part of state employment was military service. The presence of those who served in the armed forces increased in importance in British society as Britain engaged in a series of wars with France. As discussed by Roger

[21] Philip Harling and Peter Mandler, 'From "Fiscal-Military" State to Laissez-Faire State, 1760–1850', *Journal of British Studies*, 32 (1993), 54; House of Commons, *Return of Number of Persons Employed and Salaries in Public Offices, 1797, 1805, 1810, 1815, 1819 and 1827, Showing Increase and Diminution* (1830). For the wartime expansion of the state's economic activity, see Patrick K. O'Brien, 'The Contributions of Warfare with Revolutionary and Napoleonic France to the Consolidation and Progress of the British Industrial Revolution' (Economic History Working Papers No. 264/2017, London School of Economics and Political Science, 2011), 15–16.

[22] House of Commons, *Return of Number of Persons Employed*, 2–3.

[23] Harling and Mandler, 'From "Fiscal-Military" State to Laissez-Faire State', 54–9.

[24] *Memoirs and Correspondence of Viscount Castlereagh, Second Marquess of Londonderry*, ed. Charles Vane (London, 1848), i, 84–5.

[25] Frank W. Fetter, *The Irish Pound 1797–1826: A Reprint of the Report of the Committee of 1804 of the British House of Commons on the Condition of the Irish Currency* (London, 1955), 28.

[26] House of Commons, *Accounts of Net Public Income and Expenditure of Great Britain and Ireland, 1688–1869* (1869), 217; House of Commons, *Reports from the Committee of Secrecy on the Outstanding Demands of the Bank and the Restriction of Cash Payments* (1797), 41.

[27] The Bank dividend was increased to £1.4 million in 1805 and then reduced to £1.16 million in 1807, with occasional bonus payments. In 1799, it paid out £1,169,140 to the proprietors. House of Commons, *Report from the Committee of Secrecy on the Bank of England Charter* (London, 1832), appendix, 42.

Morriss, Patrick O'Brien and Nuno Palma, the British navy was a vital institution not just for the nation's military survival but also as the engine of the wartime economy.[28] During the French and Napoleonic wars, state expenditure on military forces constantly increased. In 1801, out of the £50 million total state expenditure, the government spent £14.7 million and £15.3 million on the navy and the army, respectively, in addition to the ordnance, the outlay of which was £1.7 million.[29] Overall, this military expenditure represented 63 per cent of the state's spending, which had a tremendous implication for British society. Those transactions involving relatively large sums, such as payments by the Victualling and Ordnance Board, were normally settled with bills of exchange.[30] In contrast, for payments by the navy, commercial instruments were rarely used; albeit a special form of paper, navy pay tickets were used in the process of wage payments and often traded by sailors at a discount.[31]

Monetary payment was the dominant mode of transaction for the navy's expenditure on wages. As one of the nation's largest employers, the scale of employment in the navy was significant, with the number of voted seamen and marines increasing from 85,000 in 1794 to 145,000 in 1812.[32] In addition to the large number of sailors, there were clerical staff and workers at ports and docks. Arguably, Britain's military mobilisation during the war brought a significant number of the working-age population on to a money wage, paid by the Bank note (the preferred mode of official payment), who may otherwise have been locally employed, for which coins, tokens or local notes were common modes of wage payment. To pay for the large and growing body of employees, the total size of the navy's wage payment increased, and so did the pay per man.[33]

---

[28] Roger Morriss, *The Foundations of British Maritime Ascendancy: Resources, Logistics and the State, 1755–1815* (Cambridge, 2010), 3; Patrick K. O'Brien, 'Fiscal and Financial Preconditions for the Rise of British Naval Hegemony, 1485–1815' (Economic History Working Papers, 91/05, London School of Economics and Political Science, 2005), 37; Patrick K. O'Brien and Nuno Palma, 'Not an Ordinary Bank but a Great Engine of State: The Bank of England and the British Economy', *Economic History Review*, 76 (2023), 315–16.

[29] Morriss, *Foundations of British Maritime Ascendancy*, 97.

[30] Morriss, *Foundations of British Maritime Ascendancy*, 90–2.

[31] Christopher P. Magra, *Poseidon's Curse: British Naval Impressment and Atlantic Origins of the American Revolution* (Cambridge, 2016), 164.

[32] House of Commons, *Statement of Number of Seamen, Boys and Marines Voted for Naval Service and Number of Ships, 1756–1859* (1860), 4. For 1797, see abstract of the monthly list, 1 Mar. 1797, TNA, ADM 8/73.

[33] However, the gap in the pay scale between high-ranking officers and low-paid seamen remained. Daniel A. Baugh, 'The Eighteenth-Century Navy as a National Institution', in Bryan Ranft and J. R. Hill, eds., *The Oxford Illustrated History of the Royal Navy* (Oxford,

In 1797, as the result of the naval mutinies at Spithead and Nore, the monthly pay for ordinary seamen, which had been frozen since 1653, increased from 19s to £1 3s 6d and for able seamen from £1 4s to £1 9s 6d, and there were further pay increases in 1801 and 1806.[34]

The Bank of England note became a chief means of wage payment for the navy due to the suspension of cash payments, which reduced the availability of regal coins. The government needed to manage carefully how it spent the limited amount of precious metals, which was also required, for example, to pay for continental allies. Prior to the suspension, the navy received the largest amount of the Bank's cash payments, and that was why the Bank Restriction Act allowed the Bank to make cash payments, in exceptional cases, for the services of the army, the navy or the ordnance.[35] Nonetheless, when the entire nation was required to be frugal with its coins, the navy had to reduce its cash transactions, and wage payments were an area where cash payments traditionally dominated. Although the navy had introduced wage payments in Bank notes in the late eighteenth century, when seamen had a choice between the Bank note and coins, most of them preferred coins. In 1781, Henry Martin, navy commissioner of Portsmouth, reported that 'our having so large a Sum in Bank notes is likely to prove a considerable embarrassment, as we find great difficulty in getting them off at the payment of ships'.[36] In contrast, from 1797 onwards, the cash option was offered much less often, if at all. To make it work, sailors' preference for hard currency had to be overcome, which was a challenge in 1797, a year when two major mutinies occurred.

The severely restricted specie supply left the navy with no choice but to make its wage payments in paper currency for both high-ranking officials and relatively low-paid sailors. In 1798, expenditure on wages – for officers, seamen, administrators, half-pay and superannuated officers – amounted to £3,299,330, which was approximately 25 per cent of the total navy expenditure and about 7 per cent of Britain's public expenditure.[37] The amount of cash available to the navy was miniscule. Henry

---

1995), 145; Roger Morriss, *Naval Power and British Culture, 1760–1850: Public Trust and Government Ideology* (Abingdon, 2017), 93–4.

[34] J. Ross Dancy, *The Myth of the Press Gang: Volunteers, Impressment and the Naval Manpower Problem in the Late Eighteenth Century* (Martlesham, 2015), 3.

[35] 37 Geo. III, c. 45 s. 3; House of Lords, *Report of the Lords' Committee of Secrecy* (1797), 66.

[36] Henry Martin's letter, 3 Feb. 1781, TNA, ADM 106/1266/64.

[37] House of Commons, *Thirty-First Report from the Select Committee on Finance* (1798), appendix A. Cf. Roger Morriss, 'The British Fiscal-Military State in the Late Eighteenth Century: A Naval Historical Perspective', in Aaron Graham and Patrick Walsh, eds., *British Fiscal-Military States* (London, 2016), 214. See also House of Commons, *Thirty-*

Dundas, then treasurer of the navy, secured £48,000 of specie in that year's navy budget for paying seamen's wages, with additional specie of £16,000 to pay for artificers' and labourers' work at victualling yards, £18,000 to pay allotments to seamen's wives and children and £2,000 to pay fractional parts of navy bills.[38] The total amount of specie the navy secured was £84,000, equivalent to only 2.5 per cent of the navy's wage payments in that year. With such a small amount of coin available, Dundas had to handle a growing number of complaints, especially from sailors and soldiers being deployed overseas. In October 1799, Admiral Lord Keith reported that at some foreign ports, Bank of England notes were discounted by 10–40 per cent and 'in many places they will not take Paper at all'.[39] However sympathetic they may have been to the sailors' situation, the Navy Office was unable to make wage payments entirely in specie. Dundas made a desperate appeal to the Privy Council to allocate the Navy Office £200,000 of specie annually in order that those who were going abroad could be paid part of their wages in specie.[40] This was still a tiny amount for the navy's vast scale of operation.[41] Even with the increase in the navy's specie allocation for wages, it still accounted for only one-tenths of the total wage payments – a substantial part of the rest was made up by the Bank note.

With Britain's war machine sustained by paper-currency circulation, the impact of the navy's wage payments on the geographical penetration of the Bank note was wide ranging. The payments made the economy of port towns inseparable from the paper system, as sailors and navy-related workers earned and spent their pay in Bank notes.[42] Not only active navy employees but, as shown by a warrant issued by the Admiralty in 1799, also superannuated artificers were paid with the Bank of England note.[43]

First Report from the Select Committee on Finance, 17–18; House of Commons, *Twenty-Fourth Report from the Select Committee on Finance* (1798), 50–3.

[38] Dundas to William Fawkener, 9 Jan. 1798, TNA PC 1/40/133; Bank of England, minutes of the Committee of Directors (hereafter CD), 25 Jan. 1798, BE, G4/27, fols. 334–5.

[39] To Henry Dundas, 19 Aug. 1799, TNA, PC1/44/159.

[40] Hope, Palmers and Marsh to Henry Dundas, 19 Aug. 1799, TNA PC1/44/159; Henry Dundas to W. Fawkener, 4 Oct. 1799, TNA PC1/44/159; CD, 9 Oct. 1799, BE, G4/28, fol. 176; E. M. Kelly, *Spanish Dollars and Silver Tokens: An Account of the Issues of the Bank of England, 1797–1816* (London, 1976), 44.

[41] Portions of the metallic currency thus obtained were to be sent to Portsmouth, Plymouth and Sheerness. A. S. Hamond, P. Henslow, W. Rule to Dundas, 20 Sept. 1799, TNA PC1/44/159. Nonetheless, this only amounted to between £5,000 and £10,000 for each town, far from sufficient for the seamen's wages. For the annual figures for workmen's wages at Plymouth dockyards, see House of Commons, *The Commissioners of Naval Enquiry: Sixth Report (Plymouth and Woolwich Yards)* (1804), 8.

[42] William Robinson, *Jack Nastyface: Memoirs of an English Seaman* (London, 2002), 95–6.

[43] Navy board minutes, 26 Apr. 1805, TNA ADM 106/2668.

Navy employees' use of the Bank note went far beyond the ship decks and port towns. Since 1758, the Navy Pay Office had permitted sailors a facility to remit money directly from their entitled wages to their dependents, and government officials at naval ports could act as agents for remitting money.[44] Sailors could also use the ordinary postal service to remit money to their family and to pay for goods and services.[45] Some of these transactions were recorded in the Bank's Lost Note Books. For instance, in September 1797 Joseph Humphreys, on board HMS *Royal William*, and Sara, his wife, jointly claimed for a £5 note lost by post.[46] Similarly, in 1810, the long-serving navy captain James Fynmore's £2 note, sent from HMS *Africa* at Plymouth, did not reach his wife, Frances, in Rochester, Kent.[47] These episodes of Bank-note remittances bring to light the monetary transactions between sailors and indirect beneficiaries of the navy's wage payments, especially those who depended on seamen's income. The scale of this type of transaction should not be underestimated. In his account of the social structure of England and Wales, Patrick Colquhoun calculates that, in 1801–3, there were 165,000 dependents for 41,175 naval officers, seamen and marines.[48] Soldiers and seamen contributed to the circulation of inconvertible paper money by sending Bank notes that they had earned to those who depended on their income, thereby expanding the sphere of note circulation beyond their immediate locality.[49]

Compared to the navy, the British army's dependence on Bank notes was less pronounced. Although during foreign campaigns metallic currency was the most reliable form of payment, within the British Isles army forces were closely connected to the places they were stationed and the use of local banknotes was more feasible for the army than for the mobile

---

[44] Stephen Gradish, *The Manning of the British Navy during the Seven Years' War* (London, 1980), 97–8. Similarly, as Rediker notes, advance pay for merchant seamen was used to pay off debts and help sustain a family during the absence of a wage earner. Marcus Rediker, *Between the Devil and the Deep Blue Sea: Merchant Seamen, Pirates and the Anglo-American Maritime World, 1700–1750* (Cambridge, 1987), 125.

[45] After 1795, in addition to the system of remitting money to families instituted in 1758, officers and seamen could allocate part of their pay for the maintenance of their wives and families. 35 Geo. III, c. 28 (1758). This scheme was further enhanced in 1797 by 37 Geo. III, c. 53.

[46] Lost Note Books, BE, C101/22, fol. 87.   [47] Lost Note Books, BE, C101/34, fol. 372.

[48] Patrick Colquhoun, *A Treatise on Indigence* (London, 1806), 23. Lindert and Williamson's revised figures for the equivalent group is 59,906. No estimate of dependents is given. Peter H. Lindert and Jeffrey G. Williamson, 'Revising England's Social Tables 1688–1812', *Explorations in Economic History*, 19 (1982), 401.

[49] For instance, in 1808 Benjamin Soden, a purser on HMS *Thetis*, sent a £5 note by post, which went missing. The recipient was not specified. 'Navy Pay Office: Ships' Pay Books', *Thetis*, 1808–12, TNA ADM 35/3175; Lost Note Books, BE, C101/31, fol. 177.

employees of the navy. Nonetheless, odd amounts had to be paid in either regal coins, silver or official tokens. In Ipswich in 1811 some local tokens were issued specifically for the 'Convenience of the Army and Public'.[50] Still, there is evidence that the suspension of cash payments led to the introduction of the Bank note into army soldiers' pay.[51] In the immediate aftermath of the suspension in 1797, the Treasury sent drafts to provincial excise collectors and instructed them to pay those drafts in small Bank notes and coins, thereby releasing the reserve of currency from the provincial tax collection system by redirecting it to provincial paymasters.[52] The Treasury repeated the same operation in 1798 and in 1800, through which tax collectors mediated the conversion of Bank of England notes into local notes and specie.[53] By 1803, payments in metallic currency had become the exception rather than the rule in the army.[54] The Duke of York, commander-in-chief of the army, prepared an emergency plan in that year, which included an arrangement to shift army pay from a paper to a metallic basis when an enemy invasion materialised. In his letter to Prime Minister Henry Addington, he explained the risk of the Bank note being refused or depreciated where enemy troops landed, which would lead to a difficulty in obtaining subsistence for British soldiers. Anticipating such a situation, he recommended empowering the paymaster general to send specie to places that were most exposed to attack.[55]

During the French wars, the navy's wage payments were the most conspicuous use of the Bank note for war-related purposes. Between 1806 and 1816, naval expenditure on wages remained high, with its peak in 1814 at £5,397,208 (Table 3.1). The end of the French wars in 1815 contributed to a reduction of naval expenditure, but in 1817 and

---

[50] Glyn Davies, *A History of Money: From Ancient Times to the Present Day* (Cardiff, 2002), 297.

[51] For example, CD, 1 Oct. 1812, BE, G4/35, fols. 152–3; CD, 20 Jan. 1814, BE, G4/36, fol. 198.

[52] George Rose to Commissioners of Excise, 23 Mar. 1797, TNA CUST 48/29, fol. 377.

[53] For 1798, see George Rose to the Excise Board, TNA CUST 48/30, fols. 336–7. For a similar episode in 1800, see Pressnell, *Country Banking*, 63.

[54] This appears to have been the case in Ireland as well, though Irish soldiers were paid chiefly in Bank of Ireland notes and Irish private banknotes. Court of Directors Transaction Book, 17 Nov. 1812, BIAC, bk. 6, fols. 291–2; House of Commons, *Select Committee on State of Ireland as to Circulating Paper, Specie and Current Coin, and Exchange between Ireland and Great Britain* (1804), 11; House of Commons, *Minutes of Evidence Taken before the Committee Appointed to Enquire into the Select Committee on State of Ireland as to Circulating Paper, Specie and Current Coin, and Exchange between Ireland and Great Britain* (1804), 74–5.

[55] Duke of York to Henry Addington, 19 Oct. 1803, Devon Heritage Centre, 152M/C/ 1803/OZ/124.

Table 3.1 *Navy spend on wages, etc., 1797–1820 (£)*

Year	Salaries to the Admiralty, the navy and navy pay officers	Wages to officers and seamen	Half pay to sea officers and bounty to chaplains	Pensions to sea officers and their widows and to superannuated artificers	Wages to HM dock and rope yards	Marines' pay, etc.	Pilotage	Wages for victualling yard employees	Navy spend on salaries, wages, and pensions	Navy total spend	Navy wages and salaries as % of total (%)
1797	85,037	1,352,910	111,812	118,425	757,599	272,895	31,584		2,645,225	14,065,980	18.81
1798	70,000	1,665,000	130,463	17,386	956,686	306,692	29,500		3,175,727	12,591,728	25.22
1799*											
1800	46,000	2,129,000	140,642	76,943	857,875	362,265	35,000	151,050	3,798,775	14,809,445	25.65
1801	76,000	1,920,000	160,502	77,128	941,129	327,000	31,000	142,900	3,675,659	17,303,371	21.24
1802	54,000	2,308,000	181,502	72,833	721,835	219,000	23,000	83,594	3,663,764	11,704,400	31.30
1803	56,000	1,468,000	313,437	83,193	714,709	287,000	17,000	88,012	3,027,351	7,979,878	37.94
1804	84,000	1,155,000	231,750	91,206	816,235	287,000	29,000	124,900	2,859,091	11,759,351	24.31
1805	94,000	1,660,000	191,830	109,934	923,152	403,300	35,000	125,300	3,542,516	14,466,998	24.49
1806	123,600	2,035,000	201,895	105,195	931,718	437,500	35,000	135,100	4,005,008	16,084,028	24.90
1807	130,000	2,117,308	206,404	138,724	1,051,000	412,100	38,000	135,100	4,228,636	16,775,761	25.21
1808**		2,320,000	248,000	34,962	1,038,600			112,400	3,753,962	17,467,893	21.49
1809		2,450,000	215,000		1,016,500			67,400	3,748,900	19,236,037	19.49
1810		2,780,000	200,000	43,401	1,020,000				4,043,401	20,058,412	20.16
1811		2,721,000	291,000	39,548	918,000				3,969,548	19,540,679	20.31
1812		2,976,000	332,000	43,747	1,264,000				4,615,747	20,500,339	22.52
1813		2,678,000	362,000	44,070	1,360,000				4,444,070	21,996,624	20.20
1814		3,676,100	436,900	47,208	1,237,000				5,397,208	21,961,567	24.58
1815		2,838,500	501,500	27,924	1,315,000				4,682,924	16,373,870	28.60
1816		1,594,500	861,500	12,576	989,000				3,457,576	9,516,325	36.33
1817		602,000	990,000		932,000				2,524,000	6,473,063	38.99
1818		573,800	912,000		939,000				2,424,800	6,521,714	37.18
1819		610,500	885,500		785,000				2,281,000	6,395,552	35.67
1820		526,000	901,000		874,000				2,301,000	6,387,799	36.02

* No data for this year.
** Format changes.

Sources: House of Commons, *Accounts Presented to the House of Commons Respecting the Public Income of Great Britain* (1799–1804); House of Commons, *Finance Accounts of Great Britain* (1805–21); House of Commons, *Twenty-Fourth Report from the Select Committee on Finance* (1798).

1818 the navy was still spending around £2.5 million for its officers, seamen and other workers – and the majority of them received their pay in paper currency. According to a comment by John Smith, paymaster of the navy, in 1817, Bank notes were the principal medium of wage payments that were made 'very much in one and two pound notes'.[56]

The royal navy's wage payment was particularly important for the way it expanded the geographical and social reach of the Bank note. At one end of transactions were navy officers, sailors and other navy workers, who were the initial users of Bank notes. At the other end, there were those who did business with the navy and its employees, such as suppliers, local merchants and retailers. When both the navy employees and local businesses accepted the Bank note, they helped create an economic sphere in which the Bank note was an accepted means of payment. This interdependency is revealed in the episode of John Bounden's stolen Bank notes, which we briefly examined at the beginning of this chapter. In April 1805, Bounden, a shipwright who worked in the Plymouth dockyard, received his wages, mostly in the form of Bank of England notes. His intention was to pay £20 to a local victualler to cancel his accumulated debt, but the notes were stolen by Mary Folley, who had no problem disposing of a Bank note at a local hatter. Evidently, all of these people in the south-western port town were accustomed to accepting Bank of England notes.[57] In other words, the war economy was a major factor in the penetration of paper money into Britain's national life because the military economy and non-military sectors were deeply intertwined.[58] Starting with the introduction of inconvertible paper currency into the state's military outlays, wartime mobilisation of financial resources had a far-reaching impact on the composition of circulating media in wartime Britain.

---

[56] House of Commons, *Select Committee on Income and Expenditure of United Kingdom, Sixth Report (Navy)* (1817), 218.

[57] Depositions of John Bounden of Stoke Damerel, shipwright, and William Kingdon of Plymouth, hatter, against Mary Folley for stealing a Bank of England note, 8 Apr. 1805, Plymouth and West Devon RO, 1/695/43.

[58] For the historical linkage between war and currency, and the significance of military transactions for the monetisation of the economy in medieval and early modern period, see Nigel Dodd, *The Social Life of Money* (Princeton, NJ, 2014), 96; David Glasner, 'An Evolutionary Theory of the State Monopoly over Money', in Kevin Dowd and Richard H. Timberlake, eds., *Money and the Nation State: The Financial Revolution, Government, and the World Monetary System* (New Brunswick, NJ, 1998), 36; Muldrew, 'Hard Food for Midas', 99; Peter Spufford, *Money and Its Use in Medieval Europe* (Cambridge, 1989), 235–6.

Provincial Note Reserves and Interregional Payments

The penetration of the Bank of England note into diverse geographical areas of Britain was in part predicated on the need for interregional payments. Inasmuch as the war-induced expansion of central government's financial operations created a channel for paper currency to enter the local economy, Britain's economic growth in the late eighteenth century increased the frequency of interregional transactions. The scarcity of metallic currency after the Bank's suspension of cash payments highlighted the need for a currency with universal acceptability. Country banknotes and local tokens did not serve as interregional currency because they were usually only accepted in and around the place of their issue.[59] In contrast, the Bank of England note was used for clearing purposes among bankers based in London, which rendered it a preferred medium for interregional transactions, including payments across provinces and those between provinces and London.[60]

The Bank's Lost Note Books offer many instances of interregional transactions between London and the provinces that were conducted using the medium of Bank of England notes. In the record for 1800, seventy-seven out of eighty-five interregional transactions involved London. Yet, it is also important to note that a constant number of transactions between provinces were recorded in the Lost Note Books. In June 1801, Reverend Edward Healy of Patrington near Hull reported to the Bank that a £5 note he had sent to a plasterer in Litchfield, Hampshire, had gone missing.[61] In the same year, an ironmonger of Woodstock, Oxfordshire, claimed for a £20 note he had sent to Birmingham.[62] Despite the existence of the Bank Post Bill, a dedicated means for money transfer between distant locations, numerous note users chose instead to send Bank notes by post, usually cutting notes into halves and sending them separately for security against theft and loss.[63] The Bank of England, itself often resorting to the method of sending notes by post, officially acknowledged the practice in 1805 by

---

[59] Francis Baring, *Further Observations on the Establishment of the Bank of England, and on the Paper Circulation of the Country* (London, 1797), 5.

[60] Rondo Cameron, 'England, 1750–1844', in Rondo Cameron, ed., *Banking in the Early Stages of Industrialization: A Study in Comparative Economic History* (New York, 1967), 22; John H. Clapham, *The Bank of England: A History* (Cambridge, 1944), i, 116; Ron Harris, *Industrializing English Law: Entrepreneurship and Business Organization, 1720–1844* (Cambridge, 2000), 212.

[61] Lost Note Books, BE, C101/25, fol. 147.

[62] Lost Note Books, BE, C101/25, fol. 226.

[63] Iain Black, 'Geography, Political Economy and the Circulation of Finance Capital in Early Industrial England', *Journal of Historical Geography*, 15 (1989), 370.

printing a vertical line in the middle of the note, clearly intended as a guide for cutting notes in half.[64] The popular practice of remitting Bank notes by post continued, as shown in the Lost Note Books for 1810, which records interregional transactions between, for example, Shropshire, Lancashire, Cornwall, Devon, Dorset, Durham, Cambridgeshire, Warwickshire, Sussex and Hertfordshire.[65] The prevalence of the practice of sending Bank notes by post was also acknowledged by the General Post Office, which frequently appeared in lost-note records as a claimant.

A well-known method for interregional or international payment was the bill of exchange. Especially for commercial transactions, the use of bills of exchange was widespread and the volume of their circulation was significant. While Henry Thornton remarked in 1802 that the volume of bills of exchange was greater than that of paper currency and guinea coins combined, William Leatham's relatively more concrete estimate was £477 million for inland bills of exchange that were drawn in 1815.[66] However, a large share of these bills could have been for credit-creation purposes and not for general circulation. Nor were they available for the majority of private individuals, as the bill of exchange was a method chiefly, if not exclusively, reserved for the business community. Furthermore, the tripartite relationship of payer, payee and acceptor, on which the system of bills of exchange rested, did not always work in an age that was without any instant mode of communication. In 1799, a Cork distilling firm, Hewitt, Teulon, Blunt & Co., sent a bill of exchange to Messrs John and Thomas Winwood, Bristol ironfounders. When the payee in Bristol brought the bill to the acceptor, the latter, who was supposed to make the payment for the Cork firm, refused to honour the bill for an unknown reason. Having been informed of what had happened in Bristol, the Cork distiller sent a £5 Bank of England note across the Irish Channel.[67] As this case illustrates, payment by bill of exchange required an existing financial arrangement at the destination of

---

[64] Letter to Messrs William Jones, Loyd & Co., 6 May 1821, letter books, BE, C82/2; Derrick Byatt, *Promises to Pay: The First Three Hundred Years of the Bank of England Notes* (London, 1994), 40; Howard Robinson, *Britain's Post Office: A History of Development from the Beginnings to the Present Day* (London, 1953), 97–8; John Trusler, *The London Adviser and Guide: Containing Every Instruction and Information Useful and Necessary to Persons Living in London, and Coming to Reside There* (London, 1786), 85.

[65] Lost Note Books, BE, C101/34–6.

[66] The figure excludes Irish bills and foreign bills. Shizuya Nishimura, *The Decline of Inland Bills of Exchange in the London Money Market, 1855–1913* (Cambridge, 1971), 86.

[67] Letter to John and Thomas Winwood, 25 July 1799, Hewitt, Teulon, Blunt & Company Distillers, Cork City and County Archives, Irish Distillers Copy Letter Book, 1794–1802, U15B/B/3.

the payment. When it was not available or did not work as intended, the Bank note and the Bank Post Bill served as alternative modes of payment that did not require the involvement of a third party.

Country banks, with their own note-issuing power, were not always hostile to the circulation of the Bank note in their provinces. From time to time, they actively sought the Bank note as a form of asset. Country banks' Bank-note holdings functioned as reserve currency, a contingency fund in times of hardship.[68] A temporary loss of local confidence often boosted demand for the Bank note as well as gold. In 1816, when northern bankers suffered a financial difficulty that led to the failure of three local banks in Durham and Sunderland, the Newcastle banker Charles Loraine reported an extraordinary demand for Bank of England notes.[69] In Lancashire, where there was a general preference for Bank of England notes and bills of exchange, such a preference was most pronounced during times of financial instability.[70]

Country banks' Bank-note holdings were not solely kept as a reserve as there were constant transactions of Bank notes between London and the provinces – notes flowed in both directions. The record of an Exeter bank, Milford, Hogg, Nation, offers a rare insight into such transactions. In April, October and November 1800, the bank sent a number of Bank of England notes, amounting to £2,585 – 192 £5 notes, 230 £2 notes and 56 £1 notes – to its London agent Robarts & Co.[71] As well as sending those notes, the Exeter bank kept a share of the Bank notes accumulated in its business, and it occasionally sent a request to its London agent to send over Bank of England notes.[72] Underlining the prominence of the Bank of England note in trans-regional exchange conducted via London, the number of Bank of England notes moved between the two banks was greater than that of country banknotes: the remittance from Exeter in July 1801 contained 105 Bank of England notes, while there were only twenty country banknotes.[73]

---

[68] It virtually functioned as holding an account with the Bank of England. John A. S. L. Leighton-Boyce, *Smiths, the Bankers, 1658–1958* (London, 1958), 168; Pressnell, *Country Banking*, 198–9. See also House of Commons, *Report from the Select Committee on the High Price of Gold Bullion* (1810), 115; House of Commons, *Reports from the Select Committee on the Expediency of Resuming Cash Payments* (1819), 164; House of Lords, *Reports from the Select Committee on the Expediency of Resuming Cash Payments* (1819), 94.

[69] Loraine, Baker & Co. to Vere, Lucadou and Troughton, 23 July 1816, Royal Bank of Scotland (hereafter RBS), London, SAP/36.

[70] T. S. Ashton, 'The Bill of Exchange and Private Banks in Lancashire, 1790–1830', *Economic History Review*, 15 (1945), 31.

[71] Letter book of Milford, Hogg, Nation, RBS, London, MIL/7.

[72] Milford, Hogg, Nation to Robarts & Co., 21 Oct. 1801, RBS, London, MIL/7.

[73] Milford, Hogg, Nation to Robarts & Co., 4 July 1801, RBS, London, MIL/7.

Another instance of Bank-note use for interregional payment was travellers' money. A currency with wide geographical acceptability was indispensable for those travelling across the country. In the eighteenth century, there was a gradual shift from metallic to paper currency as the principal mode of travellers' payments, a practice that took root during the Bank Restriction period, when English innkeepers came to accept the Bank note along major travelling routes.[74] The practice was equally assisted by bankers who supplied paper currency to travellers, which is shown in the business records of some Scottish banks that regularly kept several hundred pounds of Bank of England small notes for Scottish travellers going to England. In 1801, Robert Moncrieff of the Glasgow branch of the Royal Bank of Scotland requested that its Edinburgh headquarters send £500 of 'B of E small notes' to accommodate travellers, because 'those going to England are better pleased with Paper than Gold'.[75] The weight of metallic currency was probably one major reason for travellers' general preference for paper currency, as carrying leaves of banknotes was much easier than carrying a heavy sack of coins. An additional consideration was that the procedure of lost-note claim provided additional security and safety by protecting note users against theft and loss.[76]

As there was a need for interregional transactions, both commercial and private in nature, Scottish banks constantly held Bank of England notes. The account book for the Glasgow branch of the Royal Bank of Scotland shows it normally held around £500 in Bank of England notes.[77] There is no detailed account of the nature of this small holding of Bank notes, but the fluctuations in the figure indicate that transactions involving English notes were not uncommon.[78] In addition, Bank of England notes formed part of the Scottish bank's petty cash account, which was managed separately from the bank's main business account. In 1816, included in the clerks' petty cash holding were a total of £400 of

---

[74] There was a greater chance that country banknotes would be refused outside their circulation areas. John Brown to Edward Finch Hatton, 14 Apr. 1801, TNA, HO 42/49, fol. 195.

[75] W. Simpson to the Royal Bank of Scotland, 24 Aug. 1801, RBS, Edinburgh, RB/837/335.

[76] On the inconvenience of local banknotes for travellers, see Robert Southey, *Letters from England*, ed. Jack Simmons (London, 1951), 122.

[77] RBS, extract from Moncrieff letters, University of Glasgow Archive Services, UGD/129/2/1/6. See also William Graham, *The One Pound Note in the History of Banking in Great Britain* (Edinburgh, 1911), 123–4.

[78] The weekly statement of 2 February 1807 shows that the Bank of England notes kept at the branch were only fractional. Weekly statements from Glasgow agency of RBS, February–December 1807, in RBS, extract from Moncrieff's letters, University of Glasgow Archive Services, UGD/129/2/1/6.

Bank of England notes along with Royal Bank of Scotland notes (£4,200) and silver coins (£4,900).[79] The Royal Bank's headquarters in Edinburgh held a yet greater amount in Bank notes, as it could regularly send a large amount, in the region of a few thousand pounds of 'Bank of England small notes' to the Glasgow branch.[80] Making the English notes available for customers was a normal, if not an everyday, part of banking business in Scotland, and the other leading Scottish banks, the Bank of Scotland and the Commercial Bank of Scotland, held a relatively small but constant amount of Bank of England notes, including £1 and £2 notes.[81]

The nature of the Bank of England note as a widely accepted currency stimulated demand for it in the provinces, to cater to a specific type of use. The interregional movement of the Bank note and its use as traveller's money are two prominent examples of its penetration into broader geographical areas. Prior to the Bank Restriction period, the Bank of England note was already accepted in major cities across Britain. The suspension boosted the Bank note's acceptability, and the enhanced acceptability of the Bank note further bolstered its currency across the regions, establishing its status as a preferred mode for interregional transactions. As far as interregional transactions were concerned, what modern economists recognise as the hierarchy of currency appears to have been created through money users' practice rather than the state's compulsory power, a topic that we return to in the next section.

Rents and Taxes

The diffusion of the Bank note was undoubtedly accelerated during the Bank Restriction period, but this was due to the complementarity of different circulating media; that is, the Bank of England note usually complemented rather than replaced other currencies. Two categories of payments are illustrative of the complementarity and linkage between the Bank note and other forms of payments. The first was the payment of rent, for which Bank notes were increasingly used across England, yet in the provinces, country notes remained the dominant mode of payment. The second category was the payment of taxes, for which initial payments in the provinces were usually made in local currency, and through the

---

[79] Minutes of the Court of Directors, vol. 16, 20 Sept. 1816, RBS, Edinburgh, RB/12/16, fol. 303.

[80] Minutes of the Court of Directors, vol. 17, 29 Sept. 1819, RBS, Edinburgh, RB/12/17, fols. 195–6.

[81] 'Business Peculiar to Agencies', 29 June 1815, HBOS Group Archives, 1/288/170.

process of transferring tax from the provinces to London, the collected tax money was exchanged into Bank of England notes.

Rent payment was a major item of unavoidable expenditure for many of the British population, and for landowners their principal source of income. As with wage payments, the Bank note gradually appears in contemporary accounts of rent payments in this period, which was partly related to the upward trend in rent. In the early eighteenth century, a middle-class family paid £20 and upwards for annual rent.[82] At the turn of the nineteenth century, tenants were paying about 30 per cent more.[83] According to an 1801 parliamentary report, in the relatively poor parishes of Mile End New Town in London, five-sixths of tenants were paying less than £11 per annum, while the rest were paying more.[84] Considering that rent was often paid half-yearly or quarterly, those renting a property at £10 per annum would have paid £2 10s quarterly – a sum that was likely to have been paid in paper currency during the Bank Restriction period.[85] Agricultural rents, which were more variable than house rents, were also on the rise during the French wars, when rents on agricultural lands increased on average by 90 per cent.[86] Arguably, the rising level of rents and the scarcity of coin sped up the shift to payments in paper currency outside the metropolitan area. From declarations made in 1797 in support of the suspension, one could conclude that tenants of the Duke of Northumberland and of the bishop of Durham were allowed to pay their rent in banknotes, including the Bank of England note.[87] The exact degree to which the Bank note was used in provincial rent payment is unclear, but scattered evidence suggests that it was not uncommon for provincial landowners to receive Bank notes when collecting rent.[88] The rent book for Gisburn estate in North

---

[82] Peter Earle, *The Making of the English Middle Class: Business, Society and Family Life in London, 1660–1730* (London, 1989), 208–9.

[83] Gregory Clark, 'Shelter from the Storm: Housing and the Industrial Revolution, 1550–1909', *Journal of Economic History*, 62 (2002), 495.

[84] House of Commons, *Fifth Report from the Committee Appointed to Consider of the Present High Price of Provisions* (1801), 121; L. D. Schwarz, *London in the Age of Industrialisation: Entrepreneurs, Labour Force and Living Conditions, 1700–1850* (Cambridge, 1992), 176.

[85] Benjamin Crosby, *Crosby's Merchant's and Tradesman's Pocket Dictionary* (London, 1808), 269.

[86] François Crouzet, 'The Impact of the French Wars on the British Economy', in Harry T. Dickinson, ed., *Britain and the French Revolution, 1789–1815* (Basingstoke, 1989), 198; Glenn Hueckel, 'English Farming Profits during the Napoleonic Wars, 1793–1815', *Explorations in Economic History*, 13 (1976), 331.

[87] *Newcastle Chronicle*, 4 Mar. 1797.

[88] For example, see Account of balances due (from rentals) to Mrs Judith and George Baker, c. 4 Apr. 1803, Durham University Library Archives & Special Collections, Baker Baker Papers, 19/25.

Yorkshire for the year 1811, for example, showed occasional receipts of 'Bk of Engd' notes, and no case exceeded £10, suggesting that tenants of relatively small estates made these payments.[89]

Had it not been for the widespread practice of paying rent in paper currency, a notice issued by the aristocratic politician Lord King in June 1811 to his tenants would not have caused a fierce public debate – as will be discussed in Chapter 4 in more detail. Lord King demanded that tenants on his Surrey estates pay the year's rent in gold coins.[90] Believing that the Bank of England note had depreciated, he insisted that if tenants were to make rent payments in depreciated currency, landlords were entitled to charge a higher rate according to the market price of gold.[91] That the government rushed to enact laws prohibiting landlords from making similar demands serves as testimony that rent payments in paper currency had by then become an established practice. The resulting legislation protected tenants who tendered 'Notes of the Governor and Company of the Bank of England' from landlords' demands for specie payments.[92] In August 1811, presumably to clarify the local landlord's position on this matter, the Exeter assizes issued a statement pronouncing that its signatories would receive 'only Bank-paper in payment of their Michaelmas rents'.[93]

The Bank of England note entered provincial rent payments, but it never replaced country banknotes, and one could observe the same complementarity in the payment of taxes. While legislation and official policy generally encouraged the use of the Bank note, in practice the use of the state-sanctioned paper currency was enforced only to a limited extent.[94] As early as the 1760s, tax collectors in Bristol and Hull were

---

[89] Copy of J. Brayshay's accounts, Yorkshire Archaeological Society, H. L. Bradfer-Lawrence Collection, MD335 1/4/4/36.

[90] F. W. Fetter, 'Legal Tender during the English and Irish Bank Restrictions', *Journal of Political Economy*, 58 (1950), 241–53.

[91] Hansard, 1st ser., xx (1811), cols. 792–3, 2 July 1811; Lord King's notice to Johnson, Tallow Chandler of Ripley; Surrey, n.d., Kent History and Library Centre, U1590/C57/2.

[92] 51 Geo. III, c. 127.   [93] *Northampton Mercury*, 31 Aug. 1811.

[94] For the generally high level of British taxation, see Martin J. Daunton, 'The Fiscal Military State and the Napoleonic Wars: Britain and France Compared', in David Cannadine, ed., *Trafalgar in History: A Battle and Its Afterlife* (Basingstoke, 2006), 18–43; Peter Mathias and Patrick O'Brien, 'Taxation in Britain and France, 1715–1810: A Comparison of the Social and Economic Incidence of Taxes Collected for the Central Governments', *Journal of European Economic History*, 5 (1976), 601–50. On direct taxes such as local rates and, most importantly, the wartime income tax, see M. J. Daunton, *Trusting Leviathan: The Politics of Taxation in Britain, 1799–1914* (Cambridge, 2001), ch. 2; Roy Douglas, *Taxation in Britain since 1660* (Basingstoke, 1999), 63; Arthur Hope-Jones, *Income Tax in the Napoleonic Wars* (Cambridge, 1939); John Jeffrey-Cook, 'William Pitt and His Taxes', *British Tax Review*, 4 (2010), 386–8;

accepting Bank notes for 'Duties of all Kinds as Specie'.[95] Presumably, around the same time, country banknotes appeared in payments of taxes, including customs, excise and land tax. The extent of the use of paper media – notes and bills – in tax payments can be gauged from the fact that, in 1797, the Bank of England received only around £5,000 in cash in annual customs receipts, the total of which was about £4 million, while less than 1 per cent of excise duties, which brought about £10 million annually to the Bank, was paid in cash ('not above £50 or £60,000' according to the Bank's chief cashier).[96] The Bank Restriction Act of 1797 was virtually an official acknowledgement of the pre-existing practice of tax payment in paper currency, with a stipulation that the Bank note should be accepted at government offices at par.[97] Arguably, paper currency was further embedded in the nation's tax system with the 1799 income tax, which was introduced with an announcement that this new tax could be paid only by 'Bank of England note or Specie', theoretically precluding the use of local banknotes.[98]

During the Bank Restriction period, it was still common to pay taxes in country banknotes in the provinces, and receivers general usually remitted the collected tax money in the form of bills and drafts.[99] The state did not seek to enforce the use of the Bank of England note throughout the tax system as long as the final payment to the national coffer (practically, the Bank of England) was made in the Bank note or regal coins.[100] At the provincial end of tax collection, it was left to individual tax receivers as to what payment options they allowed taxpayers. There were some cases in which tax receivers and receivers general tried to enforce tax payments in Bank notes, but this effectively demonstrated how entrenched the use of local currency was. In 1805, a public notice by a local meeting in Plymouth warned the locals against taking any promissory notes under the value of five pounds each, except the notes of the Bank of England, as

M. E. Turner, J. V. Beckett and B. Afton, *Agricultural Rent in England, 1690–1914* (Cambridge, 1997), 21.

[95] Petition of the merchants and traders in the town of Lynn, 15 Nov. 1763, TNA, T 1/426/319.

[96] House of Lords, *Report of the Lords' Committee of Secrecy*, 66.

[97] 37 Geo. III, c. 46 (1797).

[98] CD, 2 May 1799, BE, G4/28, fol. 118; *The Bank – The Stock Exchange – The Bankers – The Bankers' Clearing House – The Minister, and the Public* (London, 1821), 76.

[99] House of Commons, *Minutes of Evidence Taken before the Select Committee on Receivers General of Land and Assessed Taxes* (1821), 111; L. S. Pressnell, 'Public Monies and the Development of English Banking', *Economic History Review*, 5 (1953), 379.

[100] House of Commons, *1797 Commons Committee on the Outstanding Demands of the Bank*, 19; House of Commons, *Minutes of Evidence Taken before the Select Committee on Receivers General of Land and Assessed Taxes*, 53.

the revenue collectors would not accept small-denomination notes that were payable only at the place of issue.[101] Similarly, in 1810 the Receiver General of North Wales announced he would refuse any country banknotes at tax collection.[102] His statement issued in the following year was slightly modified – 'No Notes whatever but Bank of England'.[103] Tax payment was a channel through which Bank-note use penetrated into the provinces, but in the early nineteenth century the practice was yet to fully take root at the provincial level. Christopher Pemberton, the land-tax receiver in Cambridgeshire in the later part of the Bank Restriction period, made it a rule 'not to take any money for taxes but in notes of the bank of England', but other tax receivers probably accepted other modes of payment.[104]

The degree of monetary standardisation through state-related monetary transactions was limited, although the role of navy wages and taxation in diffusing the use of the Bank note is unquestionable. The Bank of England note appeared in monetary transactions along with other forms of currency, such as local banknotes, bills of exchange, coins and tokens. Historians need to be cautious of ascribing a stable hierarchy to this heterogenous monetary landscape because, much as some local tax collectors and receivers general tried to make the Bank note the single standard means of payment, the system as a whole was still grounded on a mixture of local currencies and nationally circulated ones. The state's guarantee of accepting the Bank of England note at public offices was by no means a sufficient condition for the diffusion of its use across the nation; rather, the diffusion depended on the tax collectors' personal preference. The historical development was much more complicated than monetary theorists – either from a neoclassical or a chartalist standpoint – tend to suggest. What existing theories of money have overlooked is the role of money users in the formation of the monetary landscape. Money users' decisions in accepting certain media of payment while refusing others were, as an aggregate, the foundation of the general acceptability of each circulating media. The next section zooms in to the practice of Bank-note transaction and especially its modality to better

---

[101] Printed notice regarding the problems of issuing and receiving promissory notes, 1805, Plymouth and West Devon RO 1/716/3. A similar meeting was held in Exeter the following week, adopting identical resolutions. *Exeter Flying Post*, 7 Mar. 1805.

[102] *North Wales Gazette*, 27 Sept. 1810.

[103] *North Wales Gazette*, 4 Apr. 1811. For a similar case of refusing country banknotes in Berwickshire, see *Caledonian Mercury*, 18 Feb. 1808.

[104] House of Commons, *Minutes of Evidence Taken before the Select Committee on Receivers General of Land and Assessed Taxes*, 61; Pressnell, 'Public Monies', 383.

understand how note users' practical involvement made the Bank of England note a socially acceptable method of payment.

Social Endorsement

In historical records describing the contemporary practice of banknote use during the Bank Restriction period, what is striking is the care note users took in their handling of notes. They observed the notes they used in far more detail than those in later periods, and in the eighteenth century, merchants, traders and those who routinely dealt with banknotes meticulously recorded the details of their notes. Contemporary evidence suggests that many users kept a record of notes, writing down the denomination, serial number and issue date of notes that came to their hand (Figure 3.1). John Trusler's *London Adviser*, in both its 1786 and 1790 editions, instructed the public 'never to carry any bank notes ... without first entering the number and date in your book'.[105] John Richie of College Hill, London, was one of those who wisely followed such advice, and when he was pickpocketed in late January 1798, he immediately went to the Bank and informed them of the serial numbers and issue dates of the seven £5 notes that had been stolen.[106] Keeping the details of notes was a precaution against all sorts of trouble, including theft and loss, which were hardly rare occurrences, and the relatively high value of paper notes made note users attentive to the various risks associated with their use.

In the 1790s and throughout the Bank Restriction period, the prevalent view was that every Bank note was a unique object, being differentiated by a combination of serial numbers, issue dates, denomination and the clerk's signature on its surface.[107] Echoing this contemporary belief, a lawyer in *Churchill v. Littler* in February 1797 argued that a note's serial number was what 'distinguished it from the others, and fixed its identity'.[108] The case involved a £40 Bank note, which was stolen from the post and subsequently used at a shop in the Strand. When the shopkeeper, Littler, sold a gold watch to a customer, he did not notice

---

[105] Trusler, *London Adviser and Guide* (1786), 20, 147; John Trusler, *The London Adviser and Guide: Containing Every Instruction and Information Useful and Necessary to Persons Living in London and Coming to Reside There*, 2nd ed. (London, 1790), 19.

[106] Lost Note Books, BE, C101/22, fol. 192; *The Oracle*, 25 Jan. 1798.

[107] In 1801, responding to requests from 'many different Quarters', the Bank began publishing the names of clerks who signed notes in the *London Gazette* and other newspapers. CD, 4 June 1801, BE, G4/29, fol. 49; CD, 12 Nov. 1801, BE, G4/29, fol. 109.

[108] *Morning Chronicle*, 24 Feb. 1797.

Figure 3.1 List of Haverfordwest Bank notes created by John Bateman, 1815.

Source: National Library of Wales, Eaton Evans and Williams Collection (B), 11960–6.

that the note offered in payment was without the serial number as the note's edges were pared round. The plaintiff contended that Littler neglected to pay sufficient attention when he accepted the note without examining its identifiers; therefore, the note should be returned to its rightful owner. Littler's lawyer disagreed, stating that if people were required not to trust strangers or damaged notes, no one would take a Bank note and 'there would be an end from this hour of all the paper credit of the Bank of England'.[109] In this case, which set the legal standard for note users' due diligence, Lord Kenyon took the latter view, saying that Littler should be regarded as a bona fide receiver, with the comment that, to maintain the uninhibited circulation of the Bank note, one should not be burdened by the responsibility to inspect notes closely as it would impede the notes' circulation.[110]

 Churchill v. Littler highlights the tension between the traditional mode of personalised economic transactions and its gradual de-individualisation in the age of paper currency, which had important implications for the chronology of modern monetary development. In the tradition of Georg Simmel, historians and sociologists have regarded anonymity as a defining feature of modern economic transactions.[111] Paper currency, according to this view, precipitated the process of de-individualisation of economic transactions.[112] Lord Kenyon's advocacy of unimpeded note circulation, in fact, hardly marked an end to note users' record-keeping, a practice that continued well into the nineteenth century. The prevalent practice of keeping a record of notes' identifiers even after the decision on *Churchill v. Littler* demonstrates that Bank Restriction Britain did not fully embrace de-individualised transactions. The fact that many users could recover their lost Bank notes – discussed in Chapter 2 – clearly indicates that, for those users, Bank notes were indeed identifiable.

 An eminent example that contradicts the alleged anonymisation of economic transactions was the contemporary practice of endorsing Bank notes. During the Bank Restriction period, it was common for note users to write their name and address when a note changed hands, a

---

[109] *Evening Mail*, 22 Feb. 1797.

[110] The verdict followed Lord Kenyon's logic and acknowledged that Littler had a legitimate claim for the monetary value from the Bank. *Evening Mail*, 22 Feb. 1797. See also Hannah Barker and Sarah Green, 'Taking Money from Strangers: Traders' Responses to Banknotes and the Risks of Forgery in Late Georgian London', *Journal of British Studies*, 60 (2021), 585–608.

[111] For criticism of the assumption of modern money's anonymity, see Zelizer, *Social Meaning of Money*, 18.

[112] Natalie Roxburgh, *Representing Public Credit: Credible Commitment, Fiction, and the Rise of the Financial Subject* (London, 2015), 130.

practice that was closely related to the material orientation of the Bank of England note, which was printed only on one side and the back of which was blank. As the negotiability of the Bank note had been established since the early eighteenth century, the endorsement on the note scarcely had any legal meaning.[113] Nevertheless, it was widely practised as part of both business and private transactions. It was an established practice for bank clerks, when they received a note, to write down the name of the person who brought in the note, along with their own name on the back of the note.[114] Merchant clerks followed the same procedure, so did shopkeepers and shop clerks, especially for note transactions involving customers that were not known to them.[115]

Legal historians, when describing the development of financial instruments, have characterised the early eighteenth century as a formative period, when the negotiability of the note was established.[116] In the early years of banking, bankers issued notes for specific transactions and the denomination of the note varied according to the monetary value involved; therefore, the note embodied a personalised promise: 'I promise to pay X'. Endorsement allowed a third party to take part in that relationship, by the original payee's transfer of the right to receive payment to another person, and this transfer was completed by writing the original note owner's name (X in the above example) along with the new owner's name on the back of the note. As paper-note circulation expanded and bankers' notes came to be used as general currency, banknotes were made assignable without endorsement, and they became payable to the bearer of the note. The Bank of England note was from the start payable to the bearer, which theoretically made endorsement redundant. However, endorsement on the Bank note and other types of notes was common in eighteenth-century England, and the practice was conspicuous during the Bank Restriction period. Offering not only an important counterexample to the anonymisation of economic transactions that historians associate with the early eighteenth century, the practice of endorsement also shows that the anonymous circulation of

---

[113] 3 & 4 Anne, c. 9; William Searle Holdsworth, *A History of English Law*, 2nd ed. (London, 1937), viii, 191. See also Bruce G. Carruthers, *City of Capital: Politics and Markets in the English Financial Revolution* (Princeton, NJ, 1996), 128.

[114] The practice was also adopted in some parts of Ireland. From Monaghan, 5 Aug. 1802, Cork City and County Archives, Irish Distillers Copy Letter Book, 1794–1802, U15/B.

[115] Based on testimony by John Cuell, a clerk to the London and Middlesex Bank. Old Bailey Proceedings, Sept. 1800, Benjamin Pooley (t18000917-11).

[116] James Steven Rogers, *The Early History of the Law of Bills and Notes: A Study of the Origins of Anglo-American Commercial Law* (Cambridge, 1995), 177–86.

goods and services, which some held as desirable in modern commercial society, was hardly a universally embraced idea. Occasional expressions of note users' discontent regarding the cumbersome process of endorsement point to the prevalence of the practice, and the tension between the ideal of uninhibited circulation and the everyday reality of personalised economic transactions. A letter to *Black Dwarf* in 1818 describes a female shopper who refused to endorse a Bank note at a haberdasher's shop, saying that she would rather not buy anything 'if you cannot sell me your goods without knowing who I am, and where I live'.[117] Such protests were relatively rare, and transactions of paper currency were usually accompanied by an exchange of personal information about the users of notes.

Undoubtedly, one major reason for the contemporary adoption of endorsement was the considerable number of forged notes in circulation.[118] At the Bank of Scotland, for instance, it became an established practice for clerks to endorse incoming notes in 1779 when there was an alarm about forged notes.[119] Attaching identity to notes was a precautionary measure against the crime of forgery, which was a crime that primarily depended on the anonymity of monetary transaction.[120] Identifying Bank notes through their endorsements often helped prosecutors of forgery crimes in the legal court, as the crime became more prevalent during the Bank Restriction period.[121] William Sadler's case in 1818 is illustrative of how the name and address written on Bank notes constituted crucial evidence in the criminal trials for Bank-note forgery.[122] When Sadler paid for his purchase at a shoemaker's shop in Westminster with two forged £1 notes, he endorsed the notes with his true name and a false address. Writing his name on the note led to his arrest, and in the subsequent trial, the prosecutor argued that Sadler gave the false address because he knew the notes were unauthentic.

---

[117] *Black Dwarf*, 28 Jan. 1818, 60–1.
[118] However, as McGowen argues, signatures had lost much of their legal value by the end of the eighteenth century. Randall McGowen, 'Knowing the Hand: Forgery and the Proof of Writing in Eighteenth-Century England', *Historical Reflections*, 24 (1998), 412–13.
[119] Business peculiar to agencies, HBOS Group Archives, 1/288/17a, Kelso branch, 5 May 1779; Inverness, 5 May 1779; Kilmarnock, 18 Dec. 1779; Commercial Bank of Scotland Board of Minute Book, 22 Nov. 1810, RBS, Edinburgh, CS/13/1.
[120] Paul Baines, *The House of Forgery in Eighteenth-Century Britain* (Aldershot, 1999), 10–11. On the rise of forgery crime, see Philip Handler, 'Forging the Agenda: The 1819 Select Committee on the Criminal Laws Revisited', *Journal of Legal History*, 25 (2004), 251–3; Randall McGowen, 'The Bank of England and the Policing of Forgery 1797–1821', *Past & Present*, 186 (2005), 81–116.
[121] *The Star*, 19 June, 22 Aug. 17 and 19 Sept. 1818.   [122] *The Star*, 19 Sept. 1818.

Recognising endorsements as a proof of Sadler's identity and his criminal intent, the court sentenced Sadler to fourteen years' transportation.[123]

Precaution against forgery could hardly be the sole reason for the widespread adoption of endorsement in Bank Restriction Britain. Many criminals must have escaped being arrested for passing forged notes by providing a false name and address, though historical records tend to highlight less accomplished criminals like Sadler. One such criminal was Mary Smith, who in July 1816 paid for her purchase (a boy's corduroy dress, a pair of shoes and stockings) with two forged £1 notes; when asked to endorse the note, she gave a fictional name and address that she claimed to be her husband's.[124] As endorsement did not guarantee the authenticity of information and the effect on preventing forgery crime was dubious to say the least, its widespread practice needs to be seen less as specifically for preventing forgery and more as a way to generally enhance the security of paper currency. The legal court accepted endorsement as evidence in a variety of cases, ranging from theft and forgery to political corruption. In the trial of John Norton, in 1798, law enforcement traced stolen notes with the help of endorsements on Bank notes. The case concerned two £10 and six £5 notes enclosed in a letter sent by a Suffolk farmer, John Robinson, and addressed to a London tea dealer.[125] Norton, an employee of the Post Office, intercepted the notes and subsequently spent them. Following contemporary custom, Robinson kept a record of the numbers and issue dates of these notes, and when the notes were eventually paid into the Bank, Robinson's record-keeping and endorsements on the notes led the authorities to Norton. Norton used the stolen notes in payment to several people, including one of his co-workers, a grocer and a publican; by the time Norton's crime came to light, the eight notes had been used in transactions that involved at least five people and two banks. At almost every step, the notes were endorsed. Even the inspector, Luke Ferguson, endorsed the notes he found when he raided the house of the thief.[126] During Norton's trial at the Old Bailey, five out of eight notes were brought in as evidence, which the witness readily identified as notes that they had received from Norton. Endorsement thus functioned as a device

---

[123] Old Bailey Proceedings, Sept. 1818, William Sadler (t18180909–92).
[124] Old Bailey Proceedings, Sept. 1818, Mary Smith (t18180909–108); *The Star*, 19 Sept. 1818. For other examples of the use of false names, see *The Star*, 19 June, 17 and 22 Sept. 1818.
[125] Old Bailey Proceedings, Jan. 1798, John Norton (t17980110–14).
[126] Ferguson was an inspector of the carriers at the General Post Office. On Ferguson, see Old Bailey Proceedings, Sept. 1792, Isaac Moore (t17920912–85).

for tracking down wrongdoing involving Bank notes, while giving additional security to note users.

Ultimately, the nature of endorsement on the Bank note was social rather than legal, and its primary social function was to enhance the general credibility of the Bank note. Criminal note forgers knew well that people were more likely to accept notes with endorsements and some of them took the trouble of adding fake endorsements to forged notes. In December 1808, John Peake used a forged £1 note at a cheesemonger on Brick Lane, London. A copper engraver by trade, Peake was a seasoned forger, who successfully manufactured and circulated about 800 forged notes from 1803 until he was arrested in January 1808. Peake's forged notes, however, were far from exact copies of authentic Bank notes. The cheesemonger Thomas Mallard recalled later that the paper of Peake's forged notes was thicker than the real Bank notes, and Mallard suspected the note might be a bad one. What dispelled Mallard's suspicion – and that of some of Peake's other victims' too – was endorsements on the back of Peake's notes. When the cheesemonger saw the names and addresses on the note, they 'removed his suspicions'.[127] When Peake was brought to trial, the court recognised that many of the endorsements that appeared on Peake's forged notes were written in the same or similar handwriting, which witnesses confirmed to be Peake's. Although his handwriting eventually gave him away, the endorsements led his victims to believe that the notes had previously been accepted by others and therefore their authenticity was assured.

What may be called *social endorsement* was prevalent during the Bank Restriction period, despite it having limited legal and practical meaning. As the poem *Adventures of a One Pound Note* (1819) illustrates, Bank notes were usually endorsed when they were passed from one hand to another.[128] In the tradition of Joseph Addison's 'Adventures of a Shilling' (1710), Charles Johnston's *Chrysal; or, the Adventures of a Guinea* (1760) and Thomas Bridge's humorous parable of *Adventures of a Bank Note* (1770–1), the anthropomorphised £1 note in *Adventures of a One Pound Note* recounts its life story, from its encounter with its first owner to its return to the Bank.[129] The note passes from hand to hand, between a 'beau', a 'lass', a tavern keeper, a tea broker and an exciseman, and the list goes on: it travels 'from house to house, both far and wide',

---

[127] Prosecution of J. Peake, 1818, BE, F2/95.
[128] *The Adventures of a One Pound Note: A Poem* (London, 1819).
[129] Joseph Addison, 'Adventures of a Shilling', *The Tatler*, 249 (11 Nov. 1710); Thomas Bridges, *Adventures of a Bank Note*, 4 vols. (London, 1770–1); Charles Johnston, *Chrysal; or, the Adventures of a Guinea*, 2 vols. (London, 1760).

from 'high life' to 'completely low'. The journey leaves visible traces, numerous endorsements, on the note: 'written o'er with many a name. / I scarcely now look like the same'. Bank notes full of endorsements were not uncommon, and the practice was so prevalent that when Jeremy Bentham proposed a new note design to the Bank he recommended that the obverse side of the note be left blank so that it would be 'free for *indorsements*, as at present'.[130]

In 1802, Henry Thornton contrasted commercial bills, the acceptability of which depended on 'the confidence placed by each receiver of it in the last indorser', with the circulation of bankers' notes, which derived from general trust in the credit of the issuing bank.[131] The popular practice of social endorsement, however, suggests that there was no sharp distinction regarding the source of confidence on which the circulation of commercial bills and that of Bank notes depended. Rather, Thornton's account of the generation of confidence by a chain of endorsements applied equally to commercial bills and to the Bank note. A note with endorsers' names was more trustworthy than one without, as endorsements served as testimonials that the note had previously been accepted by others. Just as in the case of endorsed transactions of commercial bills, endorsers of Bank notes provided a virtual guarantee of their acceptability, which by itself increased the likelihood of their acceptance in the future.[132] As such, endorsements were not merely evidence of notes' past acceptance. By implying notes' future acceptance by other note users, these writings on the back of notes reinforced inter-subjective trust within Britain's paper-based monetary system.

From a longer-term perspective, the practice of endorsing paper currency may be seen as British note users' spontaneous response to the shifting balance between personal and anonymous economic transactions, as the advocates of commercial society strove to adjust reality to the idea of uninhibited circulation of goods, services and exchange media. By recording information on Bank notes – serial numbers, issue dates and a clerk's signature – and by adding personal information to them, notes and note transactions were made traceable, identifiable and personal.[133] Social endorsement was a part of the note

[130] 'Mr Bentham's Plan for Preventing Forgery of Bank Notes &c.' University College London, Special Collections, Bentham Manuscripts, Box 3b, 36/341–57, fol. 4.

[131] Thornton, *Paper Credit*, 40.

[132] F. Stuart Jones, 'Government, Currency and Country Banks in England, 1770–1797', *South African Journal of Economics*, 44 (1976), 267.

[133] Some note users relied on the name and signature of the Bank clerks on the note as a way to determine the authenticity of a note. McGowen, 'Knowing the Hand', esp. 410–11.

users' acculturation to the new monetary regime of inconvertible paper currency, a regime that was gradually eroding the culture of personal credit. This voluntary expression of social relations by note users boosted the acceptability of the Bank note in British society. By enabling note users to ascertain the identity of their transaction partners in an increasingly anonymised commercial society, social endorsement re-socialised monetary transactions. At the same time, endorsements helped shape the imaginary geography of the monetary landscape by offering a visual representation of monetary networks in the small space on the back of a Bank note, connecting individuals to a broad community of note users.[134] When note users added their name to the chain of transactions, they participated in creating a bond between note users. This chain connecting economic actors had a far more positive resonance than its descendant, the cash nexus that was castigated by Thomas Carlyle, Karl Marx and Friedrich Engels as a degenerated form of monetised social relations.[135]

Acceptance of the Bank Note as a Political Expression

In Bank Restriction Britain, the act of accepting the Bank note took on a meaning that went beyond the mere transfer of economic value. Political meanings, among others, were often attached to currency acceptance, a dimension of the social meaning of money that stemmed from the voluntary nature of Britain's paper currency. The Bank Restriction Act stipulated that an offer of payment by Bank note constituted a legitimate reason for debtors to avoid imprisonment, which in principle made all payments in the Bank note legally valid, but as the Bank note was not legal tender its transactions still rested on a voluntary agreement. The voluntary nature of acceptance gave rise to the everyday politics of paper currency, and it manifested in cases when a user refused to accept a Bank note. A collective refusal of Bank notes was rare in eighteenth-century Britain, but runs on the Bank did happen. When a large number of note holders demanded that the Bank convert the notes into coins – as was the case in 1745 – contemporaries ascribed political motives to the rejection of paper currency. At the individual level, prior to the Bank Restriction

[134] Hoppit points out that the credit relationship had been conceived in terms of 'chain[s]' and 'links' throughout the eighteenth century. Julian Hoppit, 'The Use and Abuse of Credit in Eighteenth-Century England', in Neil McKendrick and R. B. Outhwaite, eds., *Business Life and Public Policy: Essays in Honour of D.C. Coleman* (Cambridge, 1986), 67.

[135] Niall Ferguson, *The Cash Nexus: Money and Power in the Modern World, 1700–2000* (London, 2001).

Act note users could legitimately refuse Bank notes. Indeed, there were occasional reports of Bank of England notes being refused or discounted.[136] For instance, in 1792, the diarist John Byng's £10 note was refused at a Rochdale inn. To be more precise, the inn holder refused to accept it unless Byng paid an additional 1s 6d. Byng commented bitterly, 'Is this to be justified, or is it part of their treason to decry the lawful money of the Bank of England, to serve their own notes?'[137] In his distinctively political interpretation of the event, Byng's choice of the word 'treason' plainly shows his recognition that refusing the Bank note was a subversive political act, an understanding that was couched in terms of competition between the Bank of England and provincial banking interests.[138]

With the suspension of cash payments in 1797, the dichotomy of London versus the provinces receded into the background as the Bank note was now lawful money in a country that had effectively come to embrace the paper standard. In the new regime of paper currency, contemporaries saw Bank notes and country notes as constituting a single monetary system, in which the inconvertible Bank of England note provided legitimacy to inconvertible paper currency in general. Under the new paper-based regime, British citizens came to associate the Bank of England's note issue ever more closely with quasi-sovereign power. With this understanding of the new symbolic hierarchy of currency, refusing the Bank note, which constituted no crime in law, could be construed as a political offence in denying the legitimacy of the nation's monetary order. Within this symbolic economy of paper currency, discounting of the Bank note or adding a surcharge for Bank-note payment – which came to be known as 'two prices' – was reprehensible as much for its political implications as its profiteering nature.[139] Such a political interpretation was shared by those who encountered the practice of two prices in the months following the suspension of cash payments. In March 1797, painter Ozias Humphrey experienced two prices when he went to a bookshop in London. For a book priced at £1, the bookseller asked Humphrey for a one-shilling premium if he was paying with a

---

[136] Baring, *Further Observations*, 11.

[137] John Byng, *The Torrington Diaries*, ed. C. B. Andrews (London, 1936), iii, 115–16.

[138] Thornton stated that it was often a practice of country bankers to discourage the circulation of the Bank note. House of Lords, *Report of the Lords' Committee of Secrecy*, 76.

[139] *St James's Chronicle*, 28 Feb.–2 Mar. 1797; William Cobbett, *Paper against Gold and Glory against Prosperity* (London, 1815), i, 401–2, 477–81. On the same phenomenon in revolutionary France, see Francis Baring, *Observations on the Establishment of the Bank of England, and on the Paper Circulation of the Country* (London, 1797), 78–9.

£1 Bank note. Recounting the episode to his friend Joseph Farington, Humphrey described the conduct of the bookseller as 'little short of treason'.[140] Similarly, Charles Hales, when he reported the rejection of a Bank note by an innkeeper in his *A Correct Detail of the Finances of This Country* (1797), remarked that 'the rejector of such [a] note deserved to be considered in no other light than that of a private enemy to Government'.[141] Just as the declaration movement of 1797 underlined the solidarity of Britain's money users, the political interpretation of refusing or discounting the Bank note defined note refusal as a social transgression, a threat to social order in the new paper-based regime.

The refusal of a Bank note, or any signs of its likelihood, was taken far more seriously in the front line of Britain's war against France than in other spheres of national life. The navy commander Charles Penrose wrote that wage payment in £1 and £2 Bank notes, when they were first issued in early 1797, met with sailors' reluctance to accept them. Some sailors, who sought 'political mischief' or 'emolument', tried to persuade others to refuse note payment or to sell notes to fellow sailors at a discount. Penrose ordered the fleet under his command that 'if any one offered or accepted less than a full value, that the offender should instantly be brought to me, that he might be treated as an enemy to his King and country'.[142] It is not known how far the initial reluctance to accept Bank notes was shared across the navy, but the fact that the use of paper currency was not explicitly put forward as a grievance during the Spithead and Nore mutinies in the same year suggests that its refusal was less a radical political agenda than an act of individual political disobedience or economic greed.

Politically motivated refusal of Bank notes would later grow into a genuine threat to the stability of the paper system, as it offered a new tactic for challenging the established political system via discrediting the legitimacy of the monetary order. However, it was some time before political radicals realised the potential of undermining the paper system by an organised refusal of Bank notes. In the late 1810s, William Cobbett devised what he called a puff-out scheme, a plan for discrediting the Bank note, but apart from Francis Place's 'Go for Gold' campaign in the 1830s there were only sporadic and isolated cases of refusal.[143] A radical politician in Bury St Edmunds, Joshua Grigby, caused a well-publicised

---

[140] Joseph Farington, *The Farington Diary*, ed. James Greig (London, 1922), i, 197.

[141] Charles Hales, *A Correct Detail of the Finances of This Country* (London, 1797), 36–7.

[142] Charles Penrose, *A Friendly Address to the Seamen of the British Navy* (Bodmin, 1820), 47–8.

[143] In Ireland, a collective refusal of banknotes was in fact being contemplated by the United Irishmen as an assault on the political authority through economic means. John

legal case when he rejected an offer of Bank of England notes by the local bank Oakes and Sons.[144] Also in the late 1810s, Henry 'Orator' Hunt tried another version of note refusal when he brought a £1,000 note to the Bank of England. While he demanded payment for his note, he refused to write his name and address on it, without which, according to the Bank's established practice, the Bank clerks were not supposed to receive notes.[145] With this ingenious method of disrupting social endorsement, Hunt hoped to secure a legal ground for suing the Bank for its unpaid 'debt', which was narrowly avoided by the Bank's decision to bend the rule and accept Hunt's note without endorsement.

At the end of the eighteenth century, many British citizens held that the value of the Bank of England note rested on its voluntary nature, and on its acceptance not being enforced by political or legal authorities: Edmund Burke gave currency voluntarism an early expression in his *Reflections on the Revolution in France*. As he wrote, 'Our paper is of value in commerce, because in law it is of none. It is powerful on Change, because in Westminster Hall it is impotent'.[146] The prevalence of currency voluntarism in British society effectively left the choice over acceptance up to users, which meant that the note could be rejected, potentially destabilising the existing system of monetary value. Insisting on cash (precious metal) and refusing paper currency had a distinctive political meaning that amounted to a challenge to the social order, an act associated with a radical political creed. Yet, strictly speaking, politically motivated refusal was still within the legitimate use of the Bank note because there was no law forcing Britons to accept Bank notes. In other words, those who refused to accept the Bank note pushed the boundary of how paper currency was used beyond immediate economic purposes – an example of how users invented ways of using currency against the intention of its creators.

Conclusion: Anonymity and Paper Currency

By tracing the uses of the Bank note, this chapter illustrated the several registers of Bank-note use, covering both its practical and its symbolic –

Thomas Gilbert, ed., *Documents Relating to Ireland, 1795–1804* (Shannon, Ireland, 1970), 156.

[144] Jane Fiske, ed., *The Oakes Diaries: Business, Politics and the Family in Bury St Edmunds 1778–1827* (Woodbridge, 1990), i, 30, 82–4.

[145] Robert Huish, *The History of the Private and Political Life of the Late Henry Hunt* (London, 1836), 437–53; Henry Hunt, *Memoirs of Henry Hunt* (London, 1820), i, 141–9.

[146] Edmund Burke, *Reflections on the Revolution in France*, ed. J. C. D. Clark (Stanford, CA, 2001), 401.

or economic and social – levels. From the examination of wage payments, interregional transactions and collection of rents and taxes, we saw that the Bank of England note was becoming a widely accepted means of payment. We also saw how the spheres of Bank-note circulation expanded through monetary use. By zooming in on the point of currency use, where the practice of social endorsement took place, this chapter argued that users' practice enhanced the Bank note's security and credibility, a process that involved visualising interpersonal or communal trust.

In the multiple-currency situation, the Bank note often appeared as a special-purpose money that was preferred in certain types of payments, such as interregional payments, but not necessarily in other forms of transactions. The Bank note's limited fungibility – the degree to which it was accepted as an equivalent to other currencies – by no means inhibited its diffusion in British society. On the contrary, the limited-use purposes provided entry points through which the reach of the Bank note was expanded geographically and socially. In this selective diffusion process, note users across the British Isles encountered the Bank of England note, some for the first time. For the majority of provincial note users, handling Bank of England notes did not become an everyday experience, but they knew that, as a special form of currency, it was a semi-national currency. They equally knew very well that it was not legal tender nor was it a government-issued currency. The state played an important part in the story of inconvertible paper currency, but monetary hierarchy was not as rigid or a priori as fiat money theorists might assume.[147] The hierarchy among different forms of currency was fluid and dynamic throughout the Bank Restriction period.

From this chapter's examination of the everyday practice and politics of Bank-note acceptance, what emerges is that, despite some historian's contention, economic transactions in the age of paper were hardly deper-sonalised. Looking at the historical evidence, it is simply implausible to contrast the 'individualised' monetary exchange of the early eighteenth century with the allegedly de-individualised exchange brought about by

[147] There is an extensive academic discussion on the hierarchy of money. Stephanie Bell, 'The Role of the State and the Hierarchy of Money', *Cambridge Journal of Economics*, 25 (2001), 149–63; Benjamin J. Cohen, *The Geography of Money* (Ithaca, NY, 1998), ch. 5; Duncan Foley, 'Money in Economic Activity', in John Eatwell, Murray Milgate and Peter Newman, eds., *Money* (London, 1989), 249–50. My discussion here recognises the 'multiple hierarchies' discussed by sociologists and ethnographers and more recently by Lascaux. Alexander Lascaux, 'Money, Trust and Hierarchies: Understanding the Foundations for Placing Confidence in Complex Economic Institutions', *Journal of Economic Issues*, 46 (2012), 81; Pressnell, 'Public Monies', 383.

the 'anonymous Bank of England note'.[148] Far from being depersonalised, paper-currency transactions during the Bank Restriction period were, in fact, imbued with identity and social relations by note users. What changed from the age of personal credit to the era of paper currency was the mode of expressing the individuality of economic transactions – if anything, endorsement was clearly a way to reduce the anonymity risk.[149] In terms of social endorsement, the chain of transactions recorded in the blank space on the back side of the Bank note substituted the early modern close-knit economic community. As a medium of exchange, every Bank note had an identity given to it by its users, and as a unique object, it had a social existence that was tangible and at the same time symbolic in nature.

---

[148] James Thompson, *Models of Value: Eighteenth-Century Political Economy and the Novel* (Durham, NC, 1996), 143.
[149] Compare Niklas Luhmann, *Trust and Power: Two Works by Niklas Luhmann*, trans. Howard Davis, John Raffan and Kathryn Rooney (Chichester, 1979), 50–2.

4   Gold, Gold, Gold

The Legal Tender Question and the Bullionist Controversy

> If guineas disappear, notes may be substituted in their place; and through that general confidence which may be inspired by the agreement of bankers and other leading persons to take them, they will not fail, provided the issues are moderate, and the balance of trade is not very unfavourable to the country, to maintain exactly the gold price.   Henry Thornton, *An Enquiry into the Nature and Effects of the Paper Credit of Great Britain* (1802)

> There were some who, like parrots and magpies, could say nothing but 'Gold, gold, gold'. To believe gold necessary to a circulating medium was an idea only fit for Hottentots. To think a circulating medium of gold necessary was only shewing that we were just at the commencement of civilization, or rather on the verge of barbarism.   Charles, Third Earl Stanhope, in the House of Lords, 16 July 1811

In January 1801, Joshua Grigby, a resident of Bury St Edmunds, visited local banking house Oakes and Son, seeking payment for a five-guinea local banknote. Following the common practice adopted by banks across England, the bank's clerk offered Grigby a £5 Bank of England note and a five-shilling coin. Grigby refused to accept the note, demanding the whole sum be paid in metallic currency, a request that the bank cordially declined.[1] Discontented, Grigby resorted to the court of law, an action that was certainly controversial but not without legal grounds. The Bank Restriction Act of 1797 stipulated that payments in notes would be deemed payments in cash 'if made and accepted as such'.[2] A possible interpretation was that one could refuse to recognise Bank notes as cash, a legal ambiguity Grigby took advantage of. The son of a radical MP, Joshua III, Grigby shared his father's deep-seated antipathy to the

---

[1] Jane Fiske, ed., *The Oakes Diaries: Business, Politics and the Family in Bury St Edmunds 1778–1827* (Woodbridge, 1990), i, 30–1, ii, 3–4; Roy Workman, 'The Joshua Grigbys: Some Materials for a History of the Joshua Grigbys of Bury St Edmunds and Drinkstone in Suffolk 1659 to 1829' (unpublished typescript, Suffolk RO Bury St Edmunds, HD1339/1, 1983), 233.

[2] 37 Geo. III, c. 45, s. 8.

established political system, which led him to take direct action against the Bank Restriction as the crux of the Pittite system.[3] His intention was to question the legality of the Bank Restriction, rather than to discredit Oakes and Son's banknote, which was later made clear in his public statement.[4]

At the summer assizes in July 1801, where the case was examined, the presiding judge, Baron Hotham, and the jury saw Grigby's action as unwarranted.[5] Hotham was an ardent supporter of the declaration movement in early 1797, in which he played a leading part in his locality by urging the Essex assizes to issue a resolution to accept banknotes as money.[6] For Hotham, who firmly believed that voluntary acceptance of paper currency was the foundation of the inconvertible paper system, Grigby's action appeared as a direct threat. Hotham grudgingly acknowledged that Grigby was, in terms of the law, entitled to demand payment in cash, but he also made it clear in his concluding remarks how strongly he disapproved Grigby's conduct:

[T]he action he has bot [brought] is the most wanton, busy, officious, unprecedented & malignant attack that I have ever known in a court of Justice. It is not easy to conceive his Motive but the tendency of it is to throw this Country into inextricable confusion & to Cause a most mischievous result, to overthrow every thing in it. If I had any knowledge of Mr Grigby & an Opportunity of speak [in]g to him, I should, in the most Solemn manner, advise him, nay implore him, not to let the matter ever appear before the Public, or be mentioned again.[7]

The case was later referred to the Court of Common Pleas as it concerned the judiciary's interpretation of the Bank Restriction Act, the legal foundation for the inconvertible currency regime. There was no doubt that the Bank Restriction Act gave protection to those who offered payments in paper currency from creditors' demand for specie payment and any legal process based on such a demand.[8] However, the court's opinion was divided as to whether Bank notes should always be considered cash. Chief Justice Lord Alvanley was of the opinion that the legislature's intention was to make Bank notes a legal payment only in limited situations while, in the main, 'they should remain upon the same footing upon which they stood before the act', meaning that the Bank note was not cash in the eyes of law.[9] Any inconveniences arising from

---

[3] Workman, 'Joshua Grigbys', 246–54.   [4] *Bury and Norwich Post*, 5 Aug. 1801.
[5] *Bury and Norwich Post*, 29 July 1801.   [6] *Norfolk Mercury*, 18 Mar. 1797.
[7] Fiske, *Oakes Diaries*, ii, 11–12. The original is Diary of James Oakes of Bury St Edmunds, Suffolk RO, Bury St Edmunds, HA521/6.
[8] *The English Reports* (Edinburgh, 1900–32), cxxvi, 1422; *Bury and Norwich Post*, 25 Nov. 1801.
[9] *English Reports*, cxxvi, 1422.

that legal provision ought to be addressed by the parliament. The court, adhering to the narrow interpretation of the law, granted Grigby nominal damages of one shilling.

The court's verdict on Grigby's case acknowledged that note holders had a legal right to seek cash payments, which was at odds with the Bank of England's interpretation of its obligations under Bank Restriction. When in 1798 a marine, John Daniels, had complained to the Bank that the Norwich bank Harvey & Co. had refused to exchange his £1 Bank note for coin, the Bank replied that neither the Norwich bank nor the Bank of England was under obligation to comply with his request.[10] The Bank did make partial cash payments for small notes, but it regarded such payments as the Bank's option, not note users'.[11] Grigby's attack revealed that the legal foundation of the Bank Restriction was not unassailable. The law was ambiguous as to whether the Bank note became 'cash' for all intents and purposes. On this matter, the idea of voluntary acceptance of paper currency, which remained highly influential in the early 1800s, was a double-edged sword because if Britain's paper money was accepted 'by choice' of citizens, they would equally have the right to refuse paper.[12] Thus the currency system, by resting on voluntarist principles, left its opponents room to manoeuvre in the legal court for their cause.

In the early nineteenth century, there was no clear separation between legal thinking and economic ideas about money. Christine Desan has recently investigated the prevalence of legalist thinking in the early discussion on the management of the monetary system, tracing the emergence of the liberal legal tradition in monetary thought.[13] According to Desan, early modern English law enshrined the sovereign's arbitrary power to change monetary value, a form of monetary nominalism. With the introduction of 'bank-based currency', money underwent a reinvention process and there emerged a tension between those who saw money as a 'constitutional process' (i.e. state creation) and those who believed that the foundation of monetary value rested outside the realm of politics. The latter school of thought grew into the liberal tradition in monetary thought, which stressed the sanctity of private contracts and market operation that defied political intervention into

---

[10] Secretary's letter books, 6 Nov. 1798, BE, G23/48, fol. 80.

[11] In 1799 and in 1800, the Bank made partial cash payments for small-denomination notes. CD, 29 Jan. 1800, BE, G4/28, fol. 229; House of Lords, *Reports from the Select Committee on the Expediency of Resuming Cash Payments* (1819), second report, 1.

[12] See Introduction.

[13] Christine Desan, *Making Money: Coin, Currency, and the Coming of Capitalism* (Oxford, 2014), 9.

the monetary standard. An early proponent of this tradition was John Locke, who firmly believed in the universal validity of the metallic standard and vehemently opposed political meddling in monetary value.[14] Desan further argues that the period of compromise between the two monetary ideas ended with the suspension of cash payments in 1797, which pitted the statists against liberals.[15]

This chapter presents the paper-currency controversy in Bank Restriction Britain as not merely an intellectual debate over the nature of paper currency and its practical consequences but as a historical debate intertwined with the social and cultural situation in wartime Britain. In the debate, as Desan rightly points out, legal and constitutional aspects of paper currency loomed large, but interpreting the debate as a battle between statists and liberals misses an important third strand of monetary thought: the communal-currency perspective that was widely shared by those who discussed the paper-based currency system during the Bank Restriction period. As already discussed in the Introduction, British writers rejected the statist theory of money on paper currency in the 1790s because of its association with the French *assignat*. Far more prevalent was the idea of credit currency based on voluntary acceptance, intersubjective trust and communal solidarity. Contemporary polemics in the early part of the Bank Restriction period steered away from evoking the state's power as a source of monetary value, and the element of political authority in the operation of Britain's monetary system was recognised primarily in the state's ability to regulate the international flow of precious metal, a tangible expression of which was the mercantilist law limiting the exportation of coins and bullion. As far as paper currency was concerned, much of the legal-economic debate on paper currency was concerned with the Bank of England's role as a *non-governmental* institution, which was in theory and practice separate from the British state; hence the statist explanation of currency was largely irrelevant. The constitutional implications of currency issues were often set aside when contemporaries discussed moral constraints on the actions of private individuals that threatened the interest of the broad community, such as refusing paper currency (like Oakes did) or undervaluing paper currency through discriminating against paper in favour of the metallic form of currency. In other words, the legal-economic perspective on monetary debate cut across the constitutional, business and civic realms of British society.

In this chapter, the British debate over the nature of the inconvertible currency system is divided into two chronological periods, in each of

---

[14] Desan, *Making Money*, 16–19, 411.   [15] Desan, *Making Money*, 19.

which distinctive societal and political concerns defined how the issue was discussed and solutions were sought. Between 1796 and the mid-1800s, British writers were preoccupied with contrasting the British monetary system against the French experience of inconvertibility as they scrambled to defend the Bank Restriction by arguing that it was fundamentally different from the dismal failure of the French *assignat*. Supported by many political writers as well as economic ones, Britain's monetary exceptionalism offered a sufficiently convincing explanation for the legitimacy and sustainability of Britain's inconvertibility. Early signs of wartime inflation did not shake the basic tenet of this monetary exceptionalism, which was grounded in the voluntary acceptance of communal currency, and its critics such as Walter Boyd remained marginal figures. The deepening concerns about currency depreciation that manifested in the public discussion of smuggling and illegal currency trade heralded the second stage of paper-currency debate. Like the economic indicators of the exchange rate and the gold price, reports on smugglers' attempts to bring British guinea coins abroad were, at least by metallists, regarded as proof of international monetary adjustment in operation, indicating a depreciation of Britain's paper currency. Legal and political concerns about the illegal currency trade, as much as the theoretical debate on currency, provided impetus for the Bullion Committee's parliamentary inquiry into currency issues and the subsequent pamphlet wars on the subject. The intensity of the debate mirrored growing scepticism about the judiciousness of the Bank of England's dominance over the nation's currency as theoretical and legal opinions about currency matters polarised. As a result, it became increasingly difficult to maintain the solidarity of Britain's currency community in theory and in reality. Disintegration of the inconvertible currency system, the impact of which would have been catastrophic in wartime Britain, was narrowly avoided by the legislative measure of the Stanhope Act, which prohibited Britons from differentiating between paper and metallic currency. Through the Stanhope Act, which made the Bank note a quasi-legal tender, Britain's paper currency would in practice lose its voluntary foundation that contemporary writers had taken as the touchstone of the peculiarly British monetary system.

The Paper-Currency Debate

From 1790 until 1796, the main concern in the British currency discussion was the French *assignat*, and contemporary commentators' views on the French monetary experiment were swayed largely by their political creeds. James Mackintosh, a young admirer of the French Revolution, saw a sanguine prospect for the French paper currency when he wrote *Vindiciae Gallicae* (1791), believing that *assignats* would restore French public credit, which had been in decline during the last years of the *Ancien Régime*.[16] This ran counter to the views of Edmund Burke and other opponents of the revolution, who saw the *assignat* as a self-destructive financial chicanery that was precariously maintained by the oppressive measures of the revolutionary government.[17] As long as the British monetary system rested on the metallic standard, the contrast between the British and the French currency remained a plausible framework for both supporters and opponents to the French Revolution and its financial foundations. By 1796, however, Britain could no longer stand aloof from money-related concerns as various war-induced financial problems began to unfold. The snowballing public debt due to war financing aroused doubts over the soundness of Britain's financial system, which gave ammunition to critics abroad; the most formidable among them was Thomas Paine, a celebrated author and a proud citizen of revolutionary France. In his *Decline and Fall of the English System of Finance* (1796), Paine claimed that every war required one and half times as much money as the previous war and that the creation of an enormous amount of paper currency to finance the swelling national expenditure would inevitably drive up general prices, leading to the 'natural march of the funding system to its irredeemable dissolution'.[18] With the inflationary spiral, Paine predicted, the English financial system would collapse within twenty years.[19]

Paine's argument was a powerful rejoinder to Burke's early attack on French 'paper money despotism'.[20] In his *Reflections on the Revolution in*

---

[16] Steven Blakemore, *Intertextual War: Edmund Burke and the French Revolution in the Writings of Mary Wollstonecraft, Thomas Paine and James Mackintosh* (Madison, NJ, 1997), 204–6; James Mackintosh, *Vindiciae Gallicae: Defence of the French Revolution, and Its English Admirers, against the Accusations of the Right Hon. E. Burke* (London, 1791), 23–4, 60–4, 149–50.

[17] See Introduction.

[18] Thomas Paine, *The Decline and Fall of the English System of Finance* (Paris, 1796), 12–13. Paine's writing was based primarily on the monetary experience during the American Revolution. Financial topics were not foreign to him, and his early writing on paper currency was occasioned by a banking crisis in Philadelphia in 1786. Thomas Paine, 'Dissertations on Government, the Affairs of the Bank, and Paper-Money (1786)', in Philip S. Foner, ed., *The Complete Writings of Thomas Paine* (Philadelphia, 1945), ii, 367–439.

[19] In the period immediately following its publication, the British response was generally critical of Paine's argument. Gregory Claeys, *Thomas Paine: Social and Political Thought* (Boston, MA, 1989), 32–3; Harry T. Dickinson, 'Thomas Paine and His British Critics', *Enlightenment and Dissent*, 27 (2011), 31–2.

[20] Edmund Burke, *The Writings and Speeches of Edmund Burke*, viii: *The French Revolution*, ed. L. G. Mitchell and William B. Todd (Oxford, 1989), 278; J. G. A. Pocock, 'The

France, Burke castigated the French fiat paper-currency *assignat* by contrasting it to the Bank of England note, which circulated through the British nation's voluntary acceptance without any state coercion. Burke was never a wholehearted advocate of a paper-based economy, but he was willing to admit that paper circulation based on money users' choice was evidence of England's prosperity, a system of currency that was compatible with the spirit of the English constitution.[21] While acknowledging the British aversion to the state's arbitrary creation of paper currency, Paine did not accept Burke's distinction between England's voluntary paper and France's compulsory paper.[22] For Paine, the mode of currency acceptance was immaterial compared to the mode of repaying the state's debt that was securitised and circulated as paper currency. For that matter, Paine argued that what distinguished English finance from that of the French and American systems was the way it kept the accumulating debt 'out of sight' by postponing its repayment into the distant future.[23] The funded debt might prolong the life of the English system, Paine conceded, but the collapse was unavoidable nonetheless.

Against Paine's claim of having discovered the Newtonian law of war finance, his critics in Britain scrambled to defend English finance by reiterating the Burkean argument of English exceptionalism.[24] Daniel Wakefield questioned whether it was possible to compare English finance with French and American finances that were 'so opposite, so totally different'?[25] Similarly, Ralph Broome's attack on Paine was grounded in his distinction between two different systems of money based on compulsion and consent, or in his terminology *nolens* and *volens*.[26] Broome argued that Paine's prophesy was irrelevant to the financial system in England, where no paper was created without the nation's consent, and therefore the level of national indebtedness was maintained within what the nation could or was willing to absorb.[27] Simeon Pope of the Stock Exchange, another participant of the anti-Painite campaign, agreed that

Political Economy of Burke's Analysis of the French Revolution', *Historical Journal*, 25 (1982), 338.

[21] See Introduction. On Burke's ambivalence towards paper currency, see Tom Furniss, 'Burke, Paine, and the Language of Assignats', *Yearbook of English Studies*, 19 (1989), 63.

[22] Alfred Owen Aldridge, 'Why Did Thomas Paine Write on the Bank?', *Proceedings of the American Philosophical Society*, 93 (1949), 311.

[23] Paine, *Decline and Fall*, 3.

[24] Paine, *Decline and Fall*, 11; Mark Philp, *Paine* (Oxford, 1989), 79–81.

[25] Daniel Wakefield, *A Letter to Thomas Paine: In Reply to His Decline and Fall of the English System of Finance* (London, 1796), 24.

[26] Ralph Broome, *Observations on Mr Paine's Pamphlet, Entitled the Decline and Fall of the English System of Finance* (London, 1796), 56, 72; 'Review of Broome's Observations on Mr Paine's Pamphlet', *Gentleman's Magazine*, 80 (1796), 760.

[27] See also Dickinson, 'Thomas Paine and His British Critics', 31–2.

Britain's parliamentary oversight was the surest safeguard against the overgrowth of public debt. Pope wrote, 'Under the mild and happier sway of BRITAIN, where Finance rests not on the dictatorial mandate of a MONARCH, but originates with the REPRESENTATIVES of the PEOPLE – where every article of the Revenue is subject to be scrutinized in open Senate, and consequently with the eye of the whole nation'.[28] Generally, British critics of Paine believed that voluntary acceptance of the Bank of England note functioned as a sufficient check on the volume of monetary circulation, a system that was secured by the free government of Britain.[29] Under the democratic system of national finance, Lieutenant-Colonel James Chalmers added, in his *Strictures on a Pamphlet Written by Thomas Paine* (1796), the Bank of England Note had never been legal tender and had never been forced on its citizens.[30]

Contrary to Paine's ominous prognosis, Broome saw no danger in expanding paper currency as long as 'the people have faith in each other', and a similar opinion was expressed by English politicians and financiers at the time.[31] Not only was there a belief that paper currency should be expanded to keep pace with economic growth – an idea that was supported by Francis Baring, John Sinclair, Edward Tatham and the Earl of Rosse – there was also a growing concern that the Bank was failing to meet the nation's liquidity needs.[32] Following the introduction of credit rationing at the Bank in December 1795, which aimed at contracting its commercial discounts, Tatham called for greater credit creation by establishing a new national bank.[33] In the same vein, in 1798 the social

[28] Simeon Pope, *A Letter to the Right Hon. William Curtis, Lord Mayor of the City of London, on the National Debt and Resources of Great Britain* (London, 1796), 11.

[29] James Chalmers, *Strictures on a Pamphlet Written by Thomas Paine* (London, 1796), 28; Wakefield, *Letter to Thomas Paine*, 29.

[30] Chalmers, *Strictures*, 28. There is no direct evidence that Chalmers' pamphlet was sponsored by the British government despite the insinuation made by, for instance, Conway in *The Writings of Thomas Paine*, ed. Moncure Daniel Conway (New York, 1967), iii, 286. Cf. Claeys, *Thomas Paine*, 20.

[31] Broome, *Observations on Mr Paine's Pamphlet*, 45.

[32] Arnold D. Harvey, *Collision of Empires: Britain in Three World Wars, 1793–1945* (London, 1992), 77.

[33] John H. Clapham, *The Bank of England: A History* (Cambridge, 1944), i, 269. For example, see a group of London merchants' resolution on 2 April 1796 in the appendix of Boyd's pamphlet. Walter Boyd, *A Letter to the Right Honourable William Pitt: On the Influence of the Stoppage of Issues in Specie at the Bank of England, on the Prices of Provisions, and Other Commodities* (London, 1801), 86–90. The general opinion was that the temptation to overissue notes was stronger in the case of government notes than with notes issued by responsible corporation. Edward Tatham, *A Second Letter to the Right Hon. William Pitt, Chancellor of the Exchequer, on a National Bank* (London, 1797), 12 et seq. See also Francis Baring, *Observations on the Establishment of the Bank of England, and on the Paper Circulation of the Country* (London, 1797), 74; John Sinclair, *Letters Written to*

reformer Sir Frederick Eden announced his intention of establishing a new corporation, Globe Insurance, a multifunctional financial institution with the plan of handling insurance, taking deposits (for working-class customers) and issuing small-denomination notes.[34] For most of the 1790s, British commentators worried less about the expansion of paper currency than its being in short supply, dismissing Paine's critique as irrelevant to what Britain was experiencing.

The first glimpse of wartime inflation came in 1799, a year of bad harvest and high price of provisions.[35] According to Thomas Tooke, the wheat price rose from 71s 8d per Winchester quarter in May 1799 to 94s 2d at the end of the year, advancing further to 134s 5d by June 1800.[36] After a brief period of eased food supply during the summer, the grain price rose again until it reached 157s 2d in March 1801.[37] The situation spawned social instability, and there were more than a hundred food riots, notably in the Midlands and the south-west and north-west of England.[38] Initial discussions on the rise in food prices, such as the Select Committee on the High Price of Provisions, saw it as a problem solely concerning grain production. Thomas Malthus, in his 1800 pamphlet on the same subject, did consider monetary circulation, but only as a side effect rather than the cause of inflation.[39]

Since the suspension of cash payments, both supporters and opponents of the Bank Restriction had discussed the possibility of the Bank being tempted to overissue its notes under the system of inconvertible paper currency.[40] At the time, however, no one outside the Bank could

---

the Governor and Directors of the Bank of England on the Pecuniary Distresses of the Country (London, 1797), 28–30.

[34] Robin Pearson, Insuring the Industrial Revolution: Fire Insurance in Great Britain, 1700–1850 (Aldershot, 2004), 157. Due to the Bank's vigorous campaign, Globe Insurance was established as an insurance company without the note-issuing privilege. CD, 7 Nov. 1799, BE, G4/28, fol. 190; CD, 2 Apr. 1801, BE, G4/29, fol. 14.

[35] Donald Grove Barnes, A History of the English Corn Laws from 1660–1846 (London, 1930), 77–86; L. S. Pressnell, Country Banking in the Industrial Revolution (Oxford, 1956), 463.

[36] Thomas Tooke, History of Prices and of the State of Circulation (London, 1838), i, 214, 216. See also Alan Booth, 'Food Riots in the North-West of England 1790–1801', Past & Present (1977), 89.

[37] Tooke, History of Prices, i, 224.

[38] John Bohstedt, The Politics of Provisions: Food Riots, Moral Economy, and Market Transition in England, c.1550–1850 (Farnham, 2010), 190, 207. See also Mark Harrison, Crowds and History: Mass Phenomena in English Towns, 1790–1835 (Cambridge, 1988), 240.

[39] Frank W. Fetter, Development of British Monetary Orthodoxy, 1797–1875 (Cambridge, MA, 1965), 30; Thomas Robert Malthus, An Investigation of the Cause of the Present High Price of Provisions (London, 1800).

[40] Baring, Observations on the Establishment, 72; Sinclair, Letters Written to the Governor, 26.

speak confidently about the Bank's overissue because, after the 1797 parliamentary inquiry, the Bank had not provided any information regarding
the volume of its note issue. In December 1801, when Whig MP George
Tierney attributed the economic depression to the suspension of cash
payments, accusing the Bank of printing money to sustain 'the most
extravagant and unprincipled expenditure' by the state, he did not have
any solid evidence of the level of Bank-note circulation.[41] Henry
Thornton made an impassioned defence of the Bank against Tierney's
accusation, claiming that there was no overissue of Bank notes, nor was
there any direct link between the volume of paper currency and the price
of provisions.[42] Only after the parliamentary debate did the Bank issue a
statement on its note circulation, which showed that Bank-note circulation in December 1800 was 30 per cent greater than the three-year
average of 1792–5.[43]

Against British commentators' preoccupation with distinguishing
between the English and French currency regimes, banker and loan
contractor Walter Boyd, who had just returned from Paris in 1792,
became one of the first writers to challenge British currency
exceptionalism chiefly from an economic ground, though his discussion
had a clear political agenda. Boyd overturned the argument of British
currency exceptionalism by contending that the Bank Restriction Act,
which released the Bank from its obligation to make cash payments,
made the Bank note a forced currency as it no longer rested on 'pure,
unmixed confidence'.[44] In doing so, Boyd cleared the ground for discussing the British inconvertible-currency system by drawing upon the
quantity theory of money, a theory that British writers so far had applied
only to the 'forced' paper currency in France. Boyd wrote the major part
of his pamphlet *Letter to the Right Honourable William Pitt* in
November 1800 without having the benefit of the Bank's statement on
note circulation.[45] He therefore based his text on the conjecture that note

---

[41] *Parliamentary Register*, xiii (1800), 279.   [42] *Parliamentary Register*, xiii (1800), 303.

[43] Boyd, *Letter to Pitt*, p. iv.; House of Commons, 'An Account of the Amount of Bank of
England Notes in Circulation, 15 December 1800', in Sheila Lambert, ed., *House of
Commons Sessional Papers of the Eighteenth Century*, cxxx: *Reports and Papers (1715–1800)*
(Wilmington, DE, 1975), 585–6.

[44] Arie Arnon, *Monetary Theory and Policy from Hume and Smith to Wicksell: Money, Credit,
and the Economy* (Cambridge, 2011), 82; Boyd, *Letter to Pitt*, 48.

[45] Boyd, whose previously successful loan-contracting business collapsed in 1800, had an
axe to grind against the Bank, which did not rescue his firm. Clapham, *Bank of England*,
ii, 16, 40; S. R. Cope, *Walter Boyd: A Merchant Banker in the Age of Napoleon*
(Gloucester, 1983), 95–9. For Boyd's early expression of his views on currency, see
House of Commons, *Reports from the Committee of Secrecy on the Outstanding Demands of
the Bank and the Restriction of Cash Payments* (1797), 35–9; House of Lords, *Report of the
Lords' Committee of Secrecy* (1797), 106–17.

issue had increased substantially after the suspension and, based on this supposition, he attributed the ongoing inflation to the workings of a 'universally recognised' principle: that an undue argumentation of a nation's circulating media, without being called for by expanding industry and trade, would invariably lead to currency depreciation. This was a classic statement of the quantity theory of money as developed by David Hume, Richard Cantillon and Joseph Harris.[46] Largely because of the lack of available data, Boyd stumbled upon what became the bullionists' two touchstones of currency depreciation: an increase in the price of gold and a drop in the exchange rate. From these two symptoms of currency devaluation Boyd deduced an overissue of Bank notes, the multiplication of the 'representative signs of money'.[47] These two tests of devaluation were later adopted by bullionists like Lord King and David Ricardo and eventually attained the status of monetary orthodoxy. It should also be pointed out that Boyd's theoretical exposition of the causal link between the value of currency, the international price of gold and the exchange rate was tied up with Boyd's *political* argument that the Bank reaped benefit from circulating an excessive amount of paper currency. The Bank's circulation figures, only made public when he was finishing the pamphlet, convinced Boyd that both his theoretical and his political claims were vindicated.[48] Boyd's quantity theory of money had the strength of being simple and clear, but such features did not necessarily appeal to those who were conversant with the intricacies of the banking world.

Francis Baring, a leading London banker, retorted to Boyd's claim that the Bank's overissue was the cause of general inflation, arguing that the £3 million increase in the Bank-note circulation was too small to affect the general price level in the British economy.[49] Baring did not dispute the plausibility of quantity theory, but he argued that the quantity of circulating media would cause inflation only when paper circulation was pushed 'much beyond reasonable and proper bounds'.[50] As if to prove Baring's point, the exchange rate for the pound sterling on the Hamburg exchange saw a favourable turn in early January 1801, but such evidence did not terminate the debate in which theory was hardly separate from political views.[51] The debate over currency exceptionalism, which

[46] Boyd, *Letter to Pitt*, 7; D. P. O'Brien, *The Classical Economists Revisited* (Princeton, NJ, 2004), 169–70.

[47] Boyd, *Letter to Pitt*, 3–7, 25–32.   [48] Boyd, *Letter to Pitt*, p. iv.

[49] Francis Baring, *Observations on the Publication of Walter Boyd* (London, 1801), 10–11; Boyd, *Letter to Pitt*, 3.

[50] Baring, *Observations on the Publication of Walter Boyd*, 6.

[51] *Anti-Jacobin*, Feb. 1801, 184; Baring, *Observations on the Publication of Walter Boyd*, 20–1.

formed the British response to Paine's 1796 pamphlet, continued to define the terms of the discussion. Boyd and his followers, such as William Frend, believed that the difference between English paper credit and that in France and America was one of degree – the degree of disparity between the metallic reserve and the paper issue – as they recognised no fundamental dissimilarity between them.[52] On the other hand, Thomas Surr, a writer who was also a clerk in the Bank of England's drawing office, insisted on the distinctive nature of Britain's paper circulation, a contention supported by his elaborate account of the process of the Bank's note issue.[53] Contradicting Boyd's accusation that the Bank profited by printing notes, Surr contended that the Bank created paper currency only in response to the need for commercial discounting, bullion purchases, dividend payments and advances for businesses and the government.[54] As long as the Bank limited its note issue to this responsive mode, there was no abuse of its note-issuing privilege, no forced circulation of paper. Surr's belief in the judicious management of the Bank's note issue echoed the abstract trust in the Bank's prudential operation.[55] In terms of his theoretical outlook, Surr's discussion of the Bank's self-regulation was broadly based on the so-called real-bills doctrine, most famously set out in Adam Smith's *Wealth of Nations*.[56] According to this doctrine, as long as banks avoided accepting 'fictitious' bills for pure credit creation and only took bills that were based on 'real' transactions, their paper issue would be kept within proper limits and the value of notes would be maintained.[57] In his

---

[52] William Frend, *The Effect of Paper Money on the Price of Provisions: Or, the Point in Dispute between Mr Boyd and Sir Francis Baring Examined* (London, 1801), 16.

[53] Surr is listed as a junior clerk in CD, 30 Apr. 1801, BE, G4/29, fol. 32.

[54] Thomas Surr, *Refutation of Certain Misrepresentations Relative to the Nature and Influence of Bank Notes* (London, 1801), 23–7.

[55] Abramson notes that the Bank's organisational culture of trust and duty, rather than competence and initiative, remained its primary trait. Daniel M. Abramson, *Building the Bank of England: Money, Architecture, Society, 1694–1942* (New Haven, CT, 2005), 168.

[56] Surr, *Refutation of Certain Misrepresentations*, 23.

[57] Adam Smith, *An Inquiry into the Nature and Causes of the Wealth of Nations*, ed. R. H. Campbell, A. S. Skinner, and W. B. Todd (Oxford, 1976), 304. The real-bills doctrine has been extensively discussed in numerous studies. Arnon, *Monetary Theory and Policy*, 40–4; David Glasner, 'The Real-Bills Doctrine in the Light of the Law of Reflux', *History of Political Economy*, 24 (1992), 867–94; David Laidler, 'Misconceptions about the Real-Bills Doctrine: A Comment on Sargent and Wallace', *Journal of Political Economy*, 92 (1984), 149–55; Nick Mayhew, 'The Quantity Theory of Money in Historical Perspective', in Mark Casson and Nigar Hashimzade, eds., *Large Databases in Economic History: Research Methods and Case Studies* (London, 2013), 62–96; Lloyd W. Mints, *A History of Banking Theory in Great Britain and the United States* (Chicago, IL, 1945), 25–30; O'Brien, *Classical Economists Revisited*, 179–81; Morris Perlman, 'Adam Smith and the Paternity of the Real Bills Doctrine', *History of Political Economy*, 21 (1989), 77–90; Thomas J. Sargent and Neil Wallace, 'The Real-Bills Doctrine versus

account of the Bank's currency creation, Surr acknowledged this doctrine as the guideline for the Bank's discounting business, constituting an essential part of the Bank's judicious management of note issue. This was one of the earliest expressions of what later came to be known as anti-bullionism.[58]

At the beginning of the 1800s, the broad contours of the paper currency debate gradually emerged, with competing ideas about the nature and effect of inconvertible currency discussed in the British context. The French monetary experience still cast a deep shadow on the British debate, but early English currency exceptionalism came under attack not only from Paine and his followers but also from those like Boyd who tried to explain the new monetary regime by extending the metallist monetary theories of previous generations. In response, advocates of inconvertibility elaborated what they believed to be the distinctive features of Britain's paper currency. Surr sardonically remarked that Frend's conflation of the French *assignat* and the Bank of England note was based on the crude idea that they were comparable because both *assignats* and Bank notes were made of paper. Such a false comparison would, Surr continued, only persuade 'an ignorant mob' who had no 'patience to be told the difference of their [Bank of England notes] origin and value'.[59] The disagreement over inconvertible paper was much deeper rooted than a mere lack of understanding about the Bank's note-issuing process. It was ultimately grounded in the long struggle between metallist and non-metallist ideas of money, and the chasm between the two would widen over the following decades.

Theorising Confidence: Henry Thornton

In many ways, Henry Thornton's *An Enquiry into the Nature and Effects of the Paper Credit* (1802) was a culmination of British intellectual engagement with paper currency through the long eighteenth century. This seminal work's contribution to the field of banking and monetary theory was wide ranging. For one thing, the book shifted the general discussion on paper currency away from somewhat naive trust in the Bank's judicious management to what was more akin to modern central banking

---

the Quantity Theory: A Reconsideration', *Journal of Political Economy*, 90 (1982), 1212–36.

[58] Murray N. Rothbard, *Classical Economics: An Austrian Perspective on the History of Economic Thought* (Cheltenham, 1995), ii, 168–9. A similar view was expressed by Boase: Henry Boase, *Guineas an Unnecessary and Expensive Incumbrance on Commerce; Or, the Impolicy of Repealing the Bank Restriction Bill* (London, 1802).

[59] Surr, *Refutation of Certain Misrepresentations*, 27–8.

principles.[60] An embryonic idea of the Bank being the lender of last resort had already appeared in Baring's 1797 pamphlet, but it was Thornton who gave the idea a more systematic expression.[61] Thornton, a prominent banker, an independent MP and a leading figure of the evangelical Anglican group Clapham Sect, was widely acknowledged as an authority on monetary issues by his contemporaries.[62] His understanding of banking and finance was firmly grounded in his first-hand experience as a London banker, which included acting as an agent for a number of provincial banks and the Royal Bank of Scotland. Thornton's extensive knowledge about the nation's banking system and its workings was amply demonstrated by his evidence given to the 1797 parliamentary committee on the Bank's financial situation, in which he offered a lucid account of the Bank's distinctive position in the nation's finance. In times of economic distress, Thornton explained, it was generally wise for private banks to reduce their note circulation to weather the storm, but the same strategy did not always apply to the Bank of England because its existence was deeply intertwined with public credit.[63] Under 'external' drain (asset outflow to foreign markets), the Bank had a legitimate reason to contract its credit to protect the domestic market; in the case of 'internal' drain (demand for liquidity from the domestic market), however, the Bank ought to act as a provider of liquidity.[64] In order to make the right choice between contractionary and expansionary policies, the Bank needed to always keep an eye on the general price level, the demand for commercial discounts, the international price of gold and exchange rates. As financial historian Arie Arnon states, Thornton's major contribution to economic literature was his clear statement on the need for the Bank of England to 'implement discretion, that is, monetary policy'.[65] The Bank would only embrace these responsibilities, Thornton pointed

[60] Friedrich A. von Hayek, 'Introduction', in Friedrich A. von Hayek, ed., *An Enquiry into the Nature and Effects of the Paper Credit of Great Britain (1802)* (London, 1939), 11–63.

[61] Thomas M. Humphrey, 'The Classical Concept of the Lender of Last Resort', *Federal Reserve Bank of Richmond Economic Review*, 61 (1975), 3–5; D. P. O'Brien, 'The Lender-of-Last-Resort Concept in Britain', *History of Political Economy*, 35 (2003), 2–5.

[62] Ernest Marshall Howse, *Saints in Politics: The 'Clapham Sect' and the Growth of Freedom* (London, 1971); Standish Meacham, *Henry Thornton of Clapham, 1760–1815* (Cambridge, 1964); Charles F. Peake, 'Henry Thornton and the Development of Ricardo's Economic Thought', *History of Political Economy*, 10 (1978), 193–212; Neil T. Skaggs, 'Thomas Tooke, Henry Thornton, and the Development of British Monetary Orthodoxy', *Journal of the History of Economic Thought*, 25 (2003), 177–97.

[63] House of Commons, *1797 Commons Committee on the Outstanding Demands of the Bank*, 76–9.

[64] Neil T. Skaggs, 'Henry Thornton and the Development of Classical Monetary Economics', *Canadian Journal of Economics*, 28 (1995), 1214–20.

[65] Arnon, *Monetary Theory and Policy*, 99.

out, if it recognised that it had 'no safety for themselves, except by seeking it in the safety of the commercial world, in the general support of Government credit, and of the general prosperity of the Nation'.[66] As the Bank's safety and the stability of public credit were inseparable, there was no temptation for the Bank to overissue its notes – an argument that effectively countered Boyd's accusation of profit-driven expansion of note issue.[67]

Thornton's modern analysis of English currency and banking was equally accompanied by an element of continuity from the currency debate in the 1790s. He characterised the Bank of England as independent from the government, sharply distinguishing it from the banks of Petersburg, Copenhagen, Stockholm, Vienna, Madrid and Lisbon, which were, according to Thornton, 'all in the most and strict sense government banks'.[68] These government banks were often subjected to pressure from their political masters, who were tempted to increase note circulation in times of financial hardship, and there was no mechanism to correct politically motivated overissue of paper currency.[69] In contrast, the Bank of England was largely free from direct meddling from the government; hence there was 'a fundamental difference between the paper of the Bank of England, and that of all the national or government banks on the continent'.[70] Another contemporary idea Thornton adopted from previous British monetary discussions was voluntary currency acceptance. Diametrically opposing Boyd's contention that the Bank Restriction had fundamentally changed the character of English paper currency to a forced currency, Thornton argued that the voluntary agreement was the foundation of the new monetary regime of inconvertible currency.

There is, indeed, both among them [the Bank proprietors] and among the whole commercial world, who make so large a portion of this country, a remarkable determination to sustain credit, and especially the credit of the bank; and this

---

[66] House of Commons, *1797 Commons Committee on the Outstanding Demands of the Bank*, 77.

[67] Thornton's criticism against Boyd was chiefly at the factual level of overissue. Thornton maintained that the alleged increase of the Bank-note issue could largely be attributed to the substitution of coins by small notes – around £2 million – and when that was taken into consideration, the increased quantity of the Bank note was only moderate. Henry Thornton, *An Enquiry into the Nature and Effects of the Paper Credit of Great Britain* (London, 1802), 312–13.

[68] Thornton, *Paper Credit*, 61–7. He maintained the distinction between the British and the French paper currencies in later speeches. Henry Thornton, *Substance of Two Speeches of Henry Thornton in the House of Commons, on the Report of the Bullion Committee* (London, 1811), 33–9.

[69] Thornton, *Paper Credit*, 63–4, 188–90.   [70] Thornton, *Paper Credit*, 65–6.

general agreement to support the bank is one of the pillars of its strength, and one pledge of its safety.[71]

Thornton's emphasis on collective will ('determination') and communal consensus ('agreement') resonated with the contemporary discussion on confidence as the foundation of credit-based currency. Joseph Smith, for instance, argued that 'active' confidence was the essence of public credit and any increase in paper circulation stemmed chiefly from 'the mutual confidence and convenience of the people'.[72] Confidence was at the heart of Thornton's analysis of contemporary monetary circulation and of his genealogical account of the development of commercial credit. When confidence rose to a certain height in a country, Thornton wrote, paper currency gained ground and began to circulate widely.[73] Still, the traditional vocabulary was modified by Thornton, who elaborated the function of confidence in a way that aligned with his analysis of the financial system. In contrast to Burke and the anti-Painite English writers, who regarded public confidence in the voluntary currency as a guarantee of monetary stability, Thornton saw two dimensions of confidence: its static and its dynamic dimensions. The value of inconvertible currency at any point of time was determined, as Thornton stated, by the combination of the level of confidence/credit and the state of note circulation: 'A non-convertible Paper *which is limited* and is in full credit may maintain its price just as if it were convertible'.[74] Confidence and note circulation had a dynamic relation as the velocity of note circulation was affected by the level of confidence.[75] In other words, Thornton redefined the traditional language of confidence to refer to what modern economists call liquidity preference, which determines the velocity of circulation.[76] He thus gave a new lease of life to the language of confidence by giving it a place in his systematic analysis of the financial system.

Thornton was an outstanding theorist of banking and currency, a pragmatic banker and an active politician, whose views were firmly grounded in his empirical observation of Britain's financial world. Pragmatism dominated his theoretical discussion, including that related

[71] Thornton, *Paper Credit*, 68.

[72] Joseph Smith, *An Examination of Mr Paine's Decline and Fall of the English System of Finance* (London, 1796), 22–4, 31.

[73] Thornton, *Paper Credit*, 13, 37.

[74] Friedrich A. von Hayek, 'Manuscript Notes by Henry Thornton to Thoughts on the Effects of the Bank Restrictions by Lord King', in Hayek, *Paper Credit of Great Britain (1802)*, 317.

[75] Thornton, *Paper Credit*, 47–8.

[76] Friedrich A. von Hayek, *The Collected Works of F. A. Hayek*, iii: *The Trend of Economic Thinking: Essays on Political Economists and Economic History*, eds. W. W. Bartley III and Stephen Kresge (Abingdon, 1991), 342.

to the Bank of England's fiscal and monetary operations, though his roundabout writing style tended to obscure his policy recommendations. For instance, Thornton stated that it was possible to substitute metallic currency with paper currency based on 'the general confidence which may be inspired by the agreement of bankers and other leading persons to take them'.[77] However, his statement had the proviso that 'the issues are moderate, and the balance of trade is not very unfavourable to the country'. Therefore, Thornton admitted the possibility of price inflation through excessive note issue, whereas the connection between the volume of note circulation and currency devaluation was seen as less immediate than in the accounts put forward by the advocates of the quantity theory of money.[78] Thornton's eclectic theoretical standpoint can also be observed in his attitude towards the metallic standard: although he did not consider convertibility to be a fundamental requirement for a stable currency, he was ready to acknowledge that the metallic standard might be employed as a stabilising mechanism. For his instrumental view on the metallic standard, Thornton was a practical bullionist rather than a theoretical bullionist.[79]

In contrast to Thornton's cautious mix of new theoretical perspectives and pragmatic policy prescription under the Bank Restriction, Lord Peter King was driven more strongly by his political agenda and his claim of theoretical legitimacy for the metallist tradition. King's theoretical argument was similar to Boyd's in that he focused on the gold price and the exchange rate as the two principal indicators of the Bank's overissue. As a proud descendant of John Locke's family, King's quantity theory of money was inseparably linked with liberal political thinking that viewed any political intervention into monetary value with suspicion or disdain. For that matter, his bullionism was closer to late seventeenth-century metallism than to the Humean quantity theory of money. Translated into policy terms, King's bullionism aimed to limit the Bank's political power by minimising its discretion in currency creation, just as Locke had tried to limit the sovereign's power to manipulate monetary value. For King, the Bank's discretionary power could only be effectively limited by putting it under the obligation of convertibility. He was much less concerned about the voluntary nature of English paper currency than his contemporaries

---

[77] Thornton, *Paper Credit*, 87–90; Neil T. Skaggs, 'Credit Where Credit Is Due: Henry Thornton and the Evolution of the Theory of Fiduciary Money', *History of Political Economy*, 44 (2012), 458–9.

[78] Thornton, *Paper Credit*, 280–2.

[79] 'Practical metallist' is a term used by Schumpeter to describe theoretical and practical levels of metallism and chartalism/cartalism. Joseph A. Schumpeter, *History of Economic Analysis* (London, 1954), 288.

because, for him, any system of inconvertible currency was illegitimate.[80] The 'unlimited paper currency of the bank' King wrote 'is, in itself, directly repugnant to every just and sound principle of political economy'.[81] While wartime exigencies made an immediate return to convertibility an impractical policy option, King took every opportunity at parliament to keep the Bank's activities in check.[82]

The broad social and economic situation served to polarise the British debate on paper currency. The Peace Treaty of Amiens in March 1802 improved the exchange rate of the pound sterling on the Hamburg market, a situation that lasted until 1805.[83] The favourable exchange buoyed the English economy, but this economic upturn did not extend to Ireland and the monetary issues there became a major agenda in the post-Union British parliament. Before 1797, thirteen Irish pounds were worth twelve British pounds. Over the subsequent five years, the Irish pound depreciated against the British pound, a trend that was accelerated when the latter's value rose on the international market in 1802. The premium on the British pound increased from 7–8 per cent prior to the suspension to 12 per cent in early 1803, reaching 20 per cent later that year.[84] The rapid depreciation of the Irish pound led to the establishment of a parliamentary committee in March 1804, and King took an active interest in the Irish currency problem partly as an absentee landlord and partly as a monetary polemicist.[85] The Irish case provided a good illustration of how overissue of currency caused a depression of the exchange rate, a causal connection underlined in King's pamphlet *Thoughts on the Restriction of Payments in Specie at the Banks of England and Ireland*, published in 1803.[86] That the Irish currency committee's report, to

[80] Peter King, *Thoughts on the Restriction of Payments in Specie at the Banks of England and Ireland* (London, 1803), 4–5; Hayek, 'Manuscript Notes', 313.

[81] *Parliamentary Register*, ii (1802), 78.

[82] He led parliament pressure on the Bank to regularly report its note circulation, at a time when the Bank was not officially required to submit annual accounts to parliament. See, for example, *Parliamentary Register*, i (1805), 308.

[83] Frank W. Fetter, *The Irish Pound 1797–1826: A Reprint of the Report of the Committee of 1804 of the British House of Commons on the Condition of the Irish Currency* (London, 1955), 26.

[84] Fetter, *Irish Pound*, 21–5; House of Commons, *Appendix to Minutes of Irish Exchange Committee* (1804), appendix A, 1; George O'Brien, 'The Last Years of the Irish Currency', *Economic Journal*, 37 (1927), 250–1.

[85] Hansard, 1st ser., i (1803–4), cols. 662–3.

[86] A revised edition of the pamphlet was published in the following year as *Thoughts on the Effects of the Bank Restrictions*, 2nd ed. (London, 1804). On King, see Clapham, *Bank of England*, i, 22; Fetter, *Irish Pound*, 25; F. G. Hall, *The Bank of Ireland, 1783–1946* (Dublin, 1949), 87. See also *The Horner Papers: Selections from the Letters and Miscellaneous Writings of Francis Horner, MP 1795–1817*, ed. Kenneth Bourne and William Banks Taylor (Edinburgh, 1994), 328–9. An anti-bullionist response to

which Thornton was the leading contributor, attributed the Irish currency's depreciation to the Bank of Ireland's overissue, appeared to King as confirmation of his metallist theory.[87] However, the Irish currency report cannot be read as an official endorsement of metallism, let alone as evidence for Thornton's support for the quantity theory of money. To be sure, Thornton did not subscribe to the extreme psychologism of the London merchant Borrows, who stated before the committee that the depreciation of the Irish currency was due to a loss of confidence.[88] Yet, the extent of the increase in Irish note issue – the Bank of Ireland's note circulation rose from £621,917 in January 1797 to £2,986,999 in January 1804 – was such that even those who did not uphold the strict correspondence between note issue and monetary value would point to overissue as a cause of the Irish paper currency's depreciation.[89] By any standard, a more than fourfold increase in paper circulation clearly fits Thornton's acknowledgment of the inflationary tendency arising from paper circulation beyond a 'moderate' amount, but this hardly constitutes a wholehearted support of the quantity theory of money.[90]

In the early 1800s, what started as esoteric discussions on currency steadily broadened their audience.[91] One particularly influential format that contributed to the popularisation of the debate was contemporary review literature. New review periodicals, such as the *Edinburgh Review*, first published in 1802, gained a wide readership by offering an intellectual tool for the reading public to navigate the diverse knowledge, opinions and views expressed in ever-growing published volumes on literature, science, politics and economic issues. The *Edinburgh Review*,

---

King's pamphlet came from Boase. Boase, *Guineas an Unnecessary and Expensive Incumbrance*; D. P. O'Brien, ed., *Foundations of Monetary Economics*, iii: *The Anti-Bullionists* (London, 1994), pp. viii–x.

[87] Fetter, *British Monetary Orthodoxy*, 39; Fetter, *Irish Pound*, 45.

[88] House of Commons, *Select Committee on State of Ireland as to Circulating Paper, Specie and Current Coin, and Exchange between Ireland and Great Britain* (1804), 11–12. Ó Gráda's analysis of the Irish monetary depreciation attributes its cause to pressure from the Irish government on the Bank of Ireland to expand note circulation. Cormac Ó Gráda, 'Reassessing the Irish Pound Report of 1804', *Bulletin of Economic Research*, 43 (1991), 5–19. See also Fetter, *Irish Pound*, 42–4, 82.

[89] O'Brien, 'Last Years of the Irish Currency', 250; Ó Gráda, 'Reassessing the Irish Pound Report', 9–11.

[90] The committee's recommendations – a remedy suggested also by King, Henry Parnell and John Leslie Foster – of suppressing Irish note issue and obliging the Bank of Ireland to redeem its notes by Bank of England note were not adopted, but the Dublin–London exchange improved in late 1804. Fetter, *Irish Pound*, 52–3, 55–60; O'Brien, 'Last Years of the Irish Currency', 252–3.

[91] Alexander Dick, *Romanticism and the Gold Standard: Money, Literature, and Economic Debate in Britain 1790–1830* (Basingstoke, 2013), 63; Francis Horner, 'Thornton on the Paper Credit of Great Britain', *Edinburgh Review*, 1 (1802), 172–4.

with its distinctive leaning towards the Scottish Enlightenment and Whig politics, was a major outlet for the emerging monetary debate. Francis Horner, a lawyer and a student of Dugald Stewart, wrote an in-depth review of Thornton's *Paper Credit* in the inaugural issue of the *Edinburgh Review*.[92] Horner's summary of *Paper Credit*, while written in a more easily digestible style, reframed Thornton's argument in a way that brought Thornton much closer to the metallist position by highlighting the danger of overissue by the Bank of England.[93] To Horner, Thornton's book was a building block in the construction of his own theoretical exposition on paper currency. Such was the discursive style of contemporary review literature, and Horner felt no qualm about digressing from a faithful representation of Thornton's theoretical outlook. Horner repeated the same intellectual exercise in his review of King's *Thoughts on the Restriction* a year later in the same periodical.[94] Again, King's rigid bullionism was tempered by Horner's explanation of additional causes of currency devaluation other than overissue, while Horner maintained King's 'two simple and satisfactory tests' of devaluation (i.e. the gold price and the foreign exchange).

In his two reviews, Horner paid particular attention to the role of the Bank of England within the nation's currency and banking system. Thornton's description of the linkage between the Bank of England and country banks clearly made a strong impression on Horner, based on which he developed his own ideas about policy prescription for the Bank. After pointing out that the issue of country banknotes was limited by 'their accustomed convertibility' into the Bank note, Horner explained that the Bank of England's regulation of its note issue virtually served as a check upon country banks' note circulation. He continued,

If the Bank of England must now be considered as a national establishment, not merely influencing, by the superior magnitude of its capital, the state of

---

[92] Horner, 'Thornton on the Paper Credit', 172–201.

[93] Biancamaria Fontana, *Rethinking the Politics of Commercial Society: The Edinburgh Review 1802–1832* (Cambridge, 1985), 57; *Memoirs and Correspondence of Francis Horner MP*, ed. Leonard Horner (London, 1843), i, 203; Horner, 'Thornton on the Paper Credit', 176. Horner set himself apart from the two extreme views on currency – one based solely on confidence and one based on metallic basis alone – and advocated a 'well-regulated paper currency'. Donald Rutherford, *In the Shadow of Adam Smith: Founders of Scottish Economics, 1700–1900* (Basingstoke, 2012), 91. *Edinburgh Review* writers' general leaning towards metallism can be seen in Brougham's scathing attack on Boase's pamphlet. Henry Brougham, 'Review of *Guineas an Unnecessary and Expensive Incumbrance on Commerce*', *Edinburgh Review*, 2 (1802), 101–16. See also, *Horner Papers*, 278–80.

[94] Francis Horner, 'Review of Lord King's *Thoughts on the Restriction of Payments in Specie at the Banks of England and Ireland*', *Edinburgh Review*, 2 (1803), 402–21.

commercial circulation, but guiding its movements according to views of public policy, an important revolution has taken place since the first erection of that corporation as a banking establishment.[95]

Horner reiterated the same point in his review of Lord King's pamphlet, referring to Thornton's 'excellent work' that elucidated 'in what manner the higher branches of national currency regulate and limit the rest'.[96] This was in fact a narrative rather than a descriptive statement with a hint of speculative history in the tradition of the Scottish Enlightenment, which Horner was familiar with. Horner was at his best when he translated theory into policy recommendations, as he expressed in much clearer terms than Thornton the need for the Bank of England's active involvement in monetary policy. As far as the Bank's role in implementing control of paper circulation was concerned, Horner and Thornton were in full agreement, likewise in their shared understanding that the Bank's expanding role called for a closer scrutiny of its operation. In fact, the two-pronged policy agenda – the Bank's greater oversight of the monetary system and public scrutiny – was pursued through Horner's and Thornton's parliamentary activities. In 1807, Thornton led a parliamentary inquiry into the Bank's role in public finance, probing the profits that the Bank derived from the management of public funds.[97] Horner would also bring his theoretical discussion into the policy field to cause a major parliamentary debate on paper currency. Theoretical discussion, for Thornton and Horner, never entirely belonged to the realm of metaphysics but was inseparable from their ambition of restructuring national finance involving the government, the Bank and parliamentary oversight.[98]

The internationalisation of finance was another major factor that defined the agenda in theory and policy discussions at a time when cross-border movements of capital had a direct bearing on the real economy and how it was understood in theory. In late 1807, as a result of the Portuguese royal family fleeing to Rio from Napoleon's aggression, new markets opened in South America, which was welcomed in Britain as a breakthrough for the country's industry and trade, which had suffered from the loss of international trade due to Napoleon's

[95] Horner, 'Thornton on the Paper Credit', 196; see also, Arnon, *Monetary Theory and Policy*, 109.

[96] Horner, 'Review of Lord King's *Thoughts on the Restriction*', 404.

[97] Ian C. Bradley, 'The Politics of Godliness: Evangelicals in Parliament, 1784–1832' (unpublished DPhil, University of Oxford, 1974), 146.

[98] Philip Harling, *The Waning of 'Old Corruption': The Politics of Economical Reform in Britain, 1779–1846* (Oxford, 1996), 109, 130.

Continental blockade and the American Non-Intercourse Act.[99] The ensuing speculative boom coincided with a trade upswing – the combined value of domestic exports and re-exports increased by nearly 40 per cent between 1808 and 1809.[100] The boom turned out to be a momentary blip, and an economic slump soon set in.[101] As early as the end of 1808, the price of gold began to edge up, and, and, the market price of gold being now more than £4, it diverged from the Mint price of £3 17s 10½d.[102] Simultaneously, £2 million worth of bullion reserve left the Bank's vault within six months from February 1808.[103] The ominous climate was ripe for metallists to renew their attack on the Bank Restriction. The new phase of the debate over inconvertibility was spearheaded by the successful financier David Ricardo (at the time a minor figure in the theoretical debate). Ricardo's series of letters to the *Morning Chronicle*, the first of which was in August 1809, was a full-frontal attack on the Bank's note issue, as he believed that there were clear signs that the Bank's money creation was excessive.[104] With the market price of gold having risen to £4 13s – 20 per cent higher than the Mint price – when the exchange rate turned against the pound sterling, Ricardo argued that this was a demonstration of currency depreciation caused by the Bank's overissue.[105]

Why was it the business of the Bank to regulate its note issue for the sake of stabilising the value of currency? Like Boyd and Lord King, Ricardo thought it reprehensible for the Bank to put its own interest before the stability of the nation's currency. He argued that the Bank's overissue was disrupting the monetary system by overflowing the economy with excess currency, which not only led to an unfavourable exchange but also stimulated an additional outflow of precious metal as merchants were lured into exporting British coins to profit from the high price of gold abroad. As a consequence, Britain's metallic currency

---

[99] Arthur D. Gayer, W. W. Rostow and Anna Jacobson Schwartz, *The Growth and Fluctuation of the British Economy, 1790–1850: An Historical, Statistical and Theoretical Study of Britain's Economic Development* (Hassocks, 1975), i, 91–7.

[100] William Smart, *Economic Annals of the Nineteenth Century* (London, 1910), i, 184, 203–4.

[101] Smart, *Economic Annals*, i, 226–7.

[102] House of Commons, *Report from the Select Committee on the High Price of Gold Bullion* (1810), 1. The information on the market price of gold before 1811 is incomplete. See R. G. Hawtrey, *Currency and Credit* (London, 1919), 276.

[103] House of Commons, *Second Report from the Secret Committee on Commercial Distress* (1847–8), appendix, 8; Clapham, *Bank of England*, ii, 19.

[104] *Morning Chronicle*, 29 Aug. 1809, 20 Sept. 1809 and 20 Nov. 1809. Fetter, *British Monetary Orthodoxy*, 28.

[105] Timothy S. Davis, *Ricardo's Macroeconomics: Money, Trade Cycles and Growth* (Cambridge, 2005), 12; House of Commons, *Bullion Committee Report* (1810), 1.

became scarcer, creating difficulties for internal as well as external trades. Previously, the obligation to pay in cash prevented the Bank from pursuing an expansionary policy, but the Bank Restriction took that corrective mechanism away. Ricardo further argued that the devaluation of Bank notes would harm the Bank's own business because it would also have to pay an ever-greater price for gold bars in the course of its business. In that scenario, printing more Bank notes would not work because, as Thornton described (subsequently quoted by Ricardo), the temptation for merchants and profiteers to melt down coins and send bullion to foreign markets would increase in step with the currency devaluation.[106] This discussion of illegal exportation of coins was, in fact, anything but hypothetical. Indeed, the illegal guinea trade was a pressing problem when Ricardo and his contemporaries set out what was to become one of the most celebrated debates on paper currency.

Selling Money: The De Yonge and Wright Cases

In November 1809, Prime Minister Spencer Perceval informed the Treasury board that some Dutchmen were purchasing a considerable amount of guinea coins 'at a price much above its current value'.[107] Alerted, the Treasury instructed the Mint, which was in charge of coin-related offences, to be vigilant against such activities.[108] Caleb Powell, assistant solicitor to the Mint, immediately set to work, and in the following month, he sent two of his employers to the house of James De Yonge in Aldgate, one of London's Jewish neighbourhoods.[109] The Mint's agents introduced themselves as Call and Bushe, a supercargo of a Dutch vessel and his Italian interpreter, seeking to buy guineas. Negotiation concluded, and the two agent provocateurs purchased fifty pieces of guinea coins, at the price of £57 5s – paying a premium of

---

[106] In his pamphlet *The High Price of Bullion*, the preface of which was dated December 1809, Ricardo further explained the operation of melting coins by quoting Smith and Thornton. David Ricardo, *The High Price of Bullion: A Proof of the Depreciation of Bank Notes* (London, 1810), 9; Thornton, *Paper Credit*, 125.

[107] Treasury board minute book, 14 Nov. 1809, TNA T 29/103, fol. 167.

[108] Denis Gray, *Spencer Perceval: The Evangelical Prime Minister, 1762–1812* (Manchester, 1963), 368. In September 1809, Lord Folkestone noted that guineas changed hands at a value equivalent to 22 shillings. *The Creevey Papers: A Selection from the Correspondence and Diaries of the Late Thomas Creevey*, ed. Herbert Maxwell (London, 1903), i, 97.

[109] *English Reports*, civ, 657. Around 1809–11, activity of the solicitors at the mint reached such a high point that the expenditure of the prosecution amounted to around £3,000 a year. Royal Mint record book (1809–12), TNA, MINT 1/16–17. Expenditure for the Bank's prosecution was far greater: £16,414 9s 3d in 1809 and £8,070 19s 9d in 1810. House of Commons, *Account of Expense Incurred by Bank of England in Prosecutions for Forging Bank Notes, 1797–1818* (1818).

eighteen pence for each guinea coin.[110] Once the transaction was completed, the two agents sent a prearranged sign to Powell, who was hidden outside the house accompanied by a police officer and a city marshal. In this successful raid, the Mint agents arrested Mr and Mrs De Yonge and seized more than 100 guinea coins, in addition to the 50 guineas in the agents' hands.[111] The De Yonges were engaged in the trade of buying and selling guineas at a premium, for themselves and for customers, with a view to profiting from the price differentials of gold between Britain and abroad. Such illicit transactions of guineas, according to Lord Folkestone in parliament, were hardly uncommon, as they had been practised by merchants and bankers in London since the early 1800s and the inducement was daily increasing.[112] The De Yonge case was undoubtedly intended as a test case by the Mint solicitors, who were intensifying their policing activities in 1809.[113]

Despite the tightened restrictions on the export of precious metals due to the French wars, it was common knowledge that smugglers were illegally exporting gold coins and gold bullion.[114] The smuggling of precious metals and other goods was a major illicit activity as well as part of the economic warfare encouraged by the French to try to strip its enemy of as much cash as possible. The vigour of the coastal patrol, which served as a guard against the illicit trade and invasion fleets, did not subdue smugglers' trade, nor did Napoleon's Continental Blockade suspend intercourse between the two sides of the Channel. The smuggling of guinea coins increased in 1809, stimulated by the exchange rate against the pound.[115] It was not only that smugglers brought gold coins to sell abroad; guinea coins also changed hands when smugglers paid for

---

[110] This was equivalent to a 7.14 per cent premium. The mint's agents made payments in Bank of England notes and Bank dollars – all of them had a secret mark.

[111] CWPR, 11 Aug. 1810, 163–5; *The Examiner*, 5 and 11 Aug. 1810; *The Times*, 4 Aug. 1810.

[112] Gray, *Spencer Perceval*, 368; Hansard, 1st ser., xix (1811), cols. 723–4; *Taunton Courier*, 29 July 1810.

[113] Hansard, 1st ser., xix (1811), col. 724.

[114] Exporting gold was illegal, and the operation of the legal prohibition was tightened in 1797, the origin of which can be traced back to a series of fourteenth-century legislation, chiefly that of 1336, prohibiting the exportation of coins and precious metal. Legislation in 1696 stipulated that only bullion bars that were stamped at the Goldsmith's Hall and accompanied with an oath stating that they were not made of melted coins could be exported. John Craig, *The Mint; A History of the London Mint from AD 287 to 1948* (Cambridge, 1953), 61–2; Albert Edgar Feaveryear, *The Pound Sterling: A History of English Money* (Oxford, 1931), 4–5. See also House of Commons, *Communications between Bank of England, Treasury and Attorney-General Respecting Execution of Laws Prohibiting Exportation of Gold and Silver, 1772* (1811).

[115] Katherine Aaslestad and Johan Joor, *Revisiting Napoleon's Continental System: Local, Regional and European Experiences* (Basingstoke, 2014), 7; Gavin Daly, 'English

French products ranging from grain, lace, silk and leather to brandy and gin, as French merchants preferred to be paid in hard currency.[116] The international trade of guinea coins received further encouragement in June 1810 from Napoleon, who deliberately exploited smugglers to extract precious gold from Britain.[117] In late 1810, the illicit coin trade brought 139,338 guineas to Dunkirk, and in the following year, the annual French 'import' of English coins increased to 1,876,617 guineas.[118]

Smugglers were far from the only ones who profited from the illicit export of coins. The exportation of bullion and coins, both authorised and unauthorised, was also mediated by merchants who had recourse to the system of international remittances via British or neutral vessels, a conduit that probably carried a far larger amount of precious metal than the smugglers did. Some French merchants in London, for instance, regularly sent bullion to France on the pretence of paying for bills drawn in the Baltic countries.[119] The British authorities hardly turned a blind eye to the ongoing illegal trade. In November 1808, the custom house commissioners expressed their concern about the prevalence of the 'evil practices' of guinea trade.[120] In early August 1809, the customs officers made at least two seizures, one of which concerned 32,000 guineas 'artfully concealed in the linings of the cabin' of a vessel at Gravesend and the other a box containing 20,000 undeclared guineas on a Dutch schooner.[121] Despite these attempts to suppress the illicit trade, the smugglers were undeterred.[122] This was the background to the authorities' turning to the sources of the guinea trade. The expanding domestic

---

Smugglers, the Channel, and the Napoleonic Wars, 1800–1814', *Journal of British Studies*, 46 (2007), 35.

[116] S. Gramshaw to Custom House, 3 Dec. 1800, TNA CUST 54/13, fol. 126.

[117] Daly, 'English Smugglers', 33–4; Gavin Daly, 'Napoleon and the "City of Smugglers," 1810–1814', *Historical Journal*, 50 (2007), 338–9.

[118] Daly, 'Napoleon and the "City of Smugglers"', 345.

[119] Bank of England, *Proceedings at the General Court of Proprietors, Held at the Bank of England, on the 19th of March, 1812; with an Appendix, Containing Some Observations on the Conduct of Lord King* (London, 1812), 466; Herbert H. Kaplan, *Nathan Mayer Rothschild and the Creation of a Dynasty: The Critical Years 1806–1816* (Stanford, CA, 2006), ch. 3; Pressnell, *Country Banking*.

[120] House of Commons, *Correspondence on Illicit Exportation of Gold Coin, or of Gold Bullion* (1811), 1.

[121] House of Commons, *Correspondence on Illicit Exportation of Gold Coin, or of Gold Bullion*, 2; *Jackson's Oxford Journal*, 12 Aug. 1809; *Morning Chronicle*, 4 Aug. 1809.

[122] For example, *Northampton Mercury*, 18 Aug. 1810. See also the official accounts of the seized bullion and coins by customs, though they probably underestimate the extent of smuggling. House of Commons, *Account of Bullion or Coin Seized by Customs, 1810–11* (1811); House of Commons, *Account of Bullion or Coin Seized by Customs, 1811–19* (1819).

guinea trade was undoubtedly a concern for officials; in February 1810, while the De Yonge case was being considered in the court, Samuel Wright, a mail guard operating on the route between London and Buckinghamshire, was arrested for purchasing five guineas with a Bank of England note and silver coins, paying a nine pence premium per guinea.[123] As with the De Yonge case, an agent of the Mint led the prosecution – it was clearly a part of the Mint's crackdown on the guinea trade.

In the two legal cases, which drew intense public attention, De Yonge and Wright were charged under ancient legislation from 1551 that prohibited the sale of a coin at a price above its denominated value.[124] The prosecutors argued that the two accused clearly infringed the law, but the legal rule was not clear-cut as to whether the law in question, enacted when metallic coins were the only currency, could be applied to transactions involving the Bank note.[125] Wright's counsel, John King, contended that metallic currency and paper currency had been distinguished in England's case law by quoting Lord Mansfield's famous statement in 1758 that 'the notes ... are treated as money, as cash, in the ordinary course and transacting of business, by the general consent of mankind, which gives them the credit and currency of money to all intents and purposes'.[126] If paper currency required 'general consent' to be treated as cash, King reasoned, paper currency should not be regarded as money because it had no value other than that created by convention. Drawing upon the 1801 case of *Grigby v. Oakes*, King contended the judiciary had never recognised Bank notes as money.[127]

King's legal defence in the criminal court is powerful testimony that the question of monetary value was never the exclusive domain of economic thinkers and politicians, and the boundary between them could easily be crossed. In the legal court, as much as in parliament and in economic literature, some of the central premises concerning paper currency were being addressed. King's argument had a close affinity with the reasoning put forward by metallists such as Boyd and Lord King as they shared the strong belief that paper currency and metallic currency were fundamentally different. In expressing this metallism creed, King was as eloquent as any of his counterparts in economic theory:

[123] The indictment file is in King's Bench, Crown Side: London and Middlesex Indictments Files, 1809–10, TNA, KB 10/56. Wright's defence counsel John King published a pamphlet giving details of the two cases. John King, *A Report of the Cases of the King v. Wright and the King v. de Yonge, Who Were Severally Tried for Exchanging Guineas for Bank Notes* (London, 1811).
[124] 5 & 6 Edw. VI, c. 19 (1551).   [125] King, *King v. Wright*, 10; *The Times*, 4 Aug. 1810.
[126] King, *King v. Wright*, 42.   [127] King, *King v. Wright*, 50–1.

inasmuch as Bank Notes are not a tender for the sum at which they are expressed
to be payable; as their value depends entirely upon the voluntary assent of
individuals; as their currency is conventional, and as they are not money; it
follows that they are not the standard of value; and if not, that they may
themselves be valued: and if they may be valued, it must be at the option of the
receiver, and in the same way as a commodity of another kind.[128]

What is striking about King's statement is the way he questions currency
voluntarism in the context of the legal battle over how to define paper
currency's monetary value. Like metallists, King discounted voluntarism
as the source of monetary value. While King's legal argument formed an
intellectual assault on the idea that Britain's paper currency was based on
voluntary acceptance, its practical aim was to force the court to recognise
that the Bank note ought to be treated as a commodity with variable price
rather than money with a stable value. As a commodity, people were free
to exchange notes for the amount in coin that accorded to their valuation.
This logic was a serious threat to the stability of the inconvertible paper
currency, but the legal court could not refuse King's argument outright,
because if the court were to announce that the law of 1551 covered the
Bank note it would amount to bringing it on a par with regal currency,
which was beyond the power of the judiciary.[129] The judiciary's self-
restraint in avoiding infringement of sovereign power over money creation thus undermined currency voluntarism at a crucial moment in
monetary history when the nature of paper currency was discussed across
British society.

William Cobbett was one of those who were captivated by the development of the De Yonge case, which was widely reported in contemporary newspapers. In Cobbett's coverage of the De Yonge case in his
Political Register in August 1810, the incident was described as the demonstration that paper currency was subject to the natural human procliv-
ity to seek gain.[130] Recognising paper currency as an unnatural creation
and a usurper of the place of metallic money, Cobbett saw that the value
of paper currency was deservedly undercut by people, such as the
De Yonges, who discovered that paper currency's value was illusory.
If the Bank profited from circulating worthless paper, Cobbett queried,
how could they deny the De Yonges of making a small profit from trading
the same paper? Cobbett's report on the De Yonge case was a prelude to
his subsequent critique of the paper system in a series of letters entitled
'Paper against Gold', the first of which appeared in the *Political Register*
on September 1. Many of his letters made direct and indirect reference to

---

[128] King, *King v. Wright*, 58.   [129] King, *King v. Wright*, 53–4.
[130] CWPR, 4 Aug. 1810, 132.

the parliamentary discussion on paper currency, but as the genesis of 'Paper against Gold' indicates the issue of guinea sales was inseparable from the ensuing discussion in parliament in the mind of Cobbett and many of his contemporaries. Soon, however, public attention to the De Yonge case receded as the main site of debate shifted from the legal court to parliament.

The Bullionist Controversy

Shortly after the two guinea sellers were prosecuted by the Mint solicitor, Francis Horner – now an MP with a reputation for expertise in financial matters – took the initiative in setting up a parliamentary committee to 'enquire into the Cause of the High Price of Gold Bullion, and to take into consideration the State of the Circulating Medium, and of the Exchanges between Great Britain and Foreign Parts'.[131] The Bullion Committee, for which Horner served as the chair, and the report that it subsequently produced became the principal reference points for the contemporary debate on paper currency. In the accounts of economic historians, what came to be known as the Bullionist Controversy has conventionally been portrayed as a hotbed of modern theories of money and finance, out of which the theoretical orthodoxy of classical monetary economics emerged. Still, it should not be forgotten that the debate had a practical dimension, as it was triggered by a specific set of problems that confronted Britain around 1810. Among others, the problem of an inflationary economy entailed the political question of the Bank of England's role in the nation's economy and monetary system. The debate also had cultural dimensions because the language of the debate was largely defined by ideas and concepts that had been brought forward from previous discussions on currency and public credit. Departing from the conventional narrative that focuses on economic theories, the following account considers the Bullionist Controversy as a political and cultural event as an alternative mode of understanding this well-discussed debate.

The committee's bullion report served as a catalyst for a wide-ranging discussion on paper currency, both inside and outside parliament, which produced hundreds of publications in the latter part of the Bank Restriction period.[132] The twenty-two members of the committee

---

[131] As Fetter notes, *Hansard* did not record this event. Frank W. Fetter, 'The Politics of the Bullion Report', *Economica*, new ser., 26 (1959), 106. It was recorded in the *Journals of the House of Commons*, 19 Feb. 1810, and *The Times*, 20 Feb. 1810.

[132] Dick, *Romanticism and the Gold Standard*, 36.

included Prime Minister Spencer Perceval and other senior political
figures such as George Tierney and the Bank's deputy director,
William Manning. Francis Horner, Henry Thornton and William
Huskisson led the committee's investigation, and they were the principal
authors of the bullion report that was submitted to parliament in
June 1810.[133] Conventionally, historians have divided the participants
in the Bullionist Controversy into two camps.[134] Those who argued for
the existence of a direct link between the quantity of paper currency and
the price of gold were called bullionists, who generally supported the
bullion report's analysis and conclusions. The opposing group, the anti-
bullionists, did not see the correspondence between the two, and they
were mostly against the Bullion Committee's report. Bullionists blamed
the inflationary pressure that the British economy had been experiencing
since late 1808 on the Bank of England's overissue of paper currency and
ultimately on the Bank Restriction, which freed the Bank from the
obligation of convertibility. In contrast, anti-bullionists generally denied
the Bank's responsibility in causing inflation, claiming that the inflation
resulted from non-monetary factors, such as war-related price fluctuations, and they therefore advocated the continuance of the Bank
Restriction. The economic historian D. P. O'Brien further elaborates
the competing theoretical positions by identifying rigid and moderate
forms of bullionism: the former saw the gold price and the exchange rate
as the sole criteria for currency depreciation, a position represented by
Boyd, Lord King and Ricardo, and the latter position acknowledged the
possible effect of non-monetary factors while maintaining that the quantity of money was the major cause of inflation.[135]

Theoretical positions served only as a rough marker of one's relative
position in the debate. One notable example is the alleged discrepancy
between Henry Thornton's early statements as an advocate of paper
currency and the Bank Restriction and his support of the bullion report,
which recommended a return to convertibility.[136] Changing one's

---

[133] It was subsequently printed in August of that year as House of Commons, *Bullion
Committee Report (1810)*.
[134] Fetter, *British Monetary Orthodoxy*, 28.
[135] D. P. O'Brien, *The Classical Economists* (Oxford, 1975), 148–9. For concise summaries
of the two positions, see D. P. O'Brien, ed., *Foundations of Monetary Economics*, ii: *The
Bullionists* (London, 1994); O'Brien, *Anti-Bullionists*.
[136] Antoin E. Murphy, 'Paper Credit and the Multi-Personae Mr Henry Thornton',
European Journal of the History of Economic Thought, 10 (2003), 429–53; Antoin
E. Murphy, 'Rejoinder to Skaggs's Treating Schizophrenia: A Comment on Antoin
Murphy's Diagnosis of Henry Thornton's Theoretical Condition', *European Journal of
the History of Economic Thought*, 12 (2005), 329–32; Neil T. Skaggs, 'Treating
Schizophrenia: A Comment on Antoin Murphy's Diagnosis of Henry Thornton's

position in the debate was not uncommon when monetary theory was still in flux. Sir John Sinclair, who in 1797 opposed the Bank Restriction, had by 1810 become an ardent supporter of inconvertible paper currency.[137] Many MPs, and some of the committee members, had merely crude ideas of monetary theory: Perceval frankly admitted that he 'could not understand, how the reduction of the bank of England paper could affect the price of bullion'.[138] Nor did the ensuing parliamentary discussion reduce multiple understandings of currency into a few clearly defined positions. As the historian Frank Fetter plausibly summarises, '[p]robably no two members of the Bullion Committee held exactly the same views, and their differences arose from a complex of considerations that transcend conventional economic analysis'.[139]

The bullion report was an attempt to find a middle way in the cacophony of ideas and opinions, but the result was a document with an equivocal theoretical outlook. Its main considerations were divided into facts, causes and remedies concerning the high gold price, the adverse exchange for Britain and the instability of the nation's currency. The logical structure of the inquiry and the report followed that of the Irish currency report, but the Bullion Committee's task was much harder than that of its Irish precursor because, while the Irish currency problem had, in 1804, primarily been discussed through examining the Anglo-Irish economic relations and a banking system consisting of only a handful of banks, the Bullion Committee's scope covered a large and dense banking network in England, with hundreds of banks; stupendous government finance; and Britain's overseas engagements of a military and commercial nature.[140] Through its painstaking fact gathering and hearings, the committee established that unfavourable exchanges for the pound sterling and the high price of bullion coincided with a period of substantial Bank-note issue. Clearly, the committee adopted as its principal tests the exchange rate and gold prices, but the report conceded to the

---

Theoretical Condition', *European Journal of the History of Economic Thought*, 12 (2005), 321–8.

[137] John Sinclair is therefore regarded as an anti-bullionist. Rosalind Mitchison, *Agricultural Sir John: The Life of Sir John Sinclair of Ulbster, 1754–1835* (London, 1962), 241; Sinclair, *Letters Written to the Governor*; John Sinclair, *Observations on the Report of the Bullion Committee* (London, 1810).

[138] Hansard, 1st ser., xv (1810), col. 274.

[139] Fetter, 'Politics of the Bullion Report', 119. See also Anna Gambles, *Protection and Politics: Conservative Economic Discourse, 1815–1852* (London, 1999), 20.

[140] Compare Gerry Boyle and P. T. Geary, 'The Irish Currency Report of 1804' (Economics Department Working Paper Series n1341203, Department of Economics, National University of Ireland – Maynooth, 2003); Fetter, *Irish Pound*; Ó Gráda, 'Reassessing the Irish Pound Report'.

anti-bullionist view by acknowledging the possibility of 'the commercial state of this Country and the political state of the Continent' affecting the gold price and the exchanges.[141] For its consideration of non-monetary factors and its eclectic theoretical position, the report was moderately bullionist in its outlook. To be more precise, it had the hallmark of Horner's version of moderate bullionism that was articulated in his synthetic reviews of Thornton and Lord King in the *Edinburgh Review*.[142] The same moderate bullionism resulted in the committee's somewhat forgiving tone to the Bank directors' liability in the currency depreciation, on which rigid bullionists such as Boyd and Ricardo had much harsher views.[143]

The bullion report's recommended remedies were no less important than its theoretical diagnosis and were most controversial. Unlike the 1804 Irish report, which concerned the Irish currency *under* inconvertibility, the bullion report directly addressed the foundation of the inconvertible system. The report concluded that 'the system of the circulating medium of this Country ought to be brought back, with as much speed ... to the original principle of Cash payments at the option of the holder of Bank paper'.[144] For this conclusion, the committee took a hard line, suggesting a return to convertibility in two years, irrespective of the war situation.[145] This bullionist programme gave rise to concern from anti-bullionists and moderates alike, including Thornton, who only reluctantly supported the two-year deadline.[146] In essence, the report demanded an immediate adjustment of the Bank of England's note issue according to the present situation of the exchange and the bullion price, with the threat of a much more violent period of currency value realignment that would happen if convertibility was restored in two years without a significant contraction of note issue.

---

[141] House of Commons, *Bullion Committee Report (1810)*, 16, 21; Fontana, *Rethinking the Politics of Commercial Society*, 120.

[142] Fontana, *Rethinking the Politics of Commercial Society*, 119–20; *Horner Papers*, 579. On Horner's economic thought, see also Stefan Collini, Winch Donald and John Burrow, *That Noble Science of Politics: A Study in Nineteenth-Century Intellectual History* (Cambridge, 1983), 49–53; *The Economic Writings of Francis Horner in the Edinburgh Review, 1802–6*, ed. F. W. Fetter (London, 1957), 1–22.

[143] Historians are divided as to the degree of practical influence of the real-bills doctrine on the conduct of the Bank directors. Ian P. H. Duffy, 'The Discount Policy of the Bank of England during the Suspension of Cash Payments, 1797–1821', *Economic History Review*, 35 (1982), 74–7, 79; J. K. Horsefield, 'The Bankers and the Bullionists in 1819', *Journal of Political Economy*, 57 (1949), 442–8.

[144] House of Commons, *Bullion Committee Report (1810)*, 31.

[145] The law effective at that time, 44 Geo. III, c. 1 (1802), stipulated the resumption to be six months after the signing of the peace.

[146] Fetter, 'Politics of the Bullion Report', 107.

Since Britain's war with France was at a critical stage, there was good reason for some members of the committee, including Thornton, to be sceptical about the feasibility of the two-year deadline for restoring convertibility. Far from anticipating that convertibility would set everything right, the aim of the main authors of the report, Thornton and Huskisson, was probably to compel the Bank directors to accept 'the propriety of limiting the bank issues with a view to the improvement of the exchange'.[147] This was a policy that had been expressly advocated by Thornton since 1797, but it was a policy the Bank directors still found difficult to swallow.[148] Throughout the committee's examinations, the directors consistently stated that their note issue was guided by domestic demand on commercial discount rather than the international exchange rate. Such an admission of their neglect of fundamental economic indicators coupled with their adherence to the real-bills doctrine in the Bank's commercial discount activity convinced the committee, especially the advocates of monetary policy like Thornton, that the Bank's policy was not fully aligned with the broader role the Bank had come to play under Bank Restriction. Somewhat patronisingly, the bullion report remarks,

And it ought not to be urged as matter of charge against the Directors, if in this novel situation in which their commercial Company was placed by the law, and intrusted with the regulation and control of the whole circulating medium of the Country, they were not fully aware of the principles by which so delicate a trust should be executed, but continued to conduct their business of discounts and advances according to their former routine.[149]

The bullion report intended to bring to the Bank directors' attention the new policy horizon, in which the Bank had to formulate its institutional conduct. It was a drastic redirection of the Bank's policy, but Huskisson hoped that the adverse currency situation would make the Bank directors more amenable to the report's recommendations 'than they were disposed to allow to them when every thing was going on more smoothly'.[150] However, while the Bank had yet to embrace central banking functions, its directors and those who were concerned with the Bank's operations generally took the report's agenda of reorienting the

[147] Hansard, 1st ser., xx (1811), col. 81.
[148] Arnon, *Monetary Theory and Policy*, 123–4; Frank W. Fetter, 'The Bullion Report Reexamined', *Quarterly Journal of Economics*, 56 (1942), 661–2; Hansard, 1st ser., xx (1811), col. 82.
[149] House of Commons, *Bullion Committee Report (1810)*, 20.
[150] Huskisson to Horner, 1 Aug. 1810, BL, Horner/Lyell Papers, Add Ms 72844, fols. 118–19; Bradley, 'Politics of Godliness', 145–6; Harling, *Waning of 'Old Corruption'*, 93–4, 105, 108, 116.

Bank's policy as an undue intrusion into its business.[151] Stephen Cattley, a London merchant and a Bank proprietor, criticised the bullion report for its disregard of the Bank's private business and the committee members for acting as though they were 'directors of directors'.[152]

The practical dimension of the debate eventually decided the course of events, but when parliamentary debate on the bullion report commenced in May 1811 Horner clearly misjudged the situation as he overestimated the support for bullionism among MPs. His misjudgement was based on the general tone of the public debate that took place during the parliamentary recess after the publication of the bullion report nearly a year ago, which seemed to suggest the relative strength of rigid bullionism. However, the expert opinion favourable to the bullion report as it was expressed in the *Edinburgh Review* and the *Quarterly Review* did not translate into parliamentary support. Horner had to pay for his misjudgement when he proposed a set of resolutions that were based on the bullion report with its moderate tone largely stripped away.[153] Many MPs saw the resolutions' emphasis on the need for the metallic standard as a prelude to contractionary policy, a concern that was amplified in a year when the nation was narrowly saved from commercial distress by a large issue of exchequer bills.[154] As a result, the resolutions failed to attract support. Instead, the majority of MPs threw their support to the nineteen counter-resolutions proposed by Nicholas Vansittart, a self-proclaimed government spokesperson in the House of Commons.[155] The contrasting fortunes of Horner's and Vansittart's resolutions did

---

[151] Davis, *Ricardo's Macroeconomics*, 14, 20, 66. See also Timothy L. Alborn, *Conceiving Companies: Joint-Stock Politics in Victorian England* (London, 1998), 54; Michael D. Bordo, 'Commentary on "The Financial Crisis of 1825 and the Restructuring of the British Financial System"', *Review – Federal Reserve Bank of Saint Louis*, 80 (1998), 80; John A. James, 'Panics, Payments Disruptions and the Bank of England before 1826', *Financial History Review*, 19 (2012), 299; Larry Neal, 'The Financial Crisis of 1825 and the Restructuring of the British Financial System', *Review – Federal Reserve Bank of Saint Louis*, 80 (1998), 69–72.

[152] Bank of England, *Proceedings at the General Court of Proprietors*, 4. On Cattley's criticism of the bullion report, see John W. Houghton, *Culture and Currency: Cultural Bias in Monetary Theory and Policy* (London, 1991), 122.

[153] Hansard 1st ser., xix (1811), cols. 830–2; *Memoirs and Correspondence of Francis Horner*, ii, 62–8, 73–4.

[154] In March 1811, a parliamentary committee on commercial credit, of which Thornton was a member, recommended that the government issue exchequer bills to resuscitate the nation's trade. Parliament agreed to spend up to £6 million, and, consequently, £1,339,000 in exchequer bills were issued to commercial houses and manufacturers in that month. Clapham, *Bank of England*, ii, 34; House of Commons, *Report from the Select Committee on the State of Commercial Credit* (1811); Pressnell, *Country Banking*, 468.

[155] Hansard, 1st ser., xx (1811), cols. 1–74.

not reflect the relative popularity of their theoretical positions. It is likely that MPs preferred Vansittart's opposition to the recommendations of the bullion report – the resolutions were adopted almost without division – as a guarantee against contractionary policy, which was criticised by Vansittart and George Rose as an impractical course of action unfit for wartime Britain.[156]

It is notable that Vansittart's resolutions challenged Horner's bullionist resolutions by appealing to the traditional language of currency voluntarism. His third resolution stated that the Bank note was 'held in public estimation to be equivalent to the legal coin of the realm'.[157] This statement, which was derided by George Canning and some modern economic historians, in fact, resonated with the early discussion on the voluntary nature of English paper currency.[158] The statement was in line with Baron Hotham's belief, expressed when he was the presiding judge in the *Grigby v. Oakes* case, that British citizens were bound by the extralegal obligation to accept paper currency. Vansittart's appeal to 'public esteem' equally resonated with Thornton's statement:

> The law authorizing the suspension of the cash payments of the bank, seems, therefore, to have only given effect to what must have been the general wish of the nation in the new and extraordinary circumstances in which it found itself. If every bill and engagement is a contract to pay money, the two parties to the contract may be understood as agreeing, for the sake of a common and almost universal interest, to relax as to the literal interpretation of it, and as consenting that 'money should mean money's worth,' and not the very pieces of metal.[159]

Vansittart's resolutions showed how deep-rooted the voluntarist idea still was in 1811, and the leading participants in the public controversy continued to hold to some basic tenets that were established in the 1790s. Huskisson's *Question Concerning the Depreciation of Our Currency* (1810) is one example of contemporaries' continued preoccupation with the intersubjective foundation of credit currency, expressed as a system based on confidence. To Huskisson, confidence concerned paper currency's ability to represent monetary value that it did not inherently

---

[156] Fontana, *Rethinking the Politics of Commercial Society*, 123–4; Gray, *Spencer Perceval*, 384; Hansard, 1st ser., xx (1811), col. 7; David Laidler, 'Highlights of the Bullionist Controversy' (Research Report No. 2000-02, University of Western Ontario, Department of Economics, 2000), 16; *Resolutions Proposed to the House of Commons, on the Report of the Committee Appointed to Inquire into the High Price of Bullion, by Francis Horner and Nicholas Vansittart* (London, 1811), 10, 19–20; Jacob Viner, *Studies in the Theory of International Trade* (New York, 1937), 171.

[157] Hansard, 1st ser., xx (1811), col. 70.

[158] Glyn Davies, *A History of Money: From Ancient Times to the Present Day* (Cardiff, 2002), 303; Hansard, 1st ser., xx (1811), cols. 107–8.

[159] Thornton, *Paper Credit*, 112–13.

possess. Based on this understanding of the role of confidence, Huskisson distinguished two types of paper currency: one based on confidence and the other on authority.[160] Britain's Bank note belonged to the former, which he also called 'circulating credit' as opposed to the state 'paper money' in Austria and Russia (and presumably the French *assignats*).[161] He argued that paper could become money only by state sanction, a form of state coercion that was unacceptable in Britain's democratic society.[162] If ever there was a need to make paper circulation compulsory, he mused, such power ought to rest with 'every possessor of a small note'.[163] Huskisson shared with his contemporary an ingrained disdain towards state paper money, while conceding that the Bank note had lately come to bear 'so near a resemblance' to it.[164]

Intellectual opinions about the source of paper currency's value, such as those expressed by Horner, Vansittart and Huskisson, were subordinated to the policy aspects of the parliamentary discussion. If one was to follow the rigid bullionists' logic of the direct link between the quantity of the Bank's note issue and the general price level, the Bank ought to be put under strict regulation to avoid any overissue. Anti-bullionists such as Randall Jackson despised the idea of the Bank being deprived of its discretionary power. On this matter, Thornton was sympathetic to anti-bullionists as he believed that obliging the Bank to be bound by a few economic indicators (e.g. the bullion price) in a somewhat mechanical manner would incapacitate the Bank from making more complex policy decisions.[165] In the real world, theories and expectations were often frustrated by the development of historical contingencies. The bullion report's theory of monetary policy did not much change how the Bank operated: the Bank's directors continued to uphold the real-bills doctrine and kept to the institution's conventional sphere of activity by largely refraining from making any form of market intervention.[166] Nor did it have much immediate impact on Britain's monetary and fiscal policy. However, the report opened up a wide-ranging debate on not just the economic but also the social implications of high inflation. One issue that was foregrounded in the debate concerned the part of the population with a fixed income, who, because their income could not easily be

---

[160] William Huskisson, *The Question Concerning the Depreciation of Our Currency Stated and Examined* (London, 1810), 3.
[161] Huskisson, *Depreciation of Our Currency*, 107.
[162] Huskisson, *Depreciation of Our Currency*, 3.
[163] Huskisson, *Depreciation of Our Currency*, 152.
[164] Huskisson, *Depreciation of Our Currency*, 150.
[165] On this point, see Arnon, *Monetary Theory and Policy*, ch. 7.
[166] *David Ricardo on the Price of Gold, 1809*, ed. Jacob H. Hollander (1903), 25.

adjusted to price fluctuations, felt that they were carrying an undue burden in the inflationary period. Regarding this, bullionism had a straightforward solution. Given that there was no incentive for the Bank to reduce its note circulation of its own accord, restoring convertibility was the only way to force the Bank to eradicate excess note issue and bring the currency value to the level that it ought to be, thereby protecting those who depended on a fixed income. The argument was particularly appealing to landowners, who believed that their real income had declined because of currency depreciation.

Stanhope Act

Lord King, a staunch bullionist, believed that the defeat of bullionism in the legislature could be overturned by moving the battleground to the judiciary. His legal assault on the Bank Restriction was grounded in the liberal legal tradition, as he argued that the depreciation of currency injured the rights of property owners and violated 'the faith of contracts'.[167] As legal historian Christine Desan argues, the liberal tradition of Locke's metallism was, in its legal dimension, a logic to protect creditors from monetary fluctuations.[168] In mid-1811, King invoked the liberal legal tradition, which his famous ancestor had contributed to establishing, in his attempt to force parliament to recognise that the inconvertible paper system was unsustainable. As an aristocratic landlord, he was able to make his point by mobilising his power as a creditor, which he did by demanding that his tenants pay rent in metallic currency and refusing to accept Bank notes at par. Lord King's crusade for bullionism met an unexpected adversary, Charles Stanhope, third Earl Stanhope, who sounded the alarm in the House of Lords about the landlord's revolt and precipitated a legislative action that foreclosed King's liberal legal challenge. In a historical irony, King's action against inconvertible paper, which had a close similarity with what a radical Grigby attempted by refusing a Bank note in 1800, galvanised Stanhope, who was a renowned radical MP, a member of revolutionary societies and a sympathiser of the French Revolution with a connection with Christopher Wyvill and Richard Price. Unlike most of his radical friends, however, Stanhope was a strong supporter of inconvertible paper

---

[167] King, *Thoughts on the Restriction*, 81. For a similar argument by Locke, see Constantine G. Caffentzis, *Clipped Coins, Abused Words, and Civil Government: John Locke's Philosophy of Money* (Brooklyn, NY, 1989), 28.

[168] Desan, *Making Money*, 372.

currency, believing that it could be made into a workable system.[169] In his defence of the Bank Restriction, Stanhope was unconventional for he had no qualm against talking about legal tender, a topic that British politicians had long kept away from.

Stanhope first presented his somewhat eccentric idea of a new form of legal tender during the third reading of the Bank Silver Tokens Bill at the House of Lords on 24 June 1811.[170] The general opposition to making the Bank note legal tender, Stanhope stated, was due to its insufficient protection from forgery.[171] His proposal was to give the Bank's transaction record the status of legal tender by establishing a network of Bank branches across the country, between which transfers were recorded. In his system, the Bank's transfer books were deemed legal tender because such 'bank books' were well protected from forgery and were free from 'any danger of loss, from the mail being robbed, or from insurrections, or other consequences of an invasion'.[172] Stanhope, in fact, proposed an identical plan to the Marquis de Condorcet twenty years earlier in 1791, as a means to put the troubled French monetary system on a sound basis.[173] The new form of legal tender he recommended to the French in the age of *assignats* he resurrected for Bank Restriction Britain. As a preliminary to what he called the Bank book scheme, Stanhope recommended that parliament pass a law that would prohibit transactions of paper and metallic currency other than their denominated value.[174] Stanhope's proposal, as it happened, could not only offer a safeguard against illegal guinea sales but also protect tenants

---

[169] Stanhope's interest in monetary issues dated back to 1775, when he published a pamphlet on preventing 'false coining'. Charles Stanhope, *Considerations on the Means of Preventing Fraudulent Practices on the Gold Coin* (London, 1775). On Stanhope's attempts to invent a new printing process for forgery prevention in the 1800s, see, for example, the letter from Stanhope to Alexander Tilloch, 17 Aug. 1808, Kent History and Library Centre, U1590 C99/1. Stanhope's engagement with the forgery problem also stemmed from his interest in printing technology. Horace Hart, *Charles Earl Stanhope and the Oxford University Press* (London, 1966), 111; Ghita Stanhope and G. P. Gooch, *The Life of Charles, Third Earl Stanhope* (London, 1914), 209–10.

[170] The main topic of the debate, the Bank Silver Tokens Bill, concerned the new issue of silver tokens by the Bank, a practice that it had been involved in since 1797. E. M. Kelly, *Spanish Dollars and Silver Tokens: An Account of the Issues of the Bank of England, 1797–1816* (London, 1976), 79.

[171] Hansard, 1st ser., xx (1811), 24 June 1811, col. 740; Stanhope and Gooch, *Life of Third Earl Stanhope*, 206–7.

[172] Hansard, 1st ser., xx (1811), col. 741.

[173] Charles Stanhope, *Lettres de Milord Stanhope à M. de Condorcet* (Paris, 1791); Stanhope and Gooch, *Life of Third Earl Stanhope*, 207; Arthur Stanley Turberville, *The House of Lords in the Age of Reform, 1784–1837* (London, 1958), 93.

[174] Hansard, 1st ser., xx (1811), cols. 740–1 (27 June 1811). See also, Huskisson's speech on the issue in Hansard, 1st ser., xiv (1812–13), col. 281.

from landlords who refused to accept depreciated paper currency at its face value.

Lord King was no political radical himself, but his tactic of refusing the Bank note was closely aligned with that employed in Grigby's politically motivated action against the Oakes bank a decade ago. Whereas Grigby targeted the local bank to mount his claim for cash payments, King importuned his tenants by claiming his right to receive rent payments according to the pre-inflation monetary value. Threatening eviction, King demanded that his tenants pay either in guineas or Portuguese gold coin.[175] If tenants insisted on payment in Bank notes, King argued, the rent ought to be adjusted so that he would receive 'a sum sufficient to purchase the weight of standard gold requisite to discharge the rent'.[176] For instance, if a leasehold contract for annual payment of £100 was originally agreed in 1807, when the gold price was £4 2s per ounce, its real value in 1811, when gold had appreciated to £4 14s, would be £114 12s 8d.[177] King's ultimate goal was to secure legal recognition for what he regarded as the rightful claim of landlords, thereby bringing pressure on parliament to revise its policy on the Bank Restriction. 'I am so confident', King wrote to Lord Holland, 'of the strict justice and fairness of my proceeding that I should desire nothing better than to have it decided by Eldon [the Lord Chancellor] himself in his own court'.[178] To most of his Whig colleagues, including Horner, this appeared to be a risky tactic because shifting the debate to the legal court would likely invite the government's legislative action to protect the value of the Bank note.[179] Their concern deepened when Stanhope presented his bill as redress against Lord King's action. The spectre of the French *assignat* still haunted parliamentarians' mind as they saw Stanhope's bill as a step towards making the Bank-note legal tender. If such a drastic legislative measure was to be implemented, Canning warned Huskisson, 'the sure consequence of a force Paper Currency' would be the introduction of the law of maximum, followed by the rapid depreciation of currency just as happened in revolutionary France.[180]

---

[175] Hansard, 1st ser., xx (1811), col. 742; Stanhope and Gooch, *Life of Third Earl Stanhope*, 207. The original letter is John Leach to Stanhope, 26 June 1811, Kent History and Library Centre, U1590 C57/2.

[176] Hansard, 1st ser., xx (1811), cols. 792–3; Lord King's notice to Johnson, tallow chandler of Ripley; Surrey, n.d., Kent History and Library Centre, U1590 C57/2.

[177] Hansard, 1st ser., xx (1811), cols. 793, 799–800. On this calculation, see *Horner Papers*, 695.

[178] King to Holland, 29 June, BL, Holland Papers, Add Ms 51572, fol. 102.

[179] Lord Grenville was the only supporter. F. W. Fetter, 'Legal Tender during the English and Irish Bank Restrictions', *Journal of Political Economy*, 58 (1950), 245.

[180] Canning to Huskisson, 4 July 1811, BL, Huskisson Papers, Add Ms 38738.

Two events markedly heightened the urgency of legislative action. At the King's Bench on 3 July 1811, Lord Ellenborough delivered the verdict on the De Yonge case – the nine judges unanimously agreed to acquit De Yonge, which also meant that Wright, whose case was pending on the De Yonge case, would be cleared of his charge.[181] The radical press, which was generally hostile to the Bank Restriction, was elated with the news. *The Examiner* announced that the court 'declared it legal to give and take bank paper at its real value'.[182] Cobbett informed readers of his *Political Register* that the verdict was an acknowledgement of the practice of differentiating paper from gold as the court admitted that they had a different value.[183] The increasing number of supporters of Lord King among the peers in the House of Lords, including Grenville, Lauderdale, Holland, Grey and Lansdowne, and the government supporters, who were alerted by a legal decision that undermined the stability of inconvertible currency, were on a collision course.[184] The day before the De Yonge decision, the leader of the House of Lords and secretary of state for war, Lord Liverpool, announced that he was now supporting the second reading of the Stanhope's bill in order to protect Britain's paper currency.[185] The decision on the De Yonge case galvanised the pro-governmental MPs' support for Stanhope's bill.[186]

Another practical concern was that the parliamentary session was coming to a close, and without any legislative measure, the Bank note would be left defenceless against any legal attacks until the next parliamentary session. The sense of urgency swayed parliamentary opinion strongly in support of Stanhope's bill. Lord Chancellor Eldon stated that adopting the bill was rendered necessary to prevent individuals from depreciating the Bank note at their pleasure, taking advantage of the recent court decision on the legality of coin sales.[187] William Manning,

---

[181] *English Reports*, civ, 657–8; *The Times*, 4 July 1811. See also *The Courier* and *Morning Chronicle* of the same date.

[182] *The Examiner*, 7 July 1811. However, Canning wrote to Huskisson that the general feeling was strongly against Lord King. Canning to Huskisson, 4 July 1811, BL, Huskisson Papers, Add Ms 38738.

[183] CWPR, 6 July 1811, 22–3.

[184] Hansard, 1st ser., xx (1811), cols. 832–45. Perceval reported on the fluid situation and on signs of some aristocrats' willingness to follow Lord King's example. *The Correspondence of George, Prince of Wales, 1770–1812*, ed. A. Aspinall (London, 1971), viii, 36–7. Followers of Lord King were numerous in the north of Ireland. Landlords in the north of Ireland who insist on their rents being paid in gold or the difference in value between gold and bank notes, 10 July 1811, PRONI, T3228/5/57.

[185] Fetter, 'Legal Tender', 245–6; Hansard, 1st ser., xx (1811), cols. 828–31.

[186] Henry Richard Holland, *Further Memoirs of the Whig Party, 1807–1821* (London, 1905), 105.

[187] Hansard, 1st ser., xx (1811), col. 851.

the deputy governor of the Bank, was busy scaremongering, asking: if landlords were allowed to demand gold for rent payments, what would prevent clergymen and commercial creditors from insisting upon payments in coins?[188] Stanhope's bill passed two houses of parliament with a large majority.[189]

According to Frank Fetter, the Stanhope Act, which was originally a temporary legislative measure but was later extended until the end of the Bank Restriction, left the British population with no choice but to accept the Bank note.[190] It is also important to note that the government tried hard to draw a line between legal tender and legal protection against depreciation, not least because there were those like Horner who suspected that the government was aiming to make the Bank-note legal tender, and the Stanhope Act would be the first step towards it.[191] Whether it was called legal tender or not, the *Morning Chronicle* remarked, the government had now made the Bank note a forced currency.[192] For the government, the De Yonge case and Lord King's action, in effect, gave a timely excuse for making the Bank-note semi-legal tender, while avoiding the controversial issue of legal tender.[193] Equally importantly, the Stanhope Act allowed the government to keep the pretence that the Bank note was still based on a voluntary foundation.[194] Lord Liverpool was complacent when he remarked that the subject of legal tender was not fit for legislative interference because it was preferable that the value of paper currency relied upon 'the general principle of the mutual confidence and good sense of the people at large'.[195] Notwithstanding, the language of currency voluntarism was

---

[188] Hansard, 1st ser., xx (1811), col. 901.

[189] The House of Commons, on July 20, passed the Stanhope bill by a majority of 95 to 20. *Correspondence of George, Prince of Wales*, viii, 52.

[190] Fetter, *British Monetary Orthodoxy*, 59; Fetter, 'Legal Tender', 246, 250. Stanhope Act (51 Geo. III, c. 127) was amended the following year (52 Geo. III, c. 50) and subsequently extended to 1814 (53 Geo. III, c. 5) and by 54 Geo. III, c. 52 (1814) until the end of the Bank Restriction.

[191] *Horner Papers*, 693–4.   [192] *Morning Chronicle*, 4, 5, 8, 9, 10 and 11 July 1811.

[193] On contemporary comments, by Canning and Malthus, on the connection between the De Yonge case and the parliamentary debate on Stanhope's bill, see Canning to Huskisson, 4 July 1811, BL, Huskisson Papers, Add Ms 38738; Thomas Robert Malthus, 'Pamphlets on the Bullion Question', *Edinburgh Review*, 18 (1811), 464. Fetter attributed the general aversion to legal tender to 'a reflection of French Revolutionary experience with the assignats'. Fetter, 'Legal Tender', 246.

[194] In November 1811, Lord King wrote to Lord Holland that 'Perceval is the only minister who will venture to make notes legal tender'. Lord King to Lord Holland, 18 Nov. 1811, BL, Holland Papers, Add Ms 51572, fol. 106.

[195] Emmanuel Coppieters, *English Bank Note Circulation, 1694–1954* (The Hague, 1955), 44; Hansard, 1st ser., xx (1811), col. 765.

gradually losing its substance when it became a legal obligation to receive Bank notes at face value.

Currency and Community in 1810–1812

Stanhope, who set in motion a profound transformation in the nature of the Bank of England note, was among a small number of writers who advocated so-called abstract currency or ideal money.[196] As in other European countries in the eighteenth century, the monetary experiment of inconvertible paper led to a rediscovery of the theory of ideal money in Bank Restriction Britain; its European tradition, according to Luigi Einaudi, can be traced as far back as the time of Charlemagne.[197] Reiterating the earlier theory of an abstract monetary standard, its advocates in the 1790s and 1800s argued that money was fundamentally a unit of account and its moneyness did not derive from its material qualities associated with commodity money.[198] Thomas Smith, a London accountant, argued in his *Essay on the Theory of Money* (1807) that coins were merely symbols or tokens.[199] For Smith and his contemporaries, such as Perceval Eliot and Thomas Raithby, it was the abstract standard, that is the pound sterling, that determined the value of economic transactions.[200] The British discussion on ideal money was rooted both in the Bank Restriction and in the monetary debate of the 1790s. Smith explained that abstract money could maintain its value by contrasting what he called 'free' paper currency and forced currency, a contrast that was familiar to British writers from the early debate on the

[196] For the parliamentary discussion on Stanhope's proposal, Hansard, 1st ser., xx (1811), cols. 980–5.

[197] Luigi Einaudi, 'The Theory of Imaginary Money from Charlemagne to the French Revolution', in Luca Einaudi, Riccardo Faucci and Roberto Marchionatti, eds., *Luigi Einaudi: Selected Economic Essays* (London, 2006), 153–81; Geoffrey Ingham, *The Nature of Money* (Cambridge, 2004); Stefano Sgambati, 'Historicizing the Money of Account: A Critique of the Nominalist Ontology of Money', *Journal of Post Keynesian Economics*, 43 (2020), 417–44.

[198] For instance, Edward Tatham, *A Letter to the Right Honourable William Pitt on the National Debt* (Oxford, 1795), 14–15.

[199] Thomas Smith, *Essay on the Theory of Money and Exchange* (London, 1807), 5. Early writings that described money as tokens include William Potter in the mid seventeenth century and George Berkeley in the early eighteenth century. Carl Wennerlind, *Casualties of Credit: The English Financial Revolution, 1620–1720* (Cambridge, MA, 2011), 67–74, 239.

[200] Francis Perceval Eliot, *Observations on the Fallacy of the Supposed Depreciation of the Paper Currency of the Kingdom* (London, 1811), 8–12; John Raithby, *The Law and Principle of Money Considered; in a Letter to W. Huskisson* (London, 1811), 2–3; Smith, *Theory of Money and Exchange*, 14.

difference between English and French paper currency.[201] Free currency, according to Smith, was a currency that was issued 'only at the desire of the public', the value of which would not be disrupted by its issuers because they were aware that overissuing the currency would adversely affect their credit.[202] Only the issuers of forced currency would disregard the public's needs and the state of their own credit. Smith's theory of ideal money was thus directly informed by the discussion on currency exceptionalism in the 1790s. Furthermore, Smith shared with his contemporaries the belief that the circulation of paper currency rested on the confidence of its users that it would be accepted by other users (or issuers) for the fulfilment of economic obligations, including tax payments.[203]

In the light of other ideal money theories of his time, Stanhope's Bank Book scheme did not appear particularly idiosyncratic. Glocester Wilson, for example, contended that 'abstract credit' was the only natural standard of value and envisioned a unified clearing system for all economic transactions without the need for commodity currency.[204] Despite the generally scathing comments by reviewers of the *Edinburgh Review* and the *Quarterly Review*, ideal money advocates were not ignored in the wider debate on currency and their discussions were digested and circulated through the review literature.[205] In parliament, there were only two known followers of the ideal money theory, Lord Castlereagh and Stanhope.[206] Nevertheless, it should not be forgotten that the Stanhope Act, which fixed the relative value of the Bank note and metallic currency, was adopted in parliament by majority, and it was legislation originally submitted by Stanhope, whose advocacy of ideal currency was well known among fellow MPs.[207] The act was primarily intended to prohibit trading of coins and charging a premium for rent payments in paper currency, but it could potentially be applied to other forms of debt

---

[201] Smith, *Theory of Money and Exchange*, 37–49.

[202] Smith, *Theory of Money and Exchange*, 88–9.

[203] Smith, *Theory of Money and Exchange*, 168–9.

[204] Glocester Wilson, *Defence of Abstract Currencies, in Reply to the Bullion Report and Mr Huskisson* (London, 1811), 45, 149. For a brief discussion on Wilson and Eliot, see Francis A. Walker, *Money* (London, 1891), 296–8.

[205] George Canning, 'Tracts on the Report of the Bullion Committee', *Quarterly Review*, 5 (1811), 250–6; James Mill, 'Smith on Money and Exchange', *Edinburgh Review*, 13 (1809), 35–68.

[206] Hansard, 1st ser., xix (1811), cols. 1086–92; Boyd Hilton, *The Age of Atonement: The Influence of Evangelicalism on Social and Economic Thought, 1785–1865* (Oxford, 1988), 129.

[207] See, for instance, the parliamentary discussion on Stanhope's Bank Book proposal. Hansard, 1st ser., xx (1811), col. 983.

obligations such as commercial debt.[208] It is equally notable that the act's regulation of value – as far as the trading of gold coins was concerned – also covered silver tokens issued by the Bank. For that matter, the Stanhope Act effectively fixed the relative value of regal currency, Bank notes and official tokens, both made of paper and metal.

With the Stanhope Act, the idea of currency voluntarism, which had already been threatened by rigid bullionism based on liberal legal tradition, was significantly eroded. Yet, the language of voluntarism and the communal nature of currency was still very much part of the monetary debate. A notable contributor was Samuel Taylor Coleridge, who deployed the idea of reciprocity and community in his impassioned diatribe against Lord King. At the end of the Bank Restriction period, Coleridge would embrace a view on money that was close to the ideal money theory, but in 1811 his ideas resonated more strongly with the confidence-based monetary theory expressed in Thornton's *Paper Credit*, though Coleridge was much less amenable to Thornton's practical bullionism.[209] Also, unlike contemporary ideal money theorists such as Stanhope and Smith, Coleridge discussed the question of the standard for its *social* consequences rather than its function in the monetary system. Thus, for Coleridge, the bullion question concerned not the mechanism of money nor contractual justice but the community's capacity to absorb monetary fluctuations; the same sentiment was expressed in his condemnation of the 'raw theories' of bullionist writers associated with the *Edinburgh Review*.[210] In a series of articles in *The Courier*, Coleridge accused Lord King of seeking personal profit 'at the expense of the community' because demanding a premium for Bank note was, for Coleridge, to transfer the burden of inflation onto tenants.[211] Landlords forgot that their economic interests could exist only in relation to the 'just claims and interests of the tenants' as the legitimate economic community was founded on mutual respect for the rights and interests of all community members.[212] This mutual respect, Coleridge called reciprocity. Coleridge's idea of reciprocity in the monetary community followed the early discussion of currency voluntarism by Burke and

---

[208] 51 Geo. III, c. 127, s.3.

[209] Samuel Taylor Coleridge, *Essays on His Times in the Morning Post and The Courier*, ed. David V. Erdman (London, 1978), ii, 124–7, 129, 131–3. As Brantlinger suggests, it is likely that Coleridge was familiar with Thornton's *Paper Credit*. Patrick Brantlinger, *Fictions of State: Culture and Credit in Britain, 1694–1994* (Ithaca, NY, 1996), 114. On Coleridge's later views on money, which were close to the theory of ideal money, see Hilton, *Age of Atonement*, 128–9.

[210] Coleridge, *Essays on His Times*, ii, 230.

[211] Coleridge, *Essays on His Times*, iii, 120–1.   [212] *The Courier*, 8 July 1811.

Thornton, in which intersubjective trust was regarded as the foundation of currency acceptance. Thornton, in his parliamentary speech on the Stanhope Act in 1812, expressed a view similar to Coleridge's idea of reciprocity as he stated that Britain's inconvertible currency system laid the burden of currency fluctuations on the shoulder of those who were 'best able to bear it ... that would otherwise be imposed upon the poor'.[213]

Historian Boyd Hilton portrays Thornton's views as anticipating 'moral bullionism', which saw a parallel between perpetual monetary value – believed to be embodied in the metallic standard – and religious belief in immutable truth.[214] However, in 1812 Thornton's moral argument was mobilised in his opposition to the rigid bullionism of Lord King, who held that the unchangeable monetary standard was a safeguard for contractual relations. For Thornton – and Coleridge, too – moral and equity within the community took precedence over the sanctity of the contract. Thornton was not in favour of a sudden return to convertibility because such a violent repudiation of the inconvertible currency system would create injustice when 'bargains will have been made, and loans supplied, under an expectation of the continuance of the existing depreciation'.[215] Such practical considerations, according to Coleridge, were at the basis of the Stanhope Act, which crystalised 'solid knowledge, the deep and wide experience of our Merchants, Bankers, Capitalists, and Statesmen', who were well versed in the fluctuating fortunes of economic life.[216] The prevalence of moral argument in criticisms of King demonstrates that the supporters of rigid bullionism did not occupy a moral high ground in the early 1810s. At any rate, as long as contemporaries such as Coleridge and Thornton believed the inconvertible paper system could deliver a just distribution of social costs, the champions of the paper system stood as much on solid moral ground as the later advocates of the metallic standard.[217]

There was a clear tension between the communal perspective of Thornton and Coleridge, which was founded on the idea of reciprocity and equity among community members, and Lord King's individualistic liberal legalism that prioritised the contractual entitlement of creditors. As noted previously, in 1811 the language of communal currency, which British economic writers consolidated in the 1790s, was still present in

[213] Hansard, 1st ser., xxiv (1812–13), col. 234. On Coleridge's 'doubts about the upper classes' commitment' to their societal role, see John Morrow, *Coleridge's Political Thought: Property, Morality and the Limits of Traditional Discourse* (London, 1990), 112.
[214] Hilton, *Age of Atonement*, 127.   [215] Hansard, 1st ser., xx (1811), col. 918.
[216] Coleridge, *Essays on His Times*, ii, 230.   [217] Gambles, *Protection and Politics*, 111.

public discussions on paper currency. Coleridge's community-based currency vision, with the notion of reciprocity at its core, drew upon the conventional language of mutuality, which was hardly outdated.[218] As Fetter notes, the dominant view on paper currency expressed during the parliamentary debate 'amounted to the antithesis of the state theory of money'.[219] Indeed, state-issued currency remained an anathema in Britain two decades after the French experiment. In a longer historical context, communal currency belonged to what Margot Finn and Paul Johnson describe as the equity tradition in credit relations, a tradition that existed well into the nineteenth century.[220] The battle between King's rigid bullionism and the communal currency view of Thornton and Coleridge could be seen as a battle between liberal legalism and the equity tradition in Britain's social thought. In this battle of currency ideas, communal currency was not as dominant as it had been in the last two decades.

The Bullionist Controversy, the De Yonge case and the Stanhope Act created sharp divisions concerning views on paper currency. In this dynamic situation, communal currency increasingly lost ground, being eroded by the development of the mechanistic monetary theory of bullionism and also by the practical measures taken to defend the inconvertible system while the war was still ongoing. The Stanhope Act saved the Bank Restriction by fending off the liberal legal challenge, but, ironically, the legislation significantly undermined the premise of voluntary acceptance because it was now a legal obligation to accept the Bank note at par, and if acceptance was compulsory, there was little rationale for talking about the voluntary nature of paper currency. The same legislation troubled rigid bullionists, who feared the perpetuation of the inconvertibility, and antagonised popular radicals in equal measure. The introduction of a coercive element into currency circulation kindled popular radicals' suspicion that paper currency was a constituent part of the Old Corruption, the unjust political system that was sustained by an oppressive and fraudulent economic order. No longer was refusing paper currency a legitimate tactic to challenge the Bank Restriction. Prior to 1811, Joshua Grigby and Henry Hunt believed that it was their choice, freedom and right to accept or refuse paper currency; the Stanhope Act

---

[218] For the principle of mutuality, see E. P. Thompson, *The Making of the English Working Class* (London, 1963), 418–29.

[219] Fetter, 'Legal Tender', 246.

[220] Margot C. Finn, *The Character of Credit: Personal Debt in English Culture, 1740–1914* (Cambridge, 2003), 14–5; Paul Johnson, *Making the Market: Victorian Origins of Corporate Capitalism* (Cambridge, 2010), 39–40.

Figure 4.1 George Cruikshank, *The Blessing of Paper Money, or King a Bad Subject* (1811).
© Trustees of the British Museum

made it an illegal act, pure and simple.[221] Thus radicals increasingly rested their hope on the restoration of convertibility, or drastically new tactics to disrupt the paper system. In the early 1810s, anti-paper politics was at an impasse. The bullion question divided the nation, so too did the two different solutions proposed by Lord King and Lord Stanhope. The Bank Restriction fended off the assault from metallists, but with the Stanhope Act the Bank note was transformed. George Cruikshank vividly described the Bank note's transformation from a voluntarily accepted currency to a forced currency in *The Blessings of Paper Money* (1811), showing Stanhope feeding Bank notes into the mouth of chair-strapped John Bull, beside whom Perceval is reverentially holding up a bolus of 'legal tender' (Figure 4.1). In the background, Britannia laments the loss of public credit, represented by a pile of bank papers that are being blown away. The moment when voluntary acceptance of the Bank note was replaced by legal obligation, Britain's communal currency entered its period of decline.

---

[221] Robert Huish, *The History of the Private and Political Life of the Late Henry Hunt* (London, 1836), 437–53; Henry Hunt, *Memoirs of Henry Hunt* (London, 1820), i, 141–9.

5   The Forgery Crisis and the Radicalisation of Communal Currency

> In the bank note ... there is something in the neatness of the engraving and the conspicuous and emphatic display of the sum, that can not but be particularly attractive and fascinating to an ordinary eye. In the Exchequer Bill, there is no such display of the sum, and the impression of the long-winded explanation of the conditions of payment has nothing particular to recommend it.
>
> Jeremy Bentham, 'Causes. Paper-Money – why not circulated by Government without interest, as well as by Individuals' (c.1794).[1]

Historians rarely give credit to Jeremy Bentham for making a theoretical or practical contribution to Britain's monetary history. Yet, during the early part of the Bank Restriction period, Bentham, like many others of his generation, was fully engaged with the question of paper currency. One can glimpse the extent to which he invested his intellectual vigour in the monetary issue through a series of writings he produced in the 1790s and early 1800s, which pivoted around his idea of a new form of government-issued currency. Bentham's plan for what he called the 'exchequer note', and later the 'annuity note', led him to consider the risks inherent in circulating paper currency, namely monetary inflation and the crime of forgery. Bentham's writings on paper currency in this period reveal that he belonged to a small minority who envisaged a state monopoly on paper currency. He was also prescient in contemplating effective modes of preventing the crime of Bank-note forgery, which would become a major social concern in the latter part of the Bank Restriction period.

Immediately after the suspension of cash payments in 1797, the Bank was adversely affected by an unprecedented number of forged Bank

---

[1] Jeremy Bentham, 'A Plan for Augmentation of the Revenue', in *Jeremy Bentham's Economic Writings*, ed. Werner Stark (London, 1952), ii, 153; Jeremy Bentham, 'Exchequer Notes', in *Writings on Political Economy*, ii: *Financial Resources*, ed. Michael Quinn (Oxford, 2019), 333. On the dating of the manuscript, see Michael Quinn, 'Editorial Introduction', in Bentham, *Writings on Political Economy*, ii: *Financial Resources*, pp. lxxvii–lxxix.

notes entering circulation. For most of the eighteenth century, forgery of the Bank of England note had not been a particularly pressing matter for the Bank or the general public because of its limited scale. Between 1783 and 1796, there were only four prosecutions related to Bank-note forgery.[2] The situation changed dramatically in 1797, when a sudden increase in the number of forged notes brought to the Bank alerted its directors to the growing problem. Between 1797 and 1800, the annual number of forged notes identified by the Bank rose sharply from 901 to 3,947, which increased further to 7,674 in the following year (Table 5.1).[3] Compared to only two prosecutions for forgery crime in 1797, forty-four prosecutions were recorded in 1800, of which twenty-nine were capitally convicted. This first wave of forgery crime was largely due to the shift in the composition of Britain's circulating media, through which paper currency became the principal medium of payment, enticing criminals to the potentially profitable business of fabricating Bank of England notes.[4] There was a social factor in operation, as a significant number of small-denomination notes were in circulation among the population, many of whom were unaccustomed to handling paper currency on an everyday basis, making them easy prey for forgers. The poor quality of newly issued small notes exacerbated the matter, as it made it easier for forgers to manufacture and circulate inauthentic notes, and some minor modifications to the note design in 1798 did little to stem the tide of forgery.[5]

Bentham and some of his contemporaries clearly recognised that forgery was an existential challenge for the system of paper currency, which was ultimately grounded in the technology of reproducing identical prints and circulating them widely.[6] The proliferation of inauthentic notes would, as Bentham and others recognised, undermine the

---

[2] House of Commons, *Account of Number of Persons Prosecuted for Forging and Uttering Notes of Bank of England, 1783–1818* (1818); Randall McGowen, 'The Bank of England and the Policing of Forgery 1797–1821', *Past & Present*, 186 (2005), 87.

[3] 'Increase of Forgeries', *Edinburgh Review*, 28 (1818), 206; *Parliamentary Register*, xvii (1802), 511.

[4] Derrick Byatt, *Promises to Pay: The First Three Hundred Years of the Bank of England Notes* (London, 1994), 43; A. D. Mackenzie, *The Bank of England Note: A History of Its Printing* (Cambridge, 1953), 54, 57–8.

[5] The small-denomination notes (£1 and £2) issued in the immediate aftermath of the suspension of cash payments were manufactured from old and worn-out plates, resulting in poor-quality notes. Mackenzie, *Bank of England Note*, 47. The new design had a smaller printed area, and the face value was written in Roman capitals on the top of each of them. Byatt, *Promises to Pay*, 36.

[6] Werner Stark, 'Introduction', in *Jeremy Bentham's Economic Writings*, ii, 18.

Table 5.1 *Forged notes discovered by the Bank of England, 1797–1833*

Year	Number of forged £1 and £2 notes	Total number of forged notes	Nominal amount of forged notes (£)
1797	24	901	29,553
1798	838	1,179	8,483
1799	1,893	2,058	4,380
1800	3,549	3,947	7,681
1801	6,820	7,674	15,410
1802	4,338	5,018	10,407
1803	2,844	3,217	6,754
1804	2,930	3,311	6,662
1805	3,096	3,543	6,602
1806	3,441	4,008	8,103
1807	4,435	4,866	8,003
1808	4,471	4,719	7,002
1809	6,025	6,281	8,994
1810	4,953	5,341	8,923
1811	7,810	8,492	15,072
1812	15,985	17,290	28,136
1813	13,819	14,565	20,868
1814	13,420	14,446	22,154
1815	15,317	16,079	21,954
1816	22,712	23,442	29,282
1817	28,648	29,521	35,098
1818	27,420	28,351	33,551
1819	23,066	23,966	29,507
1820	29,233	30,217	35,470
1821	18,252	18,955	22,585
1822	3,312	3,756	6,179
1823	1,418	1,667	3,019
1824	835	970	2,188
1825	647	777	1,399
1826	1,668	2,053	4,004
1827	1,753	2,071	3,609
1828	759	1,187	3,343
1829	643	1,118	3,293
1830	296	614	2,119
1831	221	369	1,079
1832	238	424	1,316
1833	247	440	2,146

Source: BE, F2/111.

foundation of paper-currency circulation, as people would hesitate to accept a note when its authenticity was in doubt. Such a threat to the stability of the paper system could be minimised, Bentham believed, chiefly by introducing some preventive measures such as by equipping notes with design features that were difficult to copy.[7] From the early phase of his engagement with the topic of currency, anti-forgery measures consistently featured in Bentham's theoretical writings on money, which exhibited an interesting mix of speculative monetary thought and practical considerations on note printing. Bentham was a rare character who moved between the intellectual discussion on the currency system and the technical realms of note design and manufacturing.

State power or fiat always lurked behind Bentham's monetary thought and his note design, but the idea of 'forced' currency did not fare well in 1790s Britain, where, with the memory of the French *assignat* still fresh, writers strove to distinguish fiat currency and the British paper currency. While forgery of the state currency was a direct challenge to the sovereign power, forgery was equally a threat to a communal currency, which also had to be protected because the circulation of inauthentic currency would jeopardise the shared belief in the value of currency within the community of note users. Hence, from the communal perspective on currency, the primary aim of forgery prevention was to protect the public and their trust in circulating media. Indeed, a group of engravers who endorsed Alexander Tilloch's proposal for a new Bank-note design in 1797 stressed that the Bank had the moral responsibility to guard the public against loss from accepting false notes. Bentham, in contrast, believed that forgery prevention was ultimately to protect the issuer of paper currency, an idea that resonated with the Bank directors, who had no doubt that the problem of forgery firmly rested in the domain of their private business concern. In the main, the Bank was reluctant to make any drastic changes in note design. When Bentham sent his plans for forgery prevention to the Bank, he became one of those proposers whose forgery prevention plan was summarily turned down by the Bank's directors, who were not easily persuaded by outsiders' proposals of new designs, which they generally thought were no superior to the conventional note design they were accustomed to.[8] At a time when the public nature of Bank-note circulation was scarcely recognised by the Bank's directors, there was no means by which to challenge the Bank's decision

---

[7] Bentham was much less concerned with currency depreciation from overissue. *Collected Works of Jeremy Bentham: Correspondence*, vi: *January 1798 to December 1801*, ed. J. R. Dinwiddy (Oxford, 1984), 379. Bentham's belief in the stability of inconvertible paper currency rested on his recognition of the deferred nature of its payment. See Jeremy Bentham's letter intended for George Rose, c. June 1799, Bentham, *Collected Works*, vi, 169, 171. Compare Mary Poovey, *Genres of the Credit Economy: Mediating Value in Eighteenth- and Nineteenth-Century Britain* (Chicago, IL, 2008), 15, 73.

[8] Committee for Improvement of Bank Notes, BE, M5/250, fol. 10; Jeremy Bentham to Samuel Bentham, 26 Apr. 1800, Bentham, *Collected Works*, vi, 292.

Figure 5.1 £1 Bank note dated 14 August 1810 stamped as paid.
© Bank of England. Bank of England Museum Accession I/064

to keep its note design, which had barely changed since the early eighteenth century (Figure 5.1). Nor was there any mechanism for the state or parliament – let alone the public – to steer the way the Bank responded to the threat of forged notes. In the early years of the Bank Restriction, the Bank had a free hand in expanding its policing functions for suppressing forgery, wielding judicial violence against forgers and those who were implicated in the circulation of inauthentic notes.[9]

The issue of forgery gained renewed importance in the late 1810s, when the post-war depression led to a breeding ground for economic crimes and the circulation of forged notes saw a significant increase. The Bank's relentless prosecution of those who committed forgery-related crimes – mostly users of forged notes – infuriated law reformers and note users alike. The Bank's forgery prosecutions exacerbated the already strained relations between the note users and the Bank. As discussed in Chapter 4, the Stanhope Act of 1811 made it a legal obligation to accept the Bank note at its face value, rendering it what contemporaries recognised as a forced currency. The mutation of the Bank note, which many Britons had seen as currency based on voluntary acceptance, into a currency of authority exposed note users to the vagaries of monetary value fluctuations. Simultaneously, note users were now exposed to the greater risk of being victims of forgery crime because the Stanhope Act made it practically impossible to refuse payment in paper currency.

Discontent with the Bank's overgrown power to enforce note circulation – based on the Bank Restriction and the Stanhope Act – and its violent powers for policing and punishing users of forged notes soon became apparent in parliament, the criminal court and intensifying public hostility against the Bank. In early 1818, James Mackintosh led the law reformers' assault on the Bank by initiating a series of motions that made the Bank's forgery prosecutions subject to close public scrutiny. In the criminal court, the legitimacy of the Bank's policing and prosecutions was questioned in high-profile cases involving forged Bank notes. Daring note users such as the historical engraver Thomas Ranson, in an attempt to limit the Bank's use of judicial force, confronted the Bank over the legality and propriety of its policing activity, culminating with the case of *Brooks v. Warwick*. The forgery crisis also highlights the *public* nature of the Bank of England note, as critics of the Bank attributed the increased circulation of forged notes to a neglect of preventive measures that was rooted in the Bank's disregard of note users' plight and its refusal to consult the broad expert community of inventive minds, of which Britain had no shortage. The public backlash, which demanded curbing of the Bank's power and reassertion of the rights and roles of the British note-using public, was a manifestation of a

---

[9] Since its foundation, the Bank had long been engaged with the process of instituting penal legislation for protecting its business. See Carl Wennerlind, 'The Death Penalty as Monetary Policy: The Practice and Punishment of Monetary Crime, 1690–1830', *History of Political Economy*, 36 (2004), 131–61.

radicalised version of communal currency. While acceptance of the Bank note was no longer voluntary, Britain's note users claimed they were still part of a community on which the value of paper currency rested; hence, they ought to have some say in how the threat of forged paper currency was managed and contained. Another version of mutated communal-currency theory that was firmly linked with a radical political agenda was articulated by William Cobbett, who envisaged a political revolution through inundating Britain with forged notes and destroying all public confidence in paper currency. Thus, the debate on forgery and note improvement became a battleground for alternative ideas about paper currency, before the resumption of cash payments emerged as the most viable solution to the various ills attributed to the inconvertible currency system.

Note Design and Visions of Currency

In many ways, British views on paper currency in the early part of the Bank Restriction period were defined by the French experience of the fiat currency, the *assignat*, and this was also true regarding the debate on forgery and its prevention. It was probably the prevalence of forgery in French *assignats* that led an English inventor, Alexander Tilloch, to contemplate the implications of forgery for the English currency system. In 1790, he communicated his 'discovery' concerning a forgery-proof printing process to the undersecretary of state for the home department, Evan Nepean.[10] Tilloch wrote that it was out of sheer favour to his native country that he was offering to the British government the advantage of his invention of the 'art of producing cross hatches as artists state them, that is lines crossing one another at angle either straight, curved, or mixed'. Should it decide not to accept his offer, he would bring the plan to France 'for the security of their Assignats'.[11] Tilloch's plan mildly impressed Nepean, but it apparently failed to move Lord Hawkesbury (later the first Earl of Liverpool) to consider the proposal any further, as there was no evidence that he consulted the Bank of England on the

---

[10] A. Tilloch, 'Outlines of a Plan to Prevent the Forgery of Circulating Notes or Bank Bills', 9 Nov. 1790, TNA, HO 42/17, fol. 68. See also Virginia Hewitt and John Keyworth, *As Good as Gold: 300 Years of British Bank Note Design* (London, 1987), 48.

[11] Tilloch to Nepean, 19 Oct. 1790, TNA, HO 42/17, fol. 70. See also Alan Philip Keri Davies, 'William Blake in Contexts: Family Friendships, and Some Intellectual Microcultures of Eighteenth- and Nineteenth-Century England' (unpublished PhD thesis, University of Surrey, 2003), 148–9. Tilloch apparently offered his plan to 'the commission d'Assignats at Paris'. *Annual Register*, 1825, 223.

matter.[12] In the early 1790s, forgery of paper currency was less pressing in England than in France, where *assignats* were frequently counterfeited.[13] Thus, when another inventive mind, Lord Stanhope, proposed his somewhat idiosyncratic 'bank book' plan in 1791 – a precursor to the Stanhope Act of 1811 – it was chiefly intended as a measure to protect the French paper currency from counterfeiters.[14] In England, counterforgery measures aroused little interest among government officials and the Bank of England's directors.

The outbreak of the war with France and subsequent financial instability, which led the Bank to lower its minimum note denomination to £5 in 1794, served as a prompt for Jeremy Bentham to begin his relatively short but intensive engagement with the question of currency.[15] His early writings on currency grew out of his interest in identifying additional government revenue sources and reducing public debt; in this, he was undoubtedly influenced by contemporary discussion of the expansion of paper credit and, like many of his contemporaries, by the recent French experience of *assignats*.[16] What set Bentham apart from most of his contemporaries was that he regarded state monopoly as the centrepiece of his plan for a new paper currency. As articulated in a series of mostly unpublished writings, Bentham envisaged that a Treasury-issued interest-bearing paper currency would replace various privately issued banknotes, including those issued by the Bank of England.[17] He stressed that the state would be able to reduce its debt burden by circulating notes with low interest, while monopolising the profit from issuing paper

---

[12] Nepean to Lord Hawkesbury, 9 Nov. 1790, TNA, HO 42/17, fols. 66–7.

[13] Rebecca L. Spang, *Stuff and Money in the Time of the French Revolution* (Cambridge, MA, 2015), ch. 5.

[14] Charles Stanhope, *Lettres de Milord Stanhope à M. de Condorcet* (Paris, 1791).

[15] This period also marks his transition from philosophical phase to practical phase in his career as a political philosopher, a shift that was mirrored, in a compressed fashion, in his changing focus from the theoretical to practical aspects of money. Stark, 'Introduction', 15 and passim.

[16] Bentham was well aware of, and in some cases engaged with, contemporary discussions of the creation of additional currency-issuing institutions or new forms of paper currency, proposed, for example, by Ambrose Weston and Frederick Eden. Bentham, *Collected Works*, vi, pp. xxii, 168–74; Takuo Dōme, *The Political Economy of Public Finance in Britain, 1767–1873* (London, 2004), 78–80; Pedro Schwartz, 'Central Bank Monopoly in the History of Economic Thought: A Century of Myopia in England', in Pascal Salin, ed., *Currency Competition and Monetary Union* (The Hague, 1984), 108; Stark, 'Introduction', 28–40, 85–95.

[17] Stark, 'Introduction', 155 and passim. For the text and periodisation of Bentham's writings on exchequer notes and annuity notes, Michael Quinn's new edition is the most reliable. However, as the latest volume of Quinn's edition is yet to become available, this chapter's references are mostly to Stark's edition.

currency that bankers had enjoyed.[18] In this plan, the annuity note would at first attract investors, but as the interest on the note would subsequently be reduced its function as a circulating medium would become pronounced. Bentham embraced the idea of paper currency created *by authority*. In the initial phase of their introduction, annuity notes would require some enforcement measures by the government, such as obliging investors in public loans to accept some annuity notes and making annuity notes a chief mode of transaction at public offices.[19] It was a beneficial proposition for both the government and the public, Bentham believed, as while the government would gain a powerful economic resource, state regulation of paper circulation would reduce the risk of commercial boom and bust.

One rationale for giving the state a monopoly over paper currency was, Bentham argued, better protection for the public from 'bad paper currency' issued by private individuals with dubious credit and from the more general threat posed by forgery.[20] Rather than leaving it to private initiatives, such as the Bank of England's prosecution of forgers, the state would more effectively suppress the various criminal attempts of forgers as a threat to its sovereign power of money creation. The government had an interest in guarding against forgery as the circulation of counterfeit notes would depreciate the value of genuine notes.[21] Hence, the government would have to meet the challenge to its prerogative.

The centrality of political authority in Bentham's monetary thought clearly affected how he envisaged the physical aspect of his proposed paper currency, and his idea of authority was no more apparent than in his preoccupation with one design feature: human portraits on circulating notes. Repeatedly, Bentham stressed the importance of notes having portraits of 'some real person', an idea, interestingly, that originally came to him through his encounter with Lord Stanhope's pamphlet on the prevention of forgery of coins around 1780.[22] In his earlier government note schemes, Bentham had suggested printing multiple human figures, that of the sovereign, the lords of the Treasury, the auditor and the

[18] Jeremy Bentham, 'Abstract or Compressed View of a Tract Intituled Circulating Annuities', in *Jeremy Bentham's Economic Writings*, ii, 201–300; Stark, 'Introduction', 51–4.

[19] Jeremy Bentham, 'Proposal for the Circulation of a [New] Species of Paper Currency', in *Jeremy Bentham's Economic Writings*, ii, 171. For instance, Bentham surmised that annuity notes could possibly be introduced through the government refusing to receive banknotes at public offices. Nathalie Sigot and Ghislain Deleplace, 'From Annuity Notes to Bank Notes: A Change in Bentham's Theory of Money', *History of Economic Ideas*, 20 (2012), 58.

[20] Bentham, 'Paper Currency', 157–8.   [21] Bentham, 'Paper Currency', 191.

[22] Bentham, 'Exchequer Notes', 311.

barons of the Exchequer. Later, in his recommendation of a new design for the Bank note, Bentham similarly suggested including portraits of the Bank's governor and cashier.[23] Bentham did not view having human figures on notes just as a counter-forgery measure; it connected with his vision of a well-managed paper-currency system as a mechanism to create solidarity in a political system. His idea of a monetary system was fundamentally a political vision, the scope of which was not limited to state-issued annuity notes and the Bank of England note but applied equally to a currency that would circulate across the British Empire. In his elaboration of the annuity note, Bentham described paper currency as a security for 'the old established constitution, by engaging the purses and affections of the monied interest'.[24] Paper money would form a point of engagement for different interests, ethnicities and nationalities, from Ireland to British India:

What a sheet-anchor to British dominion ... if by insensible and voluntary steps the population of that remote, most expanded, and most expansive branch of the British empire, should be led to repose the bulk of their fortunes and their hopes on a paper bearing the image and superscription of a British governor![25]

Using his geographical imagination and his vision of a system of government, Bentham described paper currency as a material object binding together nations and peoples. It was a version of an imperialistic vision, but as Jennifer Pitts argues Bentham did not subscribe to outright authoritarian rule in the colonies.[26] To be more precise, as far as Bentham's monetary idea was concerned, a currency of authority could take the place of direct authoritarian rule, serving as a soft means of maintaining trust and goodwill among the indigenous population. Somewhat naively, Bentham envisaged an imperial currency system that was voluntarily accepted by the colonial population, believing that circulating notes bearing the image of 'a British governor' would foster popular attachment to the ruling country, thereby ensuring peace across the imperial territories.[27] When the Indian population 'from the Zemindar to the Ryot, every Hindoo, every Mussulman' came to own British paper currency, Bentham mused, they would be 'converted into a pensioner of the British government'. Here, one can observe a continuity in the stream

---

[23] 'Mr. Bentham's Plan for Preventing Forgery of Bank Notes &c.' University College London, Special Collections, Bentham Manuscripts, box 3b, 36/341–57. References here are folio numbers in the original document.

[24] Bentham, 'Circulating Annuities', 296.   [25] Bentham, 'Circulating Annuities', 297.

[26] Jennifer Pitts, *A Turn to Empire: The Rise of Imperial Liberalism in Britain and France* (Princeton, NJ, 2005), 117. See also Patrick Brantlinger, *Fictions of State: Culture and Credit in Britain, 1694–1994* (Ithaca, NY, 1996), 104–5.

[27] Bentham, 'Circulating Annuities', 297.

of thought from the eighteenth century, which regarded commerce as a logic of sociability and a civilising force.[28] Similarly, in Bentham's view of colonial monetary order, paper currency replaced commerce in creating social bonds, contributing to stability in the finances and political rule of the British Empire. His imperial vision of currency shows how intimately linked Bentham's conception of the political function of money was with the form of currency. No other theorists or inventors in the 1790s and 1800s engaged with the issue of paper currency so comprehensively as Bentham. While speculating upon the macro system of the imperial currency network, the minutest details of the materiality of paper currency did not escape his dissecting eye. Examining the appearance and texture of existing paper instruments, Bentham's comments extended to their size, thickness and physical properties – and how these factors would affect their circulation. Bentham clearly appreciated the psychological effect of Bank-note design when he approvingly remarked, 'there is something in the neatness of the engraving, and the conspicuous and emphatic display of the sum, that cannot but be particularly attractive and fascinating to an ordinary eye'.[29]

Britain's introduction of inconvertible paper currency in 1797 and the subsequent rise in forged-note circulation made forgery prevention far more urgent than in the previous period, offering an opportunity for enterprising inventors to present their forgery-proof note design to the Bank of England. In that year, it became known that the Bank's directors were willing to consider suggestions made by those outside the Bank as long as they had ingenious plans for curbing the increase in the number of forged notes.[30]

One of the first to propose a note-improvement plan was Alexander Tilloch, an inventor with a keen entrepreneurial mind.[31] Tilloch's proposal was practically identical to the one he had suggested to the British government seven years earlier, a design in which the conventional style of promissory note was surrounded by a patchwork of cross-hatching patterns produced by a process of his own invention (Figure 5.2).[32] The Bank's directors were not, however, persuaded by Tilloch's claim that his

---

[28] Albert O. Hirschman, *The Passions and the Interests: Political Arguments for Capitalism before Its Triumph* (Princeton, NJ, 1977).

[29] Bentham, 'Exchequer Notes', 333.

[30] Byatt, *Promises to Pay*, 57; Hewitt and Keyworth, *As Good as Gold*, 47; Mackenzie, *Bank of England Note*, 48.

[31] For a reappraisal of Tilloch's influence, see Davies, 'William Blake in Contexts', ch. 4.

[32] Virginia Hewitt, 'Beware of Imitations: The Campaign for a New Bank of England Note, 1797–1821', *Numismatic Chronicle*, 158 (1998), 200. On the technical aspects of Tilloch's plan, see Mark Crosby, 'Blake and the Banknote Crises of 1797, 1800, and 1818', *University of Toronto Quarterly*, 80 (2011), 817–8.

Figure 5.2 Alexander Tilloch's trial design for the £5 Bank note, 1797.
© Trustees of the British Museum

proposed design 'could not be imitated', and ordered the Bank's master engraver, Garnet Terry, to reproduce Tilloch's specimen. During an interview at the Bank in May 1797, Terry delivered a copy of Tilloch's note and, despite the inventor's protest that it was far from a perfect facsimile, the Bank's directors saw it as sufficient ground for rejecting the proposal.[33] Tilloch was not alone in being disappointed by the Bank's rejection. In the same year, the Bank turned down a plan submitted by a former employee of the French Mint, Anthony Bessemer, on the advice of Terry. Bessemer's proposal – yet another example of the coevolution of the French and English discussion on note improvement in the 1790s – was based on his invention of 'identic [sic] printing', a mechanical means to print on both sides of the note, with the lettering on one side perfectly mirroring the other.[34] Hardly impressed by Bessemer's plan, Terry commented to the Bank's Committee of Treasury that its adoption 'would be attended with very great trouble, expense and want

[33] CT, 4 and 9 May 1797, BE, G8/8, fols. 20, 23; Minutes of Committee for Improvement of Bank Notes, BE, M5/245, fol. 1. See also CT, 4 July 1797, BE, G8/8, fol. 39; Secretary's letter books, 14 Jan. and 6 July 1797, BE, G23/48, fols. 8, 11.

[34] The description of Bessemer's plan is based on his letter to the Society of Arts, to which he sent his proposal after it was rejected by the Bank. Bessemer to More, 11 Feb. 1798, Royal Society of Arts Archive, RSA/PR/AR/103/10/469.

of room', while expressing his doubt that Bessemer's plan would effectively prevent forgery.[35]

Tilloch's campaign to promote his note-improvement plan is particularly notable for including an appeal to the public interest. In 1797, he was able to enlist nineteen endorsers for his plan, including John Landseer, Francis Bartolozzi and Wilson Lowry, presenting it as a collective endeavour of the engraving and printing profession.[36] After the Bank rejected it, a public letter appeared in *Monthly Magazine*, accusing the Bank of refusing several promising proposals brought to it by able experts – Tilloch was probably behind this attempt to mobilise public opinion so that the Bank might be forced to revise its decision. The letter stressed that improvement of the Bank note design was a matter of public interest, and the engravers supported Tilloch's scheme out of their sense of 'a duty which we believe in our conscience we owe to the community, who ought to be secured, as far as possible, against the losses [from forged notes]'.[37] For the Bank's directors, the question of note design belonged exclusively to the realm of their business decisions, and they hardly thought of it as their social responsibility. The public nature of the forgery problem would return with a vengeance nearly two decades later, but in the early years of the Bank Restriction the Bank effectively fended off any intervention concerning its response to the threat of forgery, including in the design features of the Bank note.

Three years later, with the encouragement of Patrick Colquhoun, who had been in close contact with the Bank on the problem of forged coins, Bentham sent his plan 'for preventing Forgery of Bank Notes' to Threadneedle Street.[38] The plan was an extended version of the forgery prevention measures that he had described in his exchequer-note scheme, conceived around 1794.[39] As noted earlier, the principal element in Bentham's Bank-note improvement was human figures in the note design, in which different styles and techniques of engraving were

[35] CT, 8 Aug. 1797, BE, G8/8, fol. 50.
[36] Committee for Improvement of Bank Notes, BM, M5/258, fol. 23; *The Times*, 21 Mar. 1818 (original endorsement dated 4 Apr. 1797). The names on the certificate are Francis Bartolozzi, James Heath, James Fittler, J. Landseer, J. R. Smith, Francis Haward, James Basire, William Sharp, William Byrne, Thomas Holloway, W. S. Blake, John Puke, William Blake, William Skelton, Mariano Bovi, Robert Dunkarton, Wilson Lowry, John Anderson and Richard Austin. *The Star*, 31 Mar. 1818; *The Times*, 31 Mar. 1818. For more detail, see Hiroki Shin, 'The Culture of Paper Money in Britain: The Bank of England Note during the Bank Restriction Period, 1797–1821' (unpublished PhD thesis, University of Cambridge, 2009), 247–82.
[37] *The Times*, 6 July 1818.
[38] Committee for Improvement of Bank Notes, BE, M5/250; To Samuel Bentham, 26 Apr. 1800, Bentham, *Collected Works*, vi, 292.
[39] Bentham, 'Exchequer Notes', 310–15; Bentham, 'Paper Currency', 191–6.

represented. Bentham regarded the combination of multiple skills as being as important as the intricate design elements. Bentham saw that the problem with the current Bank note was that it featured only a few artistic elements of paper making, letter engraving and figure engraving.[40] To this conventional mix of arts, he introduced additional processes in letterpress, copper engraving and wood engraving. A considerable number of tools and skills would be needed to complete the entire process, which would deter forgers from replicating it.[41]

In the spring of 1800, the Bank summarily rejected Bentham's proposal, as it did the fifty or so other plans that the directors examined between 1797 and 1802. The suggestions included using coloured paper, alternative paper materials, special letter presses and stamps, to give some examples.[42] Like Bentham's, at least two proposals recommended using portraits in the note design. The Bank's directors were difficult people to convince, though they kept inspecting incoming plans throughout the Bank Restriction period. In February 1802, the Bank established a special committee to examine plans for the improvement of Bank notes, which inspected sixteen further proposals, including one submitted by a renowned wood engraver, Thomas Bewick.[43] Yet, the Bank's directors set the bar high in terms of what they regarded as an effective method for preventing forgery, leading to the conclusion that no proposal would warrant a drastic change in the design of the Bank note.[44] Although the Bank was not entirely averse to innovation, it nonetheless showed extreme caution in introducing new features in the notes or modifying their manufacturing process. Among a few exceptions was the introduction of a new watermark with waved lines in 1800, a method invented by a mould maker, William Brewer.[45] Yet, compared to the number of proposals the Bank had received, the change in the Bank note's appearance was very small, leading to the criticism, not least from those whose plans had been turned down by the Bank, that the Bank directors' reluctance to change the design was due to their sheer conservatism. John Landseer, one of the keenest supporters of Tilloch's proposal, argued that it was equally 'a point both of duty and honour, for the

[40] Mackenzie, Bank of England Note, 53; 'Mr. Bentham's Plan', fols. 5–6, 30.
[41] 'Mr. Bentham's Plan', fols. 11–12. Bentham suggested the use of Patrick Wilson's invention to transfer an original copper engraving to glass, in order to reduce expense. 'Mr. Bentham's Plan', fol. 1.
[42] 'Committee for Improvement of Bank Notes: Suggestions Considered', BE, M5/251.
[43] CD, 25 Feb. 1802, BE, G4/29, fol. 151.
[44] Thomas Bewick, A Memoir of Thomas Bewick, Written by Himself, ed. Iain Bain (London, 1975), 128.
[45] CT, 4 Aug. 1799, 13 Aug. 1799, 15 Oct. 1799, BE, G8/09, fols. 16, 18, 27; Byatt, Promises to Pay, 14; Mackenzie, Bank of England Note, 10.

Bank Directors … to call for the talents and ingenuity of the country in fair competition, by offering a handsome reward for the best practical means of preventing forgery on the bank'.[46] Landseer's exhortation did not receive any response from the Bank.

If Bentham's failure to convince the Bank was due to its directors' conservative attitude to note design, Bentham's alienation in the contemporary currency debate was probably owing to his unique combination of the two strands of monetary theory – communal currency and fiat currency. Although his emphasis later shifted, Bentham never abandoned the fiat-currency perspective.[47] There were, especially in the mid-1790s, several writers who advocated state-issued currency, but fiat currency, with its association with the French *assignat*, was anathema to most British theorists, politicians and financiers and was rarely discussed in public during the Bank Restriction period. Bentham brought his annuity scheme to government officials; it was first examined by George Rose and then by his successor Nicholas Vansittart, who, after giving it some consideration, decided not to proceed with the state currency in August 1801.[48] As it became increasingly apparent to Bentham that neither the Bank nor the government was likely to adopt his proposals, the role of political authority gradually receded into the background in his further writings on currency. Instead, he focused more on the question of private note issue and its inherent instability.[49] But this shift of attention, which brought Bentham's monetary thought a step closer to the popular idea of currency based on voluntary acceptance, did not see him fully develop his ideas as his intellectual output on currency ceased thereafter – nor did he engage in the intellectual debate on paper currency that eventually grew into the Bullionist Controversy.[50] Arguably, Bentham's marginal position in the history of monetary thought stemmed largely from his inclination towards the state theory of paper currency, which was a minority view in early nineteenth-century

---

[46] John Landseer, 'To the Editor of the Monthly Magazine', *Monthly Magazine*, 5 (1798), 5.

[47] Sigot and Deleplace argue that Bentham may not have been entirely comfortable with the idea of 'coercive measures' in his systemic vision. Sigot and Deleplace, 'From Annuity Notes to Bank Notes', 48.

[48] Stark, 'Introduction', 33–4, 95.

[49] Sigot and Deleplace argue that Bentham shifted from macro to micro because his national-currency system required compulsory measures. My discussion here sheds light on *why* Bentham avoided compulsory measures. Sigot and Deleplace, 'From Annuity Notes to Bank Notes', 48. See also Dōme, *Political Economy of Public Finance*, 83–5.

[50] Although Etienne Dumont planned to publish Bentham's 'The True Alarm' in 1810. Schwartz, 'Central Bank Monopoly', 109.

Britain. Yet, Bentham's intellectual activity across monetary theory, forgery prevention and note improvement reveals how Bentham, one of the great systemic thinkers of the age, grasped the interconnected nature of these issues, which was only vaguely recognised by his contemporaries.

The Bank and Forgery

As Bentham frankly acknowledged in his 'Plan for Preventing Forgery', improving note design and its production process alone would be insufficient for eliminating the crime. The prevention and suppression of forgery would, Bentham wrote, rely equally on the administration of penal justice because the prospect of punishment needed to be realistic and sufficiently severe for it to act as a deterrent.[51] The Bank seemed to have more faith in retribution than prevention as it became more active in seeking punishment of forgers than it was in note improvement. In the first year of the Bank Restriction, the Bank prosecuted no more than two forgers, and one was acquitted. Four years later, in 1800, forty-four Bank prosecutions were recorded, of which twenty-nine were capitally convicted (Table 5.2).[52] At the time, the Bank's policing activity was less conspicuous than that of the Royal Mint – the latter brought to court around 100 counterfeiters of regal coins per year – but the Bank's sphere of operation was expanding.[53] The more Britain's monetary system became dominated by paper currency, the starker the threat posed by note forgery was felt. There was legal protection for various forms of paper instruments, and many forgery-related crimes, including uttering (i.e. passing), altering, vending and bartering fabricated notes, were punishable by the death penalty.[54] This extensive system of judicial violence was maintained as much by the Bank as by the underdeveloped police system. As a result, the surge in the number of forgery

---

[51] 'Mr. Bentham's Plan', fols. 29–30.

[52] House of Commons, *Account of Number of Prosecutions by Mint for Counterfeiting Legal Coin of Realm, 1783–1811* (1818).

[53] House of Commons, *Account of Number of Prosecutions by Mint for Counterfeiting Legal Coin of Realm, 1797–1818* (1818). For instance, the Bank informed the Earl of Liverpool (then the master of the mint) in May 1797 that a large quantity of counterfeit silver dollars were fabricated in Birmingham and some manufactories near London. Secretary's letter books, 9 May 1797, G23/48, fol. 1.

[54] 8 & 9 William III, c. 20, and 11 Geo. I, c. 9. See Philip Handler, 'The Limits of Discretion: Forgery and the Jury at the Old Bailey 1818–1821', in J. Cairns and G. McLeod, eds., *'The Dearest Birthright of the People of England': The Jury in the History of the Common Law* (Oxford, 2002), 156; Randall McGowen, 'Making the "Bloody Code"? Forgery Legislation in Eighteenth Century England', in Norma Landau, ed., *Law, Crime and English Society, 1660–1830* (Cambridge, 2002), 129; Judy Slinn, *A History of Freshfields* (London, 1984), 19.

Table 5.2 *Prosecutions for Bank-note forgery and regal-coin forgery*

Year	Capital convictions for Bank-note forgery	Convictions for possession of forged notes	Acquittals	Total prosecutions for Bank-note forgery	Prosecutions for regal coin forgery	Convictions for regal coin forgery
1783	0		0	0	15	7
1784	2		0	2	63	33
1785	0		0	0	42	21
1786	0		0	0	33	23
1787	0		0	0	36	22
1788	1		0	1	50	26
1789	0		1	1	49	25
1790	0		0	0	60	49
1791	0		0	0	71	40
1792	0		0	0	78	60
1793	0		0	0	73	47
1794	0		0	0	76	61
1795	0		0	0	75	58
1796	0		0	0	87	65
1797	1		1	2	103	77
1798	11		1	12	108	85
1799	12		3	15	107	86
1800	29		15	44	109	89
1801	32	1	21	54	131	102
1802	32	12	19	63	108	81
1803	7	1	1	9	89	64
1804	13	8	4	25	73	51
1805	10	14	4	28	124	85
1806	0	9	1	10	97	81
1807	16	24	5	45	103	80

Table 5.2 (cont.)

Year	Capital convictions for Bank-note forgery	Convictions for possession of forged notes	Acquittals	Total prosecutions for Bank-note forgery	Prosecutions for regal coin forgery	Convictions for regal coin forgery
1808	9	23	2	34	89	72
1809	23	29	16	68	101	80
1810	10	16	3	29	127	107
1811	5	19	9	33	116	93
1812	26	26	12	64	149	118
1813	9	49	7	65	173	149
1814	5	39	3	47	134	112
1815	8	51	5	63	150	125
1816	20	84	16	120	128	103
1817	33	95	15	142	292	240
1818	62	165	33	260	272	–
1819	33	160	35	228	279	–
1820	77	275	52	404	180	–
1821	41	93	105	239	174	–
1822	16	0	–	–	185	–
1823	6	0	–	–	214	–
1824	5	0	–	–	190	–
1825	2	0	–	–	221	–
1826	18	4	–	–	290	–

Sources: A return of the number of forged notes of every denomination brought to the Bank of England for payment, BE, F2/112; House of Commons, Account of Number of Persons Prosecuted for Forging and Uttering Notes of Bank of England, 1783–1818 (1818); House of Commons, Return of Number of Persons Convicted of Forgery on Bank of England, 1791–1829 (1830); House of Commons, Account of Number of Prosecutions by Mint for Counterfeiting Legal Coin of Realm, 1797–1818 (1818); House of Commons, Account of Number of Prosecutions by Mint for Counterfeiting Legal Coin of Realm, 1818–1827 (1828).

prosecutions after the suspension of cash payments drained the Bank's human and financial resources. The Bank's legal expenses concerning forgery prosecution had increased nearly tenfold from £1,538 in 1797 to £11,394 in 1801.[55] In 1801, the Bank sought legislation that would punish possession of forged notes as a misdemeanour, which was as much to prevent indiscriminate application of the death penalty to petty criminals – who had no direct link to the production of the forged note – as to reduce the Bank's expense in prosecuting them.[56]

During the Bank Restriction period, the geographical scope of forgery crime broadened as forgers often operated across borders. In 1799, the Dublin authorities raided a house of forgery run by a publican, Henry Truffit, in Abbey Street. The search of the premises led to the discovery of 200 forged Bank of England notes, along with a copper plate that was used for manufacturing them.[57] The subsequent interrogation revealed that Truffit and his accomplices intended to travel to Liverpool and other parts of England to put the notes into circulation. As the Truffit case made evident, neither Irish nor English law could adequately deal with the cross-border nature of forgery crime as, according to Irish law, counterfeiting English notes in Ireland was merely a misdemeanour, though forging Bank of Ireland notes had been punishable by the death penalty since 1798.[58] In a similar trial in 1804, the Scottish court acquitted Richard Mindham, who sold forged Bank of England notes in northern England and Scotland, as it ruled that the English law on forgery did not cover Scotland.[59] Both Truffit's and Mindham's case prompted the

---

[55] House of Commons, *Account of Expense Incurred by Bank of England in Prosecutions for Forging Bank Notes, 1797–1818* (1818).

[56] 41 Geo. III, c. 39. For details, see Randall McGowen, 'Managing the Gallows: The Bank of England and the Death Penalty, 1797–1821', *Law and History Review*, 25 (2007), 252–5. Thenceforward, the Bank prosecution adopted a strategy of bringing two charges, felony and minor offence, and in many cases, the accused only received punishment for the minor offence on pleading guilty of possession (a form of plea bargain), for which the punishment was fourteen years' transportation. House of Commons, *Select Committee on Criminal Laws Relating to Capital Punishment in Felonies* (1819), 23; McGowen, 'Managing the Gallows', 254. Many convicted criminals offered to give information to the Bank, in an attempt to mitigate the sentence. Wilfred M. Acres, *The Bank of England from Within, 1694–1900* (London, 1931), i, 342; Handler, 'Limits of Discretion', 168; McGowen, 'Policing of Forgery', 98; Minutes of Committee for Lawsuits, 9 Apr. 1805, BE, M5/307.

[57] Winter & Kaye to John Pollock, 19 Feb. 1799, BE, F2/192.

[58] John Pollock to the Bank of England, 2 Feb. 1799, BE, F2/192. Until 1797, the penalty for forging Bank of Ireland notes was transportation for life. 37 Geo. III, c. 26 (Ir.); F. G. Hall, *The Bank of Ireland, 1783–1946* (Dublin, 1949), 55–6.

[59] 'Book of Adjournal', 3 Dec. 1804, NAS, JC4/3; *The Courier*, 19 Dec. 1804; *Edinburgh Evening Courant*, 3 and 20 Dec. 1804. For Mindham's other crimes, see trial papers relating to Richard Mindham, 14 July 1800, NAS JC26/1800/46. Note that Lord Meadowbank, who in 1797 suggested making the Bank of England note legal tender,

Bank of England to take collaborative action with the Irish and Scottish authorities to amend the legal loopholes.[60] The ensuing legislation extended the geographical reach for severe penalties for forging Bank of England notes, but it did not eradicate the crime over the border. In 1806 the Bank received information on a network of forgers, which involved an engraver in Bristol who prepared printing plates, a printer in London who produced forged notes, and two vendors who operated on both sides of the Scottish border to circulate the notes – one of the vendors was Mindham.[61]

As the legal historian Randall McGowen describes in detail, the Bank developed a network for detecting forgers, the operation of which was not confined to London.[62] During the Bank Restriction period, the Bank employed about a dozen forgery investigators. Working with the Bank's solicitors, Winter and Kaye, the investigators travelled around the country, hunting down forgers and assisting forgery prosecutions in provincial quarter sessions.[63] According to the minutes of the Bank's Committee for Lawsuits, which was established in 1802 to address the increased number of forgery prosecutions by the Bank, it received reports on ninety-seven cases of Bank-note forgery between 1802 and 1807 (Table 5.3). A mere thirteen cases related to London, while twenty-one reports came from Warwickshire and thirteen from Lancashire. If fewer in number, reports also came from various English places including Bristol, Cheshire, Dorset, Gloucestershire and Staffordshire. From the late 1800s onwards, there was a conspicuous increase in the number of reports from Lancashire, where the local preference for the Bank of England note was well known, and there was a similar increase in Hampshire, a place with war-induced Bank-note circulation. In Warwickshire, most of the reports of forgery-related crimes concerned Birmingham, a city that contemporaries often associated with forged-note circulation.[64] Indeed, between

was the only judge to support the extension of the English forgery law to Scotland. Hansard, 2nd ser., xxxiii (1818), cols. 330–1, 354; Letter to Henry Dundas, 11 Mar. 1797, NAS, GD51/5/235.

[60] Bank of England to William Wickham, 28 Feb. 1799, BE, F2/192; Winter & Kaye to John Pollock, 19 Feb. 1799, BE, F2/192; 39 Geo. III, c. 24. The Scottish act is 45 Geo. III, c. 89 (1805); David Hume and Benjamin Robert Bell, *Commentaries on the Law of Scotland: Respecting Crimes* (Edinburgh, 1986), i, 140.

[61] Minutes of Committee for Lawsuits, 11 Dec. 1806, BE, M5/307, fol. 189.

[62] Peter Cook, 'William Spurrier and the Forgery Laws', *Holdsworth Law Review*, 2 (1995–6), 2–97; McGowen, 'Policing of Forgery'; McGowen, 'Managing the Gallows'.

[63] CD, 23 Apr. 1818, G4/41, fols. 15–19.

[64] Minutes of Committee for Lawsuits, BE, M5/307–8. On the contemporary association of Birmingham with forgery crime, see Robert Southey, *Letters from England*, ed., Jack Simmons (London, 1951), letter 36. For Birmingham as the centre for the crime of forgery, Robert K. Dent, *The Making of Birmingham: Being a History of the Rise and*

Table 5.3 *Committee for Lawsuits, reports by origin and mode of crime*

Period	Place (county)	Uttering	Possession	Vending	Other offences	Total reports
1802–7	Lancashire	8	3		2	13
	London	8	3		2	13
	Warwickshire	5	4	5	2	21
	Others	51	13		3	50
	Subtotal	72	23	5	9	97
1808–13	Hampshire	11	3			14
	Lancashire	34	4	7	1	46
	London	32	6	3	2	43
	Warwickshire	5	4	4	1	12
	Others	91	13	3	10	81
	Subtotal	173	30	17	14	196
1814–19	Kent	42	3		1	46
	Surrey	41	5	5	1	52
	Lancashire	111	15	28		156
	London	448	26	14	8	497
	Warwickshire	32	9	30		71
	Yorkshire	20				20
	Wales	20	1			21
	Scotland	18	1	1		20
	Others	247	16	12	15	264
	Subtotal	979	76	90	25	1,147
1820–1	Kent	11				11
	Lancashire	36	7	19		62
	London	249	11	10		271
	Surrey	46		5		51
	Warwickshire	4	3	20		28
	Others	49	14	3	7	565
	Subtotal	395	35	57	7	988

Source: Minutes of Committee for Lawsuits, BE, M5/307–25.

1802 and 1807, the committee received five reports on the vending of forged notes, all of which were related to Birmingham.

Throughout the French wars, the Bank and the government played down the extent of forgery crimes. This was despite the Bank having begun its war against forgers in the early years of the Bank Restriction, which was sporadically mentioned in parliamentary debates, popular pamphlets and newspapers.[65] A pamphlet published in 1802, *Serious Reflections on Paper Money in General* had the subtitle 'the alarming inundation of forged Bank Notes'. Its anonymous author claimed that numerous shopkeepers and artisans were deceived by spurious Bank notes, and even when they doubted the authenticity of the notes in their hand, their precarious economic situation tempted them to pass them on to others.[66] In the same year, Denbigh MP Thomas Jones urged the parliament to suppress the spread of forged Bank notes, claiming that one-tenth or more of circulating Bank notes were forged ones.[67] One of the Bank's directors, William Manning, 'utterly denied' the prevalence of forgery, while keeping quiet about the increasing number of inauthentic notes the Bank was receiving.[68] In wartime, the Bank attributed forgery crime to French economic warfare, and there were grounds for this. Already in late 1797, there were reports of forged Bank of England notes in circulation on the continent, and the Bank's Committee of Treasury was informed, for instance, that forgers were printing inauthentic notes in Paris and selling them 'publicly' in Hamburg.[69] Accusing the French of circulating counterfeit notes in England was hardly far-fetched, since the British government employed the same tactic on its enemies.[70] It was also commonly believed that many French prisoners of war on British soil were manufacturing and circulating hand-copied Bank of England notes.[71]

[65] In 1797, John Sinclair noted that the two major threats to the paper-based monetary system were overissue and forgery. John Sinclair, *Letters Written to the Governor and Directors of the Bank of England on the Pecuniary Distresses of the Country* (London, 1797), 26.

[66] *Serious Reflections on Paper Money in General, Particularly on the Alarming Inundations of Forged Bank Notes* (London, 1802).

[67] Parliamentary Register, xvii (1802), 511–12.

[68] Acres, *Bank of England from Within*, i, 322–3; Committee of Inspection, 5 May 1801, BE, M5/354, fol. 84; Parliamentary Register, xvii (1802), 516.

[69] CT, 12 Dec. 1797, BE, G8/8, fol. 79. An earlier report is J. King to the collectors of customs of Dover, Gravesend Harwich, Yarmouth and Hull, 6 Jan. 1797, TNA, HO 42/40, fol. 187.

[70] The British government did this during the American War of Independence, and during its war with revolutionary France, it fabricated *assignats* and sent them to the continent. Peter Isaac, 'Sir John Swinburne and the Forged Assignats from Haughton Mill', *Archaeologia Aeliana*, 5 (1990), 158–63; Stephen Mihm, *A Nation of Counterfeiters: Capitalists, Con Men, and the Making of the United States* (Cambridge, MA, 2007), 41; John Philipson, 'A Case of Economic Warfare in the Late 18th Century: Three Early Paper-Moulds in the Collections of the Society', *Archaeologia Aeliana*, 5 (1990), 151–7; E. H. Stuart Jones, *The Last Invasion of Britain* (Cardiff, 1950), 5.

[71] In 1809, a secretary of the Bank of England, Robert Best, wrote to Alexander McLeay of the Transport Office expressing the need for separating the French prisoners involved in Bank-note forgery from other prisoners, in order to stop forged notes from being

The prevailing idea that note users' confidence was the foundation for the circulation of paper currency tended to obscure the true extent of forgery crime; bankers were often unwilling to divulge information about forgery to their customers as any doubt about the authenticity of circulating media would be a serious blow to a system based on trust. For the same reason, private banks in the provinces did not usually bother to return small numbers of forged notes they found to the Bank of England, instead processing them as a minor loss in the ordinary course of business.[72] With local trust in paper circulation at stake, country banks had ample reason to be secretive about the number of forged notes they had received. Similar concern about damaging local confidence often dictated country banks' response to forged Bank notes. In 1801, when Exeter was beset by rumours of forged-note circulation, Milford, Hogg, Nation – locally known as the City Bank – wrote to Winter and Kaye that it was attempting to quell local fears about forged-note circulation by 'taking any Notes which have been brought to the City Bank even though in a tattered state'.[73] A Bank inspector travelled to Exeter as much to gather information as to help restore local confidence. Collaborating with the City Bank, the investigator subsequently issued a statement that he had found no evidence of forged-note circulation in Exeter.[74] This statement, however, was at odds with the Bank of England's internal records that showed that the Bank discovered many forged and defaced notes in Exeter at the time.[75] The Exeter bank's approach – assuring the local community of the security of Bank notes by accepting notes of a dubious nature – was not as idiosyncratic as it may seem. A London banker, William Fry, commented that country bankers paid for forged notes 'for fear of affecting their credit'.[76] Contemporary records indicate that, in Scotland, there was similar reluctance to publicly acknowledge

---

circulated. Robert Best to Alexander McLeay, 14 Nov. 1809, Plymouth and West Devon RO, 413/205.

[72] McGowen, 'Policing of Forgery', 87. Thomas Babington – a nephew of Thomas Babington Macaulay – stated that the real extent of forgery was twice as much as the Bank's reported figure because 'A great number of them never found their way to the Bank. After circulation, they were either torn to pieces or put into the fire: and these amounted to more than went to the Bank'. Hansard, 2nd ser., xxxviii (1818), col. 283.

[73] To Winter & Kaye, 16 Apr. 1801, RBS, London, letter book of Milford, Hogg, Nation, MIL/7.

[74] *Exeter Flying Post*, 20 Apr. 1801; CT, 14 Apr. 1801, BE, G8/9, fol. 165.

[75] Throughout the Bank Restriction period, Exeter frequently suffered from forgery. CT, 30 June 1801, BE, G8/10, fols. 20–1; CT, 24 Feb. 1808, 24 Aug. 1808 and 14 Sept. 1808, BE, G8/14, fols. 76, 119, 123.

[76] House of Commons, *Select Committee on Criminal Laws Relating to Capital Punishment in Felonies*, 74.

forged-note circulation, and banks usually bore the damage of accepting forged notes without reporting them to the authorities.[77]

The general aversion to acknowledging forged-note circulation, grounded in the conviction that maintaining public faith in paper currency took precedence over any other concerns, defined British bankers' response to the crime of forgery in the early part of the Bank Restriction period. The remainder of this chapter will discuss how the public attitude to the forgery problem was drastically recast in the late 1810s in the face of a formidable rise in forged-note circulation, during which the Bank's extensive use of penal justice provoked the ire of Britain's note users.

The Forgery Crisis of 1818 and the Question of Property

In April 1818, Bentham's interest in the currency problem was briefly rekindled, and he contemplated publishing his early proposal on the annuity note in pamphlet form.[78] The nation's system of paper currency had developed in a way that proved most of his early premonitions were warranted: there was monetary inflation, widespread forgery and the loss of public confidence. To Bentham, the root of the problem was that the current system vested too much power in the Bank, allowing it to dominate the nation's paper currency and indeed its economic life at large. It was entirely different from Bentham's early idea of state-oriented paper currency, especially as the present system of paper currency appeared to be driven primarily by the interest of a private financial institution. Bentham found the system misconceived and harmful because 'the particular interest of that corporation is, in a way which is not now a secret to any body, subservient to the most insatiable of all lusts, the lust of power'.[79] While reaping benefit from circulating notes, he went on, the Bank barely took the trouble of protecting note users from the mischiefs caused by paper currency. His earlier respect for the Bank's directors and the Bank of England note had all but evaporated in his condemnation of the Bank, which was unable to contain the problem of forgery despite his

---

[77] S. G. Checkland, *Scottish Banking: A History, 1695–1973* (Glasgow, 1975), 186; David M. Walker, *A Legal History of Scotland* (Edinburgh, 1998), v, 715. About the 'dark figure' of the prosecutions concerning economic crimes, see V. A. C. Gatrell and T. B. Hadden, 'Criminal Statistics and Their Interpretation', in E. A. Wrigley, ed., *Nineteenth-Century Society: Essays in the Use of Quantitative Methods for the Study of Social Data* (Cambridge, 1972), 350; V. A. C. Gatrell, Bruce Lenman and Geoffrey Parker, *Crime and the Law: The Social History of Crime in Western Europe since 1500* (London, 1980), 267–8; Peter King, *Crime, Justice, and Discretion in England, 1740–1820* (Oxford, 2000), 11–12.

[78] 'Annuity Notes: Proposed Advertisement on Proposed Publication in Pamphlets', 15 Apr. 1818, UCL Bentham Manuscripts, box 2, fols. 1–14; Stark, 'Introduction', 66–95.

[79] Stark, 'Introduction', 68.

warnings nearly two decades ago. Bentham was hardly alone in accusing the Bank of refusing assistance from external experts to check the spread of forgery. Alexander Tilloch, now proprietor of *The Star* newspaper, was in a vengeful mood, refreshing his bitter memory from 1797 when the Bank's directors squarely denied his inimitable note design.[80]

In the 1810s, forgery of the Bank of England note became one of the most extensive forms of organised crime in Britain. To some extent, the great increase in forged notes was due to the significant expansion in the circulation of genuine Bank of England notes, especially small-denomination notes.[81] Between 1797 and 1810, the circulation of small Bank notes had increased tenfold, and during the same period, the number of forged notes reaching the Bank significantly increased, following a similar pattern of growth. However, while small-note circulation peaked in 1814, the number of forged notes discovered by the Bank soared in the late 1810s: the Bank identified 16,079 forged notes in 1815, 23,442 in 1816 and 29,521 in 1817.[82] The post-war increase in forgery crimes overwhelmed the Bank's Committee for Lawsuits, which received more than 1,100 reports between 1814 and 1819.[83] The geographical spread of the reports suggests that the problem of forgery was most severe in London (497 reports), Lancashire (156 reports) and Warwickshire (71 reports). The majority of reports from Lancashire concerned Manchester and Liverpool and those from Warwickshire mostly related to Birmingham. Spillover from the sizeable circulation of forged notes in the metropolis probably accounted for the relatively large number of reports concerning Kent (forty-six reports) and Surrey (fifty-two reports). Yet, the forgery problem was experienced across England as more than ten reports each came from Bristol, Cambridgeshire, Cheshire, Devon, Gloucestershire, Hampshire, Leicestershire, Norfolk, Northamptonshire, Staffordshire, Worcestershire and Yorkshire. Forgery remained a cross-border crime, as evidenced by twenty reports from Scotland, mostly from Edinburgh and Dumfries. Another twenty reports originated in various Welsh towns and ten reports came from Ireland.[84]

In 1818, for the first time, the official account of the extent of forgery crime and, no less importantly, the Bank's policing and prosecution activities became public knowledge. The ardent criminal law reformer

---

[80] *The Star*, 17 Jan. 1818, 2, 20 and 31 Mar. 1818.
[81] An account of the total number and nominal amount of forged Bank of England notes, BE, F2/111; McGowen, 'Policing of Forgery', 87.
[82] McGowen, 'Policing of Forgery', 87. Compare House of Commons, *An Account of the Total Number of Forged Bank Notes, 1812–April 1818* (1818).
[83] Minutes of Committee for Lawsuits, BE, M5/313–23.
[84] Minutes of Committee for Lawsuits, BE, M5/313–23.

James Mackintosh, in February, initiated a parliamentary motion that would in due course force the Bank to disclose information concerning forged-note circulation and its measures to suppress it, thus bringing to light what had long been a closely kept secret within the Bank.[85] The Bank initially resisted parliamentary intervention in what it regarded as a private business, but the government, mindful of the 'present state of the public mind', refused to shield the Bank from parliamentary scrutiny.[86] When the Bank reluctantly published the information concerning its prosecutions, the British public saw that Mackintosh's accusation that forgery prosecutions were part of the 'bloody code' was well founded.[87] Compared to only four forgery convictions between 1783 and 1795, 313 people had been sentenced to death between 1797 and 1818 for forgery-related crimes.[88] Forgery prosecutions became especially frequent in the post-war years. The total number of forgery convictions (including for Bank Post Bills) saw a sharp rise from 63 in 1815 to 260 in 1818, while capital convictions nearly doubled from 33 in 1817 to 62 in 1818.[89] Although some proportion of those convicted were given mitigated sentences, such ex post benevolence did not subdue the public uproar against the Bank, which was spreading like a wildfire.[90] With public support on his side, in May 1818 Mackintosh induced parliament to set up a committee to inquire into the means of preventing forgery.[91]

While Mackintosh's immediate concern in the late 1810s was criminal law reform, it should also be noted that Mackintosh, in his youth, was engaged in a public debate on paper currency. In *Vindiciae Gallicae* (1791), Mackintosh defended the French Revolution and, along with it, the French monetary system based on the fiat currency, the *assignat*. Against Edmund Burke, who despised the French paper currency as destructive of established social institutions, Mackintosh praised the

---

[85] Hansard, 2nd ser., xxxvii (1818), cols. 603–6. Previously, in 1816, General Thornton had managed to force the Bank to disclose information about the number of forged notes that had been brought into the Bank. Acres, *Bank of England from Within*, i, 336.

[86] BE, CT, 23 Apr. 1818, BE, G4/41, fols. 18–19.

[87] McGowen, 'Policing of Forgery', 83, 109.

[88] House of Commons, *Account of Number of Prosecutions by Mint for Counterfeiting Legal Coin of Realm, 1783–1811*; *Journals of the House of Commons*, lxxiii (1817–18), 761–2.

[89] In the same year, a flood of reports came into the Bank's Committee for Lawsuits, amounting to 286 reports, of which 244 were concerned with uttering, 21 with selling and 21 with forged-note possession. Minutes of Committee for Lawsuits, BE, M5/320 and M5/321.

[90] For the mitigation of sentences for Bank-note forgers, Deirdre Palk, 'Introduction', in Deirdre Palk, ed., *Prisoners' Letters to the Bank of England, 1781–1827* (London, 2007), pp. vii–xxv.

[91] Hansard, 2nd ser., xxxvii (1818), cols. 603–6; Hansard, 2nd ser., xxxviii (1818), cols. 671–703.

assignat's redistributive effect that broke the churches' monopoly of the land and made it available for French citizens.[92] The later mutation of the *assignat* into a coercive system of fiat money changed Mackintosh's mind and led to his reconciliation with Burke. It is not known how Mackintosh reacted to the introduction of inconvertible paper currency in Britain, but a parallel can be drawn between the Bank of England note of the late 1810s, which was made quasi-legal tender by the Stanhope Act, and the French paper currency that let Mackintosh down a quarter of a century previously. To Mackintosh, just as the *assignat* symbolised the degeneration of the French Revolution into tyrannical rule, the coercive power of the Bank of England must have appeared as a manifestation of a corrupt political system. What Mackintosh described as his 'vigorous war against the Bank of England' was in essence an attempt to check the Bank's arbitrary power that was supported by harsh penal law, a combination symptomatic of a degenerative political order.[93]

One clear sign of the Bank losing the support of the British public was the direct confrontation between note users and the Bank in the legal court. The Bank's prosecutors faced increasingly hostile juries and judges, who were reluctant to mete out harsh punishment to protect the Bank's privilege of issuing paper currency. The criminal justice system, upon which the Bank had depended to deter forgers, suddenly turned against the Bank. In his account of the forgery crisis in 1818, legal historian Philip Handler highlights the role of London juries in leading the judicial challenges to the Bank.[94] According to Handler, London juries reacted to the Bank's judicial violence, perceiving it as a threat to their economic interest and equally as a social injustice.[95] The Bank's prolific prosecution activity amplified the uncertainty of economic transactions, on which middle-class livelihoods depended, as anyone could be brought to justice for receiving or using forged notes, regardless of their criminal intention; this roused middle-class jurors to protest against the forgery prosecutions as a direct threat to the foundation of commercial

---

[92] Steven Blakemore, *Intertextual War: Edmund Burke and the French Revolution in the Writings of Mary Wollstonecraft, Thomas Paine and James Mackintosh* (Madison, NJ, 1997), 204–7; James Mackintosh, *Vindiciae Gallicae. Defence of the French Revolution, and Its English Admirers, against the Accusations of the Right Hon. E. Burke* (London, 1791), 149–54.

[93] Quoted in Patrick O'Leary, *Sir James Mackintosh: The Whig Cicero* (Aberdeen, 1989), 108. As a practising lawyer, Mackintosh had first-hand experience of the process. In 1802, for instance, Mackintosh wrote from Norfolk that he 'was employed from 8 till 3 in the defence of two unfortunate wretches who were convicted of uttering forged bank notes on the evidence of the miscreants who had tempted them'. Quoted in O'Leary, *Sir James Mackintosh*, 63.

[94] Handler, 'Limits of Discretion'.   [95] Handler, 'Limits of Discretion', 160.

society. While Handler's account provides a plausible explanation of the London juries' actions, the forgery crisis involved a much broader range of note users. Indeed, in 1818, not only jurors but judges and the accused vigorously confronted the Bank's prosecutors to an unprecedented extent, and their judicial challenge was generally supported by public opinion.

What was the cause of Bank-note users' growingly belligerent attitude towards the Bank's prosecutions? One explanation is the increasing public animosity against what they perceived as the Bank's tyrannical power over the nation's economic transactions, which undermined the security of private property. The language of private property frequently appeared in forgery trials and in their reports in newspapers, particularly over the issue of the ownership of forged notes. The fundamental question being, could a bona fide receiver of a forged note claim ownership of that note or did it belong to the issuer of the authentic notes, the Bank of England? With regard to genuine Bank notes, the legal precedent of *Miller v. Race* (1758) recognised that ownership lay with the possessor of the notes.[96] The matter was less clear regarding forged notes.[97] Since possession of forged notes was a criminal offence, if someone discovered a forged note in their possession they were supposed to dispose of it or bring it to the Bank. Note users had to bear all the damage from accepting inauthentic notes as the Bank did not compensate the receivers of forged notes, a situation that the British public increasingly saw as unfair and unjust. As Bentham remarked, the Bank appeared to insulate itself from the economic damage caused by forgery at the expense of note users: 'By so simple an expedient as that of depriving a man of his property, keeping the subject of the crime without paying for it, whatever be the loss by the forgery they shift it off from themselves'.[98] The recognition that the Bank's counter-forgery measure was based on trampling upon private property rights was at the heart of a series of legal battles that unravelled in early 1818.

In January that year, historical engraver Thomas Ranson set the stage for public controversy over the property of forged notes by refusing to

---

[96] See Kevin Hart's discussion of *Miller v. Race* in the context of mid eighteenth-century cultural property and forgery. Kevin Hart, *Samuel Johnson and the Culture of Property* (Cambridge, 1999), 135.

[97] Although Lord Mansfield stated in 1781 that the Bank had a right to detain forged notes, the practice at the Bank changed over time. Acres, *Bank of England from Within*, i, 346; *London Chronicle*, 19–21 June 1781.

[98] Jeremy Bentham, 'Annuity Notes: Proposed Advertisement on Proposed Publication in Pamphlets', 15 Apr. 1818, UCL Bentham Manuscripts, box 2, fol. 5. Compare Stark, 'Introduction', 69.

surrender a forged £1 Bank note to the Bank. The case concerned a debt Ranson owed to a Fleet Street publican, Mitchener. At the Court of Requests – the legal court for settling small debts – Mitchener claimed that a £1 Bank note Ranson had paid to him to clear the debt was a forged note, and as the original payment by forged note was void, the debt had not been cleared.[99] A Bank investigator, Robert Fish, appeared at the court and confirmed that the note was a forgery and the court announced that Ranson's debt was still outstanding. When the court had delivered its verdict, the Bank investigator attempted to confiscate the forged note, but Ranson refused to comply. According to the investigator's report, Ranson declared 'that it was then his property, and holding a Pistol in his Hand, said he would Blow out the Brains of any Person attempting to take it from him'.[100] Ranson left the court with the note in his pocket, then went to Mitchener's house and settled the debt. He was later arrested for illegally possessing a forged note and incarcerated in the Cold Bath Fields prison for four days.

At the subsequent examinations at the magistrates' court, which were widely reported in newspapers, Ranson doggedly refused to give up the forged £1 note.[101] Eventually, the Bank chose not to pursue Ranson's prosecution, a practical decision in a case involving a single £1 note, but to the public's eyes it looked as though the engraver's action was vindicated.[102] Thomas Wooler's radical newspaper *Black Dwarf* seized on this story in its early skirmish against the Bank, congratulating Ranson on his 'spirited conduct ... and his triumph over the bank'.[103] Ranson was not alone in claiming ownership of forged notes. In mid-February, another Londoner, Robert Boyce, sought to prosecute a Bank investigator at the Mansion House for the 'felonious' act of forcibly taking away a worn-out £1 note – which turned out to be forgery – that Boyce brought to the Bank for payment. His appeal found a sympathiser in Alderman J. J. Smith who stated that Boyce 'had a better right to it than any body else, as he had given value for it'.[104]

Just as the legitimacy of the Bank's forgery prosecutions was being questioned by increasingly hostile note users, humanitarian concerns

---

[99] Minutes of Committee for Lawsuits, 5 Feb. 1818, BE, M5/320, fols. 35–6. Maberly Phillips wrote that the note was genuine, but this is not likely, and the record at the Bank explicitly states that it was a forgery. Maberly Phillips, *A History of Banks, Bankers, and Banking in Northumberland, Durham, and North Yorkshire* (London, 1894), 84.

[100] Minutes of Committee for Lawsuits, 5 Feb. 1818, BE, M5/320, fol. 36.

[101] *Morning Chronicle*, 26 and 31 Jan. 1818.

[102] *Morning Post*, 7 Feb. 1818. See also Acres, *Bank of England from Within*, i, 347; Minutes of Committee for Lawsuits, 5 Feb. 1818, BE, M5/320, fol. 35.

[103] *Black Dwarf*, 2.6 (11 Feb. 1818), 83.

[104] *Morning Post*, 17 Feb. 1818; *The Star*, 17 Feb. 1818.

about judicial violence were converging with the critical public opinion of the Bank. On February 17, four criminals were executed at the Old Bailey, three of them for forgery. Due to the poorly adjusted ropes around their necks, the hangings took an unusually long time, and the expression of pain and agony exhibited by the four dying criminals shocked those who attended the execution and those who read reports about it, even though London spectators were normally well accustomed to public hangings.[105] As law reformer Samuel Romilly recorded, the cruelty of the executions left 'considerable impression' on Londoners' minds, an impression that echoed in the Common Council's condemnation of the event as 'injudicious and shameful'.[106] Opposition to forgery-related executions on humanitarian grounds was spreading outside London, too. A general meeting held in Birmingham in April resolved that 'numerous trials and frequent executions ... are alike shocking to the feelings of the humane and a disgrace to the character of the country'.[107] In the following month, citizens of Liverpool petitioned the parliament, requesting its intervention to arrest the increase in executions due to the Bank's prosecutions.[108] Closer to home, the Bank of England's stockholders were becoming ill at ease about the Bank's prosecutions sending so many petty criminals to the gallows, and they expressed their concern at a proprietors' meeting in March.[109]

While the humanitarian crusade against the cruelty of the death penalty undoubtedly intensified public hostility to the Bank's prosecution, note users' legal challenge to the Bank was sharply focused on the ownership of forged notes. The issue came to a head in June 1818 in the case of *Brooks v. Warwick*, which closely resembled the two previous cases of Ranson and Boyce in disputing the legitimacy of the Bank's confiscation of forged notes.[110] Brooks, a pawnbroker in High Holborn, came into possession of a forged £1 note. Without knowing it was a forged note, Brooks paid it to one Mrs Bull, who raised doubts about the note's authenticity and brought it to the Bank of England. After the Bank's inspector announced that the note was a counterfeit, Brooks offered £2 to Mrs Bull and bought back the note 'for the sake of

[105] *The Times*, 18 Feb. 1818.
[106] Letter by Romilly, dated 25 Feb. 1818, in *Memoirs of the Life of Sir Samuel Romilly* (London, 1840), iii, 332. The Common Council's comments are in *The Times*, 19 Feb. 1818.
[107] *The Star*, 24 Apr. 1818. Also in *The Times*, 25 Apr. 1818.
[108] Hansard, 2nd ser., xxxviii (1818), col. 555.
[109] The issue was raised at the Bank's General Court of Proprietors on 19 March 1818. *Morning Post*, 20 Mar. 1818.
[110] *English Reports*, clxxi, 682; *The Times*, 23 June 1818.

comparing it with good notes in course of his business'. For his action, the pawnbroker was arrested, and the Bank confiscated the note. On his release from jail, Brooks sued the Bank's inspector, Warwick, for malicious imprisonment.[111] At the King's Bench, Brooks' challenge to the Bank was supported by Chief Justice Lord Ellenborough, who stated, '[if] a man retains that which he thinks his own, he is to be deemed guilty of a felony; such a doctrine would almost put a halter round the neck of every man who takes a Bank Note in the common course of trade'.[112] The court ruled in favour of Brooks, with the jury awarding him £50 in damages. The judgement effectively established that, unless there was a criminal intention, forged notes were the property of their owners. After the court decision on *Brooks v. Warwick*, the Bank realised that it could no longer maintain the practice of confiscating forged notes, but this realisation came too late as public opinion was now decidedly against the Bank.[113]

In the series of legal challenges to the Bank, what was at issue was the Bank's de facto licence to seize any forged notes, a formidable power that was perceived as a threat to private property by those who witnessed the working of its violent machinery – Ranson, Boyce and Brooks were among them. In the court, the main question boiled down to the ownership of Bank notes: to whom did the Bank of England note, authentic and inauthentic, ultimately belong? Ranson took the Bank investigator's forceful attempt to take away the forged note that he possessed as a challenge to his rights, and he was prepared to defend it with an equally violent action.[114] At subsequent examinations, Ranson resorted to the language of private property, insisting that surrendering his claim on the note would be to 'compromise the right upon which he stood'.[115] Ranson's defiance towards the Bank's competing claim on the forged note led to his arrest, but his legal challenge laid bare the tenuous relation between the Bank's policing activity and private property, a question 'in dispute between the public and the Bank of England', as one newspaper aptly described it.[116]

The threat to private property from the Bank's expanded semi-judicial power was felt most acutely when note users were devising ways *outside*

---

[111] Bank investigators had occasionally been sued for malicious or false imprisonment. Acres, *Bank of England from Within*, i, 333.

[112] *English Reports*, clxxi, 683; *The Times*, 23 June 1818.

[113] Thereafter, a possessor of a forged note was allowed to retain the note as long as it was marked by the Bank as forged. CT, 24 June 1818, BE, G8/19, fol. 114; McGowen, 'Policing of Forgery', 114.

[114] Minutes of Committee for Lawsuits, 5 Feb. 1818, BE, M5/320, fol. 36.

[115] *Morning Chronicle*, 26 and 31 Jan. 1818.   [116] *Bury and Norwich Post*, 28 Jan. 1818.

the criminal court to redress economic losses caused by transactions involving forged notes. What Mitchener sought in the Court of Request was the court's confirmation that Ranson's payment was invalid and that the debt was still outstanding. Mitchener's intention was to recover what Ranson owed to him, without accusing him as a perpetrator of forgery crime. Circumventing penal justice was, as Mitchener's appeal to the Court of Request had shown, the solution to the forgery problem that was least disruptive to the economic community, and was devised at a time when every note user was subject to the risk of receiving and unwittingly passing on forged notes. When a forged note found its way into economic transactions between those in a close relationship (e.g. regular customers and sellers), there was no reason to appeal to the criminal law because the receiver of the note could return it to its former owners by tagging the chain of endorsements that the note normally had. The Bank's intervention in such a private mode of settlement amounted to its intrusion into the realm of private economic transactions.

The public backlash against the Bank's forgery prosecutions entailed a challenge to the Bank's authority in determining the authenticity of notes. In the early years of the Bank Restriction, no one dared to question the words of witnesses from the Bank, and according to the Bank's solicitor, Joseph Kaye, it was an established practice of English judges to admit the verbal evidence of Bank inspectors on the authenticity of Bank notes without requiring any further substantiation.[117] It was no longer the case in 1818, when juries and magistrates in the criminal courts frequently disputed evidence given by the Bank's witnesses, often demanding that Bank investigators explain in plain words how to distinguish forged from genuine notes.[118] London citizens who appeared as witnesses in the court began to claim that their judgement as to the authenticity of paper currency was as good as that of the Bank. In the Ranson case, three witnesses testified that they believed the £1 note paid by Ranson was a genuine Bank of England note. One of the witnesses, a watchmaker, did not feel any qualm about contradicting the Bank investigator when he stated that 'he should not have felt the least hesitation in taking it'.[119]

Ultimately, the forgery problem concerned the question of monetary value, and in that respect, there was a continuation from the Bullionist

---

[117] Minutes of Committee for Lawsuits, 13 Nov. 1804, BE, M5/307, BE, fols. 60–1.
[118] Handler, 'Limits of Discretion', 160–1.
[119] *Annual Register, Chronicle*, 1819, p. 201. Ranson was awarded damages of £100 for the Bank's malicious imprisonment. Acres, *Bank of England from Within*, i, 347; *The Times*, 23 Feb. 1819.

Controversy, in which the causal link between the Bank's policy and monetary stability was publicly scrutinised and disputed. Just as Bullionists saw the Bank's privilege to increase note circulation at will as jeopardising monetary stability, the Bank's critics in 1818 regarded the Bank's arbitrary power to remove Bank notes by announcing them as illegitimate – that is forged – papers as amplifying post-war economic uncertainty. As long as the Bank was allowed to invalidate economic transactions and confiscate the notes involved according to its esoteric art of identifying forged notes, it acted as the irrefutable arbiter of monetary value at the expense of the certainty of economic relations and the security of private property. The Bank's decision-making power on the authenticity of paper currency could, at any time, unsettle any economic transactions involving Bank notes. Economic relations became precarious when so many forged notes were in circulation and so much depended on the Bank's judgement. The radical press was at the fore in condemning the formidable power that the Bank had come to wield in the nation's economic life. As Cobbett's *Political Register* claimed, the Bank had mutated into a 'grand tool of tyranny'.[120]

As the Bank's policing activity extended well beyond the metropolis and forged notes were finding their way into many parts of the British Isles, the clash between the Bank and note users over forged notes could occur in any place. Indeed, the London juries were hardly alone in disputing the legitimacy of the Bank's forgery prosecutions. As early as June 1817, jurors in Edinburgh defied the Bank agent's 'clearest evidence' that Ebenezer Knox uttered forged Bank notes and gave the verdict of possession, the penalty for which was less severe than that for uttering.[121] Similarly, in September the Carnarvon session in Wales acquitted J. Jones, who was a serial offender, having been prosecuted for uttering thirty-nine forged notes.[122]

Note users' multipronged legal challenges to the Bank's authority in forgery prosecutions amid the forgery crisis had two consequences. First, the British public increasingly leaned towards the view that the Bank's excessive power, which manifested in its intervention in private transactions with the violent hand of the bloody code, ought to be curtailed. The public backlash against the Bank's policing was rooted in the widely held view that the Bank was dictating the judicial process that was supposed to protect the public rather than the Bank's private interest. The

---

[120] CWPR, 28 Nov. 1818, 285.
[121] Minutes of Committee for Lawsuits, 26 June 1817, BE, M5/319, fol. 78.
[122] *Black Dwarf*, 23 Sept. 1818, 593; Philip Handler, 'Forgery and Criminal Law Reform in England 1818–1830' (unpublished PhD thesis, University of Cambridge, 2001), 44.

intensifying opposition to the Bank's prosecutors in the criminal court mirrored the public's desire to redraw the line between private transactions and the realm of the Bank's policing, thereby reducing uncertainty by shielding economic transactions from the Bank's intrusive power. However, what the public outcry achieved – namely the Bank's concession on private individuals' retention of forged notes – was more symbolic than practical as it did not fundamentally change the Bank's prosecution policy.

Second, and more importantly, the forgery crisis intensified public pressure on the Bank to take more accountability in preventing the circulation of forged notes. The London juries and the Bank's critics argued that, in its preoccupation with the retributive justice, the Bank had neglected the development of preventive measures. In fact, there was an inherent tension between forgery prevention and punishment, which Jeremy Bentham – the advocate of preventive policing – clearly recognised.[123] Ensnaring or detective methods such as secret marks, Bentham argued, when they depended on subtle design devices, might prove useful for prosecuting forgers, but they were of little use for protecting 'the unpracticed and incurious multitude' from becoming a victim of forgery.[124] Such subtle devices, Bentham further claimed, often made the note appear easy to copy, thereby inciting rather than holding back forgery attempts. For note users who were living under constant fear of being implicated in the transaction of forged notes – and the risk was not negligible in 1818 – it was perfectly legitimate to ask the Bank to do more to prevent the circulation of forged Bank notes. Growing frustration with the Bank's limited effort in the field of forgery prevention – in particular through improving its note design – led to an erosion of public trust in the Bank and in the Bank of England note.

Facing public hostility in the early months of 1818, the Bank increasingly saw the issue of Bank-note improvement less as a war against forgers than a way to mitigate adverse public criticism, including the campaign by Tilloch's *Star*, of which the Bank's directors were fully aware. Still, the Bank's immediate concern was parliamentary intrusion into the Bank's business, which was intensified by Mackintosh's assault on the Bank's forgery prosecutions.[125] To this, the Bank responded by hastening its internal discussion on note improvement. Following

---

[123] Bentham, for instance, distinguished between 'obstructing' and 'ensnaring'. 'Mr. Bentham's Plan', fol. 9. Compare McGowen, 'Policing of Forgery', 112.

[124] 'Mr. Bentham's Plan', fol. 5.

[125] Mackintosh stated that 'the concerns of the Bank of England … should not be considered as out of the reach of the cognizance of parliament'. Hansard, 2nd ser., xxxviii, col. 671.

Mackintosh's parliamentary motions, the Bank's Committee for Note Improvement were spurred into action. The committee, having been established in December the previous year, held only three meetings in March, but it met nine times in April and eight times in May.[126] The Bank's sense of urgency can be gauged by the fact that its governor, Jeremiah Herman, joined the committee at the end of March.

In its scramble to contain the forgery crisis, the Bank suddenly took a decision that, had it not been abandoned later, could have altered the design of the Bank note drastically.[127] After rejecting numerous proposals for note improvement, the Bank's directors agreed to invest in a plan submitted by the printing firm of Augustus Applegath and Edward Cowper.[128] The firm's proposal consisted of coloured relief printing, with the intricate design on the obverse side of the note having its mirror image on the reverse (Figure 5.3).[129] The Court of Directors did not specify any reason why the Bank suddenly became eager to experiment with an entirely new note design. Nor was it consistent with the directors' general scepticism about design change as a solution to forgery – the Bank's internal discussion had consistently favoured trials on paper materials.[130] A conceivable reason for the Bank's change of heart was the prospect of a parliamentary inquiry into forgery prevention, which the Bank initially resisted as an undue intervention into its private concerns.[131] As the Bank was losing control of what it regarded as the internal matter of its note production, one may suspect it grabbed at the most promising proposal to hand in a desperate attempt to retain some sort of initiative. At any rate, the Bank's payment of £1,200 to Applegath and Cowper was extremely generous, and with it, the firm set to work at their newly established Croydon workshop.[132] Shortly after, the Bank granted support to another experiment on a 'tricolour' paper by its papermaker Portal & Bridges and the inventor William Congreve as

---

[126] 'Committee to Examine Plans for the Improvement of Bank Notes: Minutes', BE, M5/246, fol. 1.

[127] Hansard, 2nd ser., xxxvii, col. 1223–4.

[128] 'Committee to Examine Plans for the Improvement of Bank Notes: Minutes', BE, M5/246, fol. 9; CD, 23 Apr. 1818, BE, G4/41, fol. 17.

[129] Byatt, *Promises to Pay*, 60; Mackenzie, *Bank of England Note*, 58–9.

[130] 'Committee to Examine Plans for the Improvement of Bank Notes: Minutes', BE, M5/246, fols. 22, 100.

[131] CD, 23 Apr. 1818, BE, G4/41, fol. 17.

[132] 'Committee to Examine Plans for the Improvement of Bank Notes: Minutes', BE, M5/246, fol. 41. The agreement is Augustus Applegath: Proposed Agreement Concerning His Process for Forestalling Forgery of Bank Notes, BE, F15/8. See also Raymond A. Taylor, 'Applegath and Cowper: Their Importance to the English Letter Press Printing Industry in the Nineteenth Century', *Journal of Printing Historical Society*, 26 (1997), 50–1.

Figure 5.3 Applegath and Cowper's trial £1 note design, 1810s.
© Trustees of the British Museum

part of the project for developing an entirely new – and inimitable – Bank of England note.[133] These operations were kept well away from the public's prying eyes, and the Bank did not take the trouble of informing the public about what it had up its sleeve.[134]

The Bank's surreptitious manner regarding its ongoing trials suggests that its directors were carefully calculating the strategic value of a new note design. Given the low ebb of its reputation in early 1818, the Bank's directors could hardly expect that any note-improvement plan under its auspices would be welcomed by the hostile public. They had every reason to be cautious. For the Bank, the parliamentary decision to set up a Royal Commission on the prevention of Bank-note forgery, with a relatively exclusive membership, rather than a select committee, was fortuitous as the commission presented an opportunity to guide the parliamentary inquiry, which had been initiated by its fiercest critic

---

[133] CT, 11 Aug. 1819, BE, G8/20, fol. 38; William Congreve, *An Analysis of the True Principles of Security against Forgery* (London, 1820), p. iii. On contemporary interest in colour printing, see Elizabeth M. Harris, 'Experimental Graphic Processes in England, 1800–1859', *Journal of Printing Historical Society*, 4 (1968), 64.

[134] Mackenzie, *Bank of England Note*, 59.

Mackintosh, to its own advantage.[135] Presumably, the Bank's silence about its recent investment in note improvement was grounded in the expectation that if the Royal Commission were to back Applegath and Cowper's note design it would be less objectionable to those who viewed any initiatives coming from the Bank with suspicion. However, the Bank's critics questioned the commission's neutrality from the moment it was established. What was particularly controversial was that a director of the Bank, Jeremiah Harman, was among the commission's seven members.[136] With Harman's presence, one would naturally doubt the neutrality of the committee, although it primarily consisted of members of the Royal Society, including the commission's chair, the highly respected Joseph Banks. Clearly, Harman represented the Bank's interest, and he kept no secret about his contempt for what he regarded as a vulgar misconception that the Bank note was easy to imitate.[137] From the Bank's perspective, Harman's role was to steer the commission's discussion towards endorsing Applegath and Cowper's note-improvement plan.

The extent to which the Bank managed to sway the committee's conclusion is unclear, but its subsequent report was generally in line with the Bank's views on the nature of Bank-note forgery.[138] The committee's first report dismissed the widely held belief that the principal perpetrators of forgery were casual engravers without professional qualifications. Rather, forgers were 'men of skill and experience, and possessed of a very considerable command of capital'.[139] Echoing Harman's previous defence of the Bank's handling of the forgery crisis, the report exonerated the Bank from the accusation that it had neglected improving its notes because the Bank was facing a formidable enemy with technical expertise and resources who was capable of getting around most of the anti-forgery measures available to the Bank. The report also granted what the Bank desperately needed: it gave its blessing to Applegath and Cowper's trial without revealing the details of the enterprise.[140]

---

[135] Hansard, 2nd ser., xxxviii (1818), cols. 681, 699. See also David M. Batt, 'Depoliticisation, Technical Discourse, and Paper-Money: A Case Study in the Bank Restriction Period', *Journal of Cultural Economy*, 14 (2021), 233–7.

[136] 'Increase of Forgeries', 211.   [137] *The Star*, 29 Mar. 1818.

[138] At the commission's meetings, the members examined 108 proposals, most of which had previously been appraised and rejected by the Bank, and about 70 varieties of papers that were produced through the trials at the Bank's manufactory. House of Commons, *Report of the Commissioners Appointed for Inquiring into the Mode of Preventing the Forgery of Bank Notes, First Report* (1819), 1.

[139] House of Commons, *Royal Commission on Forgery, First Report*, 2.

[140] House of Commons, *Royal Commission on Forgery, First Report*, 4.

Conclusion: The Radicalisation of Communal Currency

The series of events in 1818 described in this chapter redrew the line between the Bank and the note-using British public – a line separating the Bank's power to execute retributive measures against forgery crime and note users' right to free economic activity. This confrontation manifested itself as note users' claim on the property of forged notes that came to their possession against the Bank's conventional license to remove them from circulation. In these cases, the communal idea of paper currency mutated into its radical variation, in which the communal vision of monetary value generation – one that was based upon interpersonal trust and voluntary acceptance – gave way to the radical prescription that money users were the judges and owners of the monetary value embodied in paper currency. This radicalisation of communal currency mirrored the incendiary popular politics of the period, when the clash between radical meetings and government repression culminated in the Peterloo Massacre in the summer of 1819. Just as the government's repressive policy added fuel to the radical political movement, the compulsory acceptance of paper currency, stipulated by the Stanhope Act of 1811, had the effect of crystallising radical currency ideas. R. H. Solly, at the Society of Arts, commented that the public were forced to become the sole 'losers' of the prevalent forgery because 'the circulation of the Bank of England Notes is inforced [sic] by Act of Parliament'.[141] One may argue that the transformation of communal currency into a logic of public participation in monetary value creation was a popular response to the severe erosion of the voluntary basis of paper currency.

At the extreme end of the radicalised communal-currency view was William Cobbett, who by the late 1810s was already well known for his anti-paper campaign. The forgery crisis led him to the conviction that the time was ripe for bringing down the paper system he fiercely detested. After nearly a decade of sustained attack on the paper system, Cobbett finally threw off Thomas Paine's prophesy of the natural demise of the English financial system.[142] A return to convertibility, Cobbett believed,

---

[141] Society of Arts, *Report of the Committee of the Society of Arts Relative to the Mode of Preventing the Forgery of Bank Notes* (London, 1819), 42.

[142] As David Wilson argues, Cobbett's relationship with the paper system is more complicated than many historians – who often base their discussion only on *Paper against Gold* – have assumed. David A. Wilson, *Paine and Cobbett: The Transatlantic Connection* (Kingston, Ontario, 1988), 159. See also Alex Benchimol, *Intellectual Politics and Cultural Conflict in the Romantic Period: Scottish Whigs, English Radicals and the Making of the British Public Sphere* (Farnham, 2010), 174; Kenneth Neill Cameron, 'Shelley, Cobbett, and the National Debt', *Journal of English and Germanic Philology*, 42 (1943), 198; G. D. H. Cole, *The Life of William Cobbett* (London, 1927), 173.

would not save the nation as war expenditure and the inconvertible currency had irreparably damaged its finance. Nor would improving the design of the Bank note offer any cure for note users' grievances, as it was just another ruse of the political establishment to perpetuate the unjust and unsustainable paper system. In the eyes of this staunch anti-paper controversialist, law reformers such as Mackintosh did not go far enough to mount an effective challenge to the fundamentally corrupt system of inconvertible paper currency. Calling Mackintosh a 'miserable canter', Cobbett criticised his reticence about the most obvious means to put an end to 'the everlasting hangings and transportings', which was the demolition of the paper system.[143]

What inspired the new phase in Cobbett's war against paper currency, presented in the *Political Register* in February 1818, was the uncanny resemblance between forgery crime and the Bank's arbitrary creation of paper currency. As he saw it, they were both manipulations of value through circulating paper devoid of intrinsic value. Describing Britain's paper currency as being 'forced into circulation and acceptance by divers artful and unjust contrivances', Cobbett condemned the system that was operated 'at the pleasure of those by whom it has been made, issued and managed'.[144] Then he asked, if the Bank's excessive creation of paper currency tended to diminish the value of each paper, could forgers accelerate the currency depreciation by inundating the nation with forged notes? In defiance of the Bank's policing of forgery, Cobbett proposed what he called the 'puff-out' scheme, a scheme to create artificial and deadly inflation by circulating a large volume of forged Bank notes.[145] Once numerous forged notes were put into circulation, it would undermine public confidence in both genuine and inauthentic notes, leading to the rejection of Bank notes en masse. Eventually, the paper bubble would burst, bringing down the Bank and, ultimately, Britain's financial system that depended on it.[146] This revolution would be led not by soldiers but by artisans, in particular by engravers, whose hands would forge the notes, creating the weapons for the revolution. Cobbett urged those who had the skills of engraving and printing to join this revolutionary

---

[143] CWPR, 5 Sept. 1818, 181–2.
[144] 'Petition to the Honourable the Commons of the United Kingdom of Great Britain and Ireland, in Parliament Assembled', CWPR, 7 Feb. 1818, 161–92. See also Noel W. Thompson, *The People's Science: The Popular Political Economy of Exploitation and Crisis 1816–34* (Cambridge, 1984), 114–16.
[145] Iorwerth J. Prothero, *Artisans and Politics in Early Nineteenth-Century London: John Gast and His Times* (Folkestone, 1979), 126.
[146] 'On the Puff-out of Paper-Money', CWPR, 10 Oct. 1818, 217. See also CWPR, 22 Aug. 1818, 8.

army of artisans, and the invitation was extended to those without the skills as, with some exertion, 'any man can soon become an engraver' – Cobbett himself, a soldier-turned journalist and printer, being living proof of this claim.[147] Some evidence suggests that his puff-out was not entirely an empty threat. In 1819, the Home Office received several reports from its informants that Cobbett and his associate William Benbow had acquired printing plates and were getting ready to print and circulate forged notes.[148]

Cobbett's plan of monetary revolution – although it never came to fruition – showed how close subversive popular politics and the radicalised communal-currency idea became in the late 1810s.[149] The puff-out scheme was grounded in an inverted form of confidence theory: once currency users ceased to believe in the value of the Bank note, it would no longer circulate, and no law or compulsory measures would be able to force the circulation of the discredited paper. Thus, Cobbett reverted to currency voluntarism in his attack on forced paper currency, and he did so within the distinctive political context of post-war Britain. The literary historian Kevin Gilmartin perceptively comments that Cobbett, with his puff-out scheme, invented a new mode of political resistance corresponding to the 'historical shift in repressive power from force to fraud'.[150] If the tyrannical power of the state and the Bank rested on their capacity to deceive the population about the true worth of paper promises and state finances, an effective political resistance might begin by bringing the public to the conviction that genuine Bank notes had no more value than forged notes. In Cobbett's dialectical strategy of bringing down the corrupt paper system by overwhelming the valueless paper currency issued by the Bank with equally valueless spurious notes, the manufacture of forged notes became a revolutionary act. Through this 'satirical debasement of a debased form', paper currency would destroy itself.[151]

The Bank of England's actions during the forgery crisis should be read against the social conditions of contemporary British society, in which radical politics was ubiquitous. Within the Bank's organisation, the section that had the strongest inclination to radicalism was the printing department, comprising artisanal labourers engaging in papermaking,

[147] CWPR, 10 Oct. 1818, 229.
[148] Prothero, *Artisans and Politics*, 126; Iorwerth Prothero, 'William Benbow and the Concept of the "General Strike"', *Past & Present*, 63 (1974), 152–3.
[149] In November 1819, Benbow still believed that Cobbett would implement his scheme. Norris to Sidmouth, 20 Nov. 1819, TNA, HO 42/199.
[150] Kevin Gilmartin, *Print Politics: The Press and Radical Opposition in Early Nineteenth-Century England* (Cambridge, 1996), 164.
[151] Gilmartin, *Print Politics*, 164.

engraving and printing. At a time when artisanal culture was closely associated with radical politics, the Bank's directors well knew that its note production process could be the weakest link in the practical workings of the institution.[152] Earlier, in 1807, the Bank had insisted that its superintendent of printing, Garnet Terry, who was suspected of being a sympathiser to the revolutionary principle of Thomas Paine, should relinquish his work outside the Bank, severing Terry's link with the network of radical printers.[153] Terry's successors in the Bank's printing department – J. H. Harper and William Bowtree – kept well away from associating themselves with radical politics and never expressed their political views in public. After the internalisation of its printing section, the Bank ensured the number of workers in the printing department was under constant check. Given the Bank's incremental containment of radical elements within its premises, its reluctance to enlarge its artisanal workforce may have been a major reason for its rejection of a number of note-improvement proposals that would imply a significant expansion of the printing department. For instance, the Bank's papermaker, John Portal, based his criticism of William Congreve's tricolour paper – a project that ran alongside the development of the new note design by Applegath and Cowper – on his concern about bringing in additional workers for the papermaking process. Once paper production came to depend on a large number of journeymen with their 'disposition to sedition', Portal warned, they would have the power to 'stop all further circulation of notes'.[154] This was hardly alarmist paranoia, as the Bank's printers occasionally made an appeal for better treatment, namely higher wages, with the threat of strike, as in late 1809, demonstrating that the Bank's printing department was inhabited by potentially seditious artisans of early nineteenth-century London.[155]

The radicalisation of British society undoubtedly contributed to the making of the forgery crisis in 1818 and to the escalating tension between the Bank and note users. The series of legal challenges over forged notes as property and the juries' revolt against the Bank's forgery prosecutions were unmistakable signs of the British public's appetite for making a direct intervention into what had long been regarded as the Bank's private business. Never before, since its establishment in 1694, had the Bank faced such a direct challenge to its privileges from the public. Compared to Cobbett's revolutionary plan of puff-out, the public's challenge to the Bank was moderate in nature, but it was a variation of

---

[152] Davies, 'William Blake in Contexts', ch. 4.   [153] See Shin, 'Culture of Paper Money'.
[154] J. Portal to G. Dorrien, 27 Aug. 1819, Portal papers, Hampshire RO, 132M98/D2/1.
[155] Mackenzie, Bank of England Note, 45.

radicalism, nonetheless.[156] The note users' challenge to the Bank was also subversive in the sense that it called for a drastic alteration in the relationship between the Bank and the public by changing the power balance between the two. The implication of this transformation was conveyed in an article in the *Edinburgh Review*:

[The] evils of inconvertible paper money have been mitigated, in this country, by long experience of great monied transactions – by ancient habits of commercial confidence – by thorough knowledge of the importance of mutual support, by a sort of mechanical reliance on a Bank paper which had stood the test of a century, and which, in its new state, retained a great part of the credit which it had gained by being so long exchangeable at pleasure – by the watchful guard of public opinion – and by those wholesome discussions in Parliament ... All these aids and controls, though inadequate substitutes for convertibility, must be allowed to have limited the range of the evil.[157]

In these passages, the anonymous author identified public opinion and parliamentary scrutiny as the key components upon which the credit of the inconvertible paper system depended. The article presents the public 'controls' as the latest phase of Britain's monetary development in a conjectural historicist account, an account that fused Thornton's genealogy of commercial confidence and the post-Burkean repudiation of convertibility in favour of 'mutual support'.[158] By doing so, it encapsulates the transmutation of communal-currency theory into a logic of public participation in the monetary system. In this vision of democratic money, the public had a greater role in the monetary system's operations than merely being users of paper currency. The same logic of direct public participation underpinned the actions of those who challenged the Bank in the legal court, as they – as legitimate owners of the Bank note – refused to yield to the Bank's claim of being the exclusive decision-maker in the nation's monetary order. The call for democratic reform of the monetary system was a belated backlash to the Stanhope Act of 1811, by which the Bank of England note virtually became a forced currency, while the voluntary nature of its acceptance was severely undermined. In the late 1810s, when the forgery crisis led to the public's

---

[156] See Shelley's radical attack on public debt and paper currency in the language of property, such as in his 'Masque of Anarchy'. Percy Bysshe Shelley, *The Masque of Anarchy 1832* (Oxford, 1990), 23. See also Cameron, 'Shelley, Cobbett, and the National Debt', 202–9; Kenneth Neill Cameron, *Shelley: The Golden Years* (Cambridge, MA, 1974), 137–8; Paul A. Cantor, 'The Poet as Economist: Shelley's Critique of Paper Money and the British National Debt', *Journal of Libertarian Studies*, 13 (1997), 21–44.

[157] 'Increase of Forgeries', 204.

[158] 'Increase of Forgeries', 204. This explanatory style leads one to suspect that the author was a student of Dugald Stewart, either Henry Brougham or Mackintosh.

realisation of the overgrown power of the Bank, note users reasserted their role in the monetary system. When they rejected the Bank's intervention in private transactions, note users behaved as though they were reclaiming the lost ground of voluntary currency by forcing the Bank to accept that they had an independent and direct stake in the operation of the monetary regime.

For all their trouble, note users gained little from their battle against the Bank. After the defeat in *Brooks v. Watson*, the Bank ceased confiscating forged notes from their bona fide holders. Juries continued to act sympathetically in forgery trials by sparing a number of forged-note utterers severe punishment, which took the form of delivering a verdict of the non-felonious crime of possession rather than uttering. Nonetheless, the Bank's concession on the retention of forged notes and the alleviation of forgery punishment by juries led to neither the end of the Bank's unrelenting forgery prosecutions nor a wholesale revision of the bloody code – the jury's revolt in 1818 over the Bank's prosecution had a limited impact on how the Bank handled forgery crime. In 1819, the number of forgery prosecutions by the Bank declined from the previous year's 260 to 228, but this small dip may have resulted from the public's reluctance to bring in suspected forged notes – the number of forged notes identified by the Bank dropped from 28,351 in 1818 to 23,906 in 1819 – rather than any significant change in the Bank's prosecution policy.[159] Tellingly, when the number of forged notes rebounded to 30,217 in 1820, the Bank's prosecutions shot up to an unprecedented 404.[160] In the meantime, the progress of criminal law reform in parliament slowed down appreciably. Despite forgery punishment having caused an extensive debate during the parliamentary inquiry on criminal law in early 1819, it took two years before the Forgery Punishment Mitigation bill was submitted to parliament – and then it was defeated.[161] Equally sluggish was the progress of the Royal Commission's examination of forgery prevention measures, which contributed to keeping the topic away from public scrutiny.

Growingly, the British public began to lose faith in the prospect of a forgery-proof Bank of England note, as they saw the Royal Commission and the Bank being largely detached from the broader expert community

---

[159] An account of the total number and nominal amount of forged Bank of England notes, BE, F2/111; McGowen, 'Policing of Forgery', 87.

[160] A return of the number of forged notes of every denomination brought to the Bank of England for payment, BE, F2/112; McGowen, 'Policing of Forgery', 87.

[161] Philip Handler, 'Forgery and the End of the "Bloody Code" in Early Nineteenth Century England', *Historical Journal*, 48 (2005), 691; Hansard, 2nd ser., v (1821), cols. 1099–114.

of inventors and printers and the concerns of the broad community of note users. Dismayed by the stalemate in criminal law reform and in note improvement, Mackintosh and other critics of the Bank shifted their main theatre of battle to the domain of monetary policy by questioning the continuance of the Bank Restriction. As early as April 1818, Mackintosh confided in his diary his suspicion that public attention to note improvement may serve merely to 'divert the public attention from the true remedy, the resumption of cash payments'.[162] What Mackintosh contributed to the cause of restoring convertibility was that he, by revealing the extent of the Bank's prosecutions, brought public opinion decidedly against the Bank. Having supported Francis Horner's previous attempts to check the post-war extension of the Bank Restriction Act, Mackintosh allied himself with the influential Liberal Tories spearheaded by William Huskisson and Robert Peel.[163] While Huskisson would win over the government circle on the imperative of resuming cash payments, Peel, a converted bullionist, would eventually succeed in reformulating the issue of resumption as a political mission for not only Liberal Tories but for parliamentarians across the board, thereby heralding the ascendency of metallism in monetary theory and policy. In 1818, the resumption was yet to be clearly in sight, and the Bank was fighting an uphill struggle to contain the damage to its public reputation while fending off the mounting challenge from law reformers, liberal politicians, political radicals and, above all else, the community of disenchanted note users. During the forgery crisis, the communal-currency tradition was turned on its head and against the Bank. The British public increasingly saw the Bank as a draconian power that defied the 'watchful guard of public opinion', and hence no longer deserved their trust.[164] This was the diagnosis that Mackintosh, Cobbett and Bentham – despite their differences in political opinion – came to share in 1818. When the Bank and its note lost the support of note users, the inconvertible Bank of England note became unsustainable.

---

[162] *Memoirs of the Life of the Right Honourable Sir James Mackintosh*, ed. Robert James Mackintosh (London, 1835), ii, 349.

[163] Mackintosh supported a series of parliamentary motions by Horner. Hansard, 1st ser., xxx (1814–15), col. 90; Hansard, 1st ser., xxxiv (1816), col. 167, col. 250.

[164] 'Increase of Forgeries', 204.

6   Resumption and Its Aftermath

Your scampering began
From the moment Parson Van,
Poor man, made us one in Love's fetter,
'For better or for worse'
Is the usual marriage curse:
But ours is all 'worse' and no 'better'
'Dialogue between a Sovereign and One Pound Note'
(Thomas Moore, The Times, 27 February 1826)

'Eh! It is, it is, a guinea!' In May 1821, William Cobbett welcomed back metallic currency in his article in the *Political Register*.[1] On his writing desk lay some gold coins he had just brought back from the 'dear old Lady in Threadneedle Street'. Cobbett was elated at the prospect of cheap food, low taxes and fewer victims of the Bank's prosecutions. To be sure, he was unconvinced that the Bank was able to continue its payments in coin, as he believed that the Bank's coin reserve would soon run out and therefore another suspension of convertibility was very likely – 'make hay while the sun-shines! Get the gold, and, if you can, keep it', he appealed to his readers.[2]

The Bank of England resumed its cash payments in 1821, which marked the end of the Bank Restriction period. By then, leading politicians had come to regard inconvertible paper as a relic from wartime, and supporters of inconvertibility were few and far between. It was not only anti-paper radicals like Cobbett, who deemed the Bank Restriction unnecessarily protracted, but the majority of the British nation that opted for the metallic standard. Indeed, in early 1819 two parliamentary committees on the resumption of cash payments took for granted that the nation should do away with inconvertible paper and did not consider retaining it as an option. Despite the unpopularity of Bank Restriction in its last years, however, Britain's inconvertible paper was a successful monetary experiment. Contrary to the ominous predictions of national

---

[1] CWPR, 12 May 1821, 416.   [2] CWPR, 12 May 1821, 423.

bankruptcy voiced in the 1790s, Britain with its paper currency retained its position as the world's leading economic power. Then why was inconvertible paper abandoned? How had Britain, which willingly accepted paper currency in 1797, transformed into a nation that embraced the virtue of the metallic standard, with a strong belief in the stability, reliability and legitimacy of 'the ancient standard'?

This chapter describes the final years of the communal-currency tradition in Britain. The first two sections review the social and political situations that made the resumption such a compelling case for a large part of the nation. From the resumption debate, it emerges that the decision on resumption stemmed from loss of faith in inconvertible currency and the fractured state of British society, rather than from unanimous support for the theory or policy of the gold standard. Resumptionists included staunch bullionists as well as a number of anti-bullionists who had been converted to the cause of resumption without losing their theoretical creed entirely. Equally, anti-resumptionists dismally failed to unite their campaign for perpetuating inconvertible currency. In parliament, it was not any theoretical consensus but political rhetoric about 'the ancient standard', most ably deployed by Robert Peel, that elevated metallism as the moral and righteous cause for parliamentarians. Yet, as described in the third section, despite its historical significance – laying down the keystone of Britain's gold standard – the return to cash payments was a muted affair. The remnants of communal currency were gradually chipped away in the following twelve years, a period that was punctuated by major events such as the 1825 financial crisis and the political run on the Bank of England in 1832. The chapter closes in 1833, when the fate of currency voluntarism was finally sealed as the Bank of England note became legal tender.

The End of the French Wars and the Resumption Debate

Having emerged victorious in 1815 after more than two decades of warfare against France, Britain soon had to face the challenge of transitioning from a wartime to a peacetime economy. The speculative boom fuelled by the hope of post-war recovery was ephemeral, and the British economy soon plunged into a recession.[3] The economic outlook was dire

---

[3] Ian P. H. Duffy, 'The Discount Policy of the Bank of England during the Suspension of Cash Payments, 1797–1821', *Economic History Review*, 35 (1982), 77; Arthur D. Gayer, W. W. Rostow and Anna Jacobson Schwartz, *The Growth and Fluctuation of the British Economy, 1790–1850: An Historical, Statistical and Theoretical Study of Britain's Economic Development* (Hassocks, 1975), i, 111–15.

in 1815–16, during which time sixty country banks failed.[4] When the bad harvest of 1816 pushed up food prices, the nation's hard-pressed population were directly hit.[5] As the *Edinburgh Review* bleakly reported, labourers had 'to struggle against the double calamity of low wages and dear provisions; and there is every reason to believe, that a great proportion of the people are in absolute want'.[6] The economic distress was aggravated, the same article contended, by 'the fluctuating value of money', which fell particularly on agriculture because it 'deranged' all the pecuniary relations in a sector that had seen progress in monetisation of contracts over the recent decades.[7]

The French wars left the nation with an eye-watering £788.3 million of public debt. While public creditors enjoyed the high interest rates, other taxpayers felt the burden of public indebtedness and they demanded that the government reduce public spending and remove wartime taxes.[8] In March 1816, the government's failed attempt to renew the Property Tax was followed by the loss of wartime malt duties – combined, these cost the government £18 million in annual revenue, leaving state finance in a volatile position.[9] This was the backdrop to a series of extensions of the Bank Restriction, which were defended vigorously by Vansittart as he believed that a premature return to convertibility would destabilise the nation's economy and jeopardise its post-war recovery.[10] The strong demand for metallic currency between the summer of 1817 and the spring of 1818, after the Bank commenced partial cash payments for small notes, confirmed Vansittart's suspicion that the time was not yet

---

[4] Timothy S. Davis, *Ricardo's Macroeconomics: Money, Trade Cycles and Growth* (Cambridge, 2005), 254.

[5] John H. Clapham, *The Bank of England: A History* (Cambridge, 1944), ii, 58.

[6] 'Commercial Distresses of the Country', *Edinburgh Review*, 27 (1816), 374.

[7] Clapham, *Bank of England*, ii, 59–60; 'Commercial Distresses of the Country', 387; Albert Edgar Feavearyear, *The Pound Sterling: A History of English Money* (Oxford, 1931), 210–11; R. G. Hawtrey, *Currency and Credit* (London, 1919), 124; John Hughes, *Liverpool Banks & Bankers, 1760–1837: A History of the Circumstances Which Gave Rise to the Industry, and of the Men Who Founded and Developed It* (Liverpool, 1906), 23.

[8] Martin J. Daunton, *Trusting Leviathan: The Politics of Taxation in Britain, 1799–1914* (Cambridge, 2001), 51–3; Norman Gash, 'After Waterloo: British Society and the Legacy of the Napoleonic Wars', *Transactions of the Royal Historical Society*, 28 (1978), 152–4.

[9] William Brock, *Lord Liverpool and Liberal Toryism, 1820–1827* (Cambridge, 1941), 178; Clapham, *Bank of England*, ii, 55; John Cookson, *Lord Liverpool's Administration: The Crucial Years, 1815–1822* (Edinburgh, 1975), 58–69; Boyd Hilton, *Corn, Cash, Commerce: The Economic Policies of the Tory Governments, 1815–1830* (Oxford, 1977), 32–3. On the Malt Tax, see Cookson, *Lord Liverpool's Administration*, 73; Hansard, 1st ser., xxxiii (1816), cols. 457–71.

[10] The following parliamentary acts extended the restriction: 54 Geo. III, c. 99; 55 Geo. III, c. 28; 56 Geo. III, c. 40; 58 Geo. III, c. 37; 59 Geo. III, c. 23.

ripe for note convertibility as it wiped £2.6 million from the Bank's reserve. Vansittart was still intent on prolonging the Bank Restriction, and he expressed his displeasure when, in late 1818, the Bank's governor announced that the Bank was not objecting to the resumption of cash payments – a 'foolish debate' as Vansittart wrote in a letter – which caused a stir in the money market as investors were alarmed by the prospect of the Bank's deflationary policy.[11]

In the early months of 1819, despite the Bank's gold reserve remaining at a low level, there was mounting parliamentary pressure on the government to produce a clear pathway to resumption as pro-resumption MPs were becoming increasingly impatient about the repeated renewal of the Bank Restriction.[12] Since its parliamentary defeat in 1811, support for bullionism had greatly increased in high politics. One of the three authors of the Bullion Report, William Huskisson, had become an indubitable authority on monetary issues and spearheaded the bullionist campaign in parliament by presenting the end of inconvertibility as part of a liberal Tory programme of economic policy.[13] For Huskisson, the resumption of cash payments was a sine qua non for the government to leave behind wartime fiscal policy. He was highly critical of Vansittart's management of government finance, which he saw as an unnecessary extension of wartime practice.[14] In his memorandum on resumption, Huskisson's policy prescription was clear-cut: the government debt to the Bank must be reduced, and the Bank should contract its note issue and build up its metal reserve to be ready for the return to convertibility.[15]

Prime Minister Lord Liverpool saw an opportunity to redirect financial policy along Huskissonian lines when relations between Vansittart and the Bank showed signs of strain. The direct source of the Bank's

---

[11] Vansittart to R. H. Davis, 19 Sept. 1818, Bristol RO, 41593/Co/60/6.

[12] Davis, *Ricardo's Macroeconomics*, 65; Norman Gash, *Lord Liverpool: The Life and Political Career of Robert Banks Jenkinson, Second Earl of Liverpool, 1770–1828* (London, 1984), 140.

[13] Boyd Hilton, *The Age of Atonement: The Influence of Evangelicalism on Social and Economic Thought, 1785–1865* (Oxford, 1988), 222–3; Hilton, *Corn, Cash, Commerce*, 179–80; Anthony Howe, 'Restoring Free Trade: The British Experience, 1776–1873', in Donald Winch and Patrick K. O'Brien, eds., *The Political Economy of British Historical Experience, 1688–1914* (Oxford, 2002), 198–9; David Kynaston, *The City of London* (London, 1994), i, 36–7; Nathan Sussman, 'William Huskisson and the Bullion Controversy, 1810', *European Journal of the History of Economic Thought*, 4 (1997), 237–57.

[14] Brock, *Lord Liverpool and Liberal Toryism*, 179; Clapham, *Bank of England*, ii, 64; Cookson, *Lord Liverpool's Administration*, 33–4; Hilton, *Corn, Cash, Commerce*, 35, 39.

[15] William Huskisson, 'Memorandum on the Resumption of Cash Payments', 4 Feb. 1819, BL, Liverpool Papers, Add Ms 38368, fols. 222–3.

growing frustration was that Vansittart continued to demand advances from the Bank – which was inconsistent with the government's commitment to restoring convertibility in the near future – leaving the Bank to face the disgruntled mercantile community, who were discontented with the Bank's reduction in commercial lending. The Bank's directors also felt that the government was exploiting the Bank financially without giving it protection, a recent example of which was the government's refusal to shield the Bank from hostile public opinion during the forgery crisis of 1818. Left to fend for themselves, the Bank's Court of Directors adopted a resolution in March 1818, which defended its policy at a time when 'the Conduct of the Bank has become so generally the subject of discussion and the motives by which the Directors have been actuated are either so ill understood or so much misrepresented'.[16] Although the Bank's directors and Vansittart shared concern about the deflationary consequences of its monetary contraction, the discord between them deepened as the Bank was subjected to intense public censure for its commercial policy and the government offered no help to save it from its plight. There was little the Bank could do to appease adverse public opinion as its actions were constrained by the government's continued demands on the Bank's resources.[17]

A major institutional revision on the nation's metallic standard bolstered arguments in favour of resumption. In 1816, Britain officially adopted gold as the principal standard of value as a consequence of the Privy Council's Coin Committee publishing a report addressing the long-overdue reform of the nation's metallic coin circulation.[18] There was widespread discontent about the state of silver coins, and Francis Horner was not alone when he voiced his concern that the country was inundated with 'bad English, and still worse French silver' that was 'so very base, that it would probably be better for the country to have no currency at all, than be subject to suffer by such a circulating medium'.[19] This long-neglected issue was taken up by the government of Lord Liverpool, who implemented a coinage reform – the basic framework of the reformed system had already been set out by his father more than a

---

[16] CD, 11 Mar. 1819, BE, G4/41, fols. 338–9.

[17] Gash, *Lord Liverpool*, 138–40; Hilton, *Corn, Cash, Commerce*, 39. See also *The Gorgon*, 13 Feb. 1819.

[18] Graham P. Dyer and Peter P. Gaspar, 'Reform, the New Technology, and Tower Hill, 1700–1966', in C. E. Challis, ed., *A New History of the Royal Mint* (Cambridge, 1992), 480–1; House of Commons, *Report of Committee of Council on State of Coins of United Kingdom and Establishment and Constitution of Mint* (1816).

[19] Hansard, 1st ser., xxxiv (1816), col. 147.

decade ago – by adopting the committee's recommendation to down-grade silver coin's status, making it legal tender only up to £2.[20]

The ascendency of what Boyd Hilton calls 'moral' or 'ethical' bullionism in the late 1810s was another feature that rendered the restoration of convertibility the preferred option among parliamentarians.[21] As Hilton argues, bullionist theory appealed to influential figures such as Grenville and Copleston, whose economic ideas were closely linked with their religious convictions, because of bullionism's fundamentalist approach to monetary value. The belief that gold provided an immutable and absolute standard of monetary value chimed with religious belief in the immutable truth of scriptural knowledge.[22] However, it was not until after the French wars that this moral bullionism found its full expression. Prior to that, the correspondence between evangelicalism and metallism was hardly striking. Robert Grant, for instance, a prominent member of the Clapham Sect – a group of evangelical Anglicans led by William Wilberforce and Henry Thornton – was no fundamentalist in terms of currency matters. Another example was the 'evangelical' Prime Minister Spencer Perceval, who did not seem to find any conflict between his rejection of the Bullion Report and his religious creed.[23] Only with the end of the military conflict with France did gold become a symbol of the nation's moral integrity and a barrier against the 'social, economic, and moral instability' attributed to the fictitious capital of paper credit.[24] Tellingly, the *Christian Observer*, the mouthpiece of the Clapham Sect, became far more emphatic about the prospect of the resumption of cash payments in the post-war years than it was around the time when the Bullion Report was published.[25]

[20] Frank W. Fetter, *Development of British Monetary Orthodoxy, 1797–1875* (Cambridge, MA, 1965), 64–6; A. Redish, 'The Evolution of the Gold Standard in England', *Journal of Economic History*, 50 (1990), 801–3; Richard S. Sayers, 'The Question of the Standard, 1815–44', *Economic History*, 3 (1934), 79–87; Ted Wilson, *Battles for the Standard: Bimetallism and the Spread of the Gold Standard in the Nineteenth Century* (Aldershot, 2000), 26–7.

[21] Hilton, *Age of Atonement*, 127–30; Hilton, *Corn, Cash, Commerce*, 39. See also Ian C. Bradley, 'The Politics of Godliness: Evangelicals in Parliament, 1784–1832' (unpublished DPhil, University of Oxford, 1974), 140–1.

[22] Hilton, *Age of Atonement*, 126. On Copleston's view on currency, see S. Rashid, 'Edward Copleston, Robert Peel, and Cash Payments', *History of Political Economy*, 15 (1983), 249–59; Anthony Waterman, *Revolution, Economics and Religion: Christian Political Economy, 1798–1833* (Cambridge, 1991), 186–95.

[23] Denis Gray, *Spencer Perceval: The Evangelical Prime Minister, 1762–1812* (Manchester, 1963), 368–86.

[24] Boyd Hilton, *A Mad, Bad, and Dangerous People? England 1783–1846* (Oxford, 2006), 262.

[25] *Christian Observer*, x (1810), 653–9; *Christian Observer*, xviii (1820), 340–3.

Equally as important, as Anna Gambles argues, due attention should be paid to the conservative economic discourse that was pitted against the free-trade liberalism of Christian economists.[26] The Tory critics of the gold standard such as Alexander Baring, George Rose, Lord Lauderdale, Reverend Edward Tatham and George Croly were, as Gambles rightly points out, not marginal figures in Britain's broad political arena.[27] When these anti-resumptionists voiced their concerns that adopting the gold standard would erode state power by depriving the state of its ability to conduct active monetary policy, they were setting a crucial political agenda of where to draw the boundary for the state's role in conducting monetary policy.[28] This constitutional aspect of the resumption debate was no less fundamental than the Christian doctrine of immutable value. Thus, ardent anti-resumptionist Tatham contended that it was beyond the power of the legislature to put the nation in the shackles of the gold standard.[29]

Lord Liverpool's government successfully steered parliamentary discussion generally in the direction of Huskisson's recommendations. In the meantime, the rift between the government and the Bank deepened, and after a Fife House meeting on 15 January 1819, the ministers concluded that no mode of resumption would be mutually satisfactory to them and the Bank's directors.[30] With this change of approach, the government practically abandoned the Bank, soliciting an equally hostile statement from the Bank that it preferred a parliamentary inquiry to 'inadequate' government legislation.[31] Had it not been for tactful management by the government, the subsequent parliamentary inquiry might have simply prolonged the Bank Restriction, but the government by then was able to frame the process in its own terms by setting up two secret committees with members of its nomination.[32] The chairman of the House of Commons committee was Robert Peel, who had probably already been converted to metallism through his former tutor at Oxford, Edward Copleston.[33] The Lords committee was chaired

---

[26] Anna Gambles, *Protection and Politics: Conservative Economic Discourse, 1815–1852* (London, 1999), 7.

[27] Gambles, *Protection and Politics*, 94–5.   [28] Gambles, *Protection and Politics*, 97.

[29] Gambles, *Protection and Politics*, 99.   [30] Hilton, *Corn, Cash, Commerce*, 40–1.

[31] CT, 15 Jan. 1819, BE, G8/19, fol. 177D; Cookson, *Lord Liverpool's Administration*, 155; Gash, *Lord Liverpool*, 139–40.

[32] Hilton, *Corn, Cash, Commerce*, 41–2.

[33] Davis, *Ricardo's Macroeconomics*, 65; Fetter, *British Monetary Orthodoxy*, 94–5; Gash, *Lord Liverpool*, 138–9; Norman Gash, *Mr Secretary Peel: The Life of Sir Robert Peel to 1830* (London, 1961), 241–2; Richard A. Gaunt, *Sir Robert Peel: The Life and Legacy* (London, 2010), 41–6; Rashid, 'Edward Copleston, Robert Peel, and Cash Payments'.

by Lord Harrowby, president of the council, who had long sided with the anti-bullionists and was inclined to oppose the resumption.[34]

The committee discussion was soon to be dominated by resumptionists – Huskisson, Canning and Frankland Lewis in the Commons committee, and Lord Liverpool and Lord Grenville in the Lords committee.[35] There were anti-resumptionists among the committee members and witnesses, but their views were generally ignored.[36] This was hardly surprising as the government deliberately set the remit of the committees to avoid the inquiry being dragged into another theoretical battle – the Commons committee was explicitly forbidden 'from entering into any reasoning upon the effect produced upon the value of our currency, by variations in the numerical amount of the Notes issued by the Bank of England'.[37] In April, an intense discussion by the committee's ministerial members resulted in a compromise, that is a modified version of Ricardo's resumption plan based on his 1816 pamphlet *Proposals for an Economical and Secure Currency*.[38] The anti-resumptionists in the committees, including Lord Harrowby, capitulated.[39] Unlike the Bullion Report in 1810, which recommended a policy that the government at war could not accept, the Resumption Committee's reports in 1819 were grounded in political consensus that was shaped through ministerial negotiations.

The Commons committee presented its second report on 6 May 1819, recommending that, after a seven-month preparation period, the Bank was to resume cash payments in stages.[40] The plan was, from February 1820, to oblige the Bank to exchange its notes for gold bars, with a minimum of 60 ounces per payment at the price of £4 1s per ounce. The price of ingots would be reduced to £3 19s 6d on 1 October 1820 and then to £3 17s 10½d – the mint price – from 1 May 1821 onwards. The Bank's payments in ingots would continue for two to three years,

[34] Hansard, 1st ser., xx (1810–11), cols. 873–6; Hilton, *Corn, Cash, Commerce*, 42.

[35] David Ricardo, *The Works and Correspondence of David Ricardo*, ed. Piero Sraffa and M. H. Dobb (Cambridge, 1962), v, 353–4.

[36] Cecil C. Carpenter, 'The English Specie Resumption of 1821', *Southern Economic Journal*, 5 (1938), 48. See, for example, the evidence given by Thomas Smith, House of Commons, *Reports from the Select Committee on the Expediency of Resuming Cash Payments* (1819), 257.

[37] Carpenter, 'English Specie Resumption', 49; House of Commons, *1819 Select Committee on Resumption*, 14, 20.

[38] James Bonar, 'Ricardo's Ingot Plan', *Economic Journal*, 33 (1923), 281–304; David Ricardo, *Proposals for an Economical and Secure Currency; With Observations on the Profits of the Bank of England* (London, 1816).

[39] Hilton, *Corn, Cash, Commerce*, 45; Ricardo, *Works and Correspondence*, v, 365.

[40] Hansard, 1st ser., xl (1819), cols. 152–78; Barry Gordon, *Political Economy in Parliament, 1819–1823* (London, 1976), 43.

before payments in coins were fully restored.[41] The plan was aimed at softening the impact of the resumption by a stage-by-stage transition to the old mint parity.[42]

There were some competing views as to how the resumption would change Britain's monetary situation and the economy as a whole. The resumptionists claimed that the impact of restoring convertibility would be minimal. Paper currency would, according to the Lords committee on resumption, continue to circulate alongside coins as the 'established habits of the public may operate so decidedly in favour of a paper circulation'.[43] The anti-resumptionists warned that a premature end to the Bank Restriction would bring harrowing consequences for the nation's economy and people's lives by exacerbating the economic depression. When the resumptionists were unassailable in parliament, the anti-resumptionists looked to extra-parliamentary opinions for support. To what extent did opponents of the resumption manage to consolidate their campaign against the ascendant metallist consensus?

Divided Community

Much has been written about Britain's return to convertibility as a triumph of bullionism, but monetary theory provides only an imperfect demarcation between pro- and anti-resumption opinions because both sides were composed of a heterogeneous group of people.[44] The lack of solidarity was particularly pronounced in the unorganised and largely ineffective opposition to the resumption, which was amply demonstrated by what purported to be an anti-resumptionist meeting at the London Tavern on 18 May 1819. The meeting, if anything, revealed that the anti-resumption campaign had failed to establish solid support in the metropolis as the report of its proceedings showed anti-resumptionists being outnumbered by supporters of resumption.[45]

The divided meeting at the London Tavern was a microcosm of contemporary public opinion on the resumption, which was also

[41] House of Commons, *1819 Select Committee on Resumption*, 15.

[42] Brock, *Lord Liverpool and Liberal Toryism*, 178–80.

[43] Angus W. Acworth, *Financial Reconstruction in England, 1815–1822* (London, 1925), 94; House of Lords, *1819 Select Committee*, 14. Ricardo also envisaged the continued circulation of £1 and £2 notes, and he went so far as to suggest that the Bank note should be made legal tender. House of Commons, *1819 Select Committee on Resumption*, 135.

[44] In Ricardo's own words, the 'triumph of science and truth in the great councils of the nation'. Ricardo, *Works and Correspondence*, viii, 44. See also Ghislain Deleplace, *Ricardo on Money: A Reappraisal* (London, 2017), 64.

[45] *The Times*, 19 May 1819.

reflected in equally divided views on the meeting that featured in news-papers. *The Times* asserted that the London Tavern meeting was part of the Bank directors' campaign to prolong the Bank Restriction and they were deservedly embarrassed by the failure of such a ruse.[46] Similarly, the *Morning Chronicle* insinuated that the Bank played a part in the anti-resumption campaign and predicted that, when convertibility was reinstated, the Bank would no longer be able to wield the insidious power to manipulate the value of money and property, while 'all connection between them [the Bank] and the Government must be dissolved'.[47] In contrast, the *Morning Post* took the side of anti-resumptionists, arguing that the judgement of the experienced industrialist Sir Peel, who headed the anti-resumption resolutions at the London Tavern, was more reliable than that of his inexperienced son, the chairman of the Commons committee.[48] *The Courier* initially supported anti-resumption but soon switched sides, declaring that some sort of compromise was 'necessary to produce an approximation of sentiment, and a union in practical meas-ures of the great interest of all classes of the public'.[49] Arguably, such a compromise was in keeping with the ruling mood of the day, leading to a landslide victory for the resumptionists despite, according to Boyd Hilton, the fact that 'virtually all businessmen ... opposed resumption emphatically'.[50] As a matter of fact, apart from petitions from the busi-ness communities in Leeds, Halifax, Bradford and Liverpool, there was no conspicuous extra-parliamentary opposition to the resumption.[51] British citizens were largely indifferent or implicitly supported the resumption. In parliament, anti-resumptionists were marginalised, and when Sir Peel and Lord Lauderdale brought in the London Tavern resolutions, which garnered 400–500 signatures, they fell on deaf ears.[52]

In the main, popular radicals supported the resumption because there were no viable alternatives, while expecting, as *The Examiner* expressed, 'a certain painful process' ahead.[53] Convertibility was a bitter pill to swallow, but its alternative was the status quo, which was not acceptable to the British public when popular outrage against the Bank's forgery prosecution remained strong. As the forgery crisis and the government's repressive measures on radical meetings coincided in the late 1810s, the

---

[46] *The Times*, 17 and 24 May 1819.   [47] *Morning Chronicle*, 24 May 1819.

[48] *Morning Post*, 21 May 1819.   [49] *The Courier*, 17 May 1819.

[50] Hilton, *Mad, Bad, and Dangerous People?*, 261.

[51] For these petitions, see *Journals of the House of Commons*, lxxiv (1818–19), 52, 59, 71, 72, 475, 509.

[52] Hansard, 1st ser., xl (1819), cols. 597, 672–5; *Manchester Mercury*, 25 May 1819; *The Times*, 20 May 1819.

[53] *The Examiner*, 30 May 1819, 344.

radical press's condemnation of the paper system as a constituent part of the repressive government sounded all the more convincing. The Bank's arbitrary power over the economic life of the nation was perceived as a tangible threat to liberty and property, the reaction against which was plain to see from the journalism of the *Black Dwarf* to the satirical print *The Bank Restriction Note* by William Hone and George Cruikshank.[54] These radical media appealed to the public just as the public discussion on Bank-note improvement and criminal law reform came to an impasse, stifling open discussion on paper currency. At popular political meetings, reformers urged their audience to raise their voice for the return of convertibility and wholesome currency; otherwise, as Manchester radical William Fitton put it, 'paper would go on increasing in quantity until death came in the shape of war prices'.[55]

The restoration of the ancient standard – the mint parity at £3 17s 10½d an ounce – promised neither economic nor social stability. The resumption of cash payments was a product of political endeavour to establish monetary order that was imposed on a society of competing economic interests. As far as their views on society were concerned, classical economists, including Ricardo, agreed on these fundamental divisions. Following early formulations by François Quesnay and Adam Smith, Ricardo developed his vision of an economic society in which social divisions were defined by the way economic profits were generated and distributed.[56] A perpetual competition between social classes characterised such a society with conflicting economic interests. As Murray Milgate and Sharon Stimson aptly describe, Ricardo saw competing economic interests, expressed in the political arena, as forming a dynamic equilibrium.[57] In Ricardo's interest-bound social vision, there is a distinctive echo from Lord King's argument in 1811 that currency depreciation distorted rent contracts by reducing the income of the landlord, while lightening the burden on the tenant.[58] Ricardo's *Essay on Profits* (1815), which pitted the interest of landowners against that of tenants, was effectively a sophisticated version of Lord King's account of class conflict caused by currency depreciation, extending the latter's

---

[54] Noel W. Thompson, *The People's Science: The Popular Political Economy of Exploitation and Crisis 1816–34* (Cambridge, 1984), 114–16.

[55] Donald Read, *Peterloo: The 'Massacre' and Its Background* (Manchester, 1958), 43. See also *The Medusa*, 13 Mar. 1819.

[56] Norman Russell, *The Novelist and Mammon: Literary Responses to the World of Commerce in the Nineteenth Century* (Oxford, 1986), 17.

[57] Murray Milgate and Shannon C. Stimson, *Ricardian Politics* (Princeton, NJ, 1991), 106–7.

[58] See Chapter 5.

discussion to a wider socio-economic context.[59] Such a class-based analysis, in the aftermath of the Napoleonic Wars, was compelling enough for students of political economy, who had witnessed the clash of economic interests over the Corn Laws and the violent confrontation that would eventually culminate in the Peterloo Massacre.[60] In a society fraught with instances of violent class conflict, the opponents of Ricardian theory, who sought to offer 'socially cohesive alternatives' through monetary means, appeared outdated and naive.[61] Furthermore, the emerging consensus between Liberal Tories and Whigs on liberal economic policy marginalised the old guard in monetary debate, such as Sir John Sinclair, who continued to maintain that currency was a binding force of society.[62] The intellectual foundation of currency theory had shifted from a communal ideal of reciprocity to an artificial creation of orderly currency. For those who were discussing the design of the coming monetary regime, what mattered was how the new system would discipline and arbitrate conflicting interests in a divided society as they no longer believed public trust was a sufficient guarantee for a stable currency system.

Peel's parliamentary resolutions on the resumption, based on the Commons committee report, were adopted by the House of Commons on 26 May 1819 with cross-party support, marking a decisive victory for the resumptionists.[63] Many of those who supported the resolutions, including Ricardo, were well aware of the deflationary implications of the resumption, but political and social concerns about the continuation of inconvertibility – the Bank's arbitrary power, the forgery problem and the economic uncertainty of the paper standard – overwhelmed the MPs.[64] The decision on resumption was far from a triumph for Ricardo's version of bullionism, which was clear from the way his Ingot Plan was modified in the subsequent legislation, commonly called Peel's Act of 1819.[65] Not only was the transition period extended until 1 May 1823 (instead of the proposed 1 May 1821) but also the Bank was given the choice of payment in coin (instead of ingots) from

---

[59] David Ricardo, *An Essay on the Influence of a Low Price of Corn on the Profits of Stock* (London, 1815).

[60] William Anthony Hay, *The Whig Revival, 1808–1830* (Basingstoke, 2004), ch. 4.

[61] Gambles, *Protection and Politics*, 22.   [62] Gambles, *Protection and Politics*, 22, 89.

[63] Davis, *Ricardo's Macroeconomics*, 83; Gordon, *Political Economy in Parliament*, 49–56; Hansard, 1st ser., xl (1819), cols. 802–4; Hilton, *Corn, Cash, Commerce*, 47. See also CD, 18 May 1819, BE, G4/42, fols. 43–6, 49–58.

[64] Cookson, *Lord Liverpool's Administration*, 174; Gash, 'After Waterloo', 154; Hilton, *Mad, Bad, and Dangerous People?*, 260.

[65] Clapham, *Bank of England*, ii, 70–1; Fetter, *British Monetary Orthodoxy*, 93, 95; David J. Moss, *Thomas Attwood: The Biography of a Radical* (Montreal, 1990), 83.

1 May 1822.[66] At the same time, Peel's act placated the Bank's discontent with being stripped of its discretionary power by agreeing to address its long-standing concern about the government securities that had piled up, and by recommending the government repay £10 million to reduce what the Bank deemed as 'uncontrollable securities', allowing it 'more immediate control' over its note issue by increasing the proportion of commercial securities.[67] This was made possible by the government's commitment to maintaining a budget surplus, itself a manifestation of a new entente between the government and the Bank, with state finance becoming less dependent on the Bank's short-term financing.[68]

The overhaul of the British monetary system included the repeal of an ancient law that had prohibited the melting and exporting of gold and silver coins. With this legislative revision, Britain at last abandoned its legal regulation on the international transfer of precious metal, leaving the cross-border price adjustment to work without institutional inhibition. From a long-term perspective, the liberalisation of metallic-currency export removed a vestige of mercantilism, which accelerated the internationalisation of British finance.[69] Despite the pretence of returning to the ancient standard, the combination of the gold standard and the free export of precious metals pointed to a drastic departure from any monetary system that had been known to Britain; it took Britain into uncharted terrain in its monetary history.

Making Payments

Six months after the introduction of the Ingot Plan, in mid-1820, paper currency continued to dominate Britain's monetary landscape. In August 1820, the Bank's total note circulation stood at £23 million, including £6.7 million in small notes – still at a high level compared to the average circulation of £7.6 million in small notes between 1810 and 1813.[70] Yet, in post-war Britain, with the ongoing transition from a wartime to a peacetime economy, there were some marked changes in the circulation of the Bank note. Between 1 January 1818 and

---

[66] Deleplace, *Ricardo on Money*, 64. For Ricardo's suggestion of giving the Bank 'the liberty of either paying their notes in specie or in bullion', see House of Commons, *1819 Select Committee on Resumption*, 135.

[67] CD, 6 Jan. 1820, BE, G4/42, fols. 208–9. See also Hansard, 1st ser., xl (1819), cols. 687–8; House of Commons, *1819 Select Committee on Resumption*, 10; E. Victor Morgan, *The Theory and Practice of Central Banking, 1797–1913* (Cambridge, 1943), 45.

[68] Daunton, *Trusting Leviathan*, 113; Hilton, *Corn, Cash, Commerce*, 45–6.

[69] Lawrence H. Officer, *Between the Dollar-Sterling Gold Points: Exchange Rates, Parity and Market Behavior* (Cambridge, 1996), 44.

[70] House of Commons, *1832 Committee on the Bank Charter*, appendix, 22.

30 December 1820 (the last entry of the year), the Lost Note Books recorded 2,695 claims for lost notes (Table 6.1). The predominance of claims from London/Middlesex continued from the previous periods, but, after London, Surrey and Kent, the fourth largest number of claims – 58 – came from France, most of which were associated with Paris (35) with the rest coming from Bordeaux, Dieppe, Marseilles, Normandy, Rouen and St Omer. The entries for those claims do not shed light on the purposes for which those lost notes were put to use in the former enemy country, but they do reveal that the movement of paper currency between Britain and France in the early post-war years mostly concerned private individuals rather than commercial firms. For instance, Mrs Susannah Gould of Rochester sent a £20 note to her sister in Boulogne, and Mr Sylvester sent two £10 notes to his relative at the Hotel de Boston in Paris.[71] As non-military international movements resumed in post-war Europe, the Bank of England note crossed national borders more easily than during the war. In the British Isles, too, there was a notable boost in lost-note claims from Ireland (amounting to forty-eight, mostly from Dublin) and Scotland (total twenty-one).

The post-war expansion of the reach of the Bank note took place at the same time as the number of claims from English port towns – significant in wartime Britain – declined conspicuously. Hampshire no longer stood out in the list of lost-note claims as there were only 22 claims between 1818 and 1820, including 5 from Portsmouth, compared to 59 claims from Kent. Twenty-five claims concerned Devon, but only 3 were related to the navy.[72] Unlike the previous, wartime period, no claims were filed by those who were on board a warship. In post-war Britain, lost-note claims from the English provinces were less likely to originate from navy ports than from commercial and industrial centres such as Gloucestershire (24 claims), Lancashire (38) and Yorkshire (24), where the Bank of England note had already penetrated into local commercial transactions.[73]

British society's transition to a peacetime economy was also mirrored in the occupations of lost-note claimants. The proportion of military-related occupations in the total claims saw a marked decline from 20 per cent in 1804–12 to 9 per cent in 1818–20, which was not surprising given that 332,000 soldiers and sailors were discharged from the forces between 1816 and 1817.[74] In contrast, the proportion of claimants employed in hand manufacturing increased from 12 per cent to 16 per

---

[71] Lost Note Books, BE, C101/57, fol. 228 (Gould); C101/58, fol. 118 (Sylvester).
[72] Lost Note Books, BE, C101/51, fol. 281; C101/54, fol. 259; C101/56, fol. 200.
[73] Lost Note Books, BE, C101/51–9.   [74] Gash, 'After Waterloo', 147.

Table 6.1 *Lost-note claims, 1807–1811 and 1818–1820*

Place/Year	1807–1811	1818–1820	Place/Year	1807–1811	1818–1820	Place/Year	1807–1811	1818–1820
No address	418	91	Essex	40	26	Shropshire	8	4
Bank of England	81	49	Gloucestershire	11	24	Somerset	23	12
Army	11	1	Guernsey	2	6	Staffordshire	7	5
Navy	7	6	Hampshire	50	22	Suffolk	5	13
Ship	7	0	Herefordshire	4	2	Surrey	117	112
General Post Office	25	38	Hertfordshire	16	8	Sussex	45	20
Public office	94	42	Huntingdonshire	5	1	Warwickshire	12	19
Bedfordshire	6	5	Isle of Man	0	2	Westmorland	1	0
Berkshire	11	16	Jersey	3	0	Wiltshire	7	3
Bristol	21	14	Kent	84	59	Worcestershire	6	5
Buckinghamshire	7	7	Lancashire	33	38	Yorkshire	34	24
Cambridgeshire	11	7	Leicestershire	7	7			
Cheshire	8	8	Lincolnshire	4	5	Ireland	12	48
Cornwall	5	3	London	1862	1739	Scotland	14	21
Cumberland	3	3	Norfolk	8	10	Wales	23	19
Derbyshire	2	11	Northamptonshire	5	4			
Devon	38	25	Northumberland	8	10	Other/foreign	4	68
Dorset	10	8	Nottinghamshire	2	2			
Durham	8	13	Oxfordshire	7	10	Total	3,245	2,695
			Rutlandshire	3	0			

Source: Lost Note Books, BE, C101/30–8, C101/51–9.

cent during the same period, showing that a major share of claimants were no longer sailors and soldiers but those in business and industry. Those belonging to finance and trade remained the largest group of claimants at 24 per cent in 1804–12 and 33 per cent in 1818–20. In particular, country bankers appeared in the record more frequently than in previous times, indicating that the use of the Bank of England note had taken root in the provinces. Taken as a whole, what is most striking regarding the changes in the composition of note users shown in the Lost Note Books is the significant expansion in occupational coverage, a strong demonstration of the social penetration of Bank note use during the Bank Restriction period. The Lost Note Books for 1792–6 list around 190 occupations in the claimants' description. Between 1818 and 1820, more than 300 occupations were listed. In this period, the Lost Note Books recorded claims lodged by, for instance, a biscuit baker, a coal porter, a cow keeper, an organist, a news vendor and a bricklayer, along with the usual suspects of bankers, merchants and hand manufacturers. At the end of the Bank Restriction period, those humble Britons had become legitimate members of the note users' community.[75]

In February 1821, the government informed the Bank of its intention to bring in a bill that would allow the Bank to commence cash payments ahead of schedule. The bill was intended as a measure to address the shortage of currency, which was, as Vansittart believed, caused by the contraction of note circulation by the Bank and country banks, anticipating the restoration of convertibility.[76] The Bank agreed, but, curiously, in its public statements the Bank attributed its early return to convertibility not to the nation's liquidity needs but to the unsatisfactory progress in note improvement.[77] Between late 1820 and early 1821, Applegath's firm was in frequent contact with the Bank's Committee of Treasury, which gave approval to the new design featuring coloured patterns in September 1820. When the Bank's printer, Bowtree, subsequently produced an imitation of Applegath's specimen, it cast serious doubt on Applegath's claim that his note design was forgery-proof.[78] The forgery

---

[75] Lost Note Books, BE, C101/52, fol. 201; C101/53, fols. 233, 253, 259; C101/54, fol. 283; C101/57, fol. 41; C101/58, fol. 314.

[76] Acworth, *Financial Reconstruction*, 104–5. On country banks, see L. S. Pressnell, *Country Banking in the Industrial Revolution* (Oxford, 1956), 476.

[77] CT, 21 Feb. 1821, BE, G8/20, fol. 174.

[78] Derrick Byatt, *Promises to Pay: The First Three Hundred Years of the Bank of England Notes* (London, 1994), 61; CT, 27 Sept. 1820 and 7 Feb. 1821, BE, G8/20, fols. 140, 169; A. D. Mackenzie, *The Bank of England Note: A History of Its Printing* (Cambridge, 1953), 57, 78; Raymond A. Taylor, 'Applegath and Cowper: Their Importance to the English Letter Press Printing Industry in the Nineteenth Century', *Journal of Printing Historical Society*, 26 (1997), 52.

problem itself was not a driver for Britain's adoption of the gold standard, or the restoration of convertibility, but it was a major factor in
precipitating the Bank's withdrawal of small-denomination notes.[79]
Thus, in March 1821 the Bank's proprietors learned that because of
the 'unforeseen difficulties and consequent delays having arisen in per-
fecting the New Note', the Bank intended to take an early opportunity to
recommence its cash payments.[80]

In the period following the parliamentary decision on resumption, the
broad economic conditions worked in favour of the Bank regaining its
initiative. By early 1820, the post-war capital drain from Britain had
subsided, while British investments on the continent had begun to yield
interest payments, reversing the capital flow and improving the Bank's
financial position.[81] At the beginning of May 1821, the Bank exercised
the option provided by recent legislation to end the transitory period and
announced that its notes would become convertible to coins starting on
7 May.[82] As Boyd Hilton notes, the Bank's early return to convertibility
was driven by its desire to 'escape from the inhibiting program for cash
payments'.[83] Indeed, by starting its cash payments one year early, the
Bank demonstrated that it was able to restart cash payments without
being forced to by Ricardo's prescription, and this show of initiative was
crucial for the Bank to rehabilitate its tarnished image ahead of its entry
into the new era of the gold standard. The slow progress of Applegath's
note-improvement plan gave a pretext for the Bank to repudiate its small-
note issue, which had become a drag on its business as a symbol of the
forgery problem and a source of public resentment. The Bank made it
clear that it had no intention of issuing small notes in the future, even
though it reserved the power to do so in case of emergency.[84] The Bank
thus exploited the resumption of cash payments to divorce itself from the
negative public image with which it had come to be associated during the
forgery crisis, reinventing itself as a credible institution in Britain's new
monetary order.[85]

The cash payments that began in London on May 8 excited the anti-
paper campaigner William Cobbett, but the event proceeded without

---

[79] Fetter, *British Monetary Orthodoxy*, 97. Compare Acworth, *Financial Reconstruction*,
27–8.
[80] CT, 22 Mar. 1821, BE, G8/20, fol. 180.   [81] Clapham, *Bank of England*, ii, 69.
[82] 1 & 2 Geo. IV, c. 26; Fetter, *British Monetary Orthodoxy*, 98; Hansard, 2nd ser., iv
(1821), cols. 1315–7, 1338; Hilton, *Corn, Cash, Commerce*, 89.
[83] Hilton, *Corn, Cash, Commerce*, 90–1.
[84] Clapham, *Bank of England*, ii, 73; *Jackson's Oxford Journal*, 12 May 1821.
[85] Its life having been extended by 52 Geo. III, c. 50 (1812); 53 Geo. III, c. 5 to 1814; and
then by 54 Geo. III, c. 52 (1814) until the end of the restriction, the Stanhope Act quietly
expired with the resumption.

fanfare. In the Bank's yard, those who came to exchange notes had to have their notes authenticated by the Bank's note inspectors, and those with large-denomination notes had to fill in a form with their name and address before receiving solid pieces of gold.[86] On the first day of cash payments, the Bank exchanged 97,000 £1 notes, and Cobbett was probably among the first to get his notes exchanged into coins. The initial demand for coins quickly subsided in the metropolis, and in the provinces, the demand for coins was moderate. Only in two cities, Manchester and Liverpool, did the Bank set up a station for note exchange. A group of Bank employees, consisting of a teller, an assistant teller, an investigator and two note inspectors, travelled to Manchester to set up a temporary note exchange at the local bank Jones, Loyd and Co. and started exchanging notes into coins on May 10, following the procedure in London.[87] People with notes – the large proportion of them came to exchange small-denomination notes – were admitted through the front door facing King Street, and, after their notes had been examined and paid, they left the premises through the door leading to Back King Street.[88] The team of Bank employees then went to Liverpool and repeated the same process at the banking house of Heywood, Sons & Co. By late May, they had exchanged around £200,000 of notes into coins in Manchester and £80,000 in Liverpool.[89] As Leo Grindon comments, 'the circumstance caused little or no excitement' in Manchester. Nor was there any rush for metallic currency recorded in contemporary newspapers elsewhere in England, Scotland and Ireland.[90]

Following the resumption, the circulation of small Bank notes declined, but paper currency remained a major part of Britain's circulating media. Despite the sharp fall in the amount of small-denomination notes – between May 5 and November 10, it fell from £6.7 million to less than £2 million – the total volume of Bank of England notes in circulation saw only a small reduction: less than £1 million, in the same period. Moreover, £1 and £2 notes did not disappear in the immediate

[86] *Jackson's Oxford Journal*, 12 May 1821.
[87] The Bank to Messrs William Jones Loyd & Co., letter books, 6 May 1821, BE, C82/2.
[88] Leo H. Grindon, *Manchester Banks and Bankers: Historical, Biographical, and Anecdotal* (Manchester, 1877), 104; *Manchester Courier* quoted in *Newcastle Courant* 19 May 1821.
[89] Grindon, *Manchester Banks and Bankers*, 104; *Liverpool Mercury*, 1 June 1821.
[90] Charles Munn, *The Scottish Provincial Banking Companies 1747–1864* (Edinburgh, 1981), 72. On Ireland, see Frank W. Fetter, *The Irish Pound 1797–1826: A Reprint of the Report of the Committee of 1804 of the British House of Commons on the Condition of the Irish Currency* (London, 1955), 58; T. K. Whitaker, 'Origins and Consolidation, 1783–1826', in F. S. L. Lyons, ed., *Bicentenary Essays: Bank of Ireland, 1783–1983* (Dublin, 1983), 26.

aftermath of the return to convertibility.[91] Several newspapers carried columns warning against the 'erroneous impression' that all the £1 Bank of England notes had to be exchanged at once.[92] In England and Wales, the Bank of England note continued to coexist with country notes and regal coins, though small Bank notes appeared much less frequently in transactions, if at all. Bank of England notes became a relative rarity, but paper currency remained a part of economic life. At the end of 1821, John Woodcock of Fulmer, Berkshire, reported to the Bank that he had lost a £25 note out of his pocket; John Barry of Liverpool claimed that a Dublin postman lost a £100 note enclosed in his letter; and a note sent to Mrs Mary Crabb from her brother at Plymouth Dock went missing.[93] The Bank Restriction came to an end in May 1821, but the age of paper currency was hardly over.

After the Resumption

In late September 1821, the Bank's directors judged that convertibility was here to stay and a return to the paper standard was highly unlikely. Accordingly, the Bank's Committee of Treasury recommended a 'great reduction' in the number of clerks as the discontinuation of small-note issue made a large portion of their work redundant. The Bank offered a generous retirement package to nearly 130 clerks, and by January the following year 157 – including, apparently, those who voluntarily came forward – took it and left the Bank.[94] The same committee had approved, as early as February 1820, the proposal from the chief accountant to dispose of cancelled notes that the Bank held in its vault to save on storage space.[95] As the Bank withdrew its small-denomination notes and burned old notes, regal coins and to some extent country banknotes filled the gap created in the nation's currency circulation (Figure 6.1). With the foreign exchange favourable to Britain and the market price of gold below the mint price, there was scarcely any incentive to export coins abroad. Country banknotes still circulated in large quantities, and the legislature decided to allow country banks to issue small notes until

---

[91] House of Commons, *1832 Committee on the Bank Charter*, appendix, 80.
[92] *Cowdroy's Manchester Gazette*, 26 May 1821; *Exeter Flying Post*, 17 May 1821; *Morning Chronicle*, 16 May 1821.
[93] Lost Note Books, BE, C101/61, fol. 186 (Woodcock), fol. 196 (Barry) and fol. 199 (Crabb).
[94] Wilfred M. Acres, *The Bank of England from Within, 1694–1900* (London, 1931), ii, 438–9.
[95] CT, 9 Feb. 1820, BE, G8/20, fol. 75; CT, 21 Nov. 1821, BE, G8/21, fols. 28–9.

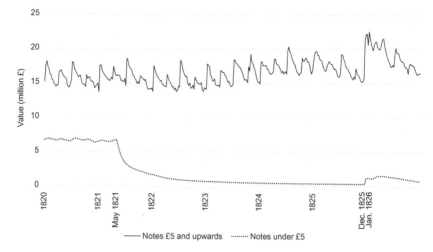

Figure 6.1 Bank of England note circulation, 1820–6.
Source: House of Commons, *Report from the Committee of Secrecy on the Bank of England Charter* (London, 1832), appendix, 79–82.

1833, as a concession to the critics of Peel's act.[96] Contemporary data on the circulation of country notes is unreliable, but the increase in stamp duty payments for small denomination country notes in 1821 indicates that the withdrawal of small Bank notes led to a greater demand for country notes. Apart from Lancashire, where local distrust of country banknotes was deep-seated, there was no organised opposition to country banks' continued engagement in small-note business. The preservation of small country notes was somewhat at odds with the public's alleged enthusiasm for returning to metallic currency as Britain's money users appeared to accept paper currency as they had done during the Bank Restriction.[97] The Marquess of Londonderry (Castlereagh) remarked in February 1822 that 'so far from being inclined to return generally to the use of gold in their dealings, the people shew a decisive preference for bank notes'.[98] This 'decisive preference' for paper

[96] This concession was struck in 1822. Thomas Doubleday, *The Political Life of the Right Honourable Sir Robert Peel, Bart: An Analytical Biography* (London, 1856), i, 275–9.

[97] Larry Neal, 'The Financial Crisis of 1825 and the Restructuring of the British Financial System', *Review – Federal Reserve Bank of Saint Louis*, 80 (1998), 61.

[98] Acworth, *Financial Reconstruction*, 94; Hansard, 2nd ser., vi (1822), col. 312; Robert Stewart (2nd Marquess of Londonderry), *Substance of the Speech of the Marquis of Londonderry Delivered on Friday, the 15th Day of February 1822, on the Subject of the Agricultural Distress of the Country and the Financial Measures Proposed for Its Relief* (London, 1822), 60.

currency undoubtedly stemmed from their twenty-four years of experience with inconvertible paper currency, showing how deeply paper currency had been embedded in everyday life in British society.

After the Bank resumed cash payments, forgery ceased to be a major threat to the credibility of Britain's paper currency. Between 1820 and 1822, when the circulation of small Bank notes fell from £6.7 million to £0.9 million, the number of forged notes brought to the Bank dropped from 30,217 to 3,756.[99] Given the proliferation of forgery crime in the late 1810s, the Bank anticipated a large inflow of inauthentic notes in the initial phase of cash payments, but it turned out to be a false alarm. In late May 1821, the Bank's chief cashier congratulated the bankers in Manchester and Liverpool for the fact that only one forged note was found among £280,000 of Bank notes that were brought back from the note-exchange stations in Lancashire.[100] While the Bank's prosecution of makers and users of forged notes continued, the sense of urgency concerning forgery crime dissipated rapidly. Criminal law reform, especially that related to forgery crime, was losing momentum, which was shown by the narrow defeat of Mackintosh's parliamentary attempt to mitigate the punishment for forgers.[101] In July 1821, the Bank's Committee of Lawsuits received only one report on forgery crime, a negligible number compared to the twenty-five reports per month it received only a year before.[102] This sudden decline in forged-note circulation gave the Bank's directors confidence to abandon the note-improvement project, deeming the threat of forgery no longer serious enough to warrant a complete redesign of the Bank note. Consequently, the contract with Applegath and Cowper was abruptly terminated on the pretext that the Bank's engraver had successfully reproduced the firm's allegedly inimitable note specimens.[103] The cancellation of the new note design also signalled the end of public discussion on improvement. The Bank's directors never liked the public's intrusion into the Bank's business, and they had cooperated with the Royal Commission of the Prevention of Forgery only to fend off further public criticism. The Bank's governor, Charles Pole, curtly remarked that as far as the forgery problem was concerned,

---

[99] An account of the total number and nominal amount of forged Bank of England notes, BE, F2/111.

[100] *Liverpool Mercury*, 1 June 1821.

[101] The Forgery Punishment Mitigation Bill was supported by 115 MPs, while 121 opposed. Philip Handler, 'James Mackintosh and Early Nineteenth-Century Criminal Law', *Historical Journal*, 58 (2015), 775–6; Hansard, 2nd ser., v (1821), col. 1114.

[102] Minutes of Committee for Lawsuits, BE, M5/325, fols. 96–105.

[103] Byatt, *Promises to Pay*, 61; Mackenzie, *Bank of England Note*, 56, 78; Taylor, 'Applegath and Cowper', 52.

'going diffusely into the subject before the public had led to more evil than good'.[104]

While there was some discontent with the Peel Act of 1819 in and outside parliament, MPs opposing convertibility remained a minority. A Whig MP for Essex, Charles Western, campaigned for the revival of the Bank Restriction as a means to provide relief for agricultural interests, but his two motions in June and July 1823 were squarely defeated in parliament.[105] Economic fluctuations, rather than political campaigns, posed a far more serious challenge to Britain's gold standard, and the financial crisis of 1825 was the severest of such challenges.[106] The way Britain's financial instability developed in 1824 and 1825 seemed to follow Thomas Attwood's prognosis that deflation and cheap money would lead to high-risk investment.[107] A series of public debt conversions in the years following the resumption reduced the yields for government bonds to less than 4 per cent, making them unattractive to investors.[108] When investors subsequently sought high-yield, and high-risk, products, they found plenty of speculative opportunities in joint-stock projects – between 1824 and 1825, more than 600 prospectuses were issued for new enterprises such as railways, canals, docks, water supply and gasworks.[109] British investors also poured money into overseas investments, among which the most popular were South American bonds with yields significantly higher than domestic bonds. These high-yielding bonds issued by governments and mining companies in Brazil, Argentina, Colombia, Guatemala and Mexico quickly found their way into investors' portfolios and built up risky assets in Britain's investor community.[110] Market volatility was also increased by a boost in the

[104] *Morning Chronicle*, 22 Sept. 1821.

[105] Alexander Brady, *William Huskisson and Liberal Reform: An Essay on the Changes in Economic Policy in the Twenties of the Nineteenth Century* (London, 1928), 36–8; Feavearyear, *Pound Sterling*, 210–11; Fetter, *British Monetary Orthodoxy*, 106–7.

[106] Turner contends that the 1825 crisis was one of the two systemic crises that Britain experienced in history. John D. Turner, *Banking in Crisis: The Rise and Fall of British Banking Stability, 1800 to the Present* (Cambridge, 2014), 12.

[107] Clapham, *Bank of England*, ii, 93.   [108] Clapham, *Bank of England*, ii, 94.

[109] Clapham, *Bank of England*, ii, 94; Gayer, Rostow and Schwartz, *Growth and Fluctuation*, 171; Ron Harris, 'Political Economy, Interest Groups, Legal Institutions, and the Repeal of the Bubble Act in 1825', *Economic History Review*, 50 (1997), 678–9; C. Hunt, 'The Joint-Stock Company in England, 1830–1844', *Journal of Political Economy*, 43 (1935), 331–64; Ranald C. Michie, *Money, Mania and Markets: Investment, Company Formation and the Stock Exchange in Nineteenth-Century Scotland* (Edinburgh, 1981), 78–100; E. Victor Morgan and William Arthur Thomas, *The Stock Exchange: Its History and Functions* (London, 1962), 83; Moss, *Thomas Attwood*, 111.

[110] Ian Bowen, 'Country Banking, the Note Issues and Banking Controversies in 1825', *Economic History*, 4 (1938), 68–88; Frank G. Dawson, *The First Latin American Debt Crisis: The City of London and the 1822–25 Loan Bubble* (New Haven, CT, 1990), ch. 4;

circulation of both country banknotes and bills of exchange, the latter to the tune of £28 million, between 1823 and 1825, overstretching Britain's commercial credit.[111]

The signs of financial volatility in the early months of 1825 soon coalesced into a series of local banking failures that eventually grew into a national financial crisis. One minor parliamentary discussion on country banks' note-convertibility obligation set the stage for the coming crisis; it was initiated by a parliamentary petition voicing the grievance of Frederick Jones, who, like Joshua Grigby in 1801, had refused to accept Bank of England notes offered by a Bristol bank.[112] The parliamentary debate showed strong support for Jones's claim, acknowledging that country banks must pay their notes in coin if so demanded. This parliamentary reinforcement of convertibility could not have come at a worse time, as demand for secure assets was increasing as the speculative boom came to an end. The financial collapse started in summer and eventually led to the first major crash under the gold standard. Along with the fall in commodity markets, the price of stocks and bonds plummeted.[113] English bankers were deluged with demand for metallic currency from customers who were trying to get hold of secure assets – with parliament having recently confirmed the legitimacy of such a demand. An early victim of the crash was a banking house, Square, Prideaux & Co., in Kingsbridge, Devon, which suspended payments in late September. In late November, not long after Thomas Attwood had written a letter to Lord Liverpool urging an issue of 10–12 million small Bank notes to ease the liquidity pressure, another bank run materialised in Plymouth, where the banking house of Sir William Elford went into administration.[114]

Across England, country banks were under strain, and as the number of bank failures increased, their impact rippled through the local economy via the bank's depositors and the numerous holders of its banknotes.

Michie, *Money, Mania and Markets*, 53–7; Morgan and Thomas, *Stock Exchange*, 81–6; Neal, 'Financial Crisis of 1825', 62.

[111] Shizuya Nishimura, *The Decline of Inland Bills of Exchange in the London Money Market, 1855–1913* (Cambridge, 1971), 86; Pressnell, *Country Banking*, 480–1; Turner, *Banking in Crisis*, 67–70. Pickering contends that the Bank's expanded circulation was a major contributor to the overheating credit. George Pickering, 'The Role of Bank of England Note Issues amongst the Causes of the Panic of 1825' (SSRN working papers, 2018), 25–34.

[112] CWPR, 16 July 1825, 129–67; Hansard, 2nd ser., xiii (1825), cols. 1271–2; Neal, 'Financial Crisis of 1825', 74; Pickering, 'Role of Bank of England Note Issues', 37; Pressnell, *Country Banking*, 482–3.

[113] Clapham, *Bank of England*, ii, 98.

[114] Henry Woollcombe II Diary, 26 Nov. 1825, Plymouth and Devon RO, 710/396; *Sherbourne and Yeovil Mercury*, 2 Dec. 1825. See also CWPR, 3 Dec. 1825, 598–604.

It did not take long before bank failures appeared in the north. The Yorkshire bank of Wentworth, Chaloner & Rishworth, and its London office, suspended payments on December 8, throwing Wakefield, Bradford, Huddersfield, Leeds, Halifax and Keighly into a panic as Wentworth & Co.'s note circulated widely in these places as a preferred currency for private and commercial transactions, particularly in the region's cattle and corn trade.[115] Provincial note users began to avoid paper currency in Bradford and elsewhere, and some country £1 notes were discounted, changing hands at 15s or less.[116] Bank failures and loss of confidence in country banknotes were reported in Southampton, Nottingham, Sheffield and Gloucester.[117] The metropolis was hardly immune to the contagious effect of the crisis. Despite a rescue attempt by the Bank of England, Pole, Thornton & Co. – a London bank with extensive provincial connections with forty-three correspondent banks – failed on December 12.[118] By mid-December, six London banks had suspended their payments.

Up to a point, the response to the 1825 crisis followed the precedent of the 1797 suspension crisis. In November 1825, immediately after Elford's bank stopped payments, a public notice with fifty-eight signatures was issued, expressing 'full and perfect confidence' in Plymouth's remaining bank of Harris, Rosdew, Harris & Co. and declaring that the signatories would accept the bank's notes 'to any amount'.[119] In Leeds, eminent members of the city issued a similar declaration of confidence, which eventually attracted the signatures of around 400 local citizens, and it was displayed on shop windows across the city.[120] In Bradford, Wakefield, Huddersfield, Nottingham and Malton, public meetings were followed by declarations that were made into placards, handbills and newspaper advertisements.[121] The analogy to the declaration movement of 1797 hardly escaped those who were witnessing the unfolding financial crisis in late 1825, and the *Morning Chronicle* refreshed the readers' memory by reproducing a copy of the 1797 London declaration that

---

[115] Steven Caunce, 'Banks, Communities and Manufacturing in West Yorkshire Textiles, c.1800–1830', in J. F. Wilson and Andrew Popp, eds., *Industrial Clusters and Regional Business Networks in England, 1750–1970* (Aldershot, 2003), 122; W. C. E. Hartley, *Banking in Yorkshire* (Clapham, N. Yorkshire, 1975), 33.

[116] *Morning Chronicle*, 17 Dec. 1825.

[117] Clapham, *Bank of England*, ii, 102; Pressnell, *Country Banking*, 487.

[118] Clapham, *Bank of England*, ii, 99; William John Lawson, *The History of Banking* (London, 1850), 114–16; Neal, 'Financial Crisis of 1825', 295; Pressnell, *Country Banking*, 486.

[119] *Plymouth and Devon Weekly Journal*, 4 Dec. 1825. See also CWPR, 3 Dec. 1825, 602.

[120] *Morning Chronicle*, 17 Dec. 1825.

[121] *Leeds Mercury*, 17 Dec. 1825; *Morning Chronicle*, 17 Dec. 1825.

expressed confidence in the nation's paper currency. On 14 December 1825, a public meeting was convened at the Mansion House, the very same place where London's merchants, bankers and tradesmen congregated in February 1797 and pledged to accept the Bank note. When they met again in late 1825, the participants, including the meeting's chair, Lord Mayor William Venables, were well aware that they were re-enacting the great meeting that took place nearly a quarter of a century before as they voiced their 'fullest confidence in the means and substance of the Banking establishments of the Capital and of the Country'.[122] The meeting called on the whole nation to organise similar gatherings in support of public credit. Some, if not many, provincial cities and towns responded to the call, such as Birmingham, where a public meeting on December 17 issued a declaration to support 5 local banks with nearly 500 signatures.[123]

The symmetry between the crises in 1825 and in 1797 was far from perfect. Unlike in 1797, public meetings did not spread across the whole country in 1825. In some provincial cities, such as Bristol, locals were reluctant to organise a collective demonstration of confidence on the grounds that such an action might arouse suspicion about the stability of local credit. For that reason, Bristolian merchants were slow to take action when two local banking houses – Ames, Cave & Co. and Haythorne & Wight – were severely affected by the failure of their London agent, Pole, Thornton & Co., and when the Merchant Venturers of Bristol proposed a declaration in support of these banks' credit, the city's mayor, John Haythorne, refused to sign the document.[124] The declaration was eventually published, but five of the banking houses in Bristol, out of ten prior to the crisis, went out of business by the end of 1826.[125] These failed Bristolian banks were among around fifty banks that went bust during the crisis. Indeed, the contrast with 1797 was most striking in the large number of failed banks in the winter of 1825–6; in 1797, most banks held their ground.[126] Business failure was widespread that winter, when the *London Gazette* listed 1,286 bankruptcy commissions.[127] Local declarations did not save English banks and businesses in the 1825 crisis, and the restoration of

---

[122] *The Times*, 15 Dec. 1825.   [123] *Aris's Birmingham Gazette*, 19 Dec. 1825.

[124] Patrick McGrath, *The Merchant Venturers of Bristol: A History of the Society of Merchant Venturers of the City of Bristol From Its Origin to the Present Day* (Bristol, 1975), 409.

[125] John A. James, 'Panics, Payments Disruptions and the Bank of England before 1826', *Financial History Review*, 19 (2012), 296.

[126] On the number of bank failures, see Clapham, *Bank of England*, ii, 102.

[127] Norman J. Silberling, 'British Prices and Business Cycles, 1779–1850', *Review of Economics and Statistics*, 5 (1923), appendix, 251.

convertibility made banks vulnerable to sudden rushes for metallic currency in times of financial uncertainty.

Amid the crisis, the Bank of England weathered the storm without recourse to a suspension of payments. The Royal Mint responded to the crisis with an important but modest contribution in producing £1.8 million sovereigns in December 1825 alone. Public esteem for the Bank of England note equalled that of gold in terms of the solidity of its value, and bankers and merchants – and ordinary citizens too – across the country were eager to get hold of the Bank of England note.[128] Within two weeks from December 10, the total circulation of Bank notes leaped from £16,235,900 to £23,359,840, as the Bank generously supplied commercial advances while country banks liquidised their assets through their London correspondent banks.[129] As its stock of notes rapidly dwindled, the Bank decided to issue £1 notes for the first time since 1821. Thanks to the discovery of chests of old notes in its vault, which had apparently escaped being burnt, the Bank was able to dispatch small notes at short notice.[130] The Bank's printing office was bustling with activity, with sixty printing machines fully employed over the weekend of December 17 and 18, and the following day, six additional clerks were hired in order to deal with the enormous amount of notes that had to be signed, packed and sent to the provinces.[131] The Bank of England notes played a vital role in restoring a sense of security among the British public until gold shipments arrived from the continent to put the gold standard back in order.[132] On December 20, John Oakes of Bury St Edmunds recorded his relief when his son returned from London at three in the morning 'most amply supplied with Sovereigns & Bank of England Notes, 4 times as much, as in all probability, we shall have need of'.[133] Gold may have saved the nation's economy in the end, but the Bank note saved numerous banks and businesses from possible ruin by providing timely liquidity for bankers and, for note users, psychological reassurance, both of which alleviated the demand for cash.

The financial crisis, which continued well into 1826, left lasting legacies. Despite the international nature of the crisis, domestic factors,

---

[128] House of Commons, *1832 Committee on the Bank Charter*, appendix, 72; Henry Dunning Macleod, *The Theory and Practice of Banking* (1856), ii, 250.

[129] Clapham, *Bank of England*, ii, 99–100.

[130] Clapham, *Bank of England*, ii, 100; *Morning Chronicle*, 20 Dec. 1825.

[131] CD, 19 Dec. 1825, BE, G4/48, fol. 161; Mackenzie, *Bank of England Note*, 82–3; *Morning Chronicle*, 20 Dec. 1825.

[132] Clapham, *Bank of England*, ii, 101; Moss, *Thomas Attwood*, 121.

[133] Jane Fiske, ed., *The Oakes Diaries: Business, Politics and the Family in Bury St Edmunds 1778–1827* (Woodbridge, 1990), ii, 304.

particularly country banks' intransigence during the boom period, were widely regarded as the primary contributor in the making of a national-scale crisis. Therefore, the ensuing parliamentary post-mortem focused on the instability of English country banks, especially their weak capital basis, as the main deficiency in the system.[134] The government pointed the finger at note-issuing country banks for spreading the impact of the crisis to their note holders, who took the brunt of market speculation that they had not been engaged in.[135] Lord Liverpool and Chancellor of the Exchequer Frederick Robinson had no doubt that the primary cause of the crisis was 'the rash Spirit of Speculation which has pervaded the Country ... supported, fostered, and encouraged by the Country Banks'.[136] Thus they shifted the blame from international speculation and the gold standard to domestic banking structure.[137] In particular, country banks' small-denomination notes were identified as the channel through which financial panic spread among the population. The Bank Note Act went swiftly through parliament in February and March, prohibiting banknotes of less than £5 in value in England – and requiring that the circulation of existing notes cease within three years.[138] The Stamp Office had begun refusing to stamp small-denomination country banknotes in early February and, thereafter, the volume of new country notes, now consisting solely of notes with the value of £5 and upwards, sharply contracted, as shown in the decrease in country banks' stamp-duty payment for reissuable notes from £114,916 1s 6d in 1825 to a mere £13,108 4s 6d in 1826.[139] The suppression of small notes had little impact on the Bank's policy, as it had mostly relinquished small-note business and it regarded the supply of £1 and £2 notes during the crisis solely as an emergency measure. The Bank was allowed to create new small notes until October, but after reaching a peak in mid-April, at a weekly average of £1.57 million, the Bank reduced its small-note circulation considerably and, by the end of that year, it was down to less than

---

[134] Clapham, *Bank of England*, ii, 108–10; Pressnell, *Country Banking*, 491.

[135] Liverpool's letter to Robinson, dated 13 Jan. 1826, is in CD, 20 Jan. 1826, BE, G4/48, fols. 200–15. See also Wilbur Devereux Jones, *'Prosperity' Robinson: The Life of Viscount Goderich, 1782–1859* (London, 1967), 116.

[136] CD, 20 Jan. 1826, BE G4/48, fols. 201–2. However, they did not see small notes as the direct cause.

[137] Caunce, 'Banks, Communities and Manufacturing', 115.

[138] 7 Geo. IV, c. 6; Clapham, *Bank of England*, ii, 106–8; Jones, *Prosperity Robinson*, 116–18; Morgan, *Theory and Practice of Central Banking*, 87–8.

[139] House of Commons, *Order to Stamp Office Prohibiting Further Stamping of Country Bank Notes under Five Pounds* (1826); House of Commons, *1832 Committee on the Bank Charter*, appendix, 114.

£800,000 (Figure 6.1).[140] In March 1826 alone, the Bank burned 2,930 boxes of £1 and £2 notes.[141]

The banking reform in 1826 brought about a profound structural transformation in the British banking system as it entailed major curtailment of the Bank's monopoly of joint-stock banking in England. The reform allowed private bankers to form joint-stock banks with no limitation on the number of proprietors; previously a maximum of six partners had been allowed for private banks.[142] In their decision to extend joint-stock incorporation to English private banking, the legislators were no doubt influenced by their observation of the remarkable resilience of Scottish banking during the recent crisis, which was attributed to the absence of regulations on the number of partnerships and branches.[143] Lord Liverpool and Robinson did not intend to copy the Scottish banking structure but envisaged a reconfigured English banking system in which a new balance would be struck between private joint-stock banking without the note-issuing privilege and the Bank of England's influence over the nation's finance and money.[144] With the legislation in late May, the Bank's monopoly of joint-stock banking came to be limited to within sixty-five miles of the City of London, while the Bank was allowed to open provincial branches.[145] The government's expectation was for the Bank to gain greater control over monetary circulation through the provincial branches' commercial operations and note circulation. The Bank was willing to take on this enhanced responsibility as long as it provided an opportunity to employ its surplus capital in a wider geographical area.[146] It subsequently opened branches in Gloucester, Manchester and Swansea in 1826, and in Birmingham, Bristol, Exeter, Hull, Leeds, Liverpool and Newcastle in the following years.[147] These provincial branches officially circulated Bank notes in the English provinces, institutionalising the Bank's provincial note circulation that, as we

---

[140] House of Commons, *1832 Committee on the Bank Charter*, appendix, 82.

[141] CT, 1 Mar. 1826, BE, G8/22, fol. 226.

[142] 7 Geo. IV, c. 46; Clapham, *Bank of England*, ii, 103; Pressnell, *Country Banking*, 507.

[143] House of Lords, *Report from the Lords Committees Appointed a Select Committee to Enquire into the State of Circulation of Promissory Notes under the Value of £5 in Scotland and Ireland* (1826), 5.

[144] CD, 20 Jan. 1826, BE G4/48, fols. 201–2. See also Hansard, 2nd ser., xiv (1826), cols. 103–11.

[145] Clapham, *Bank of England*, ii, 102–7; Pressnell, *Country Banking*, 507.

[146] Dieter Ziegler, 'Central Banking in the English Provinces in the Second Quarter of the Nineteenth Century', *Business History*, 31 (1989), 34.

[147] 'Branches of the Bank of England', *Bank of England Quarterly Bulletin*, 3 (1963), 280; Neal, 'Financial Crisis of 1825', 72.

have seen in previous chapters, had already been established since the eighteenth century.

By the late 1820s, the moral language of community had largely been dissociated from the public discussion on currency and thereafter its radicalised version was only occasionally sighted. In one rare – possibly its last – appearance in the following decade, the radicalised communal-currency tradition finally took a material form that it never did during the Bank Restriction period. This incarnation of communal currency had less to do with economic fluctuations than with political activism as it was employed as a form of political expression during the Days of May in 1832, amid the upheaval over British electoral reform. At this critical juncture in Britain's constitutional history, William IV's refusal to increase the number of seats in the House of Lords, the subsequent resignation of the Whig government and the prospect of the reform-averse Duke of Wellington forming a government triggered direct political action by popular radicals – and a run on the Bank of England was organised by Francis Place.[148] The threat to paralyse the nation's monetary system, Place reasoned, would force the king and parliament to accede to the demand for reform. The protesters held a large demonstration in Leicester Square and erected placards with the slogan 'To Stop the Duke, Go for Gold', inciting citizens to rush to the Bank of England and demand gold for every note they had at hand.[149] The call for action soon spread across England and Scotland through handbills sent by the campaigners in the metropolis.

The politically motivated bank run was hardly a novel strategy for popular radicals, having already been articulated and acted upon by radicals of the previous generation, such as Joshua Grigby, Henry Hunt and William Cobbett during the Bank Restriction period.[150] While these precedents were the sporadic actions of individuals, Place's campaign in 1832 implemented bank runs on a sufficiently large scale to embarrass the Bank of England. The 'Go for Gold' campaign started at the end of the second week of May, and in the following week, the Bank was besieged by note users demanding gold coins to the extent that it had to set up an additional gallery in its pay hall to deal with the

[148] David John Rowe, ed., *London Radicalism, 1830–1834: A Selection from the Papers of Francis Place* (London, 1970), 88–90.

[149] CWPR, 19 May 1832, 392; *Morning Chronicle*, 14 May 1832.

[150] Timothy Alborn, *Conceiving Companies: Joint-Stock Politics in Victorian England* (London, 1998), 61. For the fear of puff-out in 1821, see *A Review of the Banking System of Britain; with Observations on the Injurious Effects of the Bank of England Charter, and the General Benefit of Unrestricted Banking Companies* (Edinburgh, 1821), 226.

extraordinary number of transactions.[151] The Bank's governor later stated that £1.6 million of metallic currency was withdrawn from the Bank in that month at a time when its metallic reserve was usually less than £10 million.[152] In the provinces, note users that supported the reform joined the concerted attack on the nation's monetary order. The *Poor Man's Guardian* reported that 620 customers had withdrawn deposits amounting to £16,700 from banks in Manchester, while savings banks in Birmingham experienced a similarly extraordinary customer withdrawal of £10,000 to £20,000 during the same period.[153] Vincent Stuckey, a Somerset banker, witnessed Bank of England notes being refused by provincial note users and exchanged into country bank-notes.[154] The run continued until the public learned that the king had yielded to popular sentiment and asked Earl Grey to return to office.[155] As a matter of fact, the Go for Gold campaign made a limited contribution – if any – to the king's change of heart, and Place's self-congratulatory account of how the impact of his campaign changed the course of electoral reform was a sheer exaggeration, but, for its scale and as a self-conscious attempt to mobilise currency convertibility to change the course of electoral reform, the episode deserves a place in Britain's political as well as monetary history.[156]

It was ironic that the Go for Gold campaign in 1832 – an offshoot of the radicalised communal-currency tradition – contributed to the demise of currency voluntarism by putting the legislature on alert about the vulnerability of convertible currency to political as well as economic disturbances. This double volatility provided ample reason for the Whig government to reconsider some of the basic premises of the nation's currency system, eventually leading to a revision of the legal standing of the Bank of England note. The imminent renewal of the Bank Charter, the first renewal since 1800, offered the government an opportunity to take a step that previous governments had tried hard to avoid – giving the Bank note the status of legal tender. Coincidentally, parliamentary discussion on the Bank Charter commenced in May 1832, just

---

[151] John Francis, *History of the Bank of England: Its Times and Traditions* (London, 1847), ii, 66–7; *Morning Chronicle*, 16 May 1832; *Morning Post*, 14 and 15 Mar. 1832; Graham Wallas, *The Life of Francis Place, 1771–1854* (London, 1898), 308–10.

[152] House of Commons, *1832 Committee on the Bank Charter*, 56. See also Acres, *Bank of England from Within*, ii, 547–8.

[153] *Poor Man's Guardian*, 19 May 1832, 397.

[154] House of Commons, *Select Committee of Secrecy on Banks of Issue: Second Report* (1841), 49.

[155] Rowe, *London Radicalism*, 92–3.

[156] Joseph Hamburger, *James Mill and the Art of Revolution* (New Haven, CT, 1963), 104–5.

as the Bank's gold reserve was being drained by politically motivated withdrawals.[157] In the parliamentary committee on the Bank Charter, two types of bank run preoccupied MPs and witnesses. The financial crisis of 1825, which loomed large in the discussion about the resilience of the nation's financial system as commercial runs brought many private banks to their knees, was still fresh in people's memory. A *political* run on banks, which the nation had just experienced, was no less disturbing than commercial bank runs because, as the Go for Gold campaign demonstrated, artificial bank runs could jeopardise the stability of the political as well as the monetary order. Lord Althorp, the chancellor of the exchequer, had no doubt that legal-tender status would serve as an effective defence against the two types of run. As long as citizens were legally bound to accept the Bank note, they would be unable to prey upon metallic reserves held by the nation's banks. The legal-tender clause was only auxiliary to the charter renewal, but it caused much debate in parliament as it concerned the nature of paper currency as defined by the country's law.

The most vocal opponent to the legal-tender clause was Robert Peel, whose hostility towards it was as strong as that of the long-standing enemies of paper currency, William Cobbett and Joseph Hume. Expressing his abhorrence at the legislative deviation from the 'true principle' of the monetary system, Peel contended that metallic currency alone should be legal tender.[158] Conferring on paper currency the same status as regal coins would amount to a disavowal of the metallic standard enshrined in the Act of 1819 that ended the Bank Restriction.[159] Peel, for whom currency was as much a moral as an economic issue, condemned Althorp for succumbing to the fear of political bank runs and undermining the sound monetary system. In his response to Peel's impassioned objection, Althorp stressed that the legal-tender clause was designed with commercial bank runs in mind rather than being a product of the recent political run.[160] Despite Althorp's strenuous effort to discount it, the immediate psychological impact of the recent bank run undeniably affected the legislature's general opinion on the issue. The strong backing for the legal-tender clause in parliament suggests that the recent political run on banks consolidated support for legislation that was

[157] Clapham, *Bank of England*, ii, 121–30; Theodore E. Gregory, *Select Statutes, Documents and Reports Relating to British Banking, 1832–1928* (London, 1929), pp. xiii–xvi; Hansard, 3rd ser., xii (1832), cols. 1356–63.
[158] Emmanuel Coppieters, *English Bank Note Circulation, 1694–1954* (The Hague, 1955), 47–52.
[159] Hansard, 3rd ser., xviii (1833), col. 1345.
[160] Hansard, 3rd ser., xviii (1833), cols. 1391–2. See also Clapham, *Bank of England*, ii, 127; Hansard, 3rd ser., xviii (1833), cols. 1345–8.

not in harmony with orthodox monetary theory at the time. On 29 August 1833, in legislation that secured the Bank's legal status for another 21 years, the Bank of England note became Britain's legal tender, 139 years after the Bank's establishment.[161]

The legal-tender clause in the 1833 Bank Charter Act was the final nail in the coffin of Britain's communal currency, which had lingered on as a feeble reverberation from its heyday during the Bank Restriction period. Its principal component, voluntary acceptance, had not only lost its legal foundation but had also become irrelevant under the gold standard. Ironically, the radical version of currency voluntarism, the Go for Gold campaign in 1832, contributed to hardening the legislature's attitude to what was left of the paper currency 'of choice' as the collective refusal of the Bank note posed a tangible threat to the stability of the nation's currency system.[162] Although the legal-tender clause would serve as a defence against bank runs of the 1825 type, the 1832 political bank run was the immediate cause that led to the controversial decision to make the Bank of England note legal tender. At any rate, what the Stanhope Act implemented two decades previously in a circuitous manner – the legal obligation to accept the Bank note – was finally enshrined in the 1833 Bank Charter Act. An old Whig MP, John Wrottesley, voiced a solemn warning to the nation that it was departing from the long-established principle of paper circulation grounded in 'mutual confidence, and the good sense of the people at large'.[163] Wrottesley's comment was a perfectly legitimate description of the historical change he was witnessing, but to his contemporaries it must have sounded anachronistic – in fact, he was quoting from Lord Liverpool's speech in 1811, which was delivered in support of the Stanhope Act. Back in 1811, there was a strong feeling against making paper currency legal tender. The Stanhope Act made the Bank note a forced currency, and this was when Britain's currency debate started to move away from the language of community, pitting voluntary currency against forced currency, English paper against the French *assignat*, the nation's currency against the national currency. The political debate over legal tender in the early 1830s showed how detached Britain's currency had become from the tradition of communal currency that had been passionately debated and acted upon only a generation before.

---

[161] Acres, *Bank of England from Within*, ii, 461; Clapham, *Bank of England*, ii,127; Feavearyear, *Pound Sterling*, 251.

[162] Edmund Burke, *Reflections on the Revolution in France*, ed. J. C. D. Clark (Stanford, CA, 2001), 401; Gambles, *Protection and Politics*, 128.

[163] Hansard, 3rd ser., xviii (1833), col. 1395.

Conclusion: The Bank Note as Good as Gold

The banking reform in 1834 had a far-reaching impact on Britain's currency. With two crises in mind – 1825 and 1832 – the legislature curtailed the rights of note users, practically barring them from demanding gold for their notes. The Bank note was no longer a currency of choice; to all intents and purposes, it was a fiat currency with its acceptance mandated by law. It circulated in a currency system that was far better integrated than in any previous period, a system in which the Bank of England's presence had been enhanced by its provincial branches.[164] Some practical developments, such as improved communication through railways, the postal system and, later, the telegraph, would further change the contours of this system by providing the technical means for near-instantaneous transactions of information and monetary value.[165]

There was no immediate expansion of paper circulation under the reformed banking structure. After 1826 and throughout the 1830s, the circulation of Bank notes remained at a level below £20 million.[166] There was more than £1.5 million in Bank notes below £5 in April 1826. By 1829, when the 1826 Bank Note Act's ban on small notes took effect, the circulation had shrunk to £403,420, and three years later, it was less than £300,000 – probably a sizeable amount of the outstanding small notes were 'dead notes', that is notes that had been lost, destroyed or forgotten and therefore were unlikely to be presented for payment.[167] With the decline of small-note circulation, everyday economic transactions in paper currency became relatively uncommon, as note users reverted to payments by metallic currency or credit.[168]

The new system of banking and currency was designed to minimise the disruptive potential of crowds in times of financial instability by taking away the power of note users to refuse Britain's primary credit currency, the Bank of England note. The 1825 financial crisis and the Go for Gold campaign demonstrated the far-reaching impact of a collective refusal of paper currency on the nation's gold-anchored economy. It was also clear

---

[164] Nigel Thrift, 'Transport and Communication 1730–1914', in R. A. Dodgshon and R. A. Butlin, eds., *An Historical Geography of England and Wales*, 2nd ed. (London, 1990), 476–7; Ziegler, 'Central Banking', 38.

[165] Michael Collins, *Money and Banking in the UK: A History* (London, 1988), 20–1.

[166] Stephen Broadberry, Bruce Campbell, Alexander Klein et al., *British Economic Growth, 1270–1870* (New York, 2015), 403.

[167] Clapham, *Bank of England*, ii, 107.

[168] Margot C. Finn, *The Character of Credit: Personal Debt in English Culture, 1740–1914* (Cambridge, 2003), 80.

to the legislature that obliging banks to maintain the interchangeability of paper currency and precious metal at all times would involve a major risk of financial instability when circulating credit had grown so large compared to the metallic reserve at bankers' hands. The system of paper credit depended on the expectation that a large proportion of creditors were willing to take paper rather than coins. When convertibility was suspended in 1797, British citizens believed that voluntary support for public credit was a sufficient guarantee to buttress the acceptability of paper currency. By 1833, such belief had largely been lost. The legal-tender clause was to protect the nation's banks from the unruly behaviour of note users in times of emergency.

Another threat to the stability of the paper-currency system, the crime of forgery, had been in decline since the restoration of convertibility, which contributed to rehabilitating the Bank's public image while improving note users' general confidence in the value of the Bank note. In the last years of the Bank Restriction, 20,000–30,000 forged notes per annum were brought to the Bank of England. The number dropped to around 2,000–3,000 following the resumption, and the discontinuation of small-note issue further reduced it to less than 500 after 1829.[169] As a consequence, forgery prosecution became a minor part of the Bank's solicitors' business. In 1832, the Bank prosecuted only two criminals, and in the same year, capital punishment for Bank note forgery was abolished – a landmark legal reform that was narrowly missed by long-term campaigner James Mackintosh, who died in May that year.

Among note users, whose membership was much reduced due to the disappearance of small notes, confidence in the value of Bank notes was maintained. Under the gold standard, the legal-tender Bank note was 'as good as gold'.[170] However, that confidence was no longer based on interpersonal trust. The solidity of paper currency depended on the working of the system of interlinked banks and currency, and the state's power to compel the nation to accept specific forms of currency. Thomas Carlyle saw paper currency as an embodiment of depersonalised and dehumanised social relations in what he called the Paper Age – the origin of which he traced to the final years of the French Ancien Régime. As a sign of a corrupt nation and an unwholesome society, the proliferation of paper currency precipitated the French Revolution and culminated in the

---

[169] A return of the number of forged notes of every denomination brought to the Bank of England for payment, BE, F2/112.

[170] House of Commons, *1832 Committee on the Bank Charter*, 370.

circulation of inconvertible *assignats*.[171] There was an echo of Burke's condemnation of revolutionary France, but, unlike Burke, Carlyle did not contrast the forced paper currency in France and the English Bank notes based on voluntary acceptance. Indeed, Carlyle was to develop the theme of dehumanised monetary relations in industrialised Britain, where complex social relations had been reduced to cash payment as the 'sole nexus of man to man'.[172] Carlyle conceived the cash nexus as the antithesis to the human community, an idea that would have been alien to Britons in the 1790s and 1800s, who believed in the communal nature of paper currency. Between the 1790s and the 1830s, British ideas on paper currency transformed beyond recognition.

[171] John B. Lamb, 'The Paper Age: Currency, Crisis, and Carlyle', *Prose Studies*, 30 (2008), 28.
[172] Thomas Carlyle, *Chartism* (London, 1840), 58, 61, 66.

Conclusion

This book's examination of Britain's early experience of inconvertible paper has highlighted the communal aspects of paper currency as they were debated and acted upon by British citizens during the Bank Restriction period. The full extent of the intellectual genealogy and geographical horizon of communal currency is yet to be explored, but this book has taken a tentative step towards reincorporating the communal tradition into the history of money, which has long been dominated by the dichotomy of precious metal (by metallists) and the state (by statists or chartalists). The communal tradition also brings us closer to past money users, whose historical experiences have rarely been told in the vast literature on the development of the modern monetary system. How do the intertwined stories of communal currency and money users enrich our historical understanding of British society between the 1790s and the 1830s, a crucial turning point in British history as the nation faced multiple crises ranging from major wars, threats to political legitimacy and class struggles to a cultural crisis of representation?

No one can deny that Britain in the long eighteenth century witnessed a spectacular rise in paper credit. In 1700, the total circulation of the Bank of England note was around £1.6 million; by 1820, it was close to £25 million. A large part of this increase occurred during the Bank Restriction period. The suspension of cash payments in 1797 transformed the nature of the Bank of England note, from a promise to pay metallic currency to a currency based more firmly on interpersonal credit. The transition from convertible to inconvertible paper was not without challenges. As the Bank of England note was not legal tender, its acceptance was never guaranteed until the 1810s. Neither neoclassical economics, which rarely questions a currency's acceptability, nor state-currency theory, which presupposes that the state generally has the power to force specific forms of currency on the nation, fully captures the historical situation of Bank Restriction Britain. An alternative tradition of communal currency better explains why the acceptance of inconvertible currency in 1797 took the distinctive form of public declaration, a collective expression that British citizens accepted paper currency voluntarily – a crucial episode detailed in the first chapter of this book.

The suspension of cash payments accelerated the diffusion of the Bank of England note through British society. By the 1790s, the Bank note had become the principal paper currency in London and the home counties and, though still small in number, its users were spread across England, Wales, Scotland and Ireland. Chapter 2 challenged the conventional view of Bank-note circulation as a phenomenon limited to the metropolis and its environs by showing that its users were dispersed across the British Isles from the early part of the eighteenth century. Multiple factors underlay this historical diffusion of paper-currency use. The conventional Bank of London view stresses the absence of any institutional policy by the Bank to circulate its notes beyond the metropolitan area. However, in the absence of any explicit policy, Bank notes did move across Britain. There was no clear divide between the two spheres of currency circulation: the metropolitan area monopolised by the Bank of England note and the regional currency sphere dominated by country banknotes. As a matter of fact, the Bank note and country notes coexisted in the English provinces, understandably when the majority of country banks were still young and their credit was yet to be established. In the heyday of country banking between the 1780s and 1810s, the Bank of England note retained, or indeed enhanced, its status as the nation's foremost paper currency. As much as the geographical or horizontal reach of the Bank note progressed in the Bank Restriction period, its social or vertical penetration entered a new stage after 1797, with the introduction of small-denomination notes. The expansion of the note-user community was most pronounced in the metropolis, where there was ample evidence of paper currency reaching diverse social groups, including those with modest means. Outside the metropolitan area, penetration was uneven. Still, the degree of social penetration by the Bank note during the Bank Restriction period was unprecedented, demonstrating that it was becoming a de facto national currency.

This book's detailed study of the users and uses of the Bank note has challenged historical assumptions about the anonymous monetary relations that modern paper currency is supposed to have brought about. Historical evidence attests that note users commonly regarded paper-currency transactions as personal and identifiable. By observing, recording and adding personalised identifiers on each note, note users made Bank notes identifiable objects with distinctive histories and physical appearance. The microcosm of the monetary community inscribed on the flip side of Bank notes through what we call social endorsement demonstrates the nature of the economic community as largely an imagined, rather than tangible, form of community, but it served to consolidate the interpersonal trust that was crucial in sustaining inconvertible paper currency. There was a tension between the traditional form of interpersonal trust and the emerging ideal of commercial society, the latter privileged uninhibited currency circulation free from the burden of pre-existing social relations. Rather than a symbol of anonymised economic relations, the modes of Bank-note use examined in this book serve as a strong testimony that currency circulation retained its traditional outlook much longer than historians have hitherto acknowledged.

There were moments of change, but changes were not driven by economic factors alone. Military conflicts clearly affected how and where Bank notes circulated in Britain's wartime economy. In Portsmouth, Plymouth and other navy port towns, seamen, sailors and dockyard workers received their wages in paper currency, passing notes onto others and expanding the spheres of paper circulation. In this respect, the regional circulation of Bank notes was incidental to the state project of sustaining naval forces, which was crucial to the survival of the nation. While maintaining the war economy depended on the state's ability to make payments for munitions and provisions without drawing upon its poor metallic reserves, the government had a major stake in securing the paper system. Nonetheless, the British government largely avoided compulsory measures in circulating Bank notes, despite the fact that Bank notes were treated as official money at public offices and in tax administration. The state played a role in expanding the circulation of paper currency, but the role was accompanied by a degree of self-constraint.

Signs of inflation at the turn of the nineteenth century gave an initial spur to theoretical inquiries into the mechanism of monetary inflation. It should, however, be noted that the debate was hardly apolitical. The Bank's critics, notably Walter Boyd and Lord King, painted a picture in which they blamed the Bank's directors for reaping profit from an unrestrained note issue. Those critics, as with earlier writers on currency questions, had their own agenda, political and personal, but when the currency discussion shifted from British exceptionalism to broader monetary issues, their metallism posed a major challenge to communal currency. Although until the early 1810s communal currency and voluntary acceptance were central ideas in Britain's currency debate, the debate gradually made room for a more mechanistic mode of explanation. In this transitory period, theories were inseparable from their real-life consequences, and practical theorists such as Henry Thornton did not hesitate to modify their position in the debate to achieve policy goals. Such historical dynamics drove the focus of theoretical discussion away from the community of money users – those who accepted currency – to the actions of the issuers of currency – the Bank of England – and both critics and defenders of the Bank found something to be desired in the Bank's policymaking. The inconvertible-currency system thus precipitated the expansion of the Bank's role in the nation's currency supply when monetary policy and central banking had yet to take any solid shape.

In the long run, the theoretical debate surrounding the Bullion Report laid the foundation for monetary orthodoxy. However, when later historians looked back on the Bullionist Controversy, they took for granted the theoretical ascendency of bullionism, refusing to recognise the prevalence of what the neoclassical tradition condemned as heterodox ideas of currency. The British debate on paper currency, as shown in Chapter 4, started in the early 1790s as a response to the French currency experiment of the *assignat*, nearly a decade prior to the more domestically oriented debate that was initiated by Walter Boyd and Alexander Baring. Up to 1811, the distinction between voluntary currency and forced currency had been a key reference point for bullionists and non-bullionists alike. Forced currency was an anathema to British society because it was deemed an infringement of the nation's constitutional tradition but also a recipe for uncontrolled inflation, as the revolutionary French experienced in the early 1790s and which the British watched with distaste and horror. The broad consensus on the voluntary-currency principle was significantly undermined when the devout metallist Lord King brought a legal challenge to inconvertible currency, which left the government no option but to confer on the Bank note quasi-legal tender status. From 1811 onwards, the path was cleared for bullionism as it was no longer competing with communal currency and found an easier target in forced currency, towards which the British nation held deep-seated suspicion.

With the loss of the voluntary principle, popular support for the Bank Restriction rapidly dwindled towards the late 1810s. When paper currency was forced on them, Britain's money users traced the cause of fluctuations in monetary value to the Bank of England, which was circulating its notes without state or public oversight. The public's impression that the Bank was setting its own rules intensified when the post-war economic downturn and the surge in the circulation of forged notes made visible the Bank's draconian prosecution policy. Note users were subject to the constant fear of receiving forged notes. At any time, the Bank's investigators might confiscate inauthentic notes, and, at worst, unfortunate note users might be prosecuted and punished for passing forged notes or having them in their possession. The public backlash during the forgery crisis of 1818 was a direct response to the general uncertainty regarding the value of forced currency. Similarly, intensified public demand for note improvement was a manifestation of note users' desire to claim what remained of the communal nature of currency. Neither the Bank nor the government made much concession to these radicalised forms of communal involvement in monetary issues. Facing the choice between the continuation of forced currency and the abandonment of inconvertible paper, most of the British public, politicians and writers chose to support the resumption of cash payments.

We should not take the disappearance of the communal-money tradition as the verdict of history on this tradition's theoretical and practical shortcomings. As much as the intellectual environment of monetary debate changed its contours, Britain's social reality and economic life had transformed during the first three decades of the nineteenth century. At the beginning of the Bank Restriction period, in 1797, British citizens' declarations of their acceptance of paper currency saved the nation from national bankruptcy. In 1825, similar expressions of support for local credit proved powerless against widespread financial instability. With the growth in provincial credit supply and the extensive linkage between British and international finance, the 1825 crisis served as indisputable evidence that there was no return to the communal currency of 1797. Rather than contemplating the revival of the Bank Restriction, the government and parliament in 1826 opted to oblige private banks to hold sufficient assets to pay for their financial liabilities. From both institutional and popular memory, the idea of communal currency and voluntary acceptance was erased. In 1826, George Canning invoked the authority of 'the great man' Edmund Burke in a parliamentary speech to defend the metallic standard. Quoting Burke's passages from *Reflections on the Revolution in France*, Canning presented Burke as the defender of 'the good old system of our forefathers' when there was no 'exuberance of paper'.[1] Conveniently, Canning forgot that in the very passages he quoted, Burke's contemporaries in the 1790s found an explanation for the soundness of English paper currency. Reading Burke's statements as a prophecy of bullionist ascendancy, as Canning did in 1826, was to give the history of money a false sense of teleology.

Historical judgements often cloud our understanding of the past. For those living in the age of the gold standard, Ricardo, Lord King and Peel appeared to have always been on the winning side. If that were the case, why was the inconvertible-paper system supported for more than two

---

[1] Hansard, 2nd ser., xiv (1826), col. 323.

decades in one of Britain's most turbulent periods? Bank Restriction was supported because numerous note users believed that they would sustain the value of paper currency and, most importantly, acted accordingly by accepting and circulating it. Economic history rarely asks questions about those forgotten users of currency. While theoretical abstraction helps us understand how economic systems worked in the past, the market – the principal mode of economic abstraction – is no perfect substitute for the human community. As Robinson Crusoe well knew, money has no use for a lonely castaway on a desert island. Nor did his encounter with another living soul on the island automatically open up the possibility of monetary transactions. Unless multiple agents share the same understanding of value, money does not serve as a medium of exchange. Currency is, by nature, premised on the human community. Focusing on the communal aspect of currency reveals not only how currency operated within a community but also how a community engaged with money. Beliefs and practices concerning paper currency, such as social endorsement, tell us how British society during the Bank Restriction period dealt with the increasingly complex and anonymising world of monetised society. Nonetheless, during the same period, social, institutional and theoretical developments threw communal currency into question. Thornton and Coleridge belonged to the last generation of money users who believed that social cohesion was a sound basis for stable credit currency. In contrast, for Ricardo and his followers, trust in community was too elusive to offer a reliable foundation for the nation's currency. During the Bank Restriction period, communal or interpersonal trust was gradually replaced by trust in the system, which was to dominate the subsequent intellectual tradition in monetary theory.

Communal currency – as an idea and reality – in Bank Restriction Britain is a forgotten episode in the history of modern monetary development. It adds a new layer to the history of credit currency, which has long been discussed in relation to metallic currency and the state's fiat authority. Britain's communal-currency tradition was born of the lessons Britons had learned from their observations of the American and the French experiences of legal tender. It was equally grounded in what they thought of as the peculiarly British experience of a voluntarily accepted paper currency. When British society ventured into the uncharted territory of the inconvertible-currency system, historical experience seemed to provide a guiding light. The Bank Restriction had become another historical lesson that British people looked back on in the era of the gold standard. The Victorian populariser of political economy Harriet Martineau captured the element of historical learning about currency in her novel *Berkeley the Banker* (1833), a story based on the 1825 crisis as it was witnessed by residents of a fictional town, Haleham:

A grand crisis was thought to be at hand, and those who had profited and those who had suffered by past changes were equally eager, the one party to look forward, the other to look back, in order to gain some degree of insight into their state and prospects. All had dearly purchased the knowledge that bank-paper is not all alike, however carelessly one sort or another may pass from hand to hand. Everybody in Haleham now knew the difference between a paper currency that depends on confidence, and one that rests on authority.[2]

The distinction between the money of confidence and the money of authority was still retained in the minds of money users in Martineau's time. However, unlike the writers in the early years of the Bank Restriction period, Martineau was unequivocal when she described the Bank of England note as the money of authority as it was 'avouched by government authority'.[3] All this belonged to historical knowledge in the early 1830s, when Martineau was writing. The Bank of England's note issue was still debated in the run-up to the Bank's structural reform in 1844, but it was a debate reserved to experts in the art of political economy and monetary theory. During the Bank Restriction period, paper currency belonged to a much broader community of money users. Politicians, merchants, financiers and bankers – including the directors of the Bank of England – knew how crucial it was to gain support from that community and they often sought a public expression of confidence to buttress the nation's public credit and monetary system. Ironically, it was also during the Bank Restriction period that British people lost their faith in the voluntary foundation of paper currency. Martineau wrote that confidence in the Bank of England note was 'betrayed' because the Bank 'had not wisely regulated its issues, and had thereby impaired the sanction of government authority'.[4] The idea of paper currency – and of money – had been irrevocably changed after twenty-four years of Bank Restriction.

Modern monetary theory and the monetary system owe much to Britain. The Bank Restriction period was fertile ground for theoretical, institutional and policy development. In the ensuing decades of Britain's dominance of international finance and trade, paper currency continued to provide an essential means of carrying out trade, industry and other aspects of economic life. The gold standard was the lynchpin of Britain's economic ascendency, but it was accompanied by Victorians' belief in

---

[2] Harriet Martineau, *Berkeley the Banker: A Tale* (London, 1833), part 2, 24.
[3] Martineau, *Berkeley the Banker*, part 2, 24.
[4] Martineau, *Berkeley the Banker*, part 2, 24.

the Bank of England note being 'as good as gold'. In the long term, paper currency outlived the gold standard, and in the next century, inconvertible currency became the norm across modern nations. Paper currency was one of the most valuable assets in modern society, giving dynamism to economic transactions in a monetised society that had long been shackled by scarce metal. In the first age of paper, British citizens had a first taste of modern monetised society. The experience was not entirely sanguine, nor was it without disappointment, but when they rested their hopes on the flimsy sheets of paper, it was undoubtedly worth more than glittering gold.

Bibliography

Archival Documents

Bank of England Archives (BE), London

ADM6, Administration Department: Records of Accounts and Costing
C12, Cashier's Department: Note Issue Files
C82, Cashier's Department: Chief Cashier's Office: Letter Books
C101, Cashier's Department: Records of Bank Note Issue
F2, Freshfield Papers: Records of Forged and Other Imitation Bank Notes
F15, Freshfields Papers: Records of Machinery and Other Equipment
G4, Minutes of the Court of Directors
G6, Court Papers
G8, Minutes of the Committee of Treasury
G23, Secretary's Letter Books
M2, Cashier's Department Records
M5, Secretary's Department Records

Bank of Ireland Arts Centre, Dublin

Court of Directors Transaction Books

Bristol Record Office, Bristol

41593, Papers of the Hart-Davis family

British Library, London

Add Ms 33103, Pelham Papers
Add Ms 33113, Pelham Papers
Add Ms 38368, Liverpool Papers
Add Ms 38738, Huskisson Papers
Add Ms 51572, Holland Papers
Add Ms 72844, Horner/Lyell Papers

Cork City and County Archives, Cork

U15B, Irish Distillers Copy Letter Book, 1794–1802

Devon Heritage Centre, Exeter

47/14, Clarke of Bridwell, 1666–1800
152M/C, Political and personal papers of Henry Addington, 1st
   Viscount Sidmouth, 1705–1824
1262M, Fortescue of Castle Hill, 1158–1957

Durham University Library Archives and Special Collections

19/25, Baker Baker Papers
4-1, Cookson Papers

Glamorgan Record Office, Cardiff

D/D/GD/A, Dowlais Iron Company Letterbooks 1796–7

Hampshire Record Office, Winchester

21M57/C31, Correspondence of Charles Agar, 1st Earl of Normanton,
   1736–1809
132M98, Portals Ltd of Laverstoke and Overton

HBOS Group Archives, Edinburgh

5/1/8, Bank of Scotland, Board Minutes
1/288, Business Peculiar to Agencies

Kent History and Library Centre, Maidstone

U1590/C57, Papers of Charles, 3rd Earl Stanhope, general political
   correspondence, 1770–1811
U1590/C99, Papers of Charles, 3rd Earl Stanhope, regarding printing
   and stereotype

Lancashire Record Office, Preston

DDKE/HMC, Manuscripts of Lord Kenyon

National Archives, Kew

ADM 8/73, Admiralty: List Books, 1797
ADM 35/3175, Navy Pay Office: Ships' Pay Books, *Thetis*
ADM 106/1266, Navy Board: In-Letters, 1781–2
ADM 106/2668, Navy Board Minutes
CUST 48, Excise Board: Entry Books of Correspondence with Treasury
CUST 54, Outport Records: Dover
HO 42, Home Office: Domestic Correspondence
KB 10/56, King's Bench, Crown Side: London and Middlesex Indictments Files, 1809–10
MINT 1, Royal Mint: Record Books
PC 1, Privy Council and Privy Council Office: Miscellaneous Unbound Papers
PRO 30/8, William Pitt, 1st Earl of Chatham: Papers
PROB 11/1151, Will Registers, Prerogative Court of Canterbury
T 1/426, Treasury Board Papers
T 29, Treasury Board: Minute Books

National Archives of Scotland, Edinburgh

JC4, Book of Adjournal
JC26, High Court of Justiciary Processes
GD27, Kennedy of Dalquharran, Supplementary Inventories and Letters
GD51, Melville Castle Papers

National Library of Wales

Eaton Evans and Williams Collection (B), 11960-6

Norfolk Record Office, Norwich

MF 632/4, Mayor's Court Book

Northumberland Record Office, Ashington

ZRI 34/2, Ridley Papers

North Yorkshire County Record Office, Northallerton

QSB, North Riding Quarter Sessions
ZLB/3, Draycott Hall Manuscripts

Plymouth and West Devon Record Office, Plymouth

1/695, Plymouth Borough Records: Indictments, Depositions and General Sessions Business
1/716/3, Printed Notice Regarding the Problems of Issuing and Receiving Promissory Notes, 1805
413, Hawkins Papers
710/396, Henry Woollcombe II Diary, 1818–25

Public Record Office Northern Ireland, Belfast

T3228/5/57, Landlords in the north of Ireland who insist on their rents being paid in gold or the difference in value between gold and bank notes, 10 July 1811

Royal Bank of Scotland, London

SAP/36, Correspondence between Loraine, Baker & Co., Newcastle and Vere, Lucadou, and Troughton
MIL/7, Letterbook of Milford, Hogg, Nation

Royal Bank of Scotland, Edinburgh

CS/13/1, Commercial Bank of Scotland Board of Minute Book
RB/12, Minutes of the Court of Directors
RB/837, Royal Bank of Scotland, Correspondence

RSA Archive, London

RSA/PR/AR/103/10, Polite Arts Committee, Correspondence

Suffolk Record Office, Bury St Edmunds

HA521/6, Diary of James Oakes of Bury St Edmunds

University College London, Special Collections

Bentham Manuscripts

University of Glasgow Archive Services, Glasgow

UGD/129/2/1/6, Royal Bank of Scotland, Extract from Moncrieff Letters

West Yorkshire Archive Service, Leeds

WYL150/7/6, Diaries of Lady Amabel Yorke

Yorkshire Archaeological Society, Leeds

MD335 1/4/4/36, Yorkshire Archaeological Society, H. L. Bradfer-Lawrence Collection, Lister Family, Barons Ribblesdale, Family and Estate Records

Newspapers and Periodicals

Aberdeen Journal
Annual Register
Anti-Jacobin
Aris's Birmingham Gazette
Bath Herald and Register
Belfast Newsletter
Berrow's Worcester Journal
Black Dwarf
Bury and Norwich Post
Caledonian Mercury
Cambridge Chronicle
Christian Observer
Cobbett's Weekly Political Register
The Courier (London Courier)
Course of the Exchange
Cowdroy's Manchester Gazette
Cumberland Pacquet
Derby Mercury
Dublin Journal
Edinburgh Evening Courant
Evening Mail
The Examiner
Exeter Flying Post
Felix Farley's Bristol Journal
Freeman's Journal
Gentleman's Magazine
The Gorgon
Hampshire Chronicle
Hampshire Telegraph
Hibernian Chronicle
Ipswich Journal
Jackson's Oxford Journal
Kentish Chronicle
Leeds Mercury

Lincoln, Rutland, and Stamford Mercury
Liverpool Mercury
London Chronicle
London Gazette
Manchester Mercury
The Medusa
Moral and Political Magazine
Morning Chronicle
Morning Post
Newcastle Advertiser
Newcastle Chronicle
Newcastle Courant
Norfolk Chronicle
Norfolk Mercury
Northampton Mercury
North Wales Gazette
Norwich Mercury
Nottingham Journal
The Oracle
Parliamentary Register
Plymouth and Devon Weekly Journal
Poor Man's Guardian
Porcupine's Gazette
Portsmouth Gazette and Weekly Advertiser
Reading Mercury
Salisbury and Winchester Journal
Sheffield Courant
Sherbourne and Yeovil Mercury
Shrewsbury Chronicle
St James's Chronicle
Staffordshire Advertiser
The Star
Sussex Weekly Advertiser
Taunton Courier
The Telegraph
The Times
True Briton
York Courant

Primary Sources

Addison, Joseph. 'Adventures of a Shilling'. *The Tatler*, 249 (11 Nov. 1710).
Anon. 'Abraham Newland, Esq'. *European Magazine* (Jan. 1803): 3.
   The Adventures of a One Pound Note: A Poem (London, 1819).
   Astonishing Abraham Newland (Falkirk, 1805).
   The Bank – The Stock Exchange – The Bankers – The Bankers' Clearing House – The Minister, and the Public (London, 1821).

'Commercial Distresses of the Country', *Edinburgh Review*, 27 (1816): 373–90.

'County Banking Reports', *Banker's Magazine* (1845): 213–20.

Female Attraction; or, the Conquest of Abrm. Newland (London, 1795).

'Increase of Forgeries', *Edinburgh Review*, 28 (1818): 203–14.

Observations on Cobbett's Tremendous and Alarming Scheme (London, 1818).

'Review of Broome's Observations on Mr Paine's Pamphlet', *Gentleman's Magazine*, 80 (1796): 760–1.

A Review of the Banking System of Britain; with Observations on the Injurious Effects of the Bank of England Charter, and the General Benefit of Unrestricted Banking Companies (Edinburgh, 1821).

'Review of *The Life of Abraham Newland*', *Annual Review*, 7 (1809): 279–82.

Serious Reflections on Paper Money in General, Particularly on the Alarming Inundations of Forged Bank Notes (London, 1802).

Attwood, Thomas. *Prosperity Restored; or, Reflections on the Cause of the Public Distresses, and on the Only Means of Relieving Them* (London, 1817).

Bank of England. *Proceedings at the General Court of Proprietors, Held at the Bank of England, on the 19th of March, 1812; with an Appendix, Containing Some Observations on the Conduct of Lord King* (London, 1812).

Baring, Francis. *Further Observations on the Establishment of the Bank of England, and on the Paper Circulation of the Country* (London, 1797).

Observations on the Establishment of the Bank of England, and on the Paper Circulation of the Country (London, 1797).

Observations on the Publication of Walter Boyd (London, 1801).

Bentham, Jeremy. *Collected Works of Jeremy Bentham: Correspondence, vi: January 1798 to December 1801*, ed. J. R. Dinwiddy (Oxford, 1984).

Jeremy Bentham's Economic Writings, ed. Werner Stark. 3 vols. (London, 1952–4).

Writings on Political Economy, ii: Financial Resources, ed. Michael Quinn (Oxford, 2019).

Bewick, Thomas. *A Memoir of Thomas Bewick, Written by Himself*, ed. Iain Bain (London, 1975).

Boase, Henry. *Guineas an Unnecessary and Expensive Incumbrance on Commerce; Or, the Impolicy of Repealing the Bank Restriction Bill* (London, 1802).

Boyd, Walter. *A Letter to the Right Honourable William Pitt: On the Influence of the Stoppage of Issues in Specie at the Bank of England, on the Prices of Provisions, and Other Commodities* (London, 1801).

Bridges, Thomas. *The Adventures of a Bank Note*. 4 vols. (London, 1770–1).

Broome, Ralph. *Observations on Mr Paine's Pamphlet, Entitled the Decline and Fall of the English System of Finance* (London, 1796).

Brougham, Henry. 'Review of *Guineas an Unnecessary and Expensive Incumbrance on Commerce*', *Edinburgh Review*, 2 (1802): 101–16.

Burke, Edmund. *The Correspondence of Edmund Burke, ix: May 1796–July1797*, ed. R. B. McDowell and J. A. Woods (London, 1970).

Observations on a Late State of the Nation (London, 1769).

Reflections on the Revolution in France, ed. J. C. D. Clark (Stanford, CA, 2001).

A Third Letter to a Member of the Present Parliament, on the Proposals for Peace with the Regicide Directory of France (London, 1797).

The Writings and Speeches of Edmund Burke, viii: The French Revolution, ed. L. G. Mitchell and William B. Todd (Oxford, 1989).

Byng, John. *The Torrington Diaries*, ed. C. B. Andrews. 4 vols. (London, 1934–6).

Campbell, Alexander. *The Guinea Note, A Poem by Timothy Twig, Esquire* (Edinburgh, 1797).

Canning, George. 'Tracts on the Report of the Bullion Committee', *Quarterly Review*, 5 (1811): 242–62.

Carlyle, Thomas. *Chartism* (London, 1840).

The French Revolution: A History, ed. David Sorensen (Oxford, 1989).

Chalmers, James. *Strictures on a Pamphlet Written by Thomas Paine* (London, 1796).

Cobbett, William. *An Antidote for Tom Paine's Theological and Political Poison* (Philadelphia, PA, 1796).

Cobbett's Parliamentary History of England from the Earliest Period to the Year 1803. 36 vols. (London, 1806–20).

Paper against Gold and Glory against Prosperity. 2 vols. (London, 1815).

Rural Rides, ed. Ian Dyck (London, 2001).

Colbert Jr. *The Age of Paper; or, an Essay on Banks and Banking* (London, 1793).

Coleridge, Samuel Taylor. *Essays on His Times in the Morning Post and The Courier*, ed. David V. Erdman. 3 vols. (London, 1978).

Colquhoun, Patrick. *A Treatise on Indigence* (London, 1806).

Congreve, William. *An Analysis of the True Principles of Security against Forgery* (London, 1820).

Creevey, Thomas. *The Creevey Papers: A Selection from the Correspondence and Diaries of the Late Thomas Creevey*, ed. Herbert Maxwell. 2 vols. (London, 1903).

Critchett, B. *The Post-Office Annual Directory for 1808* (London, 1808).

Crosby, Benjamin. *Crosby's Merchant's and Tradesman's Pocket Dictionary* (London, 1808).

Davis, Michael T., ed. *The London Corresponding Society: 1792–1799*. 6 vols. (London, 2002).

Day, Robert. *Address to the Grand Jury of the Country of Dublin on the 10th of January, 1797* (Dublin, reprinted in Northallerton, 1797).

Declaration of the Merchants, Bankers, Traders, and Other Inhabitants of London, Made at Grocers' Hall, December 2nd, 1795 (London, 1795).

Declaration of the Merchants, Bankers, Traders and Other Inhabitants of London Made at Merchant Taylor's Hall December 5th, 1792 (London, 1792).

Declaration of the Merchants, Bankers, Traders, and Other Inhabitants of London, Made at the Mansion-House, February 27th, 1797: With a List of the Names and Places of Abode of the Subscribers Thereto (London, 1797).

Dibdin, Charles, Jr. *Professional and Literary Memoirs of Charles Dibdin the Younger*, ed. George Speaight (London, 1956).

Doubleday, Thomas. *The Political Life of the Right Honourable Sir Robert Peel, Bart: An Analytical Biography*. 2 vols. (London, 1856).

Eliot, Francis Perceval. *Observations on the Fallacy of the Supposed Depreciation of the Paper Currency of the Kingdom* (London, 1811).

The English Reports. 178 vols. (Edinburgh, 1900–32).

Farington, Joseph. *The Farington Diary*, ed. James Greig. 8 vols. (London, 1922).

Fielding, Henry. *The True Patriot and Related Writings*, ed. W. B. Coley (Oxford, 1987).

Fiske, Jane, ed. *The Oakes Diaries: Business, Politics and the Family in Bury St Edmunds 1778–1827*. 2 vols. (Woodbridge, 1990).

Forbes, William. *Memoirs of a Banking-House* (Edinburgh, 1859).

Frend, William. *The Effect of Paper Money on the Price of Provisions: Or, the Point in Dispute between Mr Boyd and Sir Francis Baring Examined* (London, 1801).

George III. *The Later Correspondence of George III*, ed. A. Aspinall. 5 vols. (Cambridge, 1962–70).

George IV. *The Correspondence of George, Prince of Wales, 1770–1812*, ed. A. Aspinall. 8 vols. (London, 1963–71).

Gilbert, John Thomas, ed. *Documents Relating to Ireland, 1795–1804* (Shannon, Ireland, 1970).

Hales, Charles. *A Correct Detail of the Finances of This Country* (London, 1797).

Hansard's Parliamentary Debates. 1st series (1803–20), 41 vols. 2nd series (1820–30), 25 vols. 3rd series (1830–91), 356 vols.

Hooper, Ebenezer. *Facts, Letters, and Documents (Chiefly Unpublished) Concerning W. Huntington, His Family & Friends* (London, 1872).

Horner, Francis. *The Economic Writings of Francis Horner in the Edinburgh Review, 1802–6*, ed. F. W. Fetter (London, 1957).

The Horner Papers: Selections from the Letters and Miscellaneous Writings of Francis Horner, MP 1795–1817, ed. Kenneth Bourne and William Banks Taylor (Edinburgh, 1994).

Memoirs and Correspondence of Francis Horner MP, ed. Leonard Horner. 2 vols. (London, 1843).

'Review of Lord King's *Thoughts on the Restriction of Payments in Specie at the Banks of England and Ireland*', *Edinburgh Review*, 2 (1803): 402–21.

'Thornton on the Paper Credit of Great Britain', *Edinburgh Review*, 1 (1802): 172–201.

House of Commons. *Account of Bullion or Coin Seized by Customs*, 1810–11. P.P. 1810–11, X (59).

Account of Bullion or Coin Seized by Customs, 1811–19. P.P. 1819, XVI (366).

Account of Expense Incurred by Bank of England in Prosecutions for Forging Bank Notes, 1797–1818. P.P. 1818, XVI (297).

Account of Number of Bank Notes and Post Bills Issued, and Calculation of Time of Circulation of Bank Notes, 1792 and 1818. P.P. 1819, XVI (345).

Account of Number of Bank Notes and Post Bills Issued by Bank of England, 1697–1831. P.P. 1833, XXIII (597).

Account of Number of Persons Prosecuted for Forging and Uttering Notes of Bank of England, 1783–1818. P.P. 1818, XVI (222).

Account of Number of Prosecutions by Mint for Counterfeiting Legal Coin of Realm, 1783–1811. P.P. 1818, XVI (222).

Account of Number of Prosecutions by Mint for Counterfeiting Legal Coin of Realm, 1797–1818. P.P. 1818, XVI (167).

Account of Number of Prosecutions by Mint for Counterfeiting Legal Coin of Realm, 1818–1827. P.P. 1828, XVI (509).

'An Account of the Amount of Bank of England Notes in Circulation, 15 December 1800', in Lambert, Sheila, ed., *House of Commons Sessional Papers of the Eighteenth Century, cxxx: Reports and Papers (1715–1800)* (Wilmington, DE, 1975).

Account of the Total Number of Forged Bank Notes, 1812–April 1818. P.P. 1818, XIV (296).

Accounts of Net Public Income and Expenditure of Great Britain and Ireland, 1688–1869. P.P. 1868–9, XXXV (366 366-I).

Accounts Presented to the House of Commons Respecting the Public Income of Great Britain (1799–1804).

Appendix to Minutes of Irish Exchange Committee. P.P. 1803–4, IV (86).

Commissioners of Inquiry into Collection and Management of Revenue in Ireland and Great Britain, Nineteenth Report (Post Office Revenue, Ireland). P.P. 1829, XII (353).

Commissioners of Inquiry into Fees and Emoluments Received in Public Offices in Ireland, Ninth Report (General Post Office). P.P. 1810, X (5).

The Commissioners of Naval Enquiry: Sixth Report (Plymouth and Woolwich Yards). P.P. 1803–4, III (83).

Communications between Bank of England, Treasury and Attorney-General Respecting Execution of Laws Prohibiting Exportation of Gold and Silver, 1772. P.P. 1810–11, X (68).

Correspondence on Illicit Exportation of Gold Coin, or of Gold Bullion. P.P. 1810–11, X (249).

Fifth Report from the Committee Appointed to Consider of the Present High Price of Provisions. P.P. 1800, IX.

Finance Accounts of Great Britain (1805–21).

Minutes of Evidence Taken before the Committee Appointed to Enquire into the Select Committee on State of Ireland as to Circulating Paper, Specie and Current Coin, and Exchange between Ireland and Great Britain. P.P. 1803–4, IV.1 (86).

Minutes of Evidence Taken before the Select Committee on Receivers General of Land and Assessed Taxes. P.P. 1821, VIII (667).

Order to Stamp Office Prohibiting Further Stamping of Country Bank Notes under Five Pounds. P.P. 1826, XXII (55).

Report from the Committee of Secrecy on the Bank of England Charter. P.P. 1831–2, VI.1 (722).

Report from the Select Committee on Promissory Notes in Scotland and Ireland. P.P. 1826, III (402).

Report from the Select Committee on the High Price of Gold Bullion. P.P. 1810, III (349).

Report from the Select Committee on the State of Commercial Credit. P.P. 1810–11, II (52).

Report of Committee of Council on State of Coins of United Kingdom and Establishment and Constitution of Mint. P.P. 1816, VI (411).

Report of the Commissioners Appointed for Inquiring into the Mode of Preventing the Forgery of Bank Notes, First Report. P.P. 1819, XI (2).

Report, Together with Minutes of Evidence, and Accounts, from the Select Committee on the High Price of Gold Bullion. P.P. 1810, III.1 (349).

Reports from the Committee of Secrecy on the Outstanding Demands of the Bank and the Restriction of Cash Payments (1797). P.P. 1826, III (26).

Reports from the Select Committee on the Expediency of Resuming Cash Payments. 1819. P.P. 1819, III (291).

Return of Number of Persons Convicted of Forgery on Bank of England, 1791–1829. P.P. 1830, XXIII (442).

Return of Number of Persons Employed and Salaries in Public Offices, 1797, 1805, 1810, 1815, 1819 and 1827, Showing Increase and Diminution. P.P. 1830–31, VII (214).

Second Report from the Secret Committee on Commercial Distress. P.P. 1847–8, VIII (584).

Select Committee of Secrecy on Banks of Issue: Second Report. P.P. 1841, V (410).

Select Committee on Criminal Laws Relating to Capital Punishment in Felonies. P.P. 1819, VIII (585).

Select Committee on Income and Expenditure of United Kingdom, Sixth Report (Navy). P.P. 1817, IV (410).

Select Committee on State of Ireland as to Circulating Paper, Specie and Current Coin, and Exchange between Ireland and Great Britain. P.P. 1803–4, IV (86).

Statement of Number of Seamen, Boys and Marines Voted for Naval Service and Number of Ships, 1756–1859. P.P. 1860, XLII (168).

Thirty-First Report from the Select Committee on Finance. P.P. 1798, XIII.

Twenty-Fourth Report from the Select Committee on Finance. P.P. 1797–8, CX.

House of Lords. *Report from the Lords Committees Appointed a Select Committee to Enquire into the State of Circulation of Promissory Notes under the Value of £5 in Scotland and Ireland.* P.P. 1826–7, VI (245).

Report of the Lords' Committee of Secrecy (1797).

Reports from the Select Committee on the Expediency of Resuming Cash Payments. P.P. 1819, III (291).

Huish, Robert. *The History of the Private and Political Life of the Late Henry Hunt* (London, 1836).

Hume, David. *Essays, Moral, Political, and Literary*, ed. Eugene F. Miller (Indianapolis, 1985).

Hume, David and Benjamin Robert Bell. *Commentaries on the Law of Scotland: Respecting Crimes.* 2 vols. (Edinburgh, 1986).

Hunt, Henry. *Memoirs of Henry Hunt.* 3 vols. (London, 1820).

Huskisson, William. *The Question Concerning the Depreciation of Our Currency Stated and Examined* (London, 1810).

Ibbetson, John Holt. *A Practical View of an Invention for the Better Protecting Bank-Notes against Forgery* (London, 1820).

Johnston, Charles. *Chrysal; or, the Adventures of a Guinea.* 2 vols. (London, 1760).

Jordan's Parliamentary Journal. 9 vols. (London, 1792–5).

Journals of the House of Commons (London, 1810–19).

Journals of the House of Commons of the Kingdom of Ireland. 19 vols. (Dublin, 1796–1800).

King, John. *A Report of the Cases of the King v. Wright and the King v. de Yonge, Who Were Severally Tried for Exchanging Guineas for Bank Notes* (London, 1811).

King, Peter. *Thoughts on the Effects of the Bank Restrictions*, 2nd ed. enlarged (London, 1804).

Thoughts on the Restriction of Payments in Specie at the Banks of England and Ireland (London, 1803).

Landseer, John. 'To the Editor of the Monthly Magazine', *Monthly Magazine*, 5 (1798): 4–5.

The Leeds Directory for the Year 1798 (Leeds, 1798).

Locke, John. *Locke on Money*, ed. Patrick Hyde Kelly. 2 vols. (Oxford, 1991).

The London Directory for the Year 1792; Containing an Alphabetical Arrangement of the Names of Residences of the Merchants, Manufacturers and Principal Inhabitants in the Metropolis and Its Environs (London, 1792).

A London Directory or Alphabetical Arrangement Containing the Names and Residences of the Merchants, Manufacturers and Principal Traders in the Metropolis (London, 1797).

Mackintosh, James. *Memoirs of the Life of the Right Honourable Sir James Mackintosh*, ed. Robert James Mackintosh. 2 vols. (London, 1835).

Vindiciae Gallicae: Defence of the French Revolution, and Its English Admirers, against the Accusations of the Right Hon. E. Burke (London, 1791).

Malthus, Thomas Robert. *An Investigation of the Cause of the Present High Price of Provisions* (London, 1800).

'Pamphlets on the Bullion Question', *Edinburgh Review*, 18 (1811): 448–70.

Martineau, Harriet. *Berkeley the Banker: A Tale* (London, 1833).

Melville, Lewis. *The Life and Letters of William Cobbett in England and America, Based upon Hitherto Unpublished Family Papers*. 2 vols. (London, 1913).

Midriff, John. *Observations on the Spleen and Vapours; Containing Remarkable Cases of Persons of Both Sexes, and All Ranks, from the Aspiring Director to the Humble Bubbler, Who Have Been Miserably Afflicted with Those Melancholy Disorders since the Fall of South Sea, and Other Publick Stocks* (London, 1721).

Mill, James. 'Smith on Money and Exchange', *Edinburgh Review*, 13 (1809): 35–68.

Milner, James. *Three Letters, Relating to the South-Sea Company and the Bank* (London, 1720).

Moore, Thomas. *Memoirs, Journal, and Correspondence of Thomas Moore*, ed. John Russell. 8 vols. (London, 1853–6).

Paine, Thomas. *The Decline and Fall of the English System of Finance* (Paris, 1796).

'Dissertations on Government, the Affairs of the Bank, and Paper-Money (1786)', in Philip S. Foner, ed., *The Complete Writings of Thomas Paine*, ii (Philadelphia, 1945), 367–439.

The Writings of Thomas Paine, ed. Moncure Daniel Conway. 4 vols. (New York, 1894–6).

Penrose, Charles. *A Friendly Address to the Seamen of the British Navy* (Bodmin, 1820).

Playfair, William. *A General View of the Actual Force and Resources of France* (London, 1793).

The History of Jacobinism, Its Crimes, Cruelties and Perfidies (London, 1795).

Pope, Simeon. *A Letter to the Right Hon. William Curtis, Lord Mayor of the City of London, on the National Debt and Resources of Great Britain* (London, 1796).

Proceedings of the Old Bailey Online, 1674–1913. oldbaileyonline.org.

Raithby, John. *The Law and Principle of Money Considered; in a Letter to W. Huskisson* (London, 1811).

Resolutions Proposed to the House of Commons, on the Report of the Committee Appointed to Inquire into the High Price of Bullion, by Francis Horner and Nicholas Vansittart (London, 1811).

Ricardo, David. *David Ricardo on the Price of Gold, 1809*, ed. Jacob H. Hollander (1903).

An Essay on the Influence of a Low Price of Corn on the Profits of Stock (London, 1815).

The High Price of Bullion, a Proof of the Depreciation of Bank Notes (London, 1810).

Proposals for an Economical and Secure Currency; With Observations on the Profits of the Bank of England (London, 1816).

The Works and Correspondence of David Ricardo, ed. Piero Sraffa and M. H. Dobb. 11 vols. (Cambridge, 1951–73).

Romilly, Samuel. *Memoirs of the Life of Sir Samuel Romilly*. 3 vols. (London, 1840).

Rose, George. *A Brief Examination into the Increase of the Revenue, Commerce, and Manufactures of Great Britain, from 1792 to 1799* (London, 1799).

Sanpeur, Guillaume. *On the Manufacture of Banko: With Strong Observations on the Paper Currency* (London, 1802).

Seward, William Wenman. *Collectanea Politica: Or the Political Transactions of Ireland from the Accession of George III to the Present Time* (Dublin, 1801).

Shelley, Percy Bysshe. *The Masque of Anarchy 1832* (Oxford, 1990).

Sinclair, John. *Letters Written to the Governor and Directors of the Bank of England on the Pecuniary Distresses of the Country* (London, 1797).

Observations on the Report of the Bullion Committee (London, 1810).

Smith, Adam. *An Inquiry into the Nature and Causes of the Wealth of Nations*, ed. R. H. Campbell, A. S. Skinner and W. B. Todd (Oxford, 1976).

Smith, Joseph. *An Examination of Mr Paine's Decline and Fall of the English System of Finance* (London, 1796).

Smith, Thomas. *Essay on the Theory of Money and Exchange* (London, 1807).

Society of Arts. *Report of the Committee of the Society of Arts Relative to the Mode of Preventing the Forgery of Bank Notes* (London, 1819).

Southey, Robert. *Letters from England*, ed. Jack Simmons (London, 1951).

Stanhope, Charles. *Considerations on the Means of Preventing Fraudulent Practices on the Gold Coin* (London, 1775).

Lettres de Milord Stanhope à M. de Condorcet (Paris, 1791).

Stewart, Robert. *Memoirs and Correspondence of Viscount Castlereagh, Second Marquess of Londonderry*, ed. Charles Vane. 12 vols. (London, 1848–53).

Substance of the Speech of the Marquis of Londonderry Delivered on Friday, the 15th Day of February 1822, on the Subject of the Agricultural Distress of the Country and the Financial Measures Proposed for Its Relief (London, 1822).

Surr, Thomas. *Refutation of Certain Misrepresentations Relative to the Nature and Influence of Bank Notes* (London, 1801).

Tatham, Edward. *A Letter to the Right Honourable William Pitt on the National Debt* (Oxford, 1795).

Memoirs of the Life and Ministry of the Late W. Huntington, S.S., with an Estimate of His Character. By Onesimus (London, 1813).

A Second Letter to the Right Hon. William Pitt, Chancellor of the Exchequer, on a National Bank (London, 1797).

Thomas, Hilary M. ed. *The Diaries of John Bird of Cardiff: Clerk to the First Marquess of Bute 1790–1803* (Cardiff, 1987).

Thornton, Henry. *An Enquiry into the Nature and Effects of the Paper Credit of Great Britain* (London, 1802).

Substance of Two Speeches of Henry Thornton in the House of Commons, on the Report of the Bullion Committee (London, 1811).

Tooke, Thomas. *History of Prices and of the State of Circulation.* 6 vols. (London, 1838–57).

Trusler, John. *The London Adviser and Guide: Containing Every Instruction and Information Useful and Necessary to Persons Living in London, and Coming to Reside There* (London, 1786).

The London Adviser and Guide: Containing Every Instruction and Information Useful and Necessary to Persons Living in London and Coming to Reside There, 2nd ed. (London, 1790).

Wakefield, Daniel. *A Letter to Thomas Paine: In Reply to His Decline and Fall of the English System of Finance* (London, 1796).

Whitehead, Paul. *The History of an Old Lady and Her Family* (London, 1754).

Wilson, Glocester. *Defence of Abstract Currencies, in Reply to the Bullion Report and Mr Huskisson* (London, 1811).

Wilson, Patrick. 'Copy of a Letter from Professor Wilson, of Glasgow, on the Art of Multiplying Copies of Engraved Plates and Stamps in Relief', *Journal of Natural Philosophy, Chemistry and the Arts,* 2 (1798): 60–3.

Woodforde, James. *The Diary of James Woodforde,* ed. Peter Jameson. 17 vols. (Castle Cary, Somerset, 1998).

Wright, John. *A Biographical Memoir of the Right Honourable William Huskisson* (London, 1831).

Secondary Sources

Aaslestad, Katherine and Johan Joor. *Revisiting Napoleon's Continental System: Local, Regional and European Experiences* (Basingstoke, 2014).

Abramson, Daniel M. *Building the Bank of England: Money, Architecture, Society, 1694–1942* (New Haven, CT, 2005).

Acres, Wilfred M. *The Bank of England from Within, 1694–1900.* 2 vols. (London, 1931).

Acworth, Angus W. *Financial Reconstruction in England, 1815–1822* (London, 1925).

Alborn, Timothy. *Conceiving Companies: Joint-Stock Politics in Victorian England* (London, 1998).

Aldridge, Alfred Owen. 'Why Did Thomas Paine Write on the Bank?', *Proceedings of the American Philosophical Society,* 93 (1949): 309–15.

Allen, Robert C. 'The Great Divergence in European Wages and Prices from the Middle Ages to the First World War', *Explorations in Economic History*, 38 (2001): 411–47.

Anderson, Benedict. *Imagined Communities: Reflections on the Origin and Spread of Nationalism* (London, 1983).

Angell, James W. *The Theory of International Prices: History, Criticism and Restatement* (Cambridge, 1926).

Anon. 'Bank of England Liabilities and Assets: 1696 to 1966, Appendix', *Bank of England Quarterly Bulletin*, 7 (1967): 1–86.

'The Bank of England Note: A Short History', *Bank of England Quarterly Bulletin*, 9 (1969): 211–16.

'Branches of the Bank of England', *Bank of England Quarterly Bulletin*, 3 (1963): 279–84.

Antipa, Pamfili. 'How Fiscal Policy Affects Prices: Britain's First Experience with Paper Money', *Journal of Economic History*, 76 (2016): 1044–77.

Appadurai, Arjun, ed. *The Social Life of Things: Commodities in Cultural Perspective* (Cambridge, 1986).

Appleby, Joyce. *Economic Thought and Ideology in Seventeenth-Century England* (Princeton, NJ, 1978).

'Locke, Liberalism and the Natural Law of Money', *Past & Present*, 71 (1976): 43–69.

Arnon, Arie. *Monetary Theory and Policy from Hume and Smith to Wicksell: Money, Credit, and the Economy* (Cambridge, 2011).

Ashton, John. *The History of Gambling in England* (London, 1898).

Ashton, T. S. 'The Bill of Exchange and Private Banks in Lancashire, 1790–1830', *Economic History Review*, 15 (1945): 25–35.

Economic Fluctuations in England 1700–1800 (Oxford, 1959).

Backscheider, Paula R. 'Defoe's Lady Credit', *Huntington Library Quarterly*, 44 (1981): 89–100.

Bain, George. 'Early Days of Banking in Sunderland', *Antiquities of Sunderland and Its Vicinity*, 6 (1905): 76–94.

Baines, Paul. *The House of Forgery in Eighteenth-Century Britain* (Aldershot, 1999).

Barker, Hannah and Sarah Green. 'Taking Money from Strangers: Traders' Responses to Banknotes and the Risks of Forgery in Late Georgian London', *The Journal of British Studies*, 60 (2021): 585–608.

Barnes, Donald Grove. *A History of the English Corn Laws from 1660–1846* (London, 1930).

Barry, Kevin. 'The Aesthetics of Paper Money: National Difference during the Period of Enlightenment and Romanticism', in David Duff and Catherine Jones, eds., *Scotland, Ireland, and the Romantic Aesthetic* (Lewisburg, PA, 2007), 55–76.

Batt, David M. 'Depoliticisation, Technical Discourse, and Paper-Money: A Case Study in the Bank Restriction Period', *Journal of Cultural Economy*, 14 (2021): 225–39.

Baugh, Daniel A. 'The Eighteenth-Century Navy As a National Institution', in Bryan Ranft and J. R. Hill, eds., *The Oxford Illustrated History of the Royal Navy* (Oxford, 1995), 120–60.

Beaumont, David Anthony. *Barber Beaumont* (London, 1999).

Beaven, Alfred B. *The Aldermen of the City of London.* 2 vols. (London, 1908–13).

Bell, Stephanie. 'The Role of the State and the Hierarchy of Money', *Cambridge Journal of Economics*, 25 (2001): 149–63.

Benchimol, Alex. *Intellectual Politics and Cultural Conflict in the Romantic Period: Scottish Whigs, English Radicals and the Making of the British Public Sphere* (Farnham, 2010).

Besomi, Daniele. 'Paper Money and National Distress: William Huskisson and the Early Theories of Credit, Speculation and Crises', *European Journal of the History of Economic Thought*, 17 (2010): 49–85.

Bielenberg, Andy. *Cork's Industrial Revolution 1780–1880: Development or Decline?* (Cork, 1991).

Black, Eugene. *The Association: British Extraparliamentary Political Organization, 1769–1793* (Cambridge, MA, 1963).

Black, Iain. 'Geography, Political Economy and the Circulation of Finance Capital in Early Industrial England', *Journal of Historical Geography*, 15 (1989): 366–84.

Blakemore, Steven. *Intertextual War: Edmund Burke and the French Revolution in the Writings of Mary Wollstonecraft, Thomas Paine and James Mackintosh* (Madison, NJ, 1997).

Bohannan, Paul. 'The Impact of Money on an African Subsistence Economy', *Journal of Economic History*, 19 (1959): 491–503.

Bohstedt, John. *The Politics of Provisions: Food Riots, Moral Economy, and Market Transition in England, c.1550–1850* (Farnham, 2010).

Bolton, Geoffrey. *The Passing of the Irish Act of Union: A Study in Parliamentary Politics* (London, 1966).

Bonar, James. 'Ricardo's Ingot Plan', *Economic Journal*, 33 (1923): 281–304.

Booth, Alan. 'Food Riots in the North-West of England 1790–1801', *Past & Present*, 77 (1977): 84–107.

Bordo, Michael D. 'Commentary on "The Financial Crisis of 1825 and the Restructuring of the British Financial System"', *Review – Federal Reserve Bank of Saint Louis*, 80 (1998): 77–82.

Bordo, Michael D. and Eugene White. 'A Tale of Two Currencies: British and French Finance during the Napoleonic Wars', *Journal of Economic History*, 51 (1991): 303–16.

Bourke, Richard. *Empire and Revolution: The Political Life of Edmund Burke* (Princeton, NJ, 2015).

Bowen, Ian. 'Country Banking, the Note Issues and Banking Controversies in 1825', *Economic History*, 4 (1938): 68–88.

Bowley, A. L. 'The Statistics of Wages in the United Kingdom during the Last Hundred Years. Part I. Agricultural Wages', *Journal of the Royal Statistical Society*, 61 (1898): 702–22.

Boyle, Gerry and P. T. Geary. 'The Irish Currency Report of 1804' (Economics Department Working Paper Series n1341203, Department of Economics, National University of Ireland – Maynooth, 2003).

Bradley, Ian C. 'The Politics of Godliness: Evangelicals in Parliament, 1784–1832' (unpublished DPhil, University of Oxford, 1974).

Brady, Alexander. *William Huskisson and Liberal Reform: An Essay on the Changes in Economic Policy in the Twenties of the Nineteenth Century* (London, 1928).

Brantlinger, Patrick. *Fictions of State: Culture and Credit in Britain, 1694–1994* (Ithaca, NY, 1996).

Brewer, John. *The Sinews of Power: War and the English State, 1688–1783* (London, 1989).

British Museum, Department of Prints and Drawings. *Catalogue of Prints and Drawings in the British Museum. Division 1. Political and Personal Satires*, ed. Frederic George Stephens and Mary Dorothy George. 11 vols. (1870–1954).

Broadberry, Stephen, Bruce Campbell, Alexander Klein, Mark Overton and Bas van Leeuwen. *British Economic Growth, 1270–1870* (New York, 2015).

Brock, William. *Lord Liverpool and Liberal Toryism: 1820–1827* (Cambridge, 1941).

Broz, J. Lawrence and Richard S. Grossman. 'Paying for Privilege: The Political Economy of Bank of England Charters, 1694–1844', *Explorations in Economic History*, 41 (2004): 48–72.

Bryant, Arthur. *The Years of Endurance, 1793–1802* (London, 1942).

Byatt, Derrick. *Promises to Pay: The First Three Hundred Years of the Bank of England Notes* (London, 1994).

Caffentzis, Constantine G. *Clipped Coins, Abused Words, and Civil Government: John Locke's Philosophy of Money* (Brooklyn, NY, 1989).

Cameron, Kenneth Neill. 'Shelley, Cobbett, and the National Debt', *Journal of English and Germanic Philology*, 42 (1943): 197–209.

  Shelley: The Golden Years (Cambridge, MA, 1974).

Cameron, Rondo, ed. *Banking in the Early Stages of Industrialization: A Study in Comparative Economic History* (New York, 1967).

Cannan, Edwin, ed. *The Paper Pound of 1797–1821: A Reprint of the Bullion Report* (London, 1919).

Cantor, Paul A. 'The Poet As Economist: Shelley's Critique of Paper Money and the British National Debt', *Journal of Libertarian Studies*, 13 (1997): 21–44.

Capie, Forrest. 'Money and Economic Development in Eighteenth-Century England', in Leandro Prados de la Escosura, ed., *Exceptionalism and Industrialisation: Britain and Its European Rivals, 1688–1815* (Cambridge, 2004), 216–32.

Capie, Forrest, Charles Goodhart and Norbert Schnadt. 'The Development of Central Banking', in Forrest Capie, Stanley Fischer and Norbert Schnadt, eds., *The Future of Central Banking: The Tercentenary Symposium of the Bank of England* (Cambridge, 1994), 1–231.

Carpenter, Cecil C. 'The English Specie Resumption of 1821', *Southern Economic Journal*, 5 (1938): 45–54.

Carradice, Phil. *The Last Invasion: The Story of the French Landing in Wales* (Pontypool, 1992).

Carroll, Michael. *A Bay of Destiny: A History of Bantry Bay and Bantry* (Bantry, 1996).

Carruthers, Bruce G. *City of Capital: Politics and Markets in the English Financial Revolution* (Princeton, NJ, 1996).

Cassis, Youssef and P. L. Cottrell. *Private Banking in Europe: Rise, Retreat, and Resurgence* (Oxford, 2015).

Caunce, Steven. 'Banks, Communities and Manufacturing in West Yorkshire Textiles, c.1800–1830', in J. F. Wilson and Andrew Popp, eds., *Industrial Clusters and Regional Business Networks in England, 1750–1970* (Aldershot, 2003), 112–29.

Cave, Charles Henry. *A History of Banking in Bristol from 1750 to 1899* (Bristol, 1899).

Chadha, Jagjit S. and Elisa Newby. 'Midas, Transmuting All, into Paper: The Bank of England and the Banque de France during the Revolutionary and Napoleonic Wars' (Bank of Finland Research Discussion Papers 20/2013, 2013).

Chaloner, W. H. *Industry and Innovation: Selected Essays*, ed. W. O. Henderson (London, 1990).

Chapman, Stanley D. *The Rise of Merchant Banking* (London, 1984).

Checkland, S. G. 'The Lancashire Bill System and Its Liverpool Protagonists, 1810–1827', *Economica*, 21 (1954): 129–42.

   Scottish Banking: A History, 1695–1973 (Glasgow, 1975).

Claeys, Gregory. *Thomas Paine: Social and Political Thought* (Boston, MA, 1989).

Clapham, John H. *The Bank of England: A History*. 2 vols. (Cambridge, 1944).

Clark, Gregory. 'Shelter from the Storm: Housing and the Industrial Revolution, 1550–1909', *Journal of Economic History*, 62 (2002): 489–511.

Clery, Emma J. *The Feminization Debate in Eighteenth-Century England: Literature, Commerce and Luxury* (Basingstoke, 2004).

Clews, Steven. 'Banking in Bath in the Reign of George III', *Bath History Journal*, 5 (1994): 104–24.

Cohen, Benjamin J. *The Geography of Money* (Ithaca, NY, 1998).

Cole, G. D. H. *The Life of William Cobbett* (London, 1927).

Colley, Linda. *Britons: Forging the Nation, 1707–1837* (New Haven, CT, 1992).

Collini, Stefan, Donald Winch and John Burrow. *That Noble Science of Politics: A Study in Nineteenth-Century Intellectual History* (Cambridge, 1983).

Collins, Michael. *Money and Banking in the UK: A History* (London, 1988).

Cook, Peter. 'William Spurrier and the Forgery Laws', *Holdsworth Law Review*, 2 (1995–6): 2–97.

Cookson, John. *The Friends of Peace: Anti-war Liberalism in England, 1793–1815* (Cambridge, 1982).

   Lord Liverpool's Administration: The Crucial Years, 1815–1822 (Edinburgh, 1975).

Cope, Sydney R. 'The Goldsmids and the Development of the London Money Market during the Napoleonic Wars', *Economica*, 9 (1942): 180–206.

   Walter Boyd: A Merchant Banker in the Age of Napoleon (Gloucester, 1983).

Copeland, Edward. *Women Writing about Money: Women's Fiction in England, 1790–1820* (Cambridge, 1995).

Coppieters, Emmanuel. *English Bank Note Circulation, 1694–1954* (The Hague, 1955).

Craig, John. *The Mint: A History of the London Mint from AD 287 to 1948* (Cambridge, 1953).

Crosby, Mark. 'Blake and the Banknote Crises of 1797, 1800, and 1818', *University of Toronto Quarterly*, 80 (2011): 815–36.

Cullen, L. M. *Anglo-Irish Trade 1660–1800* (Manchester, 1968).

'Landlords, Bankers and Merchants: The Early Irish Banking World, 1700–1820', in Antoin E. Murphy, ed., *Economists and the Irish Economy: From the Eighteenth Century to the Present Day* (Blackrock, Ireland, 1984), 25–44.

Daly, Gavin. 'English Smugglers, the Channel, and the Napoleonic Wars, 1800–1814', *Journal of British Studies*, 46 (2007): 30–46.

'Napoleon and the "City of Smugglers", 1810–1814', *Historical Journal*, 50 (2007): 333–52.

Dancy, J. Ross. *The Myth of the Press Gang: Volunteers, Impressment and the Naval Manpower Problem in the Late Eighteenth Century* (Martlesham, 2015).

Daunton, Martin J. 'The Fiscal Military State and the Napoleonic Wars: Britain and France Compared', in David Cannadine, ed., *Trafalgar in History: A Battle and Its Afterlife* (Basingstoke, 2006), 18–43.

Trusting Leviathan: The Politics of Taxation in Britain, 1799–1914 (Cambridge, 2001).

Davidoff, Leonore and Catherine Hall. *Family Fortunes: Men and Women of the English Middle Class, 1780–1850* (London, 1987).

Davies, Alan Philip Keri. 'William Blake in Contexts: Family Friendships, and Some Intellectual Microcultures of Eighteenth- and Nineteenth-Century England' (unpublished PhD thesis, University of Surrey, 2003).

Davies, Glyn. *A History of Money: From Ancient Times to the Present Day* (Cardiff, 2002).

Davis, Ralph. *The Industrial Revolution and British Overseas Trade* (Leicester, 1979).

Davis, Richard. *Dissent in Politics, 1780–1830: The Political Life of William Smith, MP* (London, 1971).

Davis, Timothy S. *Ricardo's Macroeconomics: Money, Trade Cycles and Growth* (Cambridge, 2005).

Dawes, Margaret and C. N. Ward-Perkins. *Country Banks of England and Wales: Private Provincial Banks and Bankers, 1688–1953*. 2 vols. (Canterbury, 2000).

Dawson, Frank G. *The First Latin American Debt Crisis: The City of London and the 1822–25 Loan Bubble* (New Haven, CT, 1990).

Deleplace, Ghislain. *Ricardo on Money: A Reappraisal* (London, 2017).

Dent, Robert K. *The Making of Birmingham: Being a History of the Rise and Growth of the Midland Metropolis* (Birmingham, 1894).

Desan, Christine. *Making Money: Coin, Currency, and the Coming of Capitalism* (Oxford, 2014).

Dick, Alexander. *Romanticism and the Gold Standard: Money, Literature, and Economic Debate in Britain 1790–1830* (Basingstoke, 2013).

Dickinson, Harry T. 'Popular Loyalism in Britain in the 1790s', in Eckhart Hellmuth, ed., *The Transformation of Political Culture: England and Germany in the Late Eighteenth Century* (Oxford, 1990), 503–33.

'Thomas Paine and His British Critics', *Enlightenment and Dissent*, 27 (2011): 19–82.

ed. *Britain and the French Revolution, 1789–1815* (Basingstoke, 1989).

Dickson, P. G. M. *The Financial Revolution in England: A Study in the Development of Public Credit, 1688–1756* (London, 1967).

Dinwiddy, J. R. *Radicalism and Reform in Britain, 1780–1850* (London, 1992).

Dodd, Nigel. 'The Social Life of Bitcoin', *Theory, Culture & Society*, 35 (2017): 35–56.

The Social Life of Money (Princeton, NJ, 2014).

Dōme, Takuo. *The Political Economy of Public Finance in Britain, 1767–1873* (London, 2004).

Douglas, Roy. *Taxation in Britain since 1660* (Basingstoke, 1999).

Dozier, Robert. *For King, Constitution, and Country: The English Loyalists and the French Revolution* (Lexington, KY, 1983).

Duckham, Baron F. 'Canals and River Navigations', in Derek Howard Aldcroft and Michael J. Freeman, eds., *Transport in the Industrial Revolution* (Manchester, 1983), 100–41.

Duffy, Ian P. H. 'The Discount Policy of the Bank of England during the Suspension of Cash Payments, 1797–1821', *Economic History Review*, 35 (1982): 67–82.

Duffy, Michael. 'William Pitt and the Origins of the Loyalist Association Movement of 1792', *Historical Journal*, 39 (1996): 943–62.

The Younger Pitt (Harlow, 2000).

Dyer, Graham P. and Peter P. Gaspar. 'Reform, the New Technology, and Tower Hill, 1700–1966', in C. E. Challis, ed., *A New History of the Royal Mint* (Cambridge, 1992), 398–606.

Earle, Peter. *The Making of the English Middle Class: Business, Society and Family Life in London, 1660–1730* (London, 1989).

Eastwood, David. 'Patriotism and the English State in the 1790s', in Mark Philp, ed., *The French Revolution and British Popular Politics* (Cambridge, 1991), 146–68.

Ehrman, John. *The Younger Pitt: The Consuming Struggle* (London, 1996).

The Younger Pitt: The Reluctant Transition (London, 1983).

Einaudi, Luigi. 'The Theory of Imaginary Money from Charlemagne to the French Revolution', in Luca Einaudi, Riccardo Faucci and Roberto Marchionatti, eds., *Luigi Einaudi: Selected Economic Essays* (London, 2006), 153–81.

Elliott, Marianne. *Partners in Revolution: The United Irishmen and France* (New Haven, CT), 1982.

Emsley, Clive. *Britain and the French Revolution* (Harlow, 2000).

British Society and the French Wars, 1793–1815 (London, 1979).

Fay, C. R. 'Locke versus Lowndes', *Historical Journal*, 4 (1933): 143–55.

Feavearyear, Albert Edgar. *The Pound Sterling: A History of English Money* (Oxford, 1931).

Ferguson, Niall. *The Cash Nexus: Money and Power in the Modern World, 1700–2000* (London, 2001).

Fetter, Frank W. 'The Authorship of Economic Articles in the Edinburgh Review, 1802–47', *Journal of Political Economy*, 61 (1953): 232–59.

'The Bullion Report Reexamined', *Quarterly Journal of Economics*, 56 (1942): 655–65.

Development of British Monetary Orthodoxy, 1797–1875 (Cambridge, MA, 1965).

The Economist in Parliament, 1780–1868 (Durham, NC, 1980).

The Irish Pound 1797–1826: A Reprint of the Report of the Committee of 1804 of the British House of Commons on the Condition of the Irish Currency (London, 1955).

'Legal Tender during the English and Irish Bank Restrictions', *Journal of Political Economy*, 58 (1950): 241–53.

'The Politics of the Bullion Report', *Economica*, new ser., 26 (1959): 99–120.

Finn, Margot C. *The Character of Credit: Personal Debt in English Culture, 1740–1914* (Cambridge, 2003).

Foley, Duncan. 'Money in Economic Activity', in John Eatwell, Murray Milgate and Peter Newman, eds., *Money* (London, 1989), 248–62.

Fontana, Biancamaria. *Rethinking the Politics of Commercial Society: The Edinburgh Review 1802–1832* (Cambridge, 1985).

Ford, Trowbridge H. *Henry Brougham and His World: A Biography* (Chichester, 1995).

Francis, John. *History of the Bank of England: Its Times and Traditions*. 2 vols. (London, 1847).

Freeman, Arthur. *John Payne Collier: Scholarship and Forgery in the Nineteenth Century* (New Haven, CT, 2004).

Frye, Susan. *Elizabeth I: The Competition for Representation* (Oxford, 1993).

Funnell, Warwick. 'The "Proper Trust of Liberty": Economical Reform, the English Constitution and the Protections of Accounting during the American War of Independence', *Accounting History*, 13 (2008), 7–32.

Furniss, Tom. 'Burke, Paine, and the Language of Assignats', *Yearbook of English Studies*, 19 (1989): 54–70.

Gambles, Anna. *Protection and Politics: Conservative Economic Discourse, 1815–1852* (London, 1999).

Gash, Norman. *Lord Liverpool: The Life and Political Career of Robert Banks Jenkinson, Second Earl of Liverpool, 1770–1828* (London, 1984).

Mr Secretary Peel: The Life of Sir Robert Peel to 1830 (London, 1961).

'After Waterloo: British Society and the Legacy of the Napoleonic Wars', *Transactions of the Royal Historical Society*, 28 (1978): 145–57.

Gatrell, V. A. C., Bruce Lenman and Geoffrey Parker. *Crime and the Law: The Social History of Crime in Western Europe since 1500* (London, 1980).

Gaunt, Richard A. *Sir Robert Peel: The Life and Legacy* (London, 2010).

Gayer, Arthur D., W. W. Rostow and Anna Jacobson Schwartz. *The Growth and Fluctuation of the British Economy, 1790–1850: An Historical, Statistical and Theoretical Study of Britain's Economic Development*. 2 vols. (Hassocks, 1975).

Gilboy, Elizabeth W. *Wages in Eighteenth Century England* (Cambridge, MA, 1934).

Gilmartin, Kevin. *Print Politics: The Press and Radical Opposition in Early Nineteenth-Century England* (Cambridge, 1996).

'In the Theater of Counterrevolution: Loyalist Association and Conservative Opinion in the 1790s', *Journal of British Studies*, 41 (2002): 291–328.

Ginter, Donald. 'The Loyalist Association Movement of 1792–93 and British Public Opinion', *Historical Journal*, 9 (1966): 179–90.

Glasner, David. 'An Evolutionary Theory of the State Monopoly over Money', in Kevin Dowd and Richard H. Timberlake, eds., *Money and the Nation State: The Financial Revolution, Government, and the World Monetary System* (New Brunswick, NJ, 1998), 21–45.

'The Real-Bills Doctrine in the Light of the Law of Reflux', *History of Political Economy*, 24 (1992): 867–94.

Glass, David V. *Numbering the People: The Eighteenth-Century Population Controversy and the Development of Census and Vital Statistics in Britain* (Farnborough, 1973).

de Goede, Marieke. 'Mastering "Lady Credit"', *International Feminist Journal of Politics*, 2 (2001): 58–81.

Goodhart, Charles. 'The Two Concepts of Money: Implications for the Analysis of Optimal Currency Areas', *European Journal of Political Economy*, 14 (1998): 407–32.

Goodspeed, Tyler Beck. *Legislating Instability: Adam Smith, Free Banking, and the Financial Crisis of 1772* (Cambridge, MA, 2016).

Gordon, Barry. *Political Economy in Parliament, 1819–1823* (London, 1976).

Gradish, Stephen. *The Manning of the British Navy during the Seven Years' War* (London, 1980).

Graeber, David. *Debt: The First 5,000 Years* (New York, 2011).

Graham, Jenny. *The Nation, the Law, and the King: Reform Politics in England, 1789–1799.* 2 vols. (Lanham, MD, 2000).

Graham, William. *The One Pound Note in the History of Banking in Great Britain* (Edinburgh, 1911).

Gray, Denis. *Spencer Perceval: The Evangelical Prime Minister, 1762–1812* (Manchester, 1963).

Gregory, Theodore E. *Select Statutes, Documents and Reports Relating to British Banking, 1832–1928* (London, 1929).

Grindon, Leo H. *Manchester Banks and Bankers: Historical, Biographical, and Anecdotal* (Manchester, 1877).

Haas, James M. *A Management Odyssey: The Royal Dockyards, 1714–1914* (Lanham, MD, 1994).

'Methods of Wage Payment in the Royal Dockyards 1775–1865', *Maritime History*, 5 (1977): 99–115.

Haggerty, Sheryllynne. 'Women, Work, and the Consumer Revolution: Liverpool in the Late Eighteenth Century', in John Benson and Laura Ugolini, eds., *A Nation of Shopkeepers: Five Centuries of British Retailing* (London, 2003), 106–26.

Hall, F. G. *The Bank of Ireland, 1783–1946* (Dublin, 1949).

Hamburger, Joseph. *James Mill and the Art of Revolution* (New Haven, CT, 1963).

Hamilton, Henry. 'The Failure of the Ayr Bank, 1772', *Economic History Review*, 8 (1956): 405–17.

Handler, Philip. 'Forgery and Criminal Law Reform in England 1818–1830' (unpublished PhD thesis, University of Cambridge, 2001).

'Forgery and the End of the "Bloody Code" in Early Nineteenth Century England', *Historical Journal*, 48 (2005): 683–702.

'Forging the Agenda: The 1819 Select Committee on the Criminal Laws Revisited', *Journal of Legal History*, 25 (2004), 249–63.

'James Mackintosh and Early Nineteenth-Century Criminal Law', *Historical Journal*, 58 (2015): 757–79.

'The Limits of Discretion: Forgery and the Jury at the Old Bailey 1818–1821', in J. Cairns and G. McLeod, eds., *'The Dearest Birthright of the People of England': The Jury in the History of the Common Law* (Oxford, 2002), 156–72.

Harling, Philip. *The Waning of 'Old Corruption': The Politics of Economical Reform in Britain, 1779–1846* (Oxford, 1996).

Harling, Philip and Peter Mandler. 'From "Fiscal-Military" State to Laissez-Faire State, 1760–1850', *Journal of British Studies*, 32 (1993): 44–70.

Harris, Elizabeth M. 'Experimental Graphic Processes in England, 1800–1859', *Journal of Printing Historical Society*, 4 (1968): 33–86.

Harris, Ron. *Industrializing English Law: Entrepreneurship and Business Organization, 1720–1844* (Cambridge, 2000).

'Political Economy, Interest Groups, Legal Institutions, and the Repeal of the Bubble Act in 1825', *Economic History Review*, 50 (1997): 675–96.

Harrison, Mark. *Crowds and History: Mass Phenomena in English Towns, 1790–1835* (Cambridge, 1988).

Hart, Horace. *Charles Earl Stanhope and the Oxford University Press* (London, 1966).

Hart, Kevin. *Samuel Johnson and the Culture of Property* (Cambridge, 1999).

Hartley, W. C. E. *Banking in Yorkshire* (Clapham, N. Yorkshire, 1975).

Harvey, Arnold D. *Collision of Empires: Britain in Three World Wars, 1793–1945* (London, 1992).

Hawtrey, R. G. *Currency and Credit* (London, 1919).

Hay, William Anthony. *The Whig Revival, 1808–1830* (New York, 2004).

Hayek, Friedrich A. von, ed. *The Collected Works of F. A. Hayek*, eds. W. W. Bartley III and Stephen Kresge. 4 vols. (Abingdon, 1988–92).

An Enquiry into the Nature and Effects of the Paper Credit of Great Britain (1802) (London, 1939).

Haywood, Ian. *Romanticism and Caricature* (Cambridge, 2013).

Haywood, Ian and John Seed, eds. *The Gordon Riots: Politics, Culture and Insurrection in Late Eighteenth-Century Britain* (Cambridge, 2012).

Heffer, Simon. *Moral Desperado: A Life of Thomas Carlyle* (London, 1995).

Helleiner, Eric. *The Making of National Money: Territorial Currencies in Historical Perspective* (Ithaca, NY, 2003).

ed. *Nation-States and Money: The Past, Present and Future of National Currencies* (London, 1999).

Hewitt, Virginia. 'Beware of Imitations: The Campaign for a New Bank of England Note, 1797–1821', *Numismatic Chronicle*, 158 (1998): 197–222.

Hewitt, Virginia and John Keyworth. *As Good as Gold: 300 Years of British Bank Note Design* (London, 1987).

Hilton, Boyd. *The Age of Atonement: The Influence of Evangelicalism on Social and Economic Thought, 1785–1865* (Oxford, 1988).

Corn, Cash, Commerce: The Economic Policies of the Tory Governments, 1815–1830 (Oxford, 1977).

'The Gallows and Mr Peel', in T. C. W. Blanning and David Cannadine, eds., *History and Biography: Essays in Honour of Derek Beales* (Cambridge, 1996), 88–112.

A Mad, Bad, and Dangerous People? England 1783–1846 (Oxford, 2006).

Hirschman, Albert O. *The Passions and the Interests: Political Arguments for Capitalism before Its Triumph* (Princeton, NJ, 1977).

Holdsworth, William Searle. *A History of English Law*, 2nd ed. 14 vols. (London, 1937).

Holland, Henry Richard. *Further Memoirs of the Whig Party, 1807–1821* (London, 1905).

Hollander, Jacob H. 'The Development of the Theory of Money from Adam Smith to David Ricardo', *Quarterly Journal of Economics*, 25 (1911): 429–70.

Hone, J. Ann. *For the Cause of Truth: Radicalism in London 1796–1821* (Oxford, 1982).

'Radicalism in London, 1796–1802: Convergences and Continuities', in John Stevenson, ed., *London in the Age of Reform* (London, 1977), 79–101.

Hope-Jones, Arthur. *Income Tax in the Napoleonic Wars* (Cambridge, 1939).

Hoppit, Julian. *Risk and Failure in English Business 1700–1800* (Cambridge, 1987).

'The Use and Abuse of Credit in Eighteenth-Century England', in Neil McKendrick and R. B. Outhwaite, eds., *Business Life and Public Policy: Essays in Honour of D. C. Coleman* (Cambridge, 1986), 64–78.

Horsefield, J. K. 'The Bankers and the Bullionists in 1819', *Journal of Political Economy*, 57 (1949): 442–8.

Houghton, John W. *Culture and Currency: Cultural Bias in Monetary Theory and Policy* (London, 1991).

Howe, Anthony. 'From "Old Corruption" to "New Probity": The Bank of England and Its Directors in the Age of Reform', *Financial History Review*, 1 (1994): 23–41.

Howse, Ernest Marshall. *Saints in Politics: The 'Clapham Sect' and the Growth of Freedom* (London, 1971).

Hueckel, Glenn. 'English Farming Profits during the Napoleonic Wars, 1793–1815', *Explorations in Economic History*, 13 (1976): 331–45.

Hughes, John. *Liverpool Banks & Bankers, 1760–1837: A History of the Circumstances Which Gave Rise to the Industry, and of the Men Who Founded and Developed It* (Liverpool, 1906).

Humphrey, Thomas M. 'The Classical Concept of the Lender of Last Resort', *Federal Reserve Bank of Richmond Economic Review*, 61 (1975): 2–9.

Humphries, Jane and Jacob Weisdorf. 'Unreal Wages? Real Income and Economic Growth in England, 1260–1850', *Economic Journal*, 129 (2019): 2867–87.

Hunt, C. 'The Joint-Stock Company in England, 1830–1844', *Journal of Political Economy*, 43 (1935): 331–64.

Hunter, Michael. *Science and Society in Restoration England* (Aldershot, 1992).

Hyde, Francis E., Bradbury B. Parkinson and Sheila Marriner. 'The Port of Liverpool and the Crisis of 1793', *Economica*, 18 (1951): 363–78.

Ingham, Geoffrey. 'Further Reflections on the Ontology of Money: Responses to Lapavitsas and Dodd', *Economy and Society*, 35 (2006): 259–78.

'Money Is a Social Relation', *Review of Social Economy*, 54.4 (1996): 507–29.

The Nature of Money (Cambridge, 2004).

Ingrassia, Catherine. *Authorship, Commerce, and Gender in Early Eighteenth-Century England: A Culture of Paper Credit* (Cambridge, 1998).

Innes, Joanna and Arthur Burns, eds. *Rethinking the Age of Reform: Britain 1780–1850* (Cambridge, 2003).

Isaac, Peter. 'Sir John Swinburne and the Forged Assignats from Haughton Mill', *Archaeologia Aeliana*, 5 (1990): 158–63.

Jackson, Gordon. 'Ports 1700–1840', in Peter Clark, ed., *The Cambridge Urban History of Britain, ii: 1540–1840* (Cambridge, 2000), 705–32.

James, John A. 'Panics, Payments Disruptions and the Bank of England before 1826', *Financial History Review*, 19 (2012): 289–309.

Jeffrey-Cook, John. 'William Pitt and His Taxes', *British Tax Review*, 4 (2010): 376–91.

Jewson, C. B. *The Jacobin City: A Portrait of Norwich in Its Reaction to the French Revolution, 1788–1802* (Glasgow, 1975).

Johnson, Paul. *Making the Market: Victorian Origins of Corporate Capitalism* (Cambridge, 2010).

Saving and Spending: The Working-Class Economy in Britain 1870–1939 (Oxford, 1985).

Johnston, Joseph. 'A Synopsis of Berkeley's Monetary Philosophy', *Hermathena*, 30 (1940): 73–86.

Jones, F. Stuart. 'The Development of Banking Institutions in Manchester, 1770–1850' (unpublished PhD thesis, University of British Columbia, 1975).

'Government, Currency and Country Banks in England, 1770–1797', *South African Journal of Economics*, 44 (1976): 252–73.

Jones, Wilbur Devereux. *'Prosperity' Robinson: The Life of Viscount Goderich, 1782–1859* (London, 1967).

Joslin, David. 'London Bankers in Wartime, 1739–84', in L. S. Pressnell, ed., *Studies in the Industrial Revolution: Presented to T. S. Ashton* (London, 1960), 156–77.

Kaplan, Herbert H. *Nathan Mayer Rothschild and the Creation of a Dynasty: The Critical Years 1806–1816* (Stanford, CA, 2006).

Keane, John. *Tom Paine: A Political Life* (London, 1995).

Kelly, E. M. *Spanish Dollars and Silver Tokens: An Account of the Issues of the Bank of England, 1797–1816* (London, 1976).

Kibbie, Anne. 'Monstrous Generation: The Birth of Capital in Defoe's *Moll Flanders* and *Roxana*', *PMLA*, 110 (1995): 1023–34.

Kindleberger, Charles P. *Manias, Panics, and Crashes: A History of Financial Crises* (London, 1978).

King, Peter. *Crime, Justice, and Discretion in England, 1740–1820* (Oxford, 2000).

Knapp, Georg Friedrich. *The State Theory of Money*, abridged edition, ed. J. Bonar (London, 1924).

Knight, Roger and Martin Wilcox. *Sustaining the Fleet, 1793–1815: War, the British Navy and the Contractor State* (Woodbridge, 2010).

Kobayashi, Noboru. 'The First System of Political Economy', in Hiroshi Mizuta, Noboru Kobayashi and Andrew S. Skinner, eds., *An Inquiry into the Principles of Political Œconomy* (London, 1998), lxix–xcix.

Kosmetatos, Paul. 'The Winding-up of the Ayr Bank, 1772–1827', *Financial History Review*, 21 (2014): 165–90.

Kynaston, David. *The City of London*. 4 vols. (London, 1994–2001).

Laidler, David. 'Highlights of the Bullionist Controversy' (Research Report No. 2000-02, University of Western Ontario, Department of Economics, 2000). 'Misconceptions about the Real-Bills Doctrine: A Comment on Sargent and Wallace', *Journal of Political Economy*, 92 (1984): 149–55.

Lamb, John B. 'The Paper Age: Currency, Crisis, and Carlyle', *Prose Studies*, 30 (2008): 27–44.

Lascaux, Alexander. 'Money, Trust and Hierarchies: Understanding the Foundations for Placing Confidence in Complex Economic Institutions', *Journal of Economic Issues*, 46 (2012): 75–100.

Latimer, John. *The Annals of Bristol* (Bath, 1970).

Lawson, William John. *The History of Banking* (London, 1850).

Lecky, William Edward Hartpole. *A History of England in the Eighteenth Century*. 8 vols. (London, 1878–90).

Leighton-Boyce, John A. S. L. *Smiths, the Bankers, 1658–1958* (London, 1958).

Lemire, Beverly. *The Business of Everyday Life: Gender, Practice and Social Politics in England, c.1600–1900* (Manchester, 2005).

Lindert, Peter H. and Jeffrey G. Williamson. 'Revising England's Social Tables 1688–1812', *Explorations in Economic History*, 19 (1982): 385–408.

Lindstrom, Eric. *Romantic Fiat: Demystification and Enchantment in Lyric Poetry* (Basingstoke, 2011).

Linebaugh, Peter. *London Hanged: Crime and Civil Society in the Eighteenth Century* (London, 1991).

Luhmann, Niklas. *Trust and Power: Two Works by Niklas Luhmann*, trans. Howard Davis, John Raffan and Kathryn Rooney (Chichester, 1979).

Mackenzie, A. D. *The Bank of England Note: A History of Its Printing* (Cambridge, 1953).

MacLeod, Christine. *Inventing the Industrial Revolution* (Cambridge, 1988).

Macleod, Emma. 'British Attitudes to the French Revolution', *Historical Journal*, 50 (2007): 689–709.

Macleod, Henry Dunning. *The Theory and Practice of Banking*. 2 vols. (London, 1855–6).

Magra, Christopher P. *Poseidon's Curse: British Naval Impressment and Atlantic Origins of the American Revolution* (Cambridge, 2016).

Mathias, Peter. 'Official and Unofficial Money in the Eighteenth Century: The Evolving Uses of Currency', *British Numismatic Journal*, 74 (2004): 68–83. *The Transformation of England: Essays in the Economic and Social History of England in the Eighteenth Century* (London, 1979).

Mathias, Peter and Patrick O'Brien. 'Taxation in Britain and France, 1715–1810: A Comparison of the Social and Economic Incidence of Taxes Collected for the Central Governments', *Journal of European Economic History*, 5 (1976): 601–50.

Mayhew, Nick. 'The Quantity Theory of Money in Historical Perspective', in Mark Casson and Nigar Hashimzade, eds., *Large Databases in Economic History: Research Methods and Case Studies* (London, 2013), 62–96.

McCavery, Trevor. 'Finance and Politics in Ireland, 1801–17' (PhD, Queen's University Belfast, 1980).

McDowell, R. B. 'The Age of the United Irishmen: Revolution and the Union, 1794–1800', in T. W. Moody and W. E. Vaughan, eds., *A New History of Ireland, iv: Eighteenth Century Ireland 1691–1800* (Oxford, 2009), 339–73.

Ireland in the Age of Imperialism and Revolution, 1760–1801 (Oxford, 1979).

McGowen, Randall. 'The Bank of England and the Policing of Forgery 1797–1821', *Past & Present*, 186 (2005): 81–116.

'Knowing the Hand: Forgery and the Proof of Writing in Eighteenth-Century England', *Historical Reflections*, 24 (1998): 385–414.

'Making the "Bloody Code"? Forgery Legislation in Eighteenth Century England', in Norma Landau, ed., *Law, Crime and English Society, 1660–1830* (Cambridge, 2002), 117–38.

'Managing the Gallows: The Bank of England and the Death Penalty, 1797–1821', *Law and History Review*, 25 (2007): 241–82.

McGrath, Patrick. *The Merchant Venturers of Bristol: A History of the Society of Merchant Venturers of the City of Bristol from Its Origin to the Present Day* (Bristol, 1975).

McNeil, Ian. *Joseph Bramah: A Century of Invention 1749–1851* (Newton Abbot, 1968).

Meacham, Standish. *Henry Thornton of Clapham, 1760–1815* (Cambridge, 1964).

Mee, Jon. *Dangerous Enthusiasm: William Blake and the Culture of Radicalism in the 1790s* (Oxford, 1992).

Michie, Ranald C. *Money, Mania and Markets: Investment, Company Formation and the Stock Exchange in Nineteenth-Century Scotland* (Edinburgh, 1981).

Miers, David. *Regulating Commercial Gambling: Past, Present, and Future* (Oxford, 2004).

Mihm, Stephen. *A Nation of Counterfeiters: Capitalists, Con Men, and the Making of the United States* (Cambridge, MA, 2007).

Milgate, Murray and Shannon C. Stimson. *Ricardian Politics* (Princeton, NJ, 1991).

Mints, Lloyd W. *A History of Banking Theory in Great Britain and the United States* (Chicago, IL, 1945).

Mitchell, Austin. 'The Association Movement of 1792–3', *Historical Journal*, 4 (1961): 56–77.

Mitchell, Brian R. *British Historical Statistics* (Cambridge, 1988).

Mitchell, Robert. *Sympathy and the State in the Romantic Era: Systems, State Finance, and the Shadows of Futurity* (London, 2007).

Mitchison, Rosalind. *Agricultural Sir John: The Life of Sir John Sinclair of Ulbster, 1754–1835* (London, 1962).

Mockford, Jack. '"They Are Exactly As Bank Notes Are": Perceptions and Technologies of Bank Note Forgery during the Bank Restriction Period, 1797–1821' (unpublished PhD thesis, University of Hertfordshire, 2014).

Mokyr, Joel. *The Enlightened Economy: An Economic History of Britain, 1700–1850* (New Haven, CT, 2009).

Morgan, E. Victor. *The Theory and Practice of Central Banking, 1797–1913* (Cambridge, 1943).

Morgan, E. Victor and William Arthur Thomas. *The Stock Exchange: Its History and Functions* (London, 1962).

Morgan, Kenneth. *Bristol and the Atlantic Trade in the Eighteenth Century* (Cambridge, 1993).

'The Economic Development of Bristol, 1700–1850', in Madge Dresser and Philip Ollerenshaw, eds., *The Making of Modern Bristol* (Tiverton, 1996), 48–75.

Morgan, L. V. 'Historical Review of Portsmouth Dockyard in Relation to Our Naval Policy', *Transactions of the Institution of Naval Architects*, 90 (1948): 18–32.

Morriss, Roger. 'The British Fiscal-Military State in the Late Eighteenth Century: A Naval Historical Perspective', in Aaron Graham and Patrick Walsh, eds., *British Fiscal-Military States* (London, 2016), 201–27.

The Foundations of British Maritime Ascendancy: Resources, Logistics and the State, 1755–1815 (Cambridge, 2010).

Naval Power and British Culture, 1760–1850: Public Trust and Government Ideology (Abingdon, 2017).

Morrow, John. *Coleridge's Political Thought: Property, Morality and the Limits of Traditional Discourse* (London, 1990).

Moss, David J. *Thomas Attwood: The Biography of a Radical* (Montreal, 1990).

Mulcaire, Terry. 'Public Credit; or, The Feminization of Virtue in the Marketplace', *PMLA*, 114 (1999): 1029–42.

Muldrew, Craig. *The Economy of Obligation: The Culture of Credit and Social Relations in Early Modern England* (Basingstoke, 1998).

'"Hard Food for Midas": Cash and Its Social Value in Early Modern England', *Past & Present*, 170 (2001): 78–120.

Muldrew, Craig and Stephen King. 'Cash, Wages and the Economy of Makeshifts in England 1650–1830', in Peter Scholliers and Leonard Schwarz, eds., *Experiencing Wages: Social and Cultural Aspects of Wage Forms in Europe since 1500* (New York, 2003), 32–56.

Munn, Charles. 'The Emergence of Joint-Stock Banking in the British Isles: A Comparative Approach', *Business History*, 30 (1988): 69–83.

The Scottish Provincial Banking Companies 1747–1864 (Edinburgh, 1981).

Murphy, Anne. 'Performing Public Credit at the Eighteenth-Century Bank of England', *Journal of British Studies*, 58 (2019): 58–78.

Murphy, Antoin. 'Paper Credit and the Multi-Personae Mr Henry Thornton', *European Journal of the History of Economic Thought*, 10 (2003): 429–53.

'Rejoinder to Skaggs's Treating Schizophrenia: A Comment on Antoin Murphy's Diagnosis of Henry Thornton's Theoretical Condition', *European Journal of the History of Economic Thought*, 12 (2005): 329–32.

Navickas, Katrina. *Loyalism and Radicalism in Lancashire, 1798–1815* (London, 2009).

Neal, Larry. 'The Financial Crisis of 1825 and the Restructuring of the British Financial System', *Review – Federal Reserve Bank of Saint Louis*, 80 (1998): 53–76.

The Rise of Financial Capitalism: International Capital Markets in the Age of Reason (Cambridge, 1990).

Nicholson, Colin E. *Writing and the Rise of Finance: Capital Satires of the Early Eighteenth Century* (Cambridge, 1994).

Nishimura, Shizuya. *The Decline of Inland Bills of Exchange in the London Money Market, 1855–1913* (Cambridge, 1971).

O'Brien, D. P. *The Classical Economists* (Oxford, 1975).

The Classical Economists Revisited (Princeton, NJ, 2004).

'The Lender-of-Last-Resort Concept in Britain', *History of Political Economy*, 35 (2003): 1–19.

ed. *Foundations of Monetary Economics, ii: The Bullionists* (London, 1994).

Foundations of Monetary Economics, iii: The Anti-Bullionists (London, 1994).

O'Brien, George. 'The Last Years of the Irish Currency', *Economic Journal*, 37 (1927): 249–58.

O'Brien, Patrick K. 'The Contributions of Warfare with Revolutionary and Napoleonic France to the Consolidation and Progress of the British Industrial Revolution' (Economic History Working Papers No: 264/2017, London School of Economics and Political Science, 2011).

'Fiscal and Financial Preconditions for the Rise of British Naval Hegemony, 1485–1815' (Economic History Working Papers, 91/05, London School of Economics and Political Science, 2005).

'Government Revenue, 1793–1815: A Study of Fiscal and Financial Policy in the Wars against France' (DPhil, University of Oxford, 1968–9).

'The Political Economy of British Taxation, 1660–1815', *Economic History Review*, 41 (1988): 1–32.

O'Brien, Patrick K. and Nuno Palma. 'Danger to the Old Lady of Threadneedle Street? The Bank Restriction Act and the Regime Shift to Paper Money, 1797–1821', *European Review of Economic History*, 24 (2020): 390–426.

'Not an Ordinary Bank but a Great Engine of State: The Bank of England and the British Economy', *Economic History Review*, 76 (2023): 305–29.

Officer, Lawrence H. *Between the Dollar-Sterling Gold Points: Exchange Rates, Parity and Market Behavior* (Cambridge, 1996).

Ó Gráda, Cormac. 'Reassessing the Irish Pound Report of 1804', *Bulletin of Economic Research*, 43 (1991): 5–19.

O'Leary, Patrick. *Sir James Mackintosh: The Whig Cicero* (Aberdeen, 1989).

Ormazabal, Kepa. 'Lowndes and Locke on the Value of Money', *History of Political Economy*, 44 (2012): 157–80.

Palk, Deirdre, ed. *Prisoners' Letters to the Bank of England, 1781–1827* (London, 2007).

Palma, Nuno. 'Money and Modernization in Early Modern England', *Financial History Review*, 25 (2018): 231–61.

Peake, Charles F. 'Henry Thornton and the Development of Ricardo's Economic Thought', *History of Political Economy*, 10 (1978): 193–212.

Pearson, Robin. *Insuring the Industrial Revolution: Fire Insurance in Great Britain, 1700–1850* (Aldershot, 2004).

Perlin, Frank. *Unbroken Landscape: Commodity, Category, Sign and Identity: Their Production as Myth and Knowledge from 1500* (Aldershot, 1994).

Perlman, Morris. 'Adam Smith and the Paternity of the Real Bills Doctrine', *History of Political Economy*, 21 (1989): 77–90.

Pesante, Maria Luisa. 'Steuart's Theory of Money and Sovereignty', in Ramón Tortajada, ed., *The Economics of James Steuart* (New York, 1999), 186–200.

Philipson, John. 'A Case of Economic Warfare in the Late 18th Century: Three Early Paper-Moulds in the Collections of the Society', *Archaeologia Aeliana*, 5 (1990): 151–7.

Phillips, Maberly. *A History of Banks, Bankers, & Banking in Northumberland, Durham, and North Yorkshire* (London, 1894).

'The Old Bank: Bell, Cookson, Carr, and Airey, Newcastle-upon-Tyne', *Archaeologia Aeliana*, 16 (1894): 452–70.

Philp, Mark. *Paine* (Oxford, 1989).

ed. *Resisting Napoleon: The British Response to the Threat of Invasion, 1797–1815* (Aldershot, 2006)

Pickering, George. 'The Role of Bank of England Note Issues amongst the Causes of the Panic of 1825' (SSRN Working Papers, 2018).

Pitts, Jennifer. *A Turn to Empire: The Rise of Imperial Liberalism in Britain and France* (Princeton, NJ, 2005).

Pocock, J. G. A. 'The Political Economy of Burke's Analysis of the French Revolution', *Historical Journal*, 25 (1982): 331–49.

Polanyi, Karl. 'The Economy as Instituted Process, Trade and Market in the Early Empires', in Karl Polanyi, Conrad M. Arensberg and Harry W. Pearson, eds., *Trade and Market in the Early Empires: Economies in History and Theory* (Glencoe, IL, 1957), 243–70.

Poovey, Mary. *Genres of the Credit Economy: Mediating Value in Eighteenth- and Nineteenth-Century Britain* (Chicago, IL, 2008).

Pressnell, L. S. *Country Banking in the Industrial Revolution* (Oxford, 1956).

'Public Monies and the Development of English Banking', *Economic History Review*, 5 (1953): 378–97.

Prothero, Iorwerth J. *Artisans and Politics in Early Nineteenth-Century London: John Gast and His Times* (Folkestone, 1979).

'William Benbow and the Concept of the "General Strike"', *Past & Present*, 63 (1974): 132–71.

Rashid, S. 'Edward Copleston, Robert Peel, and Cash Payments', *History of Political Economy*, 15 (1983): 249–59.

Read, Donald. *Peterloo: The 'Massacre' and Its Background* (Manchester, 1958).

Rediker, Marcus. *Between the Devil and the Deep Blue Sea: Merchant Seamen, Pirates and the Anglo-American Maritime World, 1700–1750* (Cambridge, 1987).

Redish, A. 'The Evolution of the Gold Standard in England', *Journal of Economic History*, 50 (1990): 789–805.

Rendall, Jane. 'The Political Ideas and Activities of Sir James Mackintosh (1765–1832): A Study of Whiggism between 1789 and 1832' (unpublished PhD thesis, University of London, 1972).

Richard, Jessica. *The Romance of Gambling in the Eighteenth-Century British Novel* (Basingstoke, 2011).

Richards, Richard David. *The Early History of Banking in England* (London, 1929).

Robertson, Frances. 'The Aesthetics of Authenticity: Printed Banknotes As Industrial Currency', *Technology and Culture*, 46 (2005): 31–50.

Robinson, Howard. *Britain's Post Office: A History of Development from the Beginnings to the Present Day* (London, 1953).

Robinson, William. *Jack Nastyface: Memoirs of an English Seaman* (London, 2002).

Rockoff, Hugh. 'Upon Daedalian Wings of Paper Money: Adam Smith and the Crisis of 1772', in Fonna Forman-Barzilai, ed., *Adam Smith Review*, vi (London, 2011), 237–68.

Rogers, James Steven. *The Early History of the Law of Bills and Notes: A Study of the Origins of Anglo-American Commercial Law* (Cambridge, 1995).

Rogers, Nicholas. *Crowds, Culture, and Politics in Georgian Britain* (Oxford, 1998). 'Popular Disaffection in London during the Forty-Five', *London Journal*, 1 (1975): 5–27.

Rothbard, Murray N. *Classical Economics: An Austrian Perspective on the History of Economic Thought*. 2 vols. (Cheltenham, 1995).

Rowe, David John, ed. *London Radicalism, 1830–1834: A Selection from the Papers of Francis Place* (London, 1970).

Rowlinson, Matthew. *Real Money and Romanticism* (Cambridge, 2010).

Roxburgh, Natalie. *Representing Public Credit: Credible Commitment, Fiction, and the Rise of the Financial Subject* (London, 2015).

Rule, John. *The Vital Century: The Developing English Economy, 1714–1815* (London, 1992).

Russell, Gillian. '"Faro's Daughters": Female Gamesters, Politics, and the Discourse of Finance in 1790s Britain', *Eighteenth-Century Studies*, 33 (2000): 481–504.
The Theatres of War: Performance, Politics, and Society, 1793–1815 (Oxford, 1995).

Russell, Norman. *The Novelist and Mammon: Literary Responses to the World of Commerce in the Nineteenth Century* (Oxford, 1986).

Rutherford, Donald. *In the Shadow of Adam Smith: Founders of Scottish Economics, 1700–1900* (Basingstoke, 2012).

Sargent, Thomas J. and François R. Velde. *The Big Problem of Small Change* (Princeton, NJ, 2002).

Sargent, Thomas J. and Neil Wallace. 'The Real-Bills Doctrine versus the Quantity Theory: A Reconsideration', *Journal of Political Economy*, 90 (1982): 1212–36.

Sayers, Richard S. 'The Question of the Standard, 1815–44', *Economic History*, 3 (1934): 79–102.

Schabas, Margaret and Carl Wennerlind. 'Retrospectives: Hume on Money, Commerce, and the Science of Economics', *Journal of Economic Perspectives*, 25 (2011): 217–30.

Schumpeter, Joseph A. *History of Economic Analysis* (London, 1954).

Schwartz, Pedro. 'Central Bank Monopoly in the History of Economic Thought: A Century of Myopia in England', in Pascal Salin, ed., *Currency Competition and Monetary Union* (The Hague, 1984), 95–126.

Schwarz, L. D. *London in the Age of Industrialisation: Entrepreneurs, Labour Force and Living Conditions, 1700–1850* (Cambridge, 1992).

'The Standard of Living in the Long Run: London, 1700–1860', *Economic History Review*, 38 (1985): 24–41.

Scott, William Robert. *Constitution and Finance of English, Scottish and Irish Joint Stock Companies to 1720.* 3 vols. (Cambridge, 1912).

Selgin, George. *Good Money: Birmingham Button Makers, the Royal Mint, and the Beginnings of Modern Coinage, 1775–1821* (Ann Arbor, MI, 2008).

'Steam, Hot Air, and Small Change: Matthew Boulton and the Reform of Britain's Coinage', *Economic History Review*, 56 (2003): 478–509.

Sgambati, Stefano. 'Historicizing the Money of Account: A Critique of the Nominalist Ontology of Money', *Journal of Post Keynesian Economics*, 43 (2020): 417–44.

Shapiro, Samuel. *Capital and the Cotton Industry in the Industrial Revolution* (Ithaca, NY, 1968).

Shell, Marc. *Art & Money* (Chicago, IL, 1995).

Money, Language and Thought: Literary and Philosophical Economies from the Medieval to the Modern Era (Berkeley, CA, 1982).

Shin, Hiroki. 'The Culture of Paper Money in Britain : The Bank of England Note during the Bank Restriction Period, 1797–1821' (unpublished PhD thesis, University of Cambridge, 2009).

'Paper Money, the Nation, and the Suspension of Cash Payments in 1797', *Historical Journal*, 58 (2015): 415–42.

Sigot, Nathalie and Ghislain Deleplace. 'From Annuity Notes to Bank Notes: A Change in Bentham's Theory of Money', *History of Economic Ideas*, 20 (2012): 45–74.

Silberling, Norman J. 'British Prices and Business Cycles, 1779–1850', *Review of Economics and Statistics*, 5 (1923): 223–61.

Simmel, Georg. 'The Metropolis and Mental Life', in Kurt H. Wolff, ed., *The Sociology of Georg Simmel* (Glencoe, IL, 1950), 409–24.

The Philosophy of Money, ed. David Frisby (London, 1990 [1978]).

Skaggs, Neil T. 'Credit Where Credit Is Due: Henry Thornton and the Evolution of the Theory of Fiduciary Money', *History of Political Economy*, 44 (2012): 451–69.

'Henry Thornton and the Development of Classical Monetary Economics', *Canadian Journal of Economics*, 28 (1995): 1212–27.

'Thomas Tooke, Henry Thornton, and the Development of British Monetary Orthodoxy', *Journal of the History of Economic Thought*, 25 (2003): 177–97.

'Treating Schizophrenia: A Comment on Antoin Murphy's Diagnosis of Henry Thornton's Theoretical Condition', *European Journal of the History of Economic Thought*, 12 (2005): 321–8.

Slinn, Judy. *A History of Freshfields* (London, 1984).

Smart, William. *Economic Annals of the Nineteenth Century.* 2 vols. (London, 1910–17).

Smith, Ernest. *Lord Grey, 1764–1845* (Oxford, 1990).

Spang, Rebecca L. *Stuff and Money in the Time of the French Revolution* (Cambridge, MA, 2015).

Spufford, Peter. *Money and Its Use in Medieval Europe* (Cambridge, 1989).

Stanhope, Ghita and G. P. Gooch. *The Life of Charles, Third Earl Stanhope* (London, 1914).

Stapleton, Barry. 'The Admiralty Connection: Port Development and Demographic Change in Portsmouth, 1650–1900', in Richard Lawton and Robert Lee, eds., *Population and Society in Western European Port-Cities, c. 1650–1939* (Liverpool, 2001), 212–51.

Stevenson, John. *Popular Disturbances in England, 1700–1870* (London, 1979).

Stuart Jones, E. H. *An Invasion That Failed: The French Expedition to Ireland, 1796* (Oxford, 1950).

  The Last Invasion of Britain (Cardiff, 1950).

Styles, John. '"Our Traitorous Money Makers": The Yorkshire Coiners and the Law, 1760–83', in John Brewer and John Styles, eds., *An Ungovernable People: The English and Their Law in the Seventeenth and Eighteenth Centuries* (London, 1980), 172–249.

Sussman, Nathan. 'William Huskisson and the Bullion Controversy, 1810', *European Journal of the History of Economic Thought*, 4 (1997): 237.

Sutherland, Lucy. *Politics and Finance in the Eighteenth Century* (London, 1984).

Taylor, Raymond A. 'Applegath and Cowper: Their Importance to the English Letter Press Printing Industry in the Nineteenth Century', *Journal of Printing Historical Society*, 26 (1997): 47–69.

Thomas, J. E. *Britain's Last Invasion: Fishguard, 1797* (Stroud, 2007).

Thompson, E. P. *The Making of the English Working Class* (London, 1963).

Thompson, James. *Models of Value: Eighteenth-Century Political Economy and the Novel* (Durham, NC, 1996).

Thompson, Noel W. *The People's Science: The Popular Political Economy of Exploitation and Crisis 1816–34* (Cambridge, 1984).

Thompson, R. H. 'French Assignats Current in Britain: The Parliamentary Debate', *British Numismatic Journal*, 51 (1981): 200–3.

Thrift, Nigel. 'Transport and Communication 1730–1914', in R. A. Dodgshon and R. A. Butlin., eds., *An Historical Geography of England and Wales*, 2nd ed. (London, 1990), 453–85.

Turberville, Arthur Stanley. *The House of Lords in the Age of Reform, 1784–1837* (London, 1958).

Turner, John D. *Banking in Crisis: The Rise and Fall of British Banking Stability, 1800 to the Present* (Cambridge, 2014).

Turner, M. E., J. V. Beckett and B. Afton. *Agricultural Rent in England, 1690–1914* (Cambridge, 1997).

Vernon, John. *Money and Fiction: Literary Realism in the Nineteenth and Early Twentieth Centuries* (Ithaca, NY, 1984).

Vickers, Douglas. *Studies in the Theory of Money, 1690–1776* (London, 1960).

Viner, Jacob. *Studies in the Theory of International Trade* (New York, 1937).

Walker, David M. *A Legal History of Scotland*. 7 vols. (Edinburgh, 1988–2003).

Walker, Francis A. *Money* (London, 1891).

Wallas, Graham. *The Life of Francis Place, 1771–1854* (London, 1898).

Ward, J. R. *The Finance of Canal Building in 18th Century England* (Oxford, 1974).

Waterman, Anthony. *Revolution, Economics and Religion: Christian Political Economy, 1798–1833* (Cambridge, 1991).

Webster, John Clarence. *Sir Brook Watson: Friend of the Loyalists, First Agent of New Brunswick in London* (Sackville, Canada, 1924).

Wells, Roger. *Insurrection: The British Experience, 1795–1803* (Gloucester, 1983).

Wennerlind, Carl. *Casualties of Credit: The English Financial Revolution, 1620–1720* (Cambridge, MA, 2011).

'The Death Penalty as Monetary Policy: The Practice and Punishment of Monetary Crime, 1690–1830', *History of Political Economy*, 36 (2004): 131–61.

'Money: Hartlibian Political Economy and the New Culture of Credit', in Philip Stern and Carl Wennerlind, eds., *Mercantilism Reimagined: Political Economy in Early Modern Britain and Its Empire* (New York, 2013), 74–93.

Whitaker, T. K. 'Origins and Consolidation, 1783–1826', in F. S. L. Lyons, ed., *Bicentenary Essays: Bank of Ireland, 1783–1983* (Dublin, 1983), 11–29.

White, Eugene N. 'The French Revolution and the Politics of Government Finance, 1770–1815', *Journal of Economic History*, 55 (1995): 227–55.

White, Jerry. *A Great and Monstrous Thing: London in the Eighteenth Century* (Cambridge, MA, 2013).

White, Stephen K. 'Burke on Politics, Aesthetics, and the Dangers of Modernity', *Political Theory*, 21 (1993): 507–27.

Wilson, David A. *Paine and Cobbett: The Transatlantic Connection* (Kingston, Ontario, 1988).

Wilson, Richard George. *Gentlemen Merchants: The Merchant Community in Leeds, 1700–1830* (Manchester, 1971).

Wilson, Ted. *Battles for the Standard: Bimetallism and the Spread of the Gold Standard in the Nineteenth Century* (Aldershot, 2000).

Winch, Donald and Patrick K. O'Brien, eds. *The Political Economy of British Historical Experience, 1688–1914* (Oxford, 2002).

Woolf, Stuart. 'Statistics and the Modern State', *Comparative Studies in Society and History*, 31 (1989): 588–604.

Workman, Roy. 'The Joshua Grigbys: Some Materials for a History of the Joshua Grigbys of Bury St. Edmunds and Drinkstone in Suffolk 1659 to 1829' (unpublished typescript, Suffolk Record Office, Bury St Edmunds, HD1339/1, 1983).

Wray, L. Randall. *Understanding Modern Money: The Key to Full Employment and Price Stability* (Cheltenham, 1998).

Wright, Thomas. *The Life of William Huntington, S. S.* (London, 1909).

Wrigley, E. A., ed. *Nineteenth-Century Society: Essays in the Use of Quantitative Methods for the Study of Social Data* (Cambridge, 1972).

Young, B. W. *The Victorian Eighteenth Century: An Intellectual History* (Oxford, 2007).

Zelizer, Viviana. *The Social Meaning of Money* (New York, 1994).

Ziegler, Dieter. 'Central Banking in the English Provinces in the Second Quarter of the Nineteenth Century', *Business History*, 31 (1989): 33–47.

Index

Printed in the United States
by Baker & Taylor Publisher Services

Printed in the United States
by Baker & Taylor Publisher Services